Patrons, Clients

MW00475990

Most models of party competition assume that citizens vote for a platform rather than narrowly targeted material benefits. However, there are many countries where politicians win elections by money, jobs, and services in direct exchange for votes. This is not just true in the developing world, but also in economically developed countries – such as Japan and Austria – that clearly meet the definition of stable, modern democracies. This book offers explanations for why politicians engage in clientelistic behaviors and why voters respond. Using newly collected data on national and subnational patterns of patronage and electoral competition, the contributors demonstrate why explanations based on economic modernization or electoral institutions cannot account for international variation in patron-client and programmatic competition. Instead, they show how the interaction of economic development, party competition, governance of the economy, and ethnic heterogeneity may work together to determine the choices of patrons, clients, and policies.

HERBERT KITSCHELT is George V. Allen Professor of International Relations in the Department of Political Science at Duke University. He is the editor of *Continuity and Change in Contemporary Capitalism* (with Peter Lange, Gary Marks, and John D. Stephens, 1999) and author of *Post-Communist Party Systems: Competition, Representation, and Inter-Party Cooperation* (with Zdenka Mansfeldova, Radoslaw Markowski, and Gabor Toka, 1999), *The Transformation of European Social Democracy* (1994), and *The Radical Right in Western Europe* (1995) which won the Woodrow Wilson Award of the American Political Science Association in 1996.

STEVEN I. WILKINSON is Associate Professor in the Department of Political Science at University of Chicago. He is the author of *Votes and Violence: Electoral Competition and Ethnic Riots in India* (2004) which won the Woodrow Wilson Award of the American Political Science Association in 2005.

Patrons, Clients, and Policies

Patterns of Democratic Accountability and Political Competition

Edited by

Herbert Kitschelt and Steven I. Wilkinson

CAMBRIDGE
UNIVERSITY PRESS

CAMBRIDGE UNIVERSITY PRESS
Cambridge, New York, Melbourne, Madrid, Cape Town, Singapore, São Paulo, Delhi

Cambridge University Press
The Edinburgh Building, Cambridge CB2 8RU, UK

Published in the United States of America by Cambridge University Press, New York

www.cambridge.org
Information on this title: www.cambridge.org/9780521690041

First published 2007

A catalogue record for this publication is available from the British Library

ISBN 978-0-521-86505-0 hardback
ISBN 978-0-521-69004-1 paperback

Transferred to digital printing 2009

Contents

Figures

Tables

Acknowledgments

This book grew out of a conference on clientelism held at Duke in 2001. The high level of interest in the topic and the excellent quality of the work being done convinced us that a more extended theoretical and empirical treatment of programmatic and clientelistic party competition was worthwhile, and over the next several years we solicited authors who spoke to these concerns – some of whom had presented at the conference and some of whom had not – to write papers for this volume. We would like to thank all of our contributors for the excellence of their contributions, their cheerfulness in making revisions and corrections, and for their willingness to shrink their papers when the original size of the volume proved too great.

At Duke University, we would like to thank the program in Democracy Institutions and Political Economy and the Department of Political Science for funding the original 2001 conference. We would also like to thank Matthew Singer for his invaluable help with the index, proofreading and production process, as well as his more substantive comments. At Cambridge, we would like to thank our editor John Haslam for his faith in the project and Carrie Cheek and Jayne Aldhouse for their help in the production process.

Herbert Kitschelt and Steven Wilkinson
Durham NC, February 9, 2006

Contributors

Kanchan Chandra is Associate Professor in the Wilf Family Department of Politics at New York University

Alberto Diaz-Cayeros is Assistant Professor in the Department of Political Science at Stanford University

Federico Estévez is Professor of Political Science at the Instituto Tecnológico Autónomo de México (ITAM)

Henry E. Hale is Assistant Professor of Political Science and International Affairs at George Washington University

Herbert Kitschelt is George V. Allen Professor of International Relations in the Department of Political Science at Duke University

Anirudh Krishna is Assistant Professor of Public Policy Studies at the Sanford Institute for Public Policy, Duke University

Steven Levitsky is Associate Professor of Government and Social Studies at Harvard University

Mona M. Lyne is Assistant Professor of Political Science at the University of South Carolina

Beatriz Magaloni is Assistant Professor in the Department of Political Science at Stanford University

Luis Fernando Medina is Assistant Professor in the Department of Politics at the University of Virginia

Wolfgang C. Müller is Professor of Political Science at the University of Mannheim

Ethan Scheiner is Associate Professor in the Department of Political Science at the University of California, Davis

Susan C. Stokes is John S. Saden Professor of Political Science and Director of the Program on Democracy at Yale University

Nicolas van de Walle is John S. Knight Professor of International Studies in the Department of Government at Cornell University

Steven I. Wilkinson is Associate Professor in the Department of Political Science, University of Chicago

1   Citizen–politician linkages: an introduction

Herbert Kitschelt and Steven I. Wilkinson

Since the 1970s, the "Third Wave" of democratic transitions has, by greatly enlarging the number and type of democracies, raised a host of new research questions on the dynamics of democratic accountability and responsiveness. After an initial period of scholarly attention to the process of regime transition, there has recently been a major effort to explain the origin and effects of democratic institutions, such as electoral laws, federalism structure, or presidential and parliamentary systems. After more than a decade's worth of research, however, it now seems that the explanatory power of formal democratic institutions for democratic process features is more limited than many had hoped. Party systems vary tremendously even among single member district plurality electoral systems. Furthermore, institutional arguments have little to say about the substantive alignments that rally citizens around rival contenders or the strategic appeals made by leading politicians in each camp.

One important area that has not received sufficient attention is the wide variation in patterns of linkages between politicians, parties and citizens. The political science literature has, since the 1950s, been dominated by the "responsible party government" model, the logic of which forms the basis of both rational choice theories (Downs 1957) as well as historical-comparative approaches (e.g., Lipset and Rokkan 1967). This model sees politics as the result of interaction of principals (citizens, voters) and agents (candidates for electoral office, elected officials), characterized by five essential ingredients. First, voters have policy preferences over a range of salient issues to allocate or redistribute scarce resources through state action. Second, vote- or executive office-seeking politicians and parties bundle issue positions in electoral platforms or programs they promise to enact, if elected into office. To simplify matters for information misers in the electorate, such programmatic bundles can be aligned in a minimally dimensional scale, with a single "left-to-right" dimension. Third, voters relate their own preferences to those offered by the partisan competitors and opt for the most compatible programmatic basket, weighted by strategic considerations such as the electability of the party and the credibility of its promises given its past performance.[1] Fourth, victorious parties or coalitions of parties with relatively similar programs then implement their promises, with an eye on the evolving preferences of their constituencies. Fifth, at the subsequent election, voters hold incumbents and opposition parties accountable for their performance during the electoral term, based upon their effort and performance.

This model of democratic representation clearly captures many of the ways in which parties' appeals and programs reflect and sometimes lead their constituencies' preferences in affluent capitalist democracies (cf. Powell 2004). Consistent with the standard responsible party model, several studies have found that the partisan complexion of governments does indeed make a difference for a wide range of social and economic policies in advanced capitalist democracies (see, e.g., Castles 1982; Esping-Andersen 1990; Huber and Stephens 2001; Klingemann, Hofferbert, and Budge 1994). In a similar vein, scholars have explored patterns of political representation according to the partisan government model and the variability of such citizen–politician relations contingent upon electoral rules and party system formats in a democratic polity (cf. Lijphart 1999; Powell 2000).

What the responsible-party model ignores, however, is that a quite different type of *patronage-based, party–voter linkage* exists in many countries, including some advanced industrial democracies. In many political systems citizen–politician linkages are based on direct material inducements targeted to individuals and small groups of citizens whom politicians know to be highly responsive to such side-payments and willing to surrender their vote for the right price. Democratic accountability in such a system does not result primarily from politicians' success in delivering collective goods such as economic growth, jobs, monetary stability, or national health care, nor does it rest on improving *overall* distributive outcomes along the lines favored by broad categories of citizens (e.g., income and asset redistribution through taxes and social benefits schemes). Instead, *clientelistic accountability represents a transaction, the direct exchange of a citizen's vote in return for direct payments or continuing access to employment, goods, and services.*

The need to understand such clientelistic linkages is particularly pressing now for three reasons. First, studies of the new democracies in Latin America, post-communist Europe, South and Southeast Asia, and parts

---

[1] Spatial models of competition (in which voters calculate the proximity of party programs to their own preference vector in terms of Euclidean distances) and directional models where they employ scalar products to gauge the distance are both only minor variants of the responsible partisan model.

of Africa have made it increasingly obvious that our general theoretical models of responsible party government fail to account for a lot of the observed variation in citizen–politician linkages. In the new democracies not all parties compete for voters based on coherent programmatic packages that can be arranged neatly on a left–right dimension or some other low-dimensional depiction of strategic configurations among parties. The programmatic positions of parties are often diffuse and erratic, but they can nevertheless attract solid support, even when emotional ties of "party identification" or a past record of competent management of economic growth appear to be unlikely sources of citizen–politician linkage.

A second theoretical reason to study clientelism is that, despite the view in the 1950s and 1960s that clientelism was a holdover from pre-industrial patterns that would gradually disappear in the modernizing West, clientelistic structures seem to have remained resilient in established party systems in advanced industrial democracies such as Italy, Japan, Austria, and Belgium. Why have these systems not made the expected full transition from patronage politics to programmatic policies?

A third reason why it is important to study clientelistic linkages now is because their pervasiveness has clear implications for economic growth and prospects for economic reform. In states in which clientelistic linkages are well entrenched, international financial institutions' attempts to liberalize developing economies and reduce the size of their states have been resisted by politicians who, not surprisingly, are determined to subvert reforms that threaten their patronage and hence their ability to win elections and stay in power. The current World Bank and bilateral donor focus on governance and transparency, in our view, is doomed to failure unless it takes more account of the often directly opposing incentives facing politicians charged with implementing reforms in patronage-based systems from Nairobi to Kuala Lumpur to Tokyo. Why should politicians dismantle the patronage networks that keep them in power in order to satisfy financial institutions whose threats to withhold aid often sound hollow and whose policy priorities and conditionality requirements seem to change every few years in any case?

There have been surprisingly few systematic comparative studies on clientelism, partly because of the origin of research on clientelism in in-depth anthropological and sociological studies. From these disciplinary perspectives, political clientelism was only a special case of a much more widespread pattern of social affiliation found in "traditional" societies from Southern Italy and Senegal to India (Clapham 1982; Cruise O'Brien 1975; Fox 1969). Clientelism was seen as a durable, face-to-face, hierarchical and thus asymmetrical exchange relation between patrons and clients supported by a normative framework. In contrast to comparative political research design, sociological and anthropological investigations favored detailed case studies and general social theory rather than "middle level" theorizing of a comparative nature about the varied incidence of clientelism across time and space.[2]

The few political scientists who examined clientelism in the late 1960s and 1970s did begin to provide a comparative perspective that examined the embeddedness of clientelistic politics in different political regimes (cf. Scott 1972; Tarrow 1977). They also realized that the stable, normative, and hierarchical character attributed to clientelism was only a special case that does not prevail at least in environments of democratic electoral competition. Electoral enfranchisement and party competition provided clients with an exit option from an existing relationship to a patron. Democracy strengthens the clients' bargaining leverage *vis-à-vis* brokers and patrons (Piattoni 2001: 7). Furthermore, electoral competition promotes a scaling up of clientelistic networks from local politics with personalistic, face-to-face relations to the national level of hierarchical political machines, starkly distinct from patrimonial political organization (Scott 1969: 1158). In the context of democratic institutional settings, clientelism thus evolves into a more symmetrical (rather than asymmetrical), intermittent (rather than stable and continuous), instrumental-rational (rather than normative) and broker-mediated (rather than face-to-face based) exchange relationship (Scott 1972; Weingrod 1968).

With some simplification, we can say that the first generation of studies exploring the causes of variance in democratic mechanisms of accountability focused on absolute levels of economic development and rates of change of economic development as the underlying conditions that induced actors to construct diverse principal–agent linkage mechanisms. In the 1970s and 1980s, this generation was displaced by a second generation of researchers with a *statist and an institutional emphasis*. Such scholars detailed how the timing of the emergence of state institutions (bureaucratic professionalization) and the nature of formal democratic institutions (electoral laws, legislative-executive relations, and political

---

[2] As documentation of the crushing predominance of case studies and general theory, see Roniger's (1981) impressive bibliography and even Eisinger and Roniger's (1984) massive tome on patron–client relationships. It develops dimensions of variation in clientelism (chapter 7) and covers just about every region on earth, but lacks a systematic analysis of how, why, and when specific forms of clientelism come into existence or fade away. Examples in political science are Banfield's (1958) study of Southern Italy and Banfield and Wilson's (1965) monograph on political machines in US cities, although the latter offers at least a subnationally comparative perspective.

decentralization) may affect principal–agent relations in democracy.[3] Chief among these studies was Martin Shefter's (1977, 1994) important comparative study of the United States, France, and Britain. First of all, Shefter's work was distinctive because he did not sample on the dependent variable, but compared clientelistic linkage mechanisms in both democracies and non-democracies. Second, by confining the comparison to polities at roughly equal levels of economic development, Shefter shows that a developmental perspective cannot be all there is to the explanation of variance among democratic linkage mechanisms. Instead, he highlights the critical role of state formation in interaction with patterns of social mobilization and political enfranchisement as key factors shaping the presence or absence of clientelistic linkage under democratic conditions. Where the rise of bureaucratic absolutism professionalized the career of state officials before democratization and made administrative office unavailable to a spoils logic of distributing benefits among supporters of the electorally successful party, parties had to compete for voters with programmatic appeals rather than with material side-payments to individuals and communities. Extension of the suffrage after the advent of industrialization and social mobilization further undercut clientelism. New "external" mass political parties, supported by working-class people who were not entitled to vote and led by politicians who could not obtain seats in parliament, had to rely on their own internal resources and their purely ideological programmatic appeal, because they had no access to state resources. After the extension of suffrage, the presence of such mass programmatic parties undercut the spread of clientelistic practices, even where bureaucratic state professionalism was vulnerable.

Shefter's perspective fed into the backlash against modernization theory and the state- and class-centered perspective advanced by comparative political theorists in the 1970s and 1980s. Unfortunately, it was published at a time when the institutional inclinations of comparative politics directed attention away from the comparative study of mass political behavior, political parties, and elections altogether. Rather than developing Shefter's arguments further, comparative theorists with a class and statist persuasion abandoned the whole research topic and instead turned to comparative political economy as the main preserve of comparative

---

[3] The critical contribution of this era is Shefter (1977; 1994). Where bureaucratic professionalization precedes both industrialization and democratic suffrage expansion, "external" parties representing peoples not permitted to vote organize programmatic parties, while "internal" parties in the legislatures of traditional authoritarian regimes prefer clientelistic payoffs, if they could avail themselves of state assets to hand out to electoral constituencies.

theorizing and empirical analysis. As a consequence, between 1978 and the late 1990s very little of theoretical consequence has been written about clientelism, except in a rather isolated literature on the effect of electoral laws on personalism and intra-party factionalism in party systems. In as much as state- and class-oriented comparative political scholars attended to political parties, their work was explicitly or tacitly steeped in the responsible party government literature and spatial models of inter-party competition based on programmatic linkages.[4]

The only notable exception to this general inattention has been an excellent recent volume edited by Piattoni on the historical origins of clientelistic democratic politics in Europe. This book combines case studies covering a much larger range of countries than those considered in Shefter's original paper with comparative historical analysis of clientelism across European politics (Piattoni 2001). These valuable studies, however, also reveal the limits of Shefter's explanatory account. The articles show that some pre-democratic legacies of bureaucracy, such as in the French case, were not as professional and impervious to clientelism as Shefter's argument suggested. Moreover, the advent of democracy may make bureaucratic professionalization reversible and endogenous to political competition that favors clientelistic patronage environments, a development also suggested by the French and Indian cases.

One aim of our book is to reorient the causal analysis of democratic accountability and responsiveness once again, and move beyond the current focus on structures and institutions. First, as in the recent literature on democratization, we propose a return to broadly *developmentalist perspectives*, but only provided this can be achieved with greater theoretical sophistication than in the past.[5] This implies close attention to the mechanisms of citizens' and politicians' strategic conduct that link their asset endowments and preferences to individual strategies and collective outcomes of political action manifesting themselves in diverse principal–agent relations of accountability and responsiveness. It also implies examining relations of contingency and endogeneity that link economic development to other attributes of democratic polities and processes affecting

---

[4] This applies, for example, to the literature on the electoral career of leftist parties, such as Przeworski and Sprague (1986) and Kitschelt (1994).

[5] In this vein, Przeworski *et al.* (2000) return to a perspective that treats development as the major predictor of democracy, albeit with amendments that concern the difference between transition rates to democracy and persistence of democracy. In a way, Boix (2003) and Boix and Stokes (2003) push the conditionality of development as a causal variable in a somewhat different direction by focusing on patterns of inequality as the mechanisms that link economic asset availability and control to political regime choice.

democratic principal–agent relations. It is the focus on these additional processes and mechanisms that constitutes the second analytical shift in the study of democratic principal–agent relations proposed in this volume. A critical mechanism shaping principal–agent accountability relations concerns the *competitiveness of democratic elections*. As we argue below, competitiveness and levels of economic development interact in contingently shaping accountability relations. In a similar vein, *political-economic governance structures and property rights regimes* mediate between development and principal–agent linkage mechanisms. Third, the mobilization of *ethnocultural divides* plays an independent role in shaping principal–agent linkages and also interacts with development and political-economic governance structures.

This introductory chapter consists of two major sections. In the first section, we conceptualize alternative democratic principal–agent linkage mechanisms of accountability within a rationalistic framework of direct (clientelistic) and indirect (programmatic, program-based) exchange. In the subsequent section, we flesh out the factors that account for variance in principal–agent linkage mechanisms across time and space.

Identifying clientelistic and programmatic linkages

We define clientelism as a particular mode of "exchange" between electoral constituencies as principals and politicians as agents in democratic systems. This exchange is focused on particular classes of goods, though the feasibility and persistence of clientelistic reciprocity is not determined by the type of goods exchanged. For the purposes of this volume we use the terms *patronage* and *clientelism* interchangeably, though we recognize that some authors use patronage in a narrower sense to refer to an exchange in which voters obtain public jobs for their services to a candidate. One problem both clients and patrons face is that the clientelistic exchange between principals and agents is not usually simultaneous, but takes place over time. This raises the obvious threat of opportunistic defection, in which either the voter or the politician reneges on the deal once he or she has been "paid." Programmatic politics does not run into this problem because the implicit exchange of votes for policies does not rely on the specific conduct of individual voters and small groups of voters. With regard to politicians, mass publics must have the possibility to observe their activities, e.g., through surveillance by free and independent mass media.

Clientelism, however, as a form of direct, contingent exchange, requires more specific contractual performance by the involved parties than programmatic linkage. Moreover, the critical contributions of the participants in exchange bargains may be unobserved or unobservable. As a consequence, clientelism can persist only if one or both of the following conditions is in place. In some instances, politicians have good reasons to expect that the target constituencies for clientelistic bargains will behave in predictable fashion and refrain from opportunism. Here, a *cognitive condition* – knowledge of the other side's motivations and payoffs from alternative courses of action – and a *motivational condition* – voluntary, spontaneous compliance of constituencies with clientelistic inducements – ensure the viability of clientelism. Absent these two conditions, politicians may develop ways to monitor defection from the bargain and capabilities to punish free-riding groups and individuals based on that knowledge. In order to do so, they have to build expensive organizational surveillance and enforcement structures.

Hence, in the case of clientelism, under conditions of democratic enfranchisement the major cost of constructing such linkages is that of building organizational hierarchies of exchange between electoral clients at the ground floor of the system, various levels of brokers organized in a pyramidal fashion, and patrons at the top. Politicians have to identify resources they can extract and offer to clients in exchange for contributions to their electoral efforts. Moreover, they must construct organizational devices and social networks of supervision that make direct individual or indirect group-based monitoring of political exchange relations viable. In this process, clients and politicians gain confidence in the viability of their relationship by iteration, i.e., the repeated success of exchange relations that makes the behavior of the exchange partner appear predictable and low risk. The evolution of party organizational forms that manage clientelistic relations is a drawn-out process, not an instant result of rational strategic interaction in single-shot games.

Under conditions of democratic competition with full enfranchisement, local exchange networks will rarely suffice to win national elections. Politicians need to organize the flow of material resources across the complex pyramidal network of client-broker-patron exchanges. By coordinating large numbers of political operatives, they must overcome challenging problems of collective action and principal–agent conflicts through finely balanced systems of incentives. For example, higher-level brokers will wish to divert as much as possible of a party's electoral resources to their private use rather than to confer them on lower-level brokers who then are in turn expected to restrain their own income-maximizing self-interests and reward external electoral clients with resources that induce the latter to contribute generously to the party through votes, labor, and financial contributions.[6] It takes complicated internal mechanisms of monitoring and control to limit the predatory behavior of party agents sufficiently so that external clientelistic exchanges can still generate the resources needed to enable a party to win electoral office and to dominate the benefits-dispensing government executive.

Programmatic exchange relations, like clientelistic exchange networks, require heavy investments on the part of politicians and voters, although each practice requires somewhat different techniques. Because programmatic party competition does not necessitate direct individual or indirect social-network-based monitoring of voters' electoral conduct, it is cheaper to construct organizational machines than in the clientelistic case. After all, programmatic parties need fewer personnel to manage exchange relations. The lower transaction costs of erecting large-scale flows of material resources up and down the organizational ladder, however, are outweighed by the imperative that the party must speak with a more or less single collective voice in order to create a measure of confidence among voters that it will pursue the policy objectives after elections it has announced before an election. Creating a common collective party program is what Aldrich (1995) calls the solution to the problem of collective choice, i.e., create agreement on and compliance with a collective partisan preference schedule that may be somewhat at variance with the many diverse preference schedules of all the party members. It takes constant "ideology work" to establish or maintain the collective preference function against the centrifugal tendencies of all individual party activists to assert their own individual or factional preference schedules. Just like clientelistic exchange networks, programmatic techniques of partisan political accountability are path dependent. In new democracies, they require pre-democratic legacies or earlier episodes of democratic competition that enabled political actors to take steps towards solving problems of social choice in the construction of programmatic alternatives. If such preconditions are absent, programmatic party competition requires the iteration of electoral contests under democratic conditions in order to allow politicians and electoral constituencies to incur the cost of overcoming problems of social choice through "ideology work."

Let us now turn to the three components that we define as constituting clientelistic exchange: *contingent direct exchange*, *predictability*, and *monitoring*. First, the exchange between principal and agent is contingent and

---

[6] For example, the Republican Party machine in Philadelphia in the 1930s complained about ward leaders who used resources to help their friends and families rather than help the party keep control of the city (Kurtzman 1935: 44).

direct. It concerns goods from which non-participants in the exchange can be excluded. Second, such exchanges become viable from the perspective of politicians, if voter constituencies respond in predictable fashion to clientelistic inducements without excessive opportunism and free-riding. Third, short of constituencies' spontaneous and voluntary compliance with the clientelistic deal, politicians can invest in organizational structures to monitor and enforce clientelistic exchanges.

Contingent direct exchange

All politicians in democratic systems target benefits to particular segments of the electorate, based upon their perception that particular groups of voters will prefer policy packages from which their own group will benefit. In a system of programmatic party competition, however, politicians announce and implement policies that create beneficiaries and losers without verifying that the beneficiaries will actually deliver their votes. Programmatic linkage therefore directs benefits at very large groups in which only a fraction of the members may actually support the candidate. In other words, politicians enter a *non-contingent, indirect political exchange.* They devise policy packages knowing that they are *likely* to benefit particular groups of voters (typically, a party's swing voters) rather than others, and that this in turn will make it more likely in general that members of these groups will vote for the party. But this policy targeting is neither accompanied by monitoring or sanctioning of voters who defect from the politician's partisan camp, nor by precise knowledge of who in the target constituency will vote for the party delivering the benefit.

In a clientelistic relationship, in contrast, the politician's delivery of a good is *contingent upon* the actions of specific members of the electorate. Here is the first difference (necessary but not sufficient) between programmatic and clientelistic politics. What makes clientelistic exchange distinctive is not simply the fact that benefits are targeted. Rather, it is the fact that politicians target a range of benefits *only* to individuals or identifiable small groups who have already delivered or who promise to deliver their electoral support to their partisan benefactor. Voters dedicate their votes *only* to those politicians who promise to deliver a particular mix of goods and services to them as individuals or small groups in return. Thus it is the contingency of targeted benefits, not the targeting of goods taken by itself, that constitutes the clientelistic exchange.

The *nature of the goods* supplied by the patron politician or party only in some cases provides definitive evidence about the nature of the linkage type at work, but not in others. For example, the politicized allocation of *private goods* that accrue to individual citizens – such as public sector jobs and promotions or preferential, discretionary access to scarce or highly subsidized goods such as land, public housing, education, utilities, or social insurance benefits (pensions, health care), and specific procurement contracts to private enterprises – signal clientelistic relations almost by definition. As well as material goods (money, jobs, other tangible goods), parties and patrons can offer clients the less immediately tangible but no less valuable private goods of power and influence. In states where individual officials and politicians have a high degree of discretion in how they enforce rules, many people regard it as crucial to have sustained access to a powerful patron who can ensure that the agents of the state either deal with the client honestly, or when required dishonestly, for example by ignoring tax regulations, building codes, anti-squatter legislation, proper procedures for charging for water and electricity, or by giving favorable legal judgments (e.g., Milne 1973).

Whereas the provision of *private goods* through political exchange invariably signals the existence of clientelism, *public goods* that are desired by everyone in society and from whose enjoyment no one can be excluded, regardless of whether they contributed to the production of the good or not, can by definition not be traded through clientelistic exchange. Public goods include the provision of external and internal security, macroeconomic growth, full employment, low inflation, and a clean environment. Just about everyone benefits from these goods. They are "valence issues" in the sense that they exhibit a popular distribution of preferences heavily skewed to one extreme. Hence politicians compete not by offering different packages of such goods, but by trying to trump each other in terms of making credible their competence and capacity to deliver such goods, if elected to office.

Many important benefits that politicians allocate through the political process have neither public nor private goods status. They belong to the murky middle ground of "*club goods*" that provide benefits for subsets of citizens and impose costs on other subsets. Citizens external to certain group boundaries can be excluded from the enjoyment of such benefits, but none of those inside the boundary. Club goods typically redistribute life chances across groups in society, and politicians engineer such redistribution so as to solidify and increase the size of their electoral coalitions. Club good character accrues to all schemes of income redistribution through the tax code and social policy insurance schemes, whether obvious or not. Redistribution is also involved in the public regulation of goods and services industries, e.g., to the advantage of consumers or producers.

When it comes to club goods, politicians can try to organize linkages to their constituencies based *either* on programmatic *or* clientelistic relations. If they go the programmatic route, they frame the disbursement of resources in terms of general rules with highly specific stipulations for policy implementation by which both administrators of the policies and recipients of the benefits have to abide, regardless of their personal party preferences. Politicians then simply hope that the distributive impact of the policies will create enough support for their party or their personal candidacy to ensure reelection. Programmatic politicians have to cast their net wide and hope for a moderate electoral yield among all the people who benefit from their office incumbency.

Clientelistic politicians, by contrast, prefer rules and regulations for the authoritative allocation of costs and benefits that leave maximum political discretion to the implementation phase, i.e., have as few precise rules of disbursement and entitlement as possible. Politicians then may cast their net narrowly and aim at identifying particular individuals and small groups whose support can be obtained by material inducements tailored to their personal needs and serviced by political appointees in public bureaucracies who do the governing parties' bidding. Rather than dispersing moderate benefits across a broad audience, clientelistic politicians concentrate a high proportion of benefits on a critical mass of voter constituencies whose support they expect to bring them victory in the next electoral contest. For this focused, concentrated strategy to work, however, either certain cognitive and motivational preconditions are vital and/or politicians must have ways and means to monitor and enforce terms of the clientelistic bargain.

Voluntary compliance as a condition of contingent exchange: predictability and elasticity of citizens' conduct

What knowledge allows politicians to be more confident when offering electoral constituencies a direct exchange involving targeted club and private goods? At a minimum, politicians need to be confident in their prediction that voters who actually receive the benefits of their actions will vote for them ("predictability" of citizens' conduct). Furthermore, politicians will go to the trouble of crafting clientelistic relations only if the direct, targeted clientelistic exchange actually makes the difference between people voting or not voting for them. Politicians would waste their scarce resources were they to focus clientelistic benefits on constituencies that support them in any case, regardless of tailored material inducements. Only where there is strong effective "elasticity" in voters' electoral conduct, contingent upon the provision of clientelistic goods, have politicians a reason to supply such goods. Vote choice predictability may be a function of the magnitude of the benefit enjoyed by the target constituency. Vote choice elasticity is a function of the probability that some competitor could offer the same or even more valuable targeted material goods to the constituency. Iteration of the political game may affect the credibility of competitors offering to deliver the club good in clientelistic fashion. Where one party or politician has done so for many rounds of the competitive game, it may be difficult for some challenger to establish credibility as a potential alternative source of benefits.

Where the conduct of individual voters or small groups of voters cannot be predicted easily, or when predictable electoral conduct is inelastic, politicians have incentives to engage only in programmatic linkage strategies with indirect, non-specific exchanges that disburse club goods to large groups of voters in the hope of swaying enough voters by the politicians' actions to win reelection. Alternatively, politicians may engage in programmatic valence competition trying to prove their competence in delivering collective goods demanded by all citizens in a polity (e.g., good economic performance) or at least club goods requested by all citizens living in a particular district ("pork"). In all of these instances, politicians save the transaction costs of monitoring and enforcing the actions of clients, but operate under conditions of uncertainty and unpredictability. Because their policy benefits are less specifically targeted and lack contingency when compared to those in clientelistic relations, they will accrue to many citizens who do not support their reelection.

Let us illustrate the impact of high predictability and elasticity in facilitating clientelistic politics with the case of the voters in the Fifth Election District in Gunma, Japan. The local economy in Gunma relies heavily upon agriculture and in particular on the local yam industry, which accounts for 80 percent of Japanese production. The Gunma yam industry is highly inefficient by international standards, and could not survive without the government's 990 percent tariff on imports. People in the district have voted overwhelmingly for the Liberal Democratic Party, which has offered strong support for the yam industry as well as for the public works projects vital to the local construction industry.[7]

Is the LDP's delivery of a club good (the yam tariff) to the voters of Gunma a clientelistic practice or not? A reasonable decision rule is to classify such a transaction as clientelistic if it satisfies the following conditions of the direct exchange: (1) *Predictability*: for the people of Gunma, protection of their local yam industry is decisive for their electoral choice. Given the size of the tariff and the profile of income sources in the district, this result is a pretty good bet. Furthermore, the fact that there have been many iterations of the electoral bargain between

---

[7] 4 "2-Party elections a foreign concept in rural Japan," *New York Times* Nov. 5, 2003, p. A-3.

LDP and Gunma district voters increases the predictability of political action. (2) *Elasticity*: the salience and material importance of the good's provision (tariff) for the local economy is sufficiently high for members of the target group to tip the balance of *most* group members' voting behavior in favor of the party that promises to provide the good. It is plausible that the extraordinary magnitude of the benefit all but certainly creates elasticity around the issue. (3) *Competition*: were the LDP to stop provision of the benefit, or were alternative credible parties promising to supply the same or a greater benefit, it is all but certain that the local voters would switch sides to other parties. With national competition among parties intensifying in Japan in the 1990s, LDP politicians know that they probably would lose the support of the local constituency were they to abandon the tariff.

By these criteria, the citizen–politician linkage in Gunma is clearly clientelistic: newspaper reports suggest local citizens vote for the powerful LDP family that controls the seat *because of* its fierce support for the tariffs that protect the prefecture's main crop, as well as the LDP's support for the local construction industry, both of which are the pillars on which other local services (such as banking, insurance, farm supplies) rely. While the LDP has been prepared to reduce other agricultural tariffs, the party has kept the yam tariff because of the high salience and economic importance of the issue in this one politically important district, which has produced a string of powerful LDP leaders, including former prime minister, Keichi Ozumi.[8]

Counteracting opportunism in clientelistic exchange: monitoring and enforcement

Monitoring voter behavior is often difficult, but without such monitoring from one election to the next, politicians run the risk of misdirecting resources to voters who will defect: in other words, take the money and run. As it turns out, there are many options to achieve this objective short of reliance on crude, coercive, violent, and therefore costly punishments of citizens' defection from clientelistic bargains. Some of them are explored in detail in the contributions to this volume by Chandra, Hale, and Levitsky. Politicians of course prefer lower-cost methods of monitoring to those that require large investments of time and money, and this biases them toward group rather than individual monitoring, and public methods of monitoring rather than reliance upon a network of private informants. First, monitoring how a group votes is less costly

---

[8] Ibid.

than monitoring how individuals vote, so individual monitoring will be used more often where the number of voters is small (hundreds or thousands, rather than tens of thousands) and geographically compact rather than dispersed. Second, private promises of support from an individual are much less valuable to a politician than public pledges, or the display of badges, party colors or signs. The advantages of requiring those who claim to be supporters to publicly pledge or display their support are obvious. This especially applies to members of ethnic, religious, or clearly identified social groups, because public pledges by influential members of these groups have multiplier effects on the voting preferences of the group as a whole. By forcing members of a group to publicly pledge support to the incumbent party rather than the opposition, for example, group members are effectively then cut off from any expectation of rewards if the opposition should win. This increases the probability that group members in general – including those who may not have agreed with the decision of their peers to support the incumbent party – will actually vote for the incumbents in order to avoid punishment if the opposition wins and increase their chances of a reward if the incumbent is reelected. We should note here that continued interaction and exchange between patrons and clients over time – for example at local celebrations – may eventually make such regular monitoring of voting unnecessary because (a) regular interaction and exchange alone effectively cuts off the clients from any expectation of rewards from a different client; (b) the interaction may be sufficient to induce cultural expectations of reciprocity inherent in any gift giving situation (see below).

Monitoring individuals

The simplest way to monitor individual voters, but also one that is relatively costly in terms of party resources is by violating the secrecy of the ballot, or as Chandra explores in this volume, by giving voters the impression that one has violated the secrecy of the ballot. For several hundred years in Europe and North America, of course, voting was public by law, allowing patrons to match punishments and rewards precisely to voter behavior, and also in some cases to maintain their hold on political power long after the underlying distribution of voters' preferences had shifted away from them (Whyte 1965: 741–49). Laws that mandated open voting, not surprisingly, were often endogenous to political elites' calculations about likely voting patterns under open and secret ballots. Dahl, for instance, describes how members of the Protestant elite in early nineteenth-century Connecticut, worried about losing power as the franchise expanded, instituted a "stand-up law" in 1801 to make voting public so that they could retaliate against new voters who voted the wrong way (Dahl 1961: 16).

Even where politicians were unable to block the introduction of a secret ballot they developed many methods to monitor voters so that they could then reward or punish people who supported or opposed them. Studies of voting in the USA in the nineteenth and twentieth centuries describe the widespread use of such tactics as marked or pre-printed ballots, party workers forcing voters to ask for help in the voting booth because they were "disabled" or "illiterate," or voting systems that required voters to publicly identify themselves if they did not wish to vote for officially approved candidates (Dahl 1961: 16; Kurtzman 1935: 121, 133–35). Political reformers and opposition politicians tried to challenge incumbents by pressing for the introduction of voting machines that, it was hoped, would make such monitoring impossible. Incumbent party machines, predictably, fought against the introduction of such technologies; for example, the ruling Republicans in Philadelphia made great efforts to fight off reform by "proving" that new voting machines were costly, complex, and unreliable.[9] But in practice even such apparently threatening technologies as voting machines could sometimes be adapted to politicians' need to monitor the way people voted. For example, in some cities machines were configured so as to allow a straight party ticket to be voted quickly with a distinctive ringing sound, whereas voting for the opposition or for a mixed slate required additional time with no accompanying ring, a combination that clearly signaled one's preferences to those outside the booth (Kurtzman 1935).

There are other methods of monitoring how individuals vote that do not require violating the secrecy of the ballot box. Door-to-door canvassing allows politicians to acquire good information on voters' party preferences, because most people either do not like to lie or else are not very good at it. Ethnographic studies of elections indicate that party workers quickly become skilled at determining from brief interviews whether particular voters support their party or not. The intentions of those who try to mask their preferences can be further uncovered by asking individuals to accept party literature, be contacted in the future, or show their support by wearing badges or displaying party colors and signs. In many electoral systems party workers also pass out goods such as sweets and liquor to their supporters outside polling places, the object being to make voters publicly declare their allegiance to one party or the other.

---

[9] As a result of these efforts Philadelphia spent more than *ten times* as much on the combined purchase and maintenance costs of each voting machine as nearby Delaware County. Kurtzman (1935: 121).

Another way in which politicians can monitor voters' preferences is by keeping track of how many voters from particular areas or groups come to ask them for favors based on their support for the politician (Kurtzman 1935).

We can think of mass party organization models as highly effective group devices for surveillance and mobilization, in which local party bosses closely monitor individuals' conduct. Contrary to Shefter's (1977, 1994) conceptualization of mass party organizations as the antithesis of clientelistic machine politics, mass parties provide the capabilities of serving clientelistic monitoring practices, provided they are placed in a democratic political context in which their leaders acquire access to public resources that fuel clientelistic distributive schemes – such as the power to appoint civil servants, to grant access to public housing, or to disburse pension and unemployment benefits.

Monitoring groups

Monitoring groups of voters – or having them monitor themselves and then rewarding or punishing the group– is much more efficient than monitoring and then rewarding and punishing individuals, especially where party organizations are weak and in elections with large numbers of voters dispersed over a wide area. In dealing with cohesive ethnic groups with clear hierarchies – the Lubavitch Hasidim in parts of New York State are a good example – the politician needs only to contract with the group leader to be assured of the support of the entire group. The certainty of the payoff to the politician helps explain why the Lubavitch Hasidim have enjoyed so much political patronage relative to their size. One Brooklyn politician described how "They go to synagogue and get their palm cards and they're bused right to the polls. Mayor Daley would be proud of them . . . They are the last deliverable bloc in the city . . . They get heavy money from everybody because they can deliver votes. They want bucks. They want programs, because programs mean jobs and power in their community. They get tons of stuff, housing particularly."[10]

Even though many groups lack this level of cohesion, politicians have other options to monitor groups' voting. Voting returns and opinion polls, if sufficiently disaggregated, can also provide sufficient information to politicians to enable them to verify a group's support with a high level of accuracy – and low transaction costs – even in the absence of public or

---

[10] "Birth of a voting bloc: Candidates pay court to Hasidic and Orthodox Jews," *New York Times*, May 2, 1989, p. B1.

private pledges or private information on voting behavior.[11] They can verify support and deliver rewards with very low transaction costs. Chandra, Hale, Scheiner, and Levitsky's articles in this volume all provide instances of geographic monitoring of groups, for instance through counting of ballots at the subdistrict level in Japan (Scheiner). Until 1971 ballots in India were counted at each local polling station, which enabled politicians to quickly determine whether a village had kept to its side of the political bargain. In Philadelphia and Chicago ward-level results similarly allowed supportive wards – often ethnically homogenous – to be rewarded and opposing wards to be punished. Opinion polls can also, if disaggregated by race, ethnicity, constituency, or other salient group attribute, facilitate clientelistic targeting by politicians. If a particular constituency, such as African Americans in the USA, ultra-Orthodox Sephardic Jews in Israel, or members of the Yadav caste in north India is known from opinion polls to vote for a particular party (the Democratic Party, Shas, the Samajwadi party) at a level of 80 percent or above, then patrons do not really need individual information on voting preferences in order to be (80 percent) sure of delivering benefits only to their supporters.

If the interaction between the patron and the clients is sustained over time, it may be unnecessary for the patron to continue to monitor the clients' votes, and we can think of clientelism in these circumstances as a self-enforcing group equilibrium. The sociologist Javier Auyero (2000) provides a good example of such an equilibrium in his study of clientelism in Argentina. He shows how clientelistic brokers (Peronist Judicialist Party local ward bosses) have developed a web of services in which they deliver tangible benefits to individuals (from food and medicines via local jobs in the party machine and the municipality to the delivery of marijuana to rallies). Participants are immersed into a system of generalized, implicit exchange in which brokers expect and encourage, but do not enforce reciprocal acts. The clients participate in PJ party rallies (where they get booze and pot) and in turn vote for the party. This *ongoing network of social relations* generates widely held cognitive expectations about appropriate behavior that in turn reduce monitoring efforts (Auyero 2000: 122–23). The instrumental exchange aspect remains tacit and is concealed in the symbolic representations of the relationship by both brokers and clients. It is an *ongoing, iterative process* in which the past behavior of parties individuals, and communities influences present expectations of the obligations of patrons to clients and vice versa. The same type of relationships exist in voting in Thailand, where older voters who regularly participate in patron–client networks explain their actions

---

[11] Assuming low geographical and social mobility on the part of the target population.

in normative terms and are reported to regard it as a *bap* (demerit) not to vote for a patron who has given them money or other rewards (Callahan and McCargo 1996). Historical analyses of voting in eighteenth and nineteenth-century England and Ireland also identify generalized ties of "deference" and "obligation" of tenant to landlord (and vice versa), sustained over time not just through reciprocal transactions but through continuing participation in local community affairs and events, as much more important in explaining voters' choices than simple threats of coercion or promises of monetary rewards at the time of an election (O'Gorman 1984: 398–403; Whyte 1965).

The monitoring and enforcement of clientelistic citizen–politician linkages is not a simple process in which patrons at every step monitor their clients and intervene to punish free-riders. Clientelism involves a complex web of relations in which monitoring and enforcement is practiced in a highly indirect and concealed fashion. The concealment of clientelism may go so far as to lead to "preference falsification" on the part of all participants.[12] Neither patrons nor clients are willing or even able to describe the clientelistic relationship as a quid-pro-quo exchange of scarce and desirable goods, but instead interpret it in flowery terms as an enactment of community relations and civic solidarity.

Alternative modes of citizen–politician linkage

Thus, clientelistic linkages are carried out either through single transactions, multiple discrete transactions, or – more frequently – through complex, continuing webs of exchange, obligation, and reciprocity. In many systems characterized by relatively high levels of poverty – such as Thailand, India, Pakistan, or Zambia – patrons directly purchase clients' votes in exchange for money, liquor, clothes, food, or other immediately consumable goods (Callahan and McCargo 1996). Much more frequent than single-shot transactions of this nature, however, are webs of exchange, obligation, and reciprocity sustained over a longer period, in which patrons provide *private goods* or *club goods* to their clients.[13]

In general, politicians target specific constituencies with clientelistic benefits when they can predict the electoral behavior of that constituency

---

[12] We are employing here Kuran's (1991) notion originally intended for citizens in communist regimes who deny that they even have a wish to abolish existing power structures, until it becomes feasible to do so.

[13] Some money, alcohol, food etc. may be given by politicians to voters on polling day as part of these more generalized networks of reciprocity and exchange but in many cases it would be a mistake to see these gifts as sufficient in themselves to determine voters' choices.

Table 1.1 *Which conditional exchange relations are most valuable to politicians in clientelistic systems?*

		Predictability of exchange: single-shot or ongoing relations?	
		single-shot	ongoing
Counteracting opportunism. *Locus of provision,* *monitoring and enforcement*	*groups*	Weakest leverage of political agent over principals	Intermediate leverage
	individuals	Intermediate leverage	Strongest leverage of political agent over principals

in response to the stimulus. Furthermore, the effectiveness of clientelistic targeting increases with the precision of monitoring constituency behavior and enforcing compliance by sanctioning free-riding, even though these may be expensive undertakings. Predictability of client behavior increases, as citizen–politician relations unfold in an iterative process in which both sides can coordinate around a cooperative solution. The precision of monitoring increases from less expensive group monitoring to more expensive monitoring of individual behavior. Hence, as we can see in the 2 × 2 representation presented in Table 1.1, clientelistic relations become more valuable to politicians as a way to gain political leverage if they can be (1) easily targeted to individuals or small groups and (2) if they can be withdrawn if the voter does not keep up his or her end of the bargain.

Obvious examples of goods that offer high leverage over voters include permission to work a landlord's land, or access to a local government job in systems without substantial civil service protections for employees. There are many historical examples, for instance, of landlords threatening tenants with the loss of agricultural credit, advances of seeds, loans, or the right to work the patron's land if they dared to vote the wrong way (Whyte 1965). In classic US party machines jobs were readily targeted to known supporters of the incumbent party and these supporters knew that their jobs – and those of their relatives – were in immediate jeopardy if they switched their support or failed to vote in sufficient numbers to keep their party in power.[14]

---

[14] Reports suggest that the "classic" US political machine still survives. The Philadelphia Democratic chairman warned thousands of city employees in August 2003 that their jobs would be given to Republicans if the Republican candidate was elected mayor. "Democrat says win by Katz would imperil patronage jobs," *The Philadelphia Inquirer*, August 27, 2003.

Table 1.2 *Modes of citizen–politician linkage*

	Strategic linkages		
	Programmatic valence policy competition	Programmatic policy competition	Clientelistic competition
1. Contingency of exchange: Benefit tied to vote? ("targeted" delivery)	No	No (indirect exchange)	Yes (direct exchange)
2. Nature of goods offered to voters: Private, club, or public goods?	Collective and club ("pork") goods ("valence competition")	Club goods ("spatial-directional" competition; redistribution)	Private or club goods
3. Predictability: Compliance of individuals/groups responding to politician's actions?	Low	Variable	High
4. Elasticity: Change in constituents' vote choice due to politician's stimulus?	Small	Medium	Large
5. Monitoring and external enforcement of the exchange?	No	No	Variable: 1. Individual surveillance 2. Group oversight and self-policing

We are now in a position to compare clientelistic politics to other types of citizen–politician linkages in competitive party democracies (Table 1.2). We are depicting here only *strategic* linkages in which the actions of principals and agents are conditional upon each other in some fashion. We set aside here non-strategic linkages where voter constituencies display unconditional loyalty to politicians. This at least applies to the social-psychological version of "party identification" based on processes of socialization and affective bonding, not so much the strategic version of party identification as result of the cumulative "running tally" of policy actions parties have performed over long periods of time to endear themselves to particular voters. The strategic image also does not apply to voter-citizen relations based on candidate personality traits ("charisma"), net of the candidate's policy preferences.

Among the strategic relations, we distinguish clientelism from two different types of programmatic policy voting, one dealing with a situation of valence goods with a skewed distribution of preferences and politicians trying to demonstrate their competence in delivering the club or collective goods most voters want, and the other dealing with plain directional and spatial competition among parties offering different programmatic packages and appealing to electoral constituencies with different policy preferences.

On two of our five aspects of the linkage relationship, there is a clear contrast between both forms of programmatic competition and linkage building, on one side, and clientelistic competition and linkage, on the other. Only in clientelistic politics are benefits implicitly or explicitly tied to delivery of political support (the vote, material contributions and time going to the party) in exchange for material benefits flowing from political office. Programmatic politicians do not engage in contingent exchange and therefore do not try to monitor and enforce conformity of voters with certain party preferences, while clientelistic patrons most definitely engage in such practices.

On the other three dimensions, we have a sliding scale ranging from programmatic valence voting via programmatic directional policy voting to clientelistic competition. Clientelistic linkages tend to involve goods with a smaller scale of disbursement and less opportunity for free-riding, but there is no hard and fast borderline. Local and regional club goods may be featured by politicians pursuing either clientelistic or programmatic linkage strategies. In a similar vein, even for programmatic policy strategies, the predictability of voters' response to policy initiatives may be sufficiently high to constitute a clientelistic exchange. Finally, while in general voter elasticity in response to programmatic initiatives may be lower than that in response to clientelistic inducements, this is a matter of degree and is often hard to measure.

The heuristic value of Table 1.2 is to clarify the conditions under which politicians may pursue clientelistic linkage building in a rational, instrumental fashion, taking the full political opportunity costs and benefits of this strategy into account. In this section, we have identified characteristics of clientelistic and programmatic linkages and institutional or behavioral preconditions for each to operate in democratic electoral party competition. Both modes of linkage building require considerable time and resources on the part of politicians to coordinate their teams of office-seekers as well as electoral constituencies around their preferred pattern of democratic accountability and responsiveness. Let us next explore the conditions under which politicians choose programmatic linkage strategies as their preferred mode of operation and those that make politicians inclined to seek out clientelistic linkage systems.

Explaining democratic linkage practices

In the previous section, we have identified three attribute dimensions that distinguish clientelistic from programmatic principal–agent accountability. They are analytically distinct, but up to a point parties can, of course, combine elements of clientelistic and programmatic accountability in an encompassing "portfolio" package.[15] First, clientelistic linkages *target* benefits to individuals (private goods) and small groups (local club goods) who have proven, or are expected, to be supporters of winning politicians with control over resources. Programmatic linkages deliver benefits to large groups (functional club goods) and the entire polity (collective goods). Targeting benefits also facilitates "credit claiming" by politicians for benefits reaching electoral constituencies. Second, clientelistic linkages rely on some kind of *monitoring or enforcement of direct exchanges,* and we have laid out the manifold techniques – from crude supervision of individual citizens in the voting booth and prepared ballot papers via organizational encapsulation of constituencies to sophisticated calculations based on precinct returns – that can achieve this objective in the end. Third, even where monitoring and enforcement may be weak or absent, a *high predictability and low elasticity of constituency partisan affiliation as a result of the supreme salience of specific targeted benefits for the group* may deliver a reasonably high level of certainty and contractual enforcement of direct exchanges, i.e., a low dissipation of politicians' resources among citizens who do not support them through their votes. In the absence of facilities to monitor and enforce direct exchange or under conditions where the benefits that constituencies deem salient are sufficiently amorphous and distributed among voter groups and variable over time to increase elasticity and decrease predictability of voting behavior, it is likely that politicians rely more on programmatic accountability.

All this presupposes, of course, that politicians have the time and resources to engage in the arduous, slow, resource-intensive undertaking to build clientelistic or programmatic political parties. Both kinds of parties have to solve collective action problems in the process of building an

---

[15] See Kitschelt (2000b) and Magaloni et al. in this volume for a more extensive discussion of this topic.

elaborate organizational infrastructure. This infrastructure may be more extensive in the case of clientelistic parties. In addition to targeting public resources on their constituencies, clientelistic parties raise "private" resources from asset-rich, but vote-poor clients in exchange for favors and in order to dole them out to asset-poor, but vote-rich other client groups (Kitschelt 2000b). Conversely, programmatic parties have to make an investment in solving problems of social choice by setting up mechanisms to deliberate collective goals in the organization and enforce compliance with collective programmatic objectives by partisan politicians in electoral office. Where democracies were recently founded and politicians cannot build on organizational infrastructures that either precede authoritarian episodes or that could grow within authoritarian regimes, neither clientelistic nor programmatic parties will instantly appear. In that case, politicians' accountability exclusively relies on short-term performance ratings ("retrospective voting") or personal qualities ("charisma").

In the following section, we lay out how different causal mechanisms may influence targeting/credit claiming for benefits, monitoring/enforcement of direct exchange, and the predictability/inelasticity of constituency vote choices. We begin with economic development and then consider its conditional relation to the competitiveness of democratic partisan contests. We then discuss institutional democratic rules, followed by the public control of the political economy and mobilized ethnocultural divides. While the democratic rules of the game should affect all parties competing in a polity in a similar fashion, all the other mechanisms we lay out may shape linkage mechanisms differentially for individual parties within the same polity or for all parties in the same way in that polity.

The role of economic development

Economic development is the most commonly confirmed predictor of differential modes of democratic accountability. Affluent democracies and parties appealing to affluent citizens in a democracy tend to operate more through programmatic accountability, while parties in poor democracies and parties appealing to the poorest electoral segments tend to practice clientelism.

Demand side factors

D-1. Scaling up of social networks: Development works through people's involvement in markets beyond the local level. At extremely low levels, most local constituencies will be highly autonomous and self-sufficient such that principal–agent exchange relations will be superfluous. Most residents of an area will be simply subject to political authority. As van de Walle (in this volume) explains, principal–agent relations of exchange will be limited to a small elite within which "prebendal" patrimonial exchange prevails. Scale upgrading and market commodification of social relations generates demands for societal coordination through centralized authoritative political decisions. This initially gives rise to new group loyalties serviced by clientelistic networks beyond the realm of kinship and family (Scott 1969, 1972). But as the process of further societal scale upgrading proceeds, clientelistic linkages – providing private and local club goods – become too narrow and give way to class, sectoral, and professional linkages in the formation of national and global markets. People demand goods from politicians who serve increasingly large clubs for whose members clientelistic linkages are too costly in terms of transactional arrangements. Some of these goods serve everyone in a polity ("collective goods").

D-2. Discount rates. Poor people cannot wait for material rewards and therefore prefer targeted handouts to the distant benefits of policy change. But, as Lyne argues in her treatment of the voter's dilemma, without further triggers originating on the demand and the supply side, even under conditions of high affluence voters should always prefer clientelistic exchange. It delivers benefits – both private and local public goods – with greater certainty than indirect exchange based on policy (large-scale club goods, collective goods). Citizens are stuck in a prisoner's dilemma: people abandoning a clientelistic exchange opportunity may therefore be punished and left empty-handed, if too few voters become "suckers" and promote a winning programmatic party rather than their personal and local benefit, however modest. Programmatic parties are attractive only to voters who have enough assets (especially human capital endowments) to become entirely indifferent to clientelistic-targeted goods and therefore incur zero opportunity cost when their favorite programmatic party loses to a clientelistic contender.[16]

D-3. Cognitive sophistication in the calculation of costs and benefits. As a cognitive complement to the discount rate and opportunity cost

---

[16] Banfield and Wilson (1963: 106) came to a similar conclusion about the reasons for the decline of the American urban party machines of the second half of the nineteenth century, "[t]he main reason for the decline and near disappearance of the city-wide machine was – and is – the growing unwillingness of voters to accept the inducements that it offered. The petty favors and 'friendship' of the precinct captains declined in value as immigrants were assimilated, public welfare programs were vastly extended, and per capita incomes rose steadily and sharply in postwar prosperity. To the voter who in case of need could turn to a professional social worker and receive as a matter of course unemployment compensation, aid to dependent children, old-age assistance, and all the rest, the precinct captain's hod of coal was a joke."

arguments, poor people may have less education and therefore less capacity to understand and trace the lengthy causal process linking policy changes to personal benefits. This may make them ignore or understate the value of large-scale club or collective goods.

D-4. Ethnocultural group salience and the valuation of local club goods. Conventional modernization theory considers ethnocultural divides as endogenous to development (e.g., Gellner 1983). While modernization might reduce ethnic divisions in some instances (Weber 1976), in others it has clearly increased them. Colonial and post-colonial states, for example, have increased them by creating inter-group inequalities and creating new dimensions for comparison and competition within the same multi-ethnic state (Bates 1983; Horowitz 1985; Rudolph and Rudolph 1967). As a countervailing force to the propensity of development to reduce actors' demand for clientelistic private and local club goods, ethnic divisions thus may boost clientelism even in the face of increasing economic affluence and modernization. Demand side conditions, however, do not tell the whole story. Politicians must be willing and able to mobilize resources and facilities that attract a constituency or may in the first place even create it.

Supply side factors

S-1. Network monitoring: Politicians will invest in clientelistic exchange under conditions of low development because citizens enjoy only limited spatial mobility and are entrapped in rigid, durable social networks increasing predictability and inelasticity of the vote. Programmatic politics takes over when mobility increases and makes the delivery of clientelistic goods unreliable.[17] For some stretch along the way to greater affluence, politicians counteract the erosion of their capacities for monitoring/enforcement and predictability of voter behavior by making investments in the organization of partisan machines. Contrary to Sheffer (1978), mass party organization may help, not hinder, clientelistic politics.

S-2. Constraints on acquiring resources to deploy in clientelistic exchange. In affluent societies, votes become exponentially more expensive to purchase, while economies may become increasingly vulnerable to the market

---

[17] This is not of course to claim that clientelism is incompatible with migration as such. When migrants in the nineteenth century moved from one country to another, clientelistic machines such as New York's Tweed ring were highly effective at integrating them into their new permanent homes. Immigrants were the source of clientelistic network growth, but only because they settled in ethnic neighborhoods once in the USA, in which dense social networks facilitated clientelistic monitoring activities.

distortions such authoritative resource reassignments to rent-seekers are generating. Building on Lyne's contribution, one might suggest a Malthusian law of democratic principal–agent linkages: whereas the costliness of clientelistic exchange increases exponentially with development, politicians' effective acquisition of resources grows only in a linear or asymptotic fashion. The initial response of politicians is to lean more on their asset-rich, but vote-poor clients to surrender private resources. This fuels corruption. Corruption, in turn, may restrain economic growth and indirectly reduce public revenues, generating an unsustainable vicious cycle.

S-3. Strategic dilemmas due to constituency heterogeneity. Relative scarcity of politicians' asset control and heterogeneity of constituencies with some favoring and others rejecting clientelistic exchange makes it difficult for politicians to maintain coherent parties. They may ultimately cut loose the remaining constituencies seeking clientelistic benefits.

S-4. Ethnocultural divisions facilitate supply of clientelistic linkage under conditions of economic development. The presence of clientelistic markers and of associated networks is relatively resistant to development and enables politicians to sustain clientelistic linkages much longer and at lower cost than in homogeneous societies. Even where networks break down or are less relevant at higher levels of political aggregation – towns, assembly and parliamentary districts, states – where there is more uncertainty about the efficacy of alternative networks to organize clientelistic exchange, risk-averse politicians and electoral constituencies may be more likely to rely on ethnocultural markers. Thus, in Chandra's chapter in this volume appeals to ethnicity are more successful because voters lack faith that they are being fairly compensated by other ethnic groups at these higher levels of geographical aggregation. Because trust in non-ethnic patronage networks wanes as well, voters and politicians may rally around ethnocultural clientelistic networks. Evidence from Madhya Pradesh (Singh, Gehlot, Start, and Johnson 2003) and New Haven (Johnston 1979: 389) illustrates that in clientelistic networks the patrons consistently overpay co-ethnics.

S-5. Media exposure of clientelistic politics. When large electoral constituencies have anti-clientelistic preference schedules and consider clientelism scandalous, the media will feed on reporting clientelistic practices, particularly where they are expensive and target highly exclusive rent-seeking constituencies. What were established practices of clientelistic political accountability now are framed as variants of cronyism, nepotism, corruption, fraud, and favoritism.

Development-based supply and demand mechanisms do not consider that politicians are immersed in differential competitive contests with rival parties. Things become more complicated, and clientelism may be sustained at higher levels of development, when certain competitive configurations prevail.

The effect of party competition

Parties make more effort to build principal–agent linkages of accountability whenever "competitiveness" is intense. Whether this competitiveness translates into more clientelistic or more programmatic responsiveness, however, is contingent upon levels of development. Competitiveness is a hard-to-specify concept and the party system literature often associates it in misleading ways with party system fragmentation and volatility.[18] We define party systems as competitive when citizens and politicians have strong incentives to try hard to win supporters at the margin for one or the other partisan camp. This is the case, when (1) elections are close between rival blocs of parties identifiable to voters as alternative governing teams *ex ante* (before elections) and (2) there is a market of uncommitted voters sufficiently large to tip the balance in favor of one or another partisan bloc. But elections must also be *relevant* from a perspective of resource control by the government. They are competitive only if small changes in electoral support might bring about large shifts in public policy or control of patronage.[19] In other words, there must be some programmatic distance between alternative party blocs competing for executive office ("polarization") and governments must have considerable institutional leverage to shift resources (e.g., among clients). Neither measures of party system fragmentation nor electoral volatility capture this conception of competitiveness well. What matters is the location of floating voters, not the size of the floaters' market that is revealed by electoral volatility. In a similar vein, not party system fragmentation, but the identifiability of alternative governing blocs is the critical ingredient of competitiveness.

Competitiveness is most intense under oligopolistic conditions when only a very small set of alternative (coalition) governments is feasible and has unimpeded control over the authoritative allocation of public resources. Competition is less in a highly fragmented and fluid party system with multiple coalition opportunities and in a hegemonic party system. It is under conditions of oligopoly that politicians have the greatest

---

[18] For an earlier more sophisticated effort to conceptualize competitiveness, see Strom (1990). More recently, Franklin's (2004) conceptualization is useful. For an extension of this literature, see Kitschelt (2006).

[19] This may entail, for example, the absence of institutional veto players that arises in systems with a division of power between independently elected executives (presidents) and legislatures and in many federalist and bicameralist systems. Cf. Tsebelis (2002).

incentive to reach out to uncommitted voters floating between the rival camps. Politicians will generally make less effort to extend benefits to "captive" segments of their electorate they can be sure will support their own party. Instead, under conditions of scarcity, they will focus their investments on marginal voters who make the difference between electoral victory and defeat.[20] As competitiveness intensifies, politicians will first target voters whose demands they can combine with those of their core electorate with the least effort in resource expenditure and/or policy concessions, and with comparatively high predictability. In policy terms, this means they will target "leaners" toward their own party rather than "indifferents."[21] Only under conditions of extreme competitiveness will politicians feel compelled to target highly uncertain and indifferent electoral prospects. In clientelistic terms, chasing uncertain prospects is likely to dissipate a great deal of resources. Politicians' expenses may go up exponentially for each additional marginal vote, whereas the cost of programmatic commitments may go up only moderately. Particularly under conditions of high development, where many voters have low regard for clientelistic inducements and thus command a very high price to be bought off, clientelistic linkage may lose its feasibility in the presence of intense competition and an expenditure constraint on politicians.

Consider our rendering of the development/competition interaction as a qualification and extension of what Geddes (1991) discussed as the conditions under which parties abandon administrative patronage – as a specific technique of clientelistic linkage – in favor of professional bureaucracy. On the face of it, her game theoretical set-up suggests that intense, balanced competition between two rival party blocs of almost equal size and probability to win elections induces politicians to abandon clientelism. Upon closer inspection, however, what tips the balance in favor of a competitive race to embrace professionalization is that *politicians in at least one party must perceive a small electoral incentive to propose and make salient administrative reform in a tight electoral race in which small shifts of voters may make the difference between winning and losing.* We interpret this to imply that demand side preference changes, induced by higher levels of development (resulting in human capital endowments, private sector labor market options, etc.) and a decreasing valuation of clientelistic payoffs among the more affluent, in the fashion introduced by Mona Lyne, drive the switch in office-seeking parties' linkage strategies. Competition

---

[20] For a detailed theoretical logic along these lines, see Lindbeck and Weibull (1987) and Dixit and Londregan (1996). Empirical confirmation can be found in Schady (2000) and Dahlberg and Johansson (2002).

[21] For the distinction between these types in a model of voting, see Stokes (2003).

is not the unique cause, but the catalyst of such strategic transformations of accountability and responsiveness.[22]

Politicians' response to intensifying competitiveness of a party system thus depends on the interaction of socioeconomic development in a polity with patterns of competition. We summarize this pattern in Figure 1.1 (a,b,c). Everywhere intense competitiveness makes politicians pursue less promising bets, subject to budget constraints. But under conditions of low development, this will induce politicians to spend marginally much more on clientelistic politics and only moderate additional amounts on programmatic commitments, starting from a negligible baseline (Figure 1.1a). Given the low cost of marginal voters, politicians may in fact not worry much about the dissipation of direct clientelistic benefits to some voters who end up supporting their competitors.[23] By contrast, under conditions of high development, increasing competitiveness may shift outlays almost entirely in favor of programmatic commitments and may make clientelistic responsiveness all but vanish (Figure 1.1b). In addition to resource constraints, here the intense aversion of many voters to clientelistic targeting, particularly among voters not firmly committed to an existing partisan camp, may compel politicians to give up on clientelistic responsiveness altogether. Under conditions of intermediate development, politicians are likely to engage in "menu diversification" contingent upon the electoral segments and the specific poverty or wealth of the location they are dealing with (Figure 1.1c). At the margin, electoral expenses and commitments in a clientelistic and programmatic fashion may initially go up, as competitiveness increases. Once very intense levels of competitiveness are reached and parties chase highly uncertain prospects among the electorate, they may rely more on intra-party investments in solving problems of social choice and demonstrating sincere commitment to programmatic objectives than additional clientelistic handouts. Nevertheless, clientelism remains an important ingredient in party strategy in many places.

---

[22] Because of the competitive nature of the process, not just one, but all major parties may abandon patronage at once to gain marginal voters and to protect their core constituencies hitherto benefiting from clientelism. In the USA in 1884, for instance, senior civil servants appointed under Republican patronage lobbied to have themselves demoted to lower-paid positions protected under new professional civil service rules, when President Cleveland's new Democratic administration came in. See "Charm in Civil Service Rules," *New York Times*, December 8, 1884.

[23] This resolves the at first sight so puzzling practice of candidates who hand out money and gifts to passers-by in public places in a candidate's electoral district in all but indiscriminant fashion.

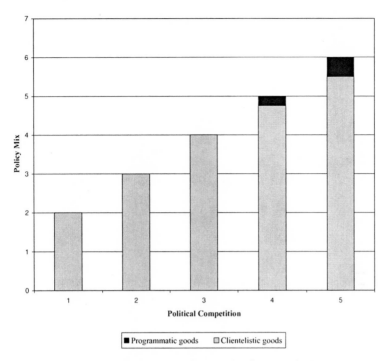

Figure 1.1a Policy mix at low levels of economic development

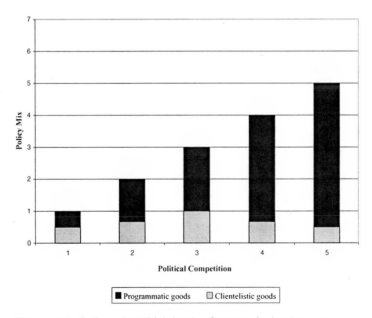

Figure 1.1b Policy mix at high levels of economic development

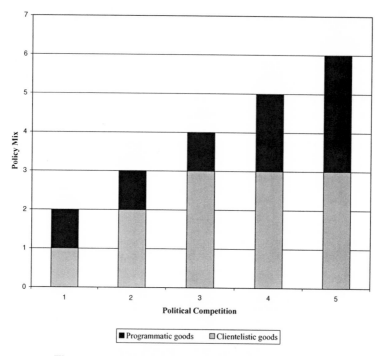

Figure 1.1c Policy mix at intermediate levels of economic development

A critical question is whether competitiveness is endogenous to linkage strategies. For example, does the existence of clientelistic politics keep clients dependent on their patrons and prevent political defection to a competitor because that competitor has little credibility to deliver the benefits guaranteed by the long-term incumbent? There is no doubt that asymmetrical relations exist in which only one party ever controls the assets of government and has additional access to private resources from wealthy, but vote-poor supporters. At the same time, the existence of highly competitive clientelistic polities with regular alternation in governing parties and intense efforts by the contenders to supply goods and to make credible their ability to supply such goods makes the endogeneity argument unlikely. From Bangladesh to Jamaica, clientelistic politics has operated through party competition. Especially among poor countries, competition enhances clientelism. Because competition intensifies ethnocultural mobilization (Wilkinson 2004), and ethnic groups promote clientelism, politicians will move to employ every imaginable strategy of attracting constituencies, subject to a general budget constraint. Within this envelope, ethnocultural mobilization induces a net increase in clientelistic patronage, amplified by democratic competition.

This point is impressively driven home by Carl Stone's (1986) and Obika Gray's (2004) splendid political-anthropological fieldwork on the power of the urban poor in the intensely competitive Jamaican partisan polity. Competition allows the urban underclass and its criminal elements to extract substantial rents from rival politicians who organize conflicting clientelistic networks. In a similar vein, municipal leaders of the urban poor in Brazil "auctioned off" the votes of their communities to the highest bidders in the electoral contest, taking pre-election tangible benefits and credibility of post-election promises into account (Gay 1994: 101–14). Multiparty competition and clientelism are also closely intertwined in Ecuador (Burgwal 1995).

How is it possible that hegemonic clientelistic systems become competitive? One path is that clientelism emerges only after democratization already in a competitive situation in which two or more parties have built up reputations to govern and deliver benefits to their constituencies before clientelism becomes a major currency of linkage building. Another path is that a clientelistic hegemonic ruling party stays in power after full democratization, but then decays both in terms of its capacity to attract private assets from wealthy supporters as well as to deliver spoils of government, for example when a country's economy faces hard times. In that instance, opposition parties with clientelistic aspirations may take over, or the clientelistic incumbent may be displaced by parties relying on different linkage strategies. In fact, very wealthy business owners, if sufficiently antagonized and disgruntled by the governance of the hegemonic party, may bring to bear their own resources on the construction of a new party that prolongs clientelistic linkage building.

Under conditions of democratic contestation also ethnocultural pluralism may be a powerful catalyst of intensifying clientelism, as competition between parties appealing to different ethnic segments heats up. The fiercer the competition, the more ethnic politics may rely on clientelistic bonds. As support of an ethnocultural group becomes *decisive* for a band of politicians to govern, they tend to offer increasing amounts of targeted clientelistic favors to assemble a winning electoral coalition. This may be one of the mechanisms that accounts for what Horowitz (1985: 306–11, 334–40) observes as an empirical reality, namely that in most polities the rise of ethnic parties drives out other non-ethnic divides based on economic class or sector. Politicians simply cannot make credible commitments to universalism in an ethnically complex polity in which some ethnic groups begin to organize in an exclusive fashion. All state assets, including the bureaucracy, instead of being seen as neutral vehicles of programmatic policy implementation, are instead perceived as deeply partisan toward one ethnic group rather than another.

The critical ingredient to bring about this dynamic of "deepening" clientelism under conditions of intensifying inter-ethnic party competition may not be necessarily the existence of ethnic markers, but the *presence of dense organizational networks configured around particular interpretations of ethnicity*. Even though ethnocultural markers may generate particularly strong social networks, as Chandra argues in her contribution, sometimes class, sector, or regional organizations may achieve equivalent levels of network properties. Krishna in his contribution therefore emphasizes the role of cross-caste village networks led by educated "new leaders" in wresting power away from traditional village-based landed elites in India.

Nevertheless, ethnicity may be a particularly powerful bond of network construction and political organization promoting clientelistic linkage building. It is therefore not by accident that most of the established affluent democratic polities with "pacified" ethnocultural divides that Lijphart (1977) refers to as "consociational" polities tend to have been heavily clientelistic, even though not all clientelistic democracies are plural in ethnocultural terms.[24] The close link between clientelism and ethnocultural divides applies to Austria and Belgium, and used to characterize the Netherlands, where since the early 1960s cultural pillarization declined in tandem with a clientelistic carving up of the state. The decline of ethnocultural divides in all three countries, in fact, may be related to the increasing political-economic difficulties these countries encountered in satisfying clientelistic claims.[25] Political-economic difficulties, in turn, boosted the salience of non-cultural divides. We will return to political-economic constraints on linkage formation shortly.

The pursuit of alternative strategies of principal–agent accountability and responsiveness at different levels of development in interaction with different modes of competition is prominently represented in many contributions to our volume. Medina's and Stokes's chapter characterizes clientelistic partisan strategies under low competition and *low to intermediate development* in general conceptual terms. Krishna and Wilkinson demonstrate with data and narratives from India that competition and

---

[24] Consider Ireland, Italy, and Japan itself.

[25] In the Netherlands, the "Dutch disease" of dependence on natural resource rents (gas) already triggered this crisis of clientelism in the 1960s, whereas in Austria and Belgium the erosion of clientelistic politics had to await the crisis of the heavy industry in the 1970s and 1980s.

clientelism go hand-in-hand in comparatively poor countries. Nevertheless, this does not lead us to deny that under conditions of single party
hegemony, clientelism may flourish and persist in the manner analyzed
by Medina and Stokes. This configuration just does not compel politicians to disburse as much in resources to their clients as does a highly
competitive partisan contest.

Contributions to this volume examining polities with diverse, and
on average intermediate development, powerfully demonstrate the logic of
portfolio diversification between clientelistic and programmatic linkage
strategies and the progressively greater propensity to support programmatic linkages, where competition creates uncertainty and interacts with
intermediate levels of development. Portfolio diversification prompted
by locally varied competitive configurations and popular demand profiles induced by differential levels of development are the main themes
of Magaloni, Diaz-Cayeros, and Estévez studying Mexico, Levitsky analyzing Argentina in comparative perspective, and Hale examining the
regional politics of national and sub-national electoral contests in Russia.
Levitsky shows how the Argentinean Peronists paid off poor communities with clientelistic compensation, while targeting the urban middle
classes with the national programmatic policy objectives of economic liberalization. In Mexico, while sub-national levels of development almost
invariably correlate with more programmatic and less clientelistic politics,
competition and what Magaloni *et al.* conceptualize as "electoral risk"
can actually be positively related to clientelism at comparatively weak or
intermediate levels of development. In a similar vein, Hale detects a net
effect of local competitive structures on clientelism in Russia's regions,
holding constant for indicators of economic development and industrial
structure.

Under conditions of high development, finally, clientelism can hold
on as long as hegemonic parties or party alliances – in countries such as
Austria, Belgium, Ireland, Italy, or Japan – remain more or less unchallenged and control a political economy penetrated by partisan politics
(see below). Societal change of preferences and performance problems
in the politicized economy often contribute to an intensifying competitiveness in the party system that translates into a partial or complete
erosion of clientelistic linkage mechanisms, as Scheiner shows for Japan,
and Kitschelt develops for a more inclusive comparison of advanced post-
industrial economies and polities. In these polities, increasing competitiveness makes clientelism prohibitively expensive just at the same time
as political-economic difficulties constrain the clientelistic largesse of the
governing parties in any case.

Public control of the political economy

Government activities are to a greater or lesser extent amenable to clientelistic targeting or universalistic programmatic allocation of costs and benefits. Governments and legislatures codify more detailed and transparent rules of authoritative allocation of costs and benefits, when incumbents intend to pursue programmatic accountability.[26] Elected politicians who appoint, confirm, instruct, or lobby administrators in the executive branch then have comparatively little leeway to target resources to their favorite supporters. But many government activities permit considerable discretion and targeting because they are inherently difficult to codify in general rules and/or the political incumbents intentionally structure them in such ways as to become amenable to clientelistic case-by-case targeting. The degrees of freedom for clientelistic linkage-building politicians tend to be particularly high in the cases of business and market regulation (safety, hygiene, and environment; anti-trust; zoning; architectural compliance; price and quantity regulations), the award of specific market advantages (subsidies, loan guarantees, export/import licenses or support, etc.) and the procurement and operating contracts for government infrastructure (transportation, public buildings for a variety of purposes, communications equipment). In a similar vein, the direct management of public enterprise under the auspices of agencies headed by elected politicians opens the door wide to the construction of clientelistic patronage networks. A thus "politicized" economic governance structure feeds directly into the partisan circuits of clientelistic principal–agent relations.

The analytical difficulty for research on principal–agent linkages, however, is to determine whether politicized economic governance is an *endogenous aspect* of clientelism or may operate as a *causal antecedent creating opportunities for clientelistic linkage building under democratic conditions*. Furthermore, there appears to be a complicated *causal interaction between politicized economic governance and other causal determinants of citizen–politician linkages, namely socioeconomic development and the intensity of inter-party competition*. Nevertheless, we insist that a partial causal autonomy of politicized economic governance in shaping principal–agent relations comes to the fore in at least two regards. First, political economic conditions that facilitate programmatic or clientelistic governance may historically precede mass enfranchisement and principal–agent linkages predicated on such democratic opening. Second, in advanced

---

[26] On this point, see the study of Huber and Shipan (2002) who measure the extent to which legislatures remove the discretion of bureaucrats by the detail that makes it into legal instructions.

post-industrial capitalist economies the decline of politicized enterprise sectors is an important trigger for bringing down clientelistic politician-voter linkages. Let us briefly sketch each of these elements and then turn to the endogenous-interactive relations among economic governance, development, and competition.

Exogenous antecedents of a politicized economy

A (de)politicized economy and public administration is not endogenous to citizen–politician linkages, *if it was established before the advent of democratic mass politics*. This was Shefter's (1977, 1994) main point about the consequences of absolutist rule, as opposed to an inter-penetration of oligarchical economic special interests and state governance. It may be no accident that all three of the most clientelistic industrialized democracies in the second half of the twentieth century – Austria, Italy, and Japan – experienced highly politicized political-economic governance under their respective authoritarian or fascist regimes.

Of course, if other conditions are favorable for clientelism, after democratization the competing parties may dismantle a professional bureaucracy and a liberal separation of private enterprise from public management in favor of more politicized arrangements. Conversely, programmatic democratic politicians may dismantle public enterprise and regulation precisely in order to seize on new opportunities to build programmatic citizen–politician linkages after the advent of democracy.[27]

Conditions of external threat to regime coherence and state survival may exogenously shape the political economy. "Politicized" economies prevail where rulers face intense immediate military threats from the environment ("total war") or none at all. In both instances, they can or must extract resources from their subjects with a short time horizon of maximization and without regard for long-term prospects of economic growth. Only where external military threats have intermediate intensity and urgency rulers may develop longer time horizons over which they assess their stream of benefits flowing from political rule. They then may calculate that the net present value of future economic wealth and military power is sufficiently large to preserve a depoliticized, if not entirely liberal economy in which private investors enjoy secure property rights and investment opportunities with moderate taxes. This arrangement encourages economic growth through private enrichment that ultimately

---

[27] Western Germany where the Allied occupying forces made the greatest effort to restructure business governance is the one outlier with relatively depoliticized post-war governance.

converts into greater tax revenue (at lower rates) and increasing military prowess of a state.[28] Where the external military threat is weak, in contrast, rulers may opt for the immediate and exhaustive exploitation of their people without much concern for the consequences for the future private wealth and power of the state. Where external military threats fade, the new security may fuel politicians' propensity to organize principal–agent relations in a clientelistic fashion. South Korea after the waning of the Chinese threat may be an example for this dynamic (Kang 2002: 158–71).

A third external condition affecting the politicization of the economy has to do with technology and market structure. It may not be an accident that in affluent capitalist democracies clientelism figured as a prominent linkage mechanism primarily in some of those polities the "variety of capitalism" literature describes as sectorally or industrial group coordinated market capitalism (cf. Hall and Soskice 2001; Soskice 1999). Economic sectors in such countries excelled that were configured around (1) heavy fixed capital investments and (2) incremental processes of innovation and learning relying on (3) a skilled labor force with human capital assets deployable only in highly specific jobs and sectors, and (4) networks of companies and associational umbrella organizations facilitating cooperative research and development. Such profiles of production and factor inputs thrived in countries with institutions that favored webs of contracts build around (1) an industrial relations regime relying on long-term labor contracts and peak-level bargaining among nationally or sectorally organized factors of production (business and labor); (2) a system of corporate governance configured around close oversight of management by capital owners; (3) a financial system based on large individual stock owners and investment banks engaged in the coordination of private enterprises within and across sectors; and (4) a cooperative regulatory public administration practicing informal negotiations with business rather than an adversarial, judicialized regulatory process. In this arrangement, either the most productive firms themselves were open to clientelistic politicization or at least they generated the public resources that enabled political parties to sustain a politicized, clientelistic sector of regulated and/or state owned companies.

This arrangement functioned as long as the world innovation frontier was centered around industries where incremental learning in large organizations was efficient. But since the 1980s, the growing significance of information and communication technologies, biotechnology, financial

---

[28] On the relationship between external threats, taxation, and organization of the public economy, see Levi (1988) and Kang (2002).

services, and personal and cultural services in post-industrial economies has made it more advantageous for firms and sectors to rely on liberal market-based economic coordination through venture capital or equity financing in stock and bond markets and more arms-length, decentralized relations between business and labor. This arrangement takes away opportunities for clientelistic linkage building. As coordinated capitalism, and especially politicized industries therein, enter a period of economic crisis, political clientelism is bound to suffer. As Kitschelt and Scheiner argue in this volume, the economic decline of politicized, state subsidized companies and entire sectors has put pressure on clientelistic partisan politics. In a similar vein, in Latin America and communist Eastern Europe, both examples of strategies of import substituting industrialization with more or less strong clientelistic linkage building that came to the fore after democratic transitions, the most politicized industrial sectors entered a deep crisis of efficiency in the 1980s that made business and labor abandon the established arrangements and opt out of clientelistic politics for either market liberalization or some vague socialist-populist political reorganization of industry. The economic costs of clientelism began to skyrocket out of control, as coordinated market capitalist governance lost its comparative advantage.[29]

A fourth, at least partially exogenous, condition for the politicization of economic enterprise results from ethnocultural mobilization. Particularly if ethnocultural pluralization goes together with an ethnic division of labor and strong ethnocultural networks, then it is likely that it promotes a politicization of the economy. Under conditions of democratic party competition, ethnocultural parties engage in a clientelistic penetration of economic governance. The presence of dense ethnic social networks makes it particularly attractive for politicians to nurture loyalties through clientelistic exchanges that are anchored in politicized economic governance. More so than in any other circumstances, from the vantage point of ethnic voters the decision of whether to join in, or abstain from support of, an ethnic party is then framed as a coordination game rather than a prisoner's dilemma. Where ethnic markers are salient and the economy is politicized, voters do not expect politicians to employ political authority in an ethnoculturally unbiased, universalistic fashion, but always in favor of some ethnic group. Supporting your ethnocultural group thus does

---

[29] This process may not be intrinsically linked to increased "globalization" of markets for goods, services, and capital, as Rosenbluth (1996) suggested, given that many of the coordinated capitalist economies were trade open and delivered globally competitive rates of return.

not have the potential downside that cooperative strategies in producing some club or collective good may incur in prisoners' dilemmas.[30]

The interaction of politicized economy, socioeconomic development and inter-party competition

Politicization of the economy, socioeconomic development and inter-party competition may all influence clientelistic or programmatic principal–agent relations in democratic politics. But this effect may be a result of complex interactive and recursive relations. We have already discussed the contingent relationship between socioeconomic development and the competitiveness of democratic party systems for citizen–politician linkage strategies. A highly politicized economic governance structure, in turn, may depress economic development and reduce inter-party competition.

The association among economic governance structures, development, and growth is quite firmly established (cf. Barro 1997; Easterly 2001; Easterly and Levine 2002; Knack 2003; Rodrik, Subramanian, and Trebbi 2002). "Good institutions" in the sense of the rule of law barring political rulers from directly intervening in the allocation of property rights on a case-by-case basis are closely intertwined with superior economic performance. This does not rule out, of course, that very different "varieties of capitalism" may yield equally favorable economic outcomes under certain circumstances (cf. Hall and Soskice 2001). Nor does it exclude the possibility that countries operating behind the world innovation frontier may have politicized economies and still be able to accelerate the process of catching up with the lead countries, particularly if they face moderately strong external threats. And, finally, good economic institutions that prevent arbitrary political intervention are no independent prime movers of economic growth all by themselves. Causally prior to them, but affecting economic outcomes only through institutions, we may discover the powerful role played by climate and geography (cf. Acemoglu *et al.* 2001). In a similar vein, prior economic development or prior bold policy initiatives by political actors may make all the difference for the emergence of economic institutions that are favorable for development at a later point in time (cf. Glaeser *et al.* 2004). What is critical for research on principal–agent relations in democratic politics is not to sort out the

---

[30] For a coordination logic of ethnic mobilization rather than a prisoner's dilemma see Hardin's (1995) discussion of ethnic violence. In a coordination game, it is always advantageous to join with your fellow group members in the production of a club good and there is little or no chance to become the "sucker" who incurs a personal cost of effort without obtaining an equivalent or greater gain.

causal priority of any of these variables for economic development. It is important, however, to keep in mind that – as a bundle – they affect the politicians' and voters' preferences over democratic principal–agent relations.

In a similar vein, a politicized economy may affect levels of democratic competition, even though at least some of these effects may be mediated through prior economic development itself. If a politicized economy undercuts competition between firms, sectors, and regions, it may not only reduce growth, but also stifle political competition, as electoral constituencies support candidates servicing "their" industries and jobs only. At least under conditions of high development, reduced competition, in turn, is likely to promote clientelistic politics even in the face of the manifest economic inefficiencies of such arrangements.

Citizen–politician linkages, in turn, may feed back to the governance of the economy. Where intense competition coincides with moderate to high levels of economic development, anti-clientelistic sentiments among voters may motivate office-seeking politicians to abandon clientelism and opt for the professionalization of public bureaucracies and a depoliticization of state-governed enterprises or entire sectors. Conversely, under conditions of weak development, intense competition may encourage politicians to seek an extension of the government's influence over economic resource allocation with the implicit or explicit objective to create clientelistic principal–agent ties. As already indicated, in the course of such political linkage building, politicians may reduce the competitiveness of democracy. They create associational "pillars" around economic groups and political parties that reduce the size of the electoral market place and may anchor the rise of a hegemonic political party or partisan cartel. As the cases of Austria, Belgium, Italy, or Japan after World War II could show, material bonds of direct citizen–politician exchange kept partisan camps afloat long after their earlier ideological moorings had weakened (Hellemans 1990). Wilkinson observes a similar process of clientelistic penetration of the public sector by a hegemonic party in India.

By contrast, in democratic polities with intense competition between two rival blocs of parties, such as in Britain or Scandinavia for much of the twentieth century as well as in Germany and France since the late 1950s, a clientelistic politicization of the economy went nowhere fast or at least was abated. Socialist parties pursued universalistic welfare state schemes, not a selective politicization of the economy. Intermediate cases are countries with dispersed competition, but fluid party systems, such as Germany during the Weimar Republic or the French Third Republic. Here clientelism played a considerable role, particularly at the local municipal level, but could not produce large-scale inter-party compacts to politicize the domestic economies for the benefit of partisan spoils.

The missing link? Formal democratic rules of the game and principal–agent relations

When we refer to democratic institutions, we mean formal, codified institutions typically detailed in democratic constitutions. In a broader sense, institutions as regular practices and rules, the violation of which actors sanction with penalties, are ubiquitous in political life and most definitely matter also for citizens' and politicians' coordination around principal–agent relations. But we wish to focus here on a narrow set of "parchment institutions" (Carey 2000) that have generated a huge and fruitful literature in comparative politics, particularly that on electoral systems (e.g., Cox 1997; Lijphart 1994; Taagepera and Shugart 1989) and on the legislative cohesiveness of parties (see Morgenstern 2004). Can we construct a causal association between electoral systems and prevailing citizen–politician linkages of accountability? Electoral systems vary according to their ballot structure, electoral formula, and district size in ways that pattern electoral contests as being more between individual candidate personalities or parties as unified competitive teams of candidates (cf. Carey and Shugart 1995). Some scholars have associated clientelism with personalized political contests that enable individual politicians to strike bargains with small target groups of voters (cf. Ames 2001; Katz 1980). Others have associated clientelism with highly centralized party machines in rigid, national-level closed-list proportional representation schemes, such as Austria and Venezuela before electoral reforms over the last twenty years. Such systems cut off the accountability of individual politicians to identifiable local constituencies of the national electorate (cf. Coppedge 1994).

Maybe it is thus "extreme" electoral systems of a personalist or collectivist type that promote clientelism over programmatic politics because they lack a balance between the personal accountability of individual politicians and of partisan collectives. They provide one or the other only, but not countervailing modes of representation that could rein in the inclinations of individual politicians or machine bosses to provide material inducements to their constituents. But, upon closer inspection, the incidence of clientelism does not appear to be closely associated with specific extreme electoral systems. Just consider a "moderate" electoral system like Belgium's with small member electoral districts, proportional representation, and a mild personal preference vote. Institutionalism has even greater difficulties explaining the subnational diversity of principal–agent linkage mechanisms across space or over time. This is a recurrent theme in our book, whether we think of Chandra's and Wilkinson's treatment of India, of Magaloni *et al.*'s study of Mexico, Hale's analysis of Russia, or Scheiner's treatment of Japan. More explicitly, the message that formal institutions cannot explain democratic linkage practices comes across in the comparative pieces by Kitschelt and Scheiner.

Given otherwise favorable conditions, it appears that politicians find a way to "work around" electoral institutions, when other imperatives make it attractive for instrumentally rational politicians to build clientelistic principal–agent relations. In this regard, electoral institutions have an indirect impact on the precise operational techniques politicians employ to build their favorite linkage patterns. Thus, in polities that effectively protect the secrecy of the vote, politicians will have to devise different indirect mechanisms of monitoring and enforcing than in polities where the vote is open and parties provide the ballot papers. In a similar vein, clientelism in a personalistic electoral system (e.g., single member district systems or PR systems with personal preference vote, but without pooling of votes for all of a candidate's party) probably relies less on national hierarchically integrated mass parties than in systems with closed-list proportional representation systems. Institutions matter for politicians' strategic choices, but not such that those institutions directly would bias linkage building toward programmatic or clientelistic options.

A similar argument about the indirect effect of institutions on the "tactics," but not the "strategy," of principal–agent linkage building could be developed for executive-legislative relations. As such, the institutions of presidential democracy, when compared to parliamentary democracy, are indifferent to the choice between more programmatic and more clientelistic linkage strategies. On the one hand, one could argue that presidents have programs and policies more on their mind, given that they rely on the support of the median voter who is captured by the provision of collective goods rather than private and club goods. On the other, one could instead claim that the single-handed leverage of presidents over discretionary funds and appointments in many polities creates tremendous capacity for patronage and favoritism that allows incumbents or candidates with the right credentials to cobble together patchwork coalitions of supporters who expect to benefit from presidential clientelistic largesse.

Hence, as long as socioeconomic, competitive, and political economic configurations are conducive to clientelism, politicians may come up with tactics to implement such linkages under all sorts of formal institutional arrangements. A shred of institutionalism can be salvaged if we examine the tactics rather than the strategy of linkage building. We are skeptical, however, about whether inflating the domain of "institutionalism" would be a helpful alternative to assert the salience of institutions for the explanation of linkage strategies. For example, to claim that

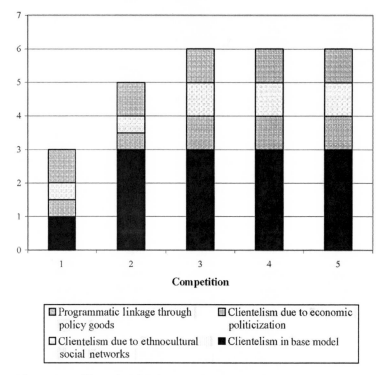

Figure 1.2a The mix of linkage mechanisms at intermediate levels of development

"informal" institutions and quasi-private choices by a party's activists, such as nomination procedures for candidates running for national legislatures, determine linkage mechanisms only begs the question of why activists play by these rather than by other rules. As political alignments change and clientelistic or programmatic exchange relations are no longer advantageous, "informal" institutions can be changed relatively easily without having to incur very high transaction costs.

In contrast to conventional predispositions in much of contemporary political science, we thus assert that – overall – formal institutions are not particularly useful in accounting for the strategic dynamics of democratic accountability and responsiveness. Our volume shows instead that the interaction of (1) economic modernization; (2) political economy; (3) levels of party competition; and (4) patterns of ethnic heterogeneity explain more about mechanisms of democratic accountability than a country's formal institutions. In Figure 1.2a and 1.2b, we visually summarize how the interaction among these factors affects patterns of

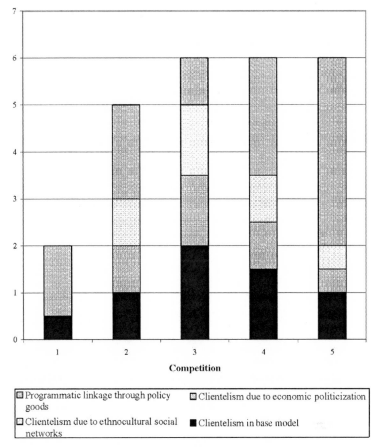

Figure 1.2b The mix of linkage mechanisms at high levels of development

programmatic and clientelistic linkages at intermediate and high levels of economic development.

Compared to the baseline models for the interaction of development and competition in Figures 1.1b. (high case) and 1.1c. (intermediate case), politicized economies add more clientelistic linkage building at low to intermediate intensities of party competition. The inverse applies to ethnocultural mobilization, but tempered by the indirect negative effect of a declining resource base for clientelistic linkage building, as economic governance structures become less politicized, and by general resource constraints on the efforts politicians can make to build citizen–politician linkages.

Ethnocultural mobilization and its impact on citizen–politician linkages in democratic polities are highly conditional on political-economic circumstances, development, and especially, partisan competition. Both greater politicization of economic governance and more intense interparty competition are likely to fuel ethnocultural mobilization such that politicians have stronger incentives to craft clientelistic principal–agent relations. Economic development may have an ambivalent influence. But most likely greater societal affluence makes more resources available for the distributive game that mobilizes ethnocultural groups around clientelistic linkages. Of course, ethnocultural mobilization remains exogenous to all these other causal factors insofar as there must be a feasibility space of cultural markers – preferably markers also associated with distributive impacts on the division of labor and distribution of economic rewards in a society – without which politicians could not even conceive a promising strategy of ethnocultural interest mobilization.

Plan of the book

The first chapters in the book – by van de Walle, Medina and Stokes, and Chandra – focus on the conditionality of linkage mechanisms, providing general theoretical accounts of how levels of economic development, party competition, and ethnocultural diversity interact to determine different levels of clientelism. Van de Walle's opening piece on democratization in sub-Saharan Africa reminds us that not only programmatic linkage mechanisms, but also clientelistic citizen–politician relations, are arrangements that presuppose material resources and organizational capacities that do not exist in every country. Under some conditions of extreme poverty and lack of democratic experience, political and economic conditions may at least initially permit only what van de Walle, following Joseph and Weber, calls "prebendal" exchange networks within a rather small political elite. Such relations of accountability may later be expanded in more full-fledged clientelistic systems, an evolution van de Walle expects to take place in the future democratization of sub-Saharan Africa. In what is a purely theoretical model, but with parameter settings that approximate most clearly to countries at intermediate levels of wealth, Medina and Stokes highlight the importance of competitive conditions between partisan incumbents and challengers in shaping linkage strategies. Economic development is a big driving force of democratic linkage formation because resource constraints shape the calculations of voters and politicians. At intermediate levels of development, however, there is sufficient socioeconomic heterogeneity and inequality to generate rather different cost–benefit calculations, such as those made by lower tiers of poor peasants and menial workers, but also those of higher tiers of well-paid engineers and professionals. Contingent upon the competitiveness of the electoral contest and the distribution of voters with different cost-benefit calculations over clientelism and programmatic policy rewards, politicians choose different linkage strategies *vis-à-vis* voters. The empirical analysis of the subsequent four chapters with cases drawn from Latin America and the post-communist region supports this general argument. Chandra adds to the analyses of van de Walle and Medina and Stokes by demonstrating how conditions of party competition and ethnocultural pluralism interact and lead strategic politicians to highlight specific ethnocultural markers as a vote-getting strategy in an overwhelmingly clientelistic setting.

The second set of chapters, by Wilkinson and Krishna, illustrate the strategic logic of linkage formation under conditions of weak development and considerable democratic experience. Here inter-party competitiveness does not reduce clientelism, but reinvigorates it. Under conditions of comparatively widespread poverty and weak development, politicians do not really have an alternative to clientelistic strategies. The intensity and specific nature of clientelistic politics, however, varies with the nature of the party system and ethnocultural mobilization. Both Wilkinson and Krishna show how the economy is politicized, at the state and national level, as a resource employed for clientelistic network building.

The following chapters deal with countries under conditions of intermediate economic development, i.e. roughly, per capita gross domestic product in the range of $5,000 to $10,000 purchasing power parity corrected in 2000. Such polities are particularly common in Latin America and post-communist Eastern Europe, the regions from which evidence is drawn in our chapters. The work of Jomo and Gomez (1999) suggests that Southeast Asia might furnish further cases of democratic linkage building under conditions of intermediate development. In these polities, conditions of living and economic rationales of citizens are sufficiently varied to open spaces for some vote-seeking politicians to abandon clientelism as the dominant linkage strategy and to add or to substitute programmatic appeals in their menus of linkage building. How exactly politicians' strategies of differentiating their mixes of linkage efforts play out, however, depends again very much on the interaction of socioeconomic conditions with our three other theoretical elements.

Lyne details how cost-benefit calculations of politicians and voters at intermediate levels of development in Brazil may eventually contribute to a change in linkage patterns. Although Brazil has electoral institutions often seen as inhibiting programmatic party competition, some voters and politicians may begin to abandon clientelism, as economic development proceeds and electoral competition intensifies. Next, Magaloni et al. demonstrate for Mexico, in an elegant comparative analysis of subnational politics, how local settings induce politicians to vary linkage strategies, contingent upon levels of local development and electoral competitiveness. With more qualitative evidence, Levitsky makes a similar point in his comparison of the linkage strategies practiced by the Argentinean Peronists over time and by four further erstwhile hegemonic parties in additional Latin American countries. Levitsky also considers political-economic governance and liberalization as a vital trigger, but also as an effect of partisan linkage strategies. Whether or not parties can find electorally promising linkage strategies in an environment of economic liberalization, however, depends on the parties' internal organization. The final chapter in this part, by Hale on Russian democratic politics in the 1990s, combines many of the Latin American themes in a statistical model of electoral success in single-member seats for the national *Duma*. Based on an ingeniously designed measure of clientelism, Hale can show that not only variance in socioeconomic development across Russia, but also ethnocultural networks and political-economic conditions play an important role in shaping the locally prevailing nature of democratic linkages.

The fourth and final set of chapters deals with postindustrial capitalist democracies, i.e., the socioeconomic conditions under which conventional developmental arguments expect the least clientelism and the greatest vulnerability of clientelism to a switch in linkage strategies. This places the greatest burden of explaining clientelistic politics on variables other than development. We therefore asked two authors to pay particular attention to the core variables featured in institutionalist explanations of linkage strategies, namely electoral systems and federalism, on which there is considerable variation within this group of countries.[31] Both Müller's cross-sectional comparative analysis and Scheiner's longitudinal analysis of electoral systems and clientelism find that institutional explanations of linkage mechanisms are rather weak. They cannot be entirely discounted, when tested against a limited sample of cases, but they leave considerable variance unexplained. Moreover, institutions may themselves be endogenous to other conditions that generate clientelistic or programmatic party competition. For this reason, Scheiner and the final cross-national contribution by Kitschelt pick up political-economic

---

[31] This leaves out executive-legislative relations ("presidentialism") on which there is rather little variance among contemporary affluent democracies, except the United States. Finland and France can be characterized at most as semi-presidential systems, and that may not fully reveal how similar their operation is to run-of-the-mill parliamentary systems.

explanations, interacted with the level of inter-party competitiveness in a polity, to account for major shifts in democratic linkage building. Performance crises of the industries and sectors most commonly exploited for clientelistic purposes generate intensified party competition and anti-clientelistic backlashes that may lead to the demise of clientelistic politics. Where competition remains lop-sided, such as in Japan until the advent of the twenty-first century, even under conditions of economic crisis in the state penetrated sector, however, clientelism can hold on tenaciously, even though in a more subdued fashion than in earlier decades.

In polities characterized by different levels of economic development linkage strategies play out differently. That much is correct about a developmentalist perspective. But in order to account for the subtle choices politicians make in designing relations of accountability and responsiveness to voters, it is indispensable to examine politicians' and voters' strategic calculations taking into account the interaction between economic resource endowments, partisan competitiveness, political-economic governance structures, and ethnocultural diversity.

2   Meet the new boss, same as the old boss?
The evolution of political clientelism in Africa

Nicolas van de Walle

Clientelism exists in all polities. The forms it takes, its extent, and its political functions vary enormously, however, across time and place. This chapter analyzes the persistence and evolution of political clientelism in sub-Saharan Africa since independence. Pervasive clientelism was a hallmark of the region's non-democratic states until their transition to multiparty politics in the 1990s. To what extent will these practices persist, now that democratic politics, however imperfect, has become the norm in the region? The second half of this chapter examines the likely evolution of political clientelism in the new multiparty electoral regimes of sub-Saharan Africa.

A comparison of this region with the regions examined by the other contributions to this book confirms an argument made by Kitschelt and Wilkinson in their introduction, that the structural characteristics of the country determine the nature of the clientelistic politics. The African cases discussed in this chapter have a lower level of economic development and smaller, poorer state structures than those discussed in the other chapters. This impacts the nature of clientelism in the region. The rest of this book uses the terms *patronage* and *clientelism* interchangeably, perhaps because most of the case material comes from middle-income countries with relatively wealthy states and extensive experience of electoral politics. It is important to note that in sub-Saharan Africa a pervasive form of elite clientelism, *prebendalism*, actually involves relatively little patronage. In a context of low levels of economic development, inadequate national integration, a history of authoritarian politics, and few organizational resources available to them, African leaders typically used state resources to co-opt different ethnic elites to maintain political stability. The clientelism that resulted was not redistributive and generally benefited only a relatively small proportion of the citizenry in more than symbolic ways. The second half of the chapter examines how the democratization wave of the early 1990s has changed these patterns. I argue that a lot of the same patterns are being sustained, at least when one party has unambiguous control over the reins of government. However, the African materials suggest that greater democratization will lead in time to more responsive forms of clientelism.

Otherwise, this chapter largely confirms the hypotheses laid out in the book's Introduction, though it offers a slightly different perspective on them. I argue below that ethnic heterogeneity does indeed affect clientelist politics, but I am skeptical that clientelism is more likely to be significantly more redistributive for in-group exchanges. Instead, I argue that African voters typically believe they have little strategic choice but to vote for their in-group candidate, and do so despite little if any material gain. I agree, finally, that growing political competition over the last ten years is likely to alter the patterns of clientelism, first by progressively circumscribing prebendal dynamics and then by replacing them with patronage-based ones. But I believe that new patterns will only slowly emerge, given the persistence of traditional dynamics, which imperfect democratization has not eliminated, and in interaction with continuing economic crisis and ethnic heterogeneity. For the time being, the dominance of presidential parties and their control over state resources help to maintain the old patterns.

Patterns of political clientelism in Africa

Three distinct forms of clientelism can be distinguished: patronage, prebends, and tribute (Lemarchand 1988: 153–55). *Tribute* describes the traditional practice of gift exchange in peasant societies, in which patron and client are engaged in bonds of reciprocity and trust. It involves real redistribution of wealth and is embedded in a communitarian ethos, even if economic anthropologists offer a perfectly rational explanation for its prevalence in terms of risk-sharing. I would argue that tribute is all but non-existent in modern Africa, although politicians evoke the practice when they engage in largely symbolic acts of munificence. This is the case notably for many alleged cases of vote buying, as I relate below.

The second form of clientelism, *patronage*, can be defined as the practice of using state resources to provide jobs and services for political clienteles. Patronage is designed to gain support for the patron that dispenses it. Overwhelmingly, and as described in the introduction to this book, the recourse to politicized patronage has been a characteristic of mass electoral politics. It is typically dispensed through political parties, which use it to gain electoral advantage. It presupposes a relatively large state with relatively substantial fiscal resources. A third type of clientelism is the practice of prebendalism (Joseph 1987). This refers to the handing out of *prebends*, in which an individual is given a public office in order for him/her to gain personal access over state resources. Prebendalism has been a feature of most early states, invariably characterized by the absence of a professional civil service and weak extractive capacity (e.g., Tilly 1975). It constitutes one of the basic fiscal institutions of the feudal state, in which the king has little choice but to allow his barons to pocket a large proportion of the revenues they have control over. Prebendalism is a characteristic of authoritarian states and is typically mediated not through political parties, but through the executive branch of government.

Prebends and patronage overlap, but I wish to emphasize their fundamental difference. Hiring a member of one's ethnic group for a senior position in the customs office is an example of patronage. Allowing the customs officer to use the position for personal enrichment by manipulating import and export taxes is an example of a prebend. Patronage is often perfectly legal, though it is frowned upon and constitutes a "gray area" of acceptable practice; it remains present in the bureaucracies of the most advanced economies of the world. Prebendalism, on the other hand, invariably entails practices in which important state agents unambiguously subvert the rule of law for personal gain.

The two central characteristics of the new states that emerged from colonialism were their lack of national integration and their low level of economic development. Various forms of authority competed with that of the state, whose reach did not necessarily extend throughout the national hinterland. Tribal chiefs often enjoyed more legitimacy than state leaders, and ethnic identities divided citizens in various ways. Poor infrastructure did not encourage political and economic integration of the territory. New state leaders needed to promote national integration to buttress their own legitimacy and to promote economic development, yet they lacked the means and capacity to reach out effectively.

As discussed in the Introduction to this book, observers like James Scott offered the "machine politics" model to explain the response of leaders in modernizing countries to this dilemma. They argued that the politicians in the new states of the developing world were in the process of emulating the machine politicians of nineteenth-century cities in the West – they were investing in strong political party organizations that could reliably mobilize a political clientele on election day, in exchange for a variety of private and club goods. After all, the political party is the perfect instrument for state leaders to overcome poor national integration. Indeed, the political elites that emerged around independence in Africa did invest in parties to consolidate political power (Morgenthau 1964; Hodgkin 1961). At the same time, economic development and the emergence of the modern state provided an increase in clientelistic possibilities. The number of public jobs was increasing, as were public works budgets.

Nonetheless, the dynamics of clientelism in post-colonial Africa proved to be distinctive. An argument of this chapter is that certain structural factors led African states to rely more on prebends than on patronage to fashion political stability. This will become clear if we analyze the difference between clientelism in electoral regimes and in non-electoral regimes, and the issue of party organization, in order to get at the precise function of clientelism in African regimes

First is the issue of party organization. To be successful, the political machine needs to be able to solve principal–agent problems by investing in monitoring and control capacity. Otherwise, as the Introduction to this book made clear, voters will not necessarily reward the machine's patronage with political support. Yet, as Bienen (1979: 62–77) and Sandbrook (1972) argued, there were no political parties in Africa in the 1960s with unambiguously enough organizational capacity to engage in the kind of "vote counting" required by the model. Few political parties were more than a couple of decades old, and after the excitement of independence had abated, few demonstrated much mobilizational capacity, certainly outside of the capitals and a handful of large towns. Even allegedly strong political parties were in fact often loose coalitions of regional elites, through which the party leadership sought to extend its reach. As Lemarchand put it in 1972:

the neo-traditional machine . . . seeks to enlist the support of micro-level clientelistic structures through bargaining with traditional patrons who act as brokers between the party elites and the masses. Vertical solidarities are maintained in part through material inducements but mainly through perpetuation of deference patterns between the brokers and their traditional clientele. Moreover, the party structure is not synonymous with the traditional clientelistic substructures but adjacent to it. (p. 114)

In sum, as the independence-era parties ventured out into the rural hinterland, they typically had little choice but to rely on traditional patrons as "intermediaries" or "brokers" between the political center and the countryside, given the initial weakness of the party, and the often greater legitimacy enjoyed by these local actors (Powell 1970; Weingrod 1977). A stronger party might have been able to marginalize these traditional local elites, but a weak party has little choice but to seek their support. In sum, the political machine model assumes that clientelism is facilitated by party organization and capacity, when in fact it is attractive to politicians who wish to compensate for the relative weakness of their party organization.

Second, even more jarring for the machine politics model is the role of clientelism *vis-à-vis* elections in post-independence Africa. Scott and others argued that the political machine was an instrument designed for electoral competition. Patronage was one instrument with which city bosses sought to manage the regular competitive elections they had to contest. "Jobs for the boys" fueled the machine to win elections and retain power, which in turn provided the public sector jobs. Losing elections was devastating for the machine, which kept it relatively responsive to its clients.

This pattern has little analytical leverage in sub-Saharan Africa. Before independence, parties found it relatively easy to mobilize people against foreign colonial occupation and material inducements were relatively unnecessary, as well as typically beyond the means of most party organizations, which did not enjoy access to state resources. The political machine model might then have fitted the African cases for the brief period after independence, during which governing parties had command over state resources and faced competitive electoral pressures, which would have put a premium on mobilizing voters. In contrast to machine politicians who had little choice but to face the voters on a regular basis, African rulers found it convenient to simply eliminate elections once they had consolidated power. Thus, within ten years of independence, only a handful of Africa's forty-eight states had not evolved to single party and no-party rule (Collier 1982; Kasfir 1971).

From the mid/late 1960s to the emergence of democratization in the early 1990s, most African countries did not hold multiparty elections with any regularity. An important point to make is that clientelism plays a very different role in such authoritarian regimes. Clearly, it is still designed to maintain support and compete for power, but just as clearly it is not designed to mobilize voters.

Clientelism in post-colonial Africa

I can now offer several basic propositions about the nature and dynamics of political clientelism in Africa in the thirty years following independence and before democratization reintroduced multiparty rule in the early 1990s.

First, *the primary function of political clientelism in Africa was to facilitate intra-elite accommodation in young, multiethnic and poorly integrated political systems.* In what Rothchild (1985) called "hegemonial exchange" and Bayart (1989) the "reciprocal assimilation of elites," political stability in Africa was constructed by using state resources to forge alliances across different social elites, often in the form of overt power-sharing arrangements. The political machine model has relatively little to say about ethnicity. Yet, the central dilemma for many African leaders was to find ways to integrate different ethnic communities. One of the most persistent themes of Africanist scholarship in the 1970s and 1980s was that clientelism was one of the instruments used to fashion cross-ethnic cooperation. As early as the mid 1960s, Zolberg had well described how the Parti Démocratique de la Côte d'Ivoire (PDCI) in Ivory Coast secured the support of different ethnic communities by providing public offices and redistributing state resources to ethnic elites, who were brought into the PDCI fold in the process. These arrangements facilitated consensus building across region and ethnicity; between the younger, more educated elites emerging from Western universities and the usually older, less educated elites that were often linked to traditional authorities; and between the individuals that emerged to take leadership roles in the different institutions of the states, not only the politicians, but also the military brass and the church hierarchy (see also Rothchild and Olorunsola 1982).

The single-party regimes that emerged by the early 1970s were thus typically broad multi-ethnic alliances in which cross-ethnic accommodation was accomplished thanks to state resources. Parties like KANU in Kenya, TANU in Tanzania, the RDPC in Cameroon, or the PDCI in Ivory Coast, provided a set of instruments to arbitrate intra-elite conflicts, such as competitive primary elections, allowing the president to manage the diverse interests of national elites.[1] These were not "mass parties," in the sense that the need to mobilize voters was extremely limited in the absence of competitive elections. Of course, these regimes undertook some patronage; but it is more useful to think of clientelistic politics as constituting primarily a mechanism for accommodation and integration of a fairly narrow political elite rather than the logic of mass party patronage. Most of the material gains from clientelism were limited to this elite. The stronger link between political elites and the citizenry is through the less tangible bonds of ethnic identity.

Arrangements to maintain these cross-ethnic alliances were often difficult to manage. They exacted a high economic cost as they promoted government consumption. One consequence was a proliferation of expensive elite offices within the state, a phenomenon I have described elsewhere (van de Walle 2001); government cabinets, the officer corps, various government councils and commissions, or legislators were all inflated to maximize the regime's ability to please different ethnic elites. The Nigerian Federation, for instance, incrementally increased from four states at independence to thirty-six states in 2000, as ethnic groups kept lobbying the federal government to get their own set of state institutions. At the same time, mass patronage would have cost African governments much more than the granting of elite offices. Some of the better-organized regimes in the region, such as the Ivory Coast or Kenya, may well have sought to

---

[1] See Widner (1992) and Bienen (1974) on Kenya, Bienen (1967) on Tanzania, Fauré and Médard (1982) on Ivory Coast, and Bayart (1979) on Cameroon.

fashion mass patronage systems. The Ghana of Nkrumah may have had this ambition as well. Unfortunately, the rapid growth of the civil service and of various social services in the 1960s and early 1970s quickly proved unsustainable, leading to debt problems and IMF stabilization programs.

Second, I argue that *prebendalism rather than patronage has been the favored form of clientelism in the region, due both to structural factors and to the absence of elections.* As these countries moved away from regular elections, patronage clearly did not disappear, though it did become somewhat less pressing for leaders, and by the 1980s became circumscribed by the economic crisis, problems in state capacity, and the growing importance of donors in the decision-making process. My argument is that both in terms of macro-economic and fiscal significance, and in terms of political importance, the salience of prebends came to exceed that of patronage for most of post-colonial Africa. The evolution of the civil service is illustrative. Though impressive in the decades following independence, growth was then largely curtailed by economic crisis, and civil services have been relatively small. Although oil wealth provides certain countries like Nigeria or Gabon with relatively larger patronage possibilities, the civil service in Africa represents on average only 2 percent of the population, compared to 6.9 percent in Eastern Europe, for example, or 7.7 percent in the countries of the OECD (van de Walle 2001: 92). In some African countries, it is close to just 1 percent. Though typically a significant share of overall formal employment, these civil services are in fact quite small: of the twenty-four countries surveyed by a 1990 IMF report, only seven had civil services of more than 100,000 individuals (Lienert and Modi 1997: 43).

In addition, the economic crisis has been particularly cruel to civil servants who lost up to 90 percent of their purchasing power in the 1970s and 1980s (Lindauer and Nunberg 1994). Far from being the core political support for the single-party regimes of which they were allegedly the main beneficiaries, civil servants were typically the first groups to rise up in political protest at the outset of the democratization episodes of the early 1990s (Bratton and van de Walle 1997: 101–05).

Even as the civil service was allowed to decay, a much smaller number of individuals atop the state apparatus benefited from substantial prebends. In some countries, every state service was up for sale, every regulation negotiable, and every asset privatizable. The sheer scale of the prebendalism can be striking; in Benin, a recent study estimated that the average customs agent had daily "parallel income" equivalent to two and a half times the monthly salary of a college professor in the late 1990s. Customs fraud resulted in the loss of state revenue amounting to a fifth of the state's total actual operating budget (Bako-Arifari 2001: 41). In

Nigeria, an official inquiry put at US$12.2 billion, or roughly 20 percent of total revenues for the period, the amount of oil revenues that were side-tracked into extra-budgetary accounts, to be used by officials with little monitoring or accountability, between 1988 and 1993 (Lewis 1996: 92). One result has been the inexorable decline of state revenues, which fell during the 1990s to an average of well under a fifth of GDP, compared to levels twice that high in the OECD countries and 50 percent higher in Latin America.

On the expenditure side, various forms of corruption greatly undermined the impact of many government programs. In Uganda in the early 1990s, for instance, only 27 percent of the central government's grants for the education sector actually reached schools (van de Walle 2001: 135–36). Other governments have chosen to explicitly limit their expenditures in the social sector. Many African governments have been characterized by a modest effort in education or health. Thus, the literacy rate in 1990 was under 50 percent in seventeen out of thirty-six states in the region with data (World Bank 2000a: 329). In 1994, similarly, only half of all Africans were immunized against the measles (World Bank 2000a: 323). Even then, perhaps as much as half of all social sector services are not provided by government at all, but by donors, NGOs, and religious organizations (van de Walle 2001: 93–101). In sum, these have not been responsive governments.

In the middle-income countries that constitute much of the empirical base of this book, clientelism is centrally controlled in the party apparatus. Instead, the clientelism that emerged in post-colonial Africa was decentralized and rarely focused on the party. Clientelistic networks were fragmented, crisscrossing all sorts of organizations in which elites exerted power and competed for supremacy (Sandbrook 1972). Every state institution appeared to benefit from them, but so did union organizations, the military, and even organized religions.

Over time, many regimes in Africa proved too weak to prevent clientelist systems from fragmenting and escaping any semblance of central control. With the onset of economic crisis in the 1980s, the political reach of the regime became more uncertain, and claims of centralized control became tenuous at best. As Lemarchand argued in the late 1980s, "in many areas, patrons have ceased to patronize . . . [and we have seen] the elimination of patronage incentives from the countryside, along with their replacement by a kind of free-for-all system in which local officials, military men and security spooks are given a blank check to use their prerogatives (and weapons) as they deem fit" (Lemarchand 1988: 155). In effect, in these states, the process can be described as the privatization of the state, in which access to state resources through various forms of prebendalism, rent-seeking, and associated forms of fraud was allowed to become endemic and only very loosely controlled from the center (see Hibou 1999; Reno 1995; van de Walle 2001).

The variation across Africa

Needless to say, these patterns varied across the region's states. Countries' natural resource endowments varied, so that oil and mineral producers like Nigeria or Gabon were more able to pursue large-scale patronage policies than were miserably poor states like Burkina Faso or Malawi. The skill of individual leaders at controlling resources also varied. In Cameroon, for example, President Ahidjo kept a tight control of both patronage and prebends during his rule from 1960 to 1982. His successor, Paul Biya, allowed the civil service to double in his first five years, bankrupting the country by 1990 (van de Walle 1993). The inability of certain leaders to manage inter-elite accommodation processes leads directly to instability and collapse of the central state, as it did in Uganda, for example, or Somalia.

It would take a much more ambitious study than the present one to track all of these variations. I shall instead focus briefly on just one question: did the level of democracy in states result in different levels of clientelism? In particular, did more democratic states exhibit different clientelistic dynamics? It is almost axiomatic that the more institutionalized the regime and the less it was patrimonial in nature, the less systematic was the recourse to prebendalism. In the Zaire of Mobutu, state resources were almost entirely privatized, to the benefit of a "political aristocracy" (Callaghy 1984). On the other hand, in Ivory Coast, greater institutionalization did result in at least some rule-based administrative behavior (Crook 1989). For the reasons discussed above, it is tempting to argue that more institutionalized regimes tended to rely more on patronage and less on prebends, simply because the latter is typically harder to make compatible with an effective legal system, whereas much patronage is perfectly legal. The comparative data on clientelism across African states is simply not good enough to prove this assertion, but it is supported by both logic and much impressionistic evidence.

Personal rule is antithetical to democracy, so that by extension I argue that *the more democratic the state, the more clientelism was circumscribed and limited to patronage.* The list of democratic states in the region is short, but the cases of Mauritius and Botswana, the two longest standing multiparty electoral regimes, offer some support for the argument. In both countries, the civil service provides substantial evidence of patronage behavior, and governments have clearly engaged in at least some politically motivated service delivery strategies, often linked to party behavior.[2] Both countries have among the largest public sectors in Africa. In both countries, party organizations appear well-oiled with patronage. At the same time, there is very little prebendal activity, which is strenuously opposed by prevailing legal and administrative norms.

Clientelism in the multiparty era

What was the impact of the democratization wave that hit Africa in the early 1990s on the patterns described in this chapter? To what extent did the return of multiparty electoral politics alter the prevailing dynamics of clientelism? To answer these questions, I start by noting several patterns that have emerged in the first decade of electoral politics. The early evidence suggests that African politicians are adapting old practices to the new circumstances of electoral competition.

The persistence of authoritarian patterns

The first point to make is that despite their regular elections, most of the new multiparty systems fall well short of the ideals of liberal democracies. Political freedoms and civil rights are imperfectly observed in practice, particularly in between electoral exercises (Diamond 1996). Elections may be nominally free, but governments engage in extensive gerrymandering, manipulation of voter registration, and harassment of opposition parties. Human rights abuses are not uncommon, even if the worst abuses are rarer than in the authoritarian past. A nominally free press is harassed in myriad ways, and the government retains a radio monopoly. Certain groups, notably key members of the executive branch and the military may, in effect, be above the law. The judiciary is officially independent, but it is poorly trained, overworked, and easily compromised.

The Freedom House rankings on political and civil rights in Africa demonstrate the extent to which multiparty elections can be combined with an illiberal political environment. In the late 1990s, two thirds of Africa's multiparty electoral systems were illiberal, if Freedom House's definitions of "Partly Free" and "Not Free" are accepted. Indeed, the twelve multiparty systems in the "Not Free" category may be more accurately termed "pseudo democracies" (Diamond 1996), so egregious is the gap between democratic ideals and current practice. Thus, only a minority of Africa's regimes can be thought of as consolidating

---

[2] On Botswana, see Good (1994) and Danevad (1995) while on Mauritius see Bräutigam (1997).

democratic politics, even though almost all now have regular multiparty elections.

The best single explanatory factor for the democratic qualities of the regime now in place is whether or not the incumbent in power in 1990 remains in power. In fact, in all, nineteen countries were led at the end of 2000 by the same leader who had been in power in the old single-party days before 1990. Incumbents lost power as a result of the democratic transition and its founding election in thirteen countries out of forty-eight in sub-Saharan Africa, in addition to the countries in which regular multiparty elections anteceded the 1990s. Seven of the thirteen are to this day classified by Freedom House as "free." The majority of the "illiberal" democracies are countries in which the transition to multiparty rule was seriously flawed or incomplete, most never really had a transition, and the turn to multiparty competition amounted to little more than an erstwhile authoritarian ruler donning the garb of democracy and tolerating regular elections as a successful strategy of holding onto power. Convening regular elections brings with it a modicum of international respectability and the resulting foreign aid, and does not threaten these leaders.

The emergence of dominant parties

The limited increase in actual political competition is also suggested by legislative elections, which are dominated by the presidential party. Of the eighty-five legislative elections conducted during the 1990s for which information is available, seventeen legislatures included ten or more parties, while another fourteen had between seven and nine parties. The average number of parties elected to the legislature actually increased between first and second elections, from 6.3 to 6.5. This actually understates the degree of apparent fragmentation, given a large number of independent candidates winning office.

Despite the large number of small parties, however, few legislatures lacked a party with at least a substantial plurality of seats; of the seventeen legislatures with ten or more parties, the minimal winning coalition required more than three parties in only four cases. Indeed, in eight of these states, the biggest party held a simple majority of seats. On average for the region's forty-one founding elections, the largest party received a comfortable 63.1 percent of the seats, and this increased to 69.6 percent for the thirty-five second elections and to 64.3 percent for third elections, that had been held by the end of 2000. Thus, the large number of parties represented in the legislature did not prevent the emergence of a large number of dominant parties. To get a better sense of the degree of fragmentation of these party systems, the standard measure, *the effective number of parties*, was calculated in order to adjust for differences in party size across political systems.[3] The calculations reveal that sixty-five of the eighty-five legislatures had an effective number of parties of three or less, while only four had one of more than six. These numbers appear to be broadly comparable to the party systems of Western Europe. Thus, the modal party system that is emerging across much of the region is a system with a large dominant party surrounded by a bevy of small, highly volatile parties. In thirty-seven of the eighty-five elections, the second biggest party in the legislature had 15 percent of the seats or less.

The continuing importance of prebendal dynamics helps to explain this peculiar type of party fragmentation. These systems create disincentives for opposition party consolidation and incentives for individual "big men" to maintain small, highly personalized parties or to join the winning party. The winning party tends to become dominant since individual politicians know that they are more likely to get access to state resources if they are in the president's party. At least some politicians believe that maintaining an independent power base will improve the deal they can strike with the president. In effect, having one's own party provides additional leverage to access state resources in negotiations with the president in power following the elections.

With a dominant party in power, opposition politicians have little incentive to coalesce with each other, since this would reduce the flexibility to strike deals with those in power and join the presidential majority. Incumbent presidents willingly encourage this party fragmentation, tacitly promoting or even sponsoring small parties or independent candidates to compete in legislative elections, presumably to divide the opposition and increase the share of the vote under its control. In some countries such as Gabon and Cameroon, the president has gone further to enhance these fissiparous tendencies by passing a law to provide public funds for parties competing in elections.

Politicians have a strong incentive to maintain the support of their own lineage or ethnic group, as their ability to capture a community's vote is what makes them useful to the presidential majority. So politicians have an incentive to mobilize ethnic identities during elections. This logic helps explain the large number of competing parties in many countries. It also explains the volatility of the party system, with the rapid appearance and disappearance of new parties around each electoral cycle, as well as the high number of independents that emerge during the course of elections. In a logic that is driven by individual clientelist strategies rather than by

---

[3] The standard formula developed by Laakso and Taagepera (Lijphart 1994: 120) for the effective number of parties was used.

institutional or legislative ambitions, politicians create parties to compete in a single election and leverage resources from the party in power, only to evaporate once the deal is struck. Clientelist politics are unstable enough that each election engenders another round of this process, in some cases with the same politicians. The consequence is that few if any parties other than the one in power undergo institutionalization over time. In turn, the absence of institutionalization makes non-clientelist strategies less likely.

Low ideological salience

A third salient feature of the emerging electoral politics in contemporary Africa has been the absence of programmatic debates. Though admittedly difficult to measure precisely, the low salience of ideology of most political parties is unmistakable. Many observers have noted the common adoption of a vague populism during elections, in which anti-corruption rhetoric, increases in public services, and general promises of a better future dominate the electoral discourse.[4] Ideological differences have been minor across parties, and debates about specific policy issues have been virtually non-existent, although opposition parties may criticize the government's management of the economy or the implementation of structural adjustment programs. A small number of parties have sought to make policy-based campaigns but with a striking lack of success. For instance, the National Lima Party (NLP) in Zambia was led by several prominent national politicians, supported by the Zambian Farmers' Association, and actively presented itself as the defender of rural interests in the 1996 elections, yet failed to get a single seat in the legislature. Similarly, in Francophone Africa, several avowedly Marxist parties regularly fail to get more than symbolic support.

Part of the low salience of ideology may well be due to the absence of labor or church-based parties. Though unions, professional associations and the churches typically played a prominent role in the democratization of the early 1990s, they quickly retreated from politics, once multiparty rule had been put in place. There is today no example of a Christian democratic party anywhere in the region. Similarly, there is no labor party, though the opposition alliance that is emerging to contest the Mugabe regime in Zimbabwe is avowedly labor-based. On the other hand, it has not staked out a policy position that is particularly to the left of the governing ZANU-PF or that puts forward labor issues (Raftopoulos 2001).

---

[4] See, for instance, Nugent (2001) and Lindberg (2001) on Ghana, Burnell (2001) on Zambia, Kaspin (1995) on Malawi, and Buijtenhuiijs (1994) on Chad.

In some cases, regional and/or ethnic identity overlaps with specific policy positions. Representatives of the Ogoni ethnic group in the oil-producing area of southeast Nigeria tend to be opponents of current federalist policies. In Kenya, Cameroon, Malawi, and Ghana, one ethnic minority is typically viewed as more pro-business than other groups, because of its alleged prominence in the private sector. Interestingly, the parties representing these communities have typically not adopted policy positions that reflect the putative economic interests of the group. Thus, in Cameroon, the SDF is viewed as the party of the Bamileke ethnic group. Bamileke businessmen are among the country's most prominent, and one reason often given for the reticence of the government to move forward with privatization is the widespread view that it would provide an advantage to the Bamileke community. Yet SDF policy positions are not particularly distinct from those of the government, and certainly not noticeably in favor of economic liberalism or privatization.

Ethnicity and the issue of vote buying

Election campaigns have been conducted almost entirely on the basis of personal and ethnoregional appeals for support. Marina Ottaway has argued that, with the end of the Cold War, "the absence of ideological or programmatic differences left ethnicity as the major characteristic by which the various parties could differentiate themselves" (1998: 311). In most countries, the single most important factor explaining party loyalty is ethnicity or region, and ethnic identity provides a remarkably precise prediction of voting behavior (e.g., on Zambia, see Posner 1998). While all party politics in Africa appears to be intensely personalized, however, it is not necessarily ethnic. Thus, in Senegal, political parties are not divided according to ethnicity, but patronage politics are just as important to the functioning of the system. In Senegal, clans around religious leaders (Marabouts), often organized along lineage, appear to shape voting behavior (Coulon 1988; Villalón 1994). In other cases, region plays the key role.

Newspaper accounts of a number of recent African elections have included stories of significant vote buying, in which citizens are given money by candidates, presumably in exchange for their vote. Most chapters in this book ascribe a high degree of instrumentality to voting in clientelist regimes. They argue that voters expect to gain in material terms for their vote. Significant segments of the citizenry in effect auction off their votes to the candidates who are willing to pay the most, also suggesting this instrumentality. This degree of instrumentality makes sense only if the candidate has the capability to ensure that the voter actually upholds his/her end of the bargain and actually casts a ballot in favor of the candidate whose money was pocketed. Much more case study work on party organization needs to be done, but the careful accounts of elections in countries like Benin (Banégas 1998) or Nigeria[5] suggests that parties generally lack this capability and do not try to enforce vote buying bargains in this manner. Banégas' careful account of elections in Benin gives the example of four out of five candidates distributing cash to the voters of one district, and makes it clear that the voters would base their vote on other criteria.

So, what is going on here? Banégas suggests that voters in Benin understand that democracy has empowered them, and understand the exchange of cash as a symbol of that empowerment. In interviews, voters argued that the politicians had stolen their money from the states, so it was only fair for the citizens now to get that money back (Banegas 1998: 78–79). At the same time, he argues that candidates' gifts provide a way for candidates to signal to the citizens their political virtues. The generous candidate will turn into a generous office-holder, who will not steal from the citizenry (p. 82; see Schatzberg 2001 for a similar argument). In this argument, the gift is a form of tribute, or a gift of munificence.

Based on Nigerian materials, Peter Lewis also views vote buying as an act of munificence, but in a more self-interested dynamic.[6] By making the gift, the candidate is signaling to voters his/her power and confidence that he/she will win. Citizens who wish to support a winner will view the payment as evidence that the candidate is very powerful or has the support of powerful forces. In neither case, however, is there a quid pro quo, which both scholars reject as highly improbable because the candidates typically lack the leverage to enforce any bargain.

The difficulties the opposition encountered in trying to gain a sizeable share of the vote in some countries are certainly compatible with a claim of voting instrumentality, since they suggest that voters believe voting for a loser will not be rewarded with access to state resources. This leads to a bandwagon effect, in which different ethnic communities seek to be part of the winning coalition. This will particularly be true of smaller ethnic groups, which are relegated to a junior partner role in successive governments, but seek to enhance their power by always being part of the presidential majority.

The ethnic calculus can lead to a very different conclusion, as well. The belief among voters in many countries that regions that do not support the winning candidate will not receive their fair share of the public expenditures in many cases leads them to "waste" their vote on losing

---

[5] Peter Lewis. Personal Communication, May 2002.   [6] Ibid.

candidates. Even in the absence of tangible benefits, citizens will choose to vote for individuals of their own ethnic group, particularly in ethnically divided societies. Less than the expectation that they will benefit directly from the vote, citizens may feel that only a member of their own ethnic group may end up defending the interests of the ethnic group as a whole, and that voting for a member of another ethnic group will certainly not do so. Thus, Kikuyu voters in Kenya take it for granted that the Moi regime will punish their prominent role in the opposition, by diverting public investments away from Kikuyu villages (Throup and Hornsby 1998). Posner suggests that voting on strictly ethnic lines in Zambia follows the same logic (Posner 1998), while my field work in Uganda in the fall of 2000 pointed to the same dynamics (van de Walle 2001). Northerners in Uganda felt sure that because the Museveni regime was southern-based and had reached power by ousting a northerner, they could not be getting their fair share of public expenditure. In turn, this perception led to much weaker support for the regime in various elections and referenda in recent years from the northern provinces (Bratton and Lambright 2001). Ironically, a careful empirical investigation offered little or no evidence that northerners were being discriminated against in various public employment positions, or that the Northern Provinces received less public investment than other regions (van de Walle 2001: Annex 3).

The Museveni regime in Uganda appears to want to continue the post-colonial pattern described above of extremely broad ethnic coalitions in power. In other regimes, however, the movement toward regular multi-party elections has resulted in a new logic of ethnic inclusiveness. Crook (1997) noted about the Ivory Coast that the move toward multiparty elections in the 1990s has brought about a greater willingness to exclude ethnic groups from the ruling alliance. Instead, the regime sought to put together a smaller "minimum winning coalition," which would be easier to manage, less expensive, and would provide leverage to the president with which to discipline disloyal groups.

The corollary of this argument is that winning candidates have no strategic interest in rewarding their in-group voters. Thus, the evidence offered in other chapters of this book that winning candidates reward their ethnic followers more than they need to finds little traction in the African cases. Instead, rewards are more likely to go to ethnic brokers and regional elites, and the rewards to voters are likely to be largely symbolic and vicarious.

In none of these cases, however, is there evidence that political parties have the organization or the inclination to monitor the vote of different communities and actually punish individual voters for their absence of support at the ballot. Bankrupt governments whose development policy-making process is micro-managed by donors do not in any event have much discretion in the allocation of social services and new patronage. Instead, clientelist punishments and rewards are meted out in the arenas of elite competition, over state offices, much as in the past. A community which did not deliver the vote is punished by seeing its three ministerial positions cut down to one in the post-election cabinet. Another community which did join the presidential majority is rewarded when one of its leading lights is named ambassador to Paris.[7]

Concluding remarks

I have argued that it is more useful to think of clientelistic politics in Africa as constituting primarily a mechanism for accommodation and integration of a fairly narrow political elite rather than a logic of mass party patronage. Most of the material gains from clientelism are limited to this elite. The stronger link between political elites and the citizenry is through the less tangible bonds of ethnic identity. Even in the absence of tangible benefits, citizens will choose to vote for individuals of their own ethnic group, particularly in ethnically divided societies. Less than the expectation that they will benefit directly from the vote, citizens may feel that only a member of their own ethnic group may end up defending the interests of the ethnic group as a whole, and that voting for a member of another ethnic group will certainly not do so.

Will this pattern change? In keeping with the arguments of the Introduction to this book, one could think that the transition to more competitive politics in the region will result in more responsive politics. However, the discussion suggests how deeply ambiguous the current evolution of the region really is. Much more systematic and comparative field research is necessary to reach a clear view of the ongoing processes. That said, the evidence does suggest that in a small number of countries, relatively liberal democracies are emerging. I would argue that in these regimes, prebendalism is in decline if not actually in the process of disappearing, at least as a systematic practice. The emergence of a free press raises the costs of evidently illegal practices. Electoral practices also force governments to be more responsive to mass demands. Thus, as systems democratize and political competition grows more lively, one can expect clientelism to become more overtly redistributive in nature. From elite offices, one would expect a move toward greater attention to welfare benefits, constituency services, and civil service positions. In countries like Botswana or Mauritius, various forms of patronage clientelism appear to remain a

---

[7] This process is well described for the case of Cameroon in Eboko (1999).

strong aspect of the electoral politics, at least if the near complete absence of programmatic parties or of ideological debate around elections is any indication. Patronage is very attractive to parties that need to compete in regular competitive elections and have no other consistent means of mobilizing voters. On the other hand, the continuing economic crisis and the micro-management of the policy reform process by the donors makes it hard for most of the regimes in the region to implement the kinds of mass patronage strategies they had aspired to in the more expansive era of the 1960s.

To explain why some parties use programmatic appeals to gain votes while others resort to promises of patronage, Martin Shefter (1994) has argued that parties with access to state resources (what he calls "internally mobilized") were more likely to eschew programmatic appeals in favor of clientelism, while outsider parties, that did not benefit from such access, were more likely to adopt programmatic appeals, as their only viable strategy to gain the support of significant segments of the population. If this analysis is correct, at least some African opposition parties will come to realize they cannot compete on the field of clientelistic politics, and will move instead to more programmatic discourse to mobilize the votes of citizens. They will adopt aggressive policy positions on economic issues, for example, and eschew the kind of ethnically driven clientelism that is their hallmark today. The fact that the experiments in this direction have been such dismal failures so far points to the difficulties involved. For one thing, the political salience of ethnicity undermines programmatic appeals. If other parties adopt an appeal to ethnic loyalties and clientelism, it is very hard for a programmatic party to win. Voters will seek to exchange their vote for the favors of a clientelist party because they know they would benefit from the programmatic party whether or not they voted for it, while they also know they will get no access to state favors if another ethnic-clientelist party they do not support wins.

In the other, less democratic, regimes, in which incumbents remain in place, the evolution to multiparty electoral regimes has probably not dramatically altered patterns of political clientelism. With some notable exceptions, political party organization remains a major constraint for the kinds of instrumental clientelist strategies described in this book for other regions of the world. My analysis suggests that incumbents continue to focus their strategy on using state resources to put together a majority coalition of ethnic elites who are assumed to be able to bring along their communities' support. The only noticeable change is that the elite coalitions have a tendency to be less inclusive than in the past.

3   Monopoly and monitoring: an approach to political clientelism

Luis Fernando Medina and Susan C. Stokes

In 1995, in a small city in northeastern Argentina, a local magnate who owned some gas stations, a transportation company, and several other businesses supported a fellow Radical Party member in the contest for mayor. But once in office the magnate's *protégé* proved too independent. In the next mayoral race, in 1999, the magnate threw his support behind a competitor. Despite the mayor's evident popularity, his supporters felt pressure to vote for the magnate's candidate and the mayor lost the election (Urquizo 1999).

In the 1950s and 1960s, the Christian Democratic Party swelled the bureaucracy of the southern Italian cities of Naples and Palermo, offering employment in return for electoral support. Chubb (1981) explains how the "vote-for-job exchange" worked:

In a highly competitive situation for both hiring and promotion, with virtually everyone recommended by one prominent politician or another, the weight of the recommendation is directly proportional to the power of the patron, which is in turn closely linked to the number of personal preference votes received in the preceding election. The employee's fate, as well as his chances of placing other family members, is thus directly dependent on the continued electoral success of the patron . . . (Chubb: 114)

These two situations have at least one thing in common: the scholars who study them describe them as instances of *clientelism*. Clientelism is one of those social science terms that mean different things to different people.

Our strategy in this chapter is not to peddle a definition that we consider the last word on clientelism. Instead we begin with a feature that is common to many settings that people identify as clientelistic, build a model of political competition around this feature, and observe whether it explains other features that people also identify with clientelism. Our independent

We are grateful to Herbert Kitschelt for his comments on an earlier draft of this chapter. Stokes's research was supported by the Russell Sage Foundation.

variable is *political monopoly*, which we mean in a particular sense explained below. Our dependent variables – the features of clientelism we hope to explain – are the entrenchment of an incumbent patron in power, despite regular and in most senses free elections; the absence of redistributive fiscal policies by the state; and economic underdevelopment.[1]

In our usage, a person holds a monopoly if she controls access to a resource or technology that is valuable to members of the polity. Access to this resource may be valuable because it reduces people's production costs and raises their incomes, or because it reduces the variability of their incomes and hence risk. We call the resource a "monopolized good." A monopolist might own the only grain elevator in a rural community, the use of which lowers risk for local farmers by smoothing out variations in production levels and the price of grains. Or the monopolist might control employment in the public sector, and offer jobs to clients that are more secure than jobs in the private sector. Whether the monopolized good reduces costs or risk, we find that, in some equilibria, the patron's control over the monopolized good allows her to keep voters from defecting to a challenger. They are kept from defecting because, in a narrow sense, they are better off under the patron; but they may be worse off than they would be if there were no monopoly and challengers could compete without disadvantage.[2]

In the next section we describe a model, analyzed more formally elsewhere (Medina and Stokes 2002), in which incumbents are monopolists. In the third part of the chapter we discuss three effects of political monopoly: it reduces (but does not eliminate) the competitiveness of elections, it discourages redistributive fiscal policies, and it discourages governments from pursuing economic growth. In the fourth section we turn our attention to the question of politicians' monitoring of voters, an important yet counterintuitive feature of our model and an implicit feature of many models of clientelism. In the final section we reflect on the differences between programmatic and clientelistic democracies.

---

[1] The lack of electoral competitiveness arises from the logic of our model, even though there is nothing in our model that violates most definitions of democracy; elections can be frequent and regularly scheduled, suffrage can be near-universal, ruling parties can lose elections and step down when they lose, people can have constitutionally protected rights to associate and speak, and the rule of law can be respected.

[2] Hence voters would have some interest in breaking the monopoly – in banning patronage or in abolishing economic monopolies. Yet it strikes us as highly plausible that voters would have difficulty doing either. Economic monopolies are often supported by legalized property rights, and no democracy on earth has found its way to barring all forms of patronage.

Outline of the model

Consider a stylized polity composed of an incumbent, whom we call the patron, and a challenger. The patron and the challenger are both office-seekers who maximize their chances of (re)election. The sequence of the game is as follows. In the lead-up to his reelection bid, the patron announces his "program." This is not a program in a traditional sense, with the politician declaring broad policies and their impact on general categories of voters.[3] Here politicians offer a deal to each voter as a quid pro quo for his or her vote. These deals can vary from one voter to the next. The economy that is the backdrop to this polity (described more fully below) generates tax revenues, and the patron announces how much of the revenues he will transfer to each voter. (We assume that the total revenues are given exogenously; politicians just decide how to distribute them.) The challenger, in turn, offers her own program, which also spells out who will receive what under her administration. Each voter has a personal endowment (labor, skills, or capital), which he or she uses to generate an income. Each one allocates his or her endowment between activities that involve the monopolized good and ones that don't. Use of the monopolized good either reduces risk, or increases income, or both.

A crucial element in our model is that patrons have some capacity to monitor voters' electoral choices, and to reward them or punish them depending on how they voted. More precisely, patrons have information that allows them to shape the voter's expected utilities in such a way that these expected utilities hinge on the voter's electoral choices.

We distinguish two sorts of monopoly: *economic monopoly* over goods that the patron controls independent of the outcome of the election (e.g., the Argentine magnate's control over employment in his firms); and *political monopoly* over goods that he controls only if he retains office (e.g., the Italian patron's control over public employment). The voter has to consider two questions when deciding how to vote: what are the relative benefits to me of the two candidates' distributive offers? And how will my vote affect my access to the monopolized good, and thus my welfare?

When the monopolized good is economic, the voter anticipates losing access to it whenever she votes for the challenger, whether the challenger wins or loses; the patron will punitively exclude her from it. In this case she only votes for the challenger when the advantages of the challenger's distributive offer outweigh the loss of access to the monopolized good.

---

[3] The model treats the programs as N-dimensional (where N is the number of voters in the polity). This implies that candidates could offer deals targeted at categories of voters, but it is also possible that they are maximally particularistic, offering a different deal to everyone.

The patron's economic monopoly, then, is like an exclusive-dealing contract – it constitutes a disincentive for voters to support a challenger and reduces competition.

When the monopolized good is political, voters will be punished only if they vote for the challenger and the challenger loses. If they vote for the patron and he wins they will not be punished: he rewards them by granting access to the monopolized good. If they vote for the patron, the patron loses, and the challenger cannot monitor votes effectively, the voters will not be punished. If they vote for the challenger and the challenger wins they are also not punished – the challenger has no motive to punish them. Note that if the monopolized good is political and the challenger *can* monitor the vote as accurately as the patron can, then an incumbent's control over the monopolized good is useless as a tool for blocking entry and politics is competitive.

Given this set-up, it is possible for us to say something about the programs which, in equilibrium, the patron and the challenger offer to voters. The patron offers some transfer to every member of the polity, whereas the challenger only makes offers to a sub-set of the electorate – a minimal winning coalition. The intuition here is that the more encompassing the patron's transfers, the higher the cost of every possible minimal winning coalition for the challenger. The challenger's minimal winning coalition is biased in favor of voters who depend little on the monopolized good and hence suffer little from forgoing access to it. The same holds true for the patron; although unlike the challenger he offers something to everyone, his offers to voters who depend less on the monopolized good are more generous than his offers to voters who rely heavily on it. Voters who are dependent on the monopolized good require less from him in transfers because, for them, access to the monopolized good is highly valuable.

Implications of the model

Monopoly and electoral competition

Intuitively it should be clear that the anticipation of loss of access to monopolized goods sometimes leads voters to support the patron even when the challenger's program (her set of distributive offers) is better for them. By extension, some challengers whose distributive offers are, for a majority of voters, superior to the patron's will be kept out of competition. The monopolized good in effect creates a barrier to entry for the challenger. It should also be clear that, all else being equal, political monopoly creates a lower barrier to entry than does economic monopoly, since voters are more likely to be punished by the patron when his monopoly does not depend on his holding on to office. Hence, the monopoly approach to clientelism predicts the suppression but not full elimination of electoral competition – in some equilibria, the challenger outbids the patron and wins.

This prediction fits nicely with many descriptions of clientelism. Many treatments of Mexican politics during the many decades of PRI hegemony, for instance, invoked the concept of clientelism to describe the relation between the party and voters. But clearly this was not a system where challengers to PRI candidates could not win – they did win local and eventually state-wide elections, as well as seats in the national legislature. Political monopoly as we conceptualize it erects obstacles for the challenger but these obstacles are surmountable.

Monopoly and redistribution

The probability that the patron wins reelection declines as tax revenues increase, and hence as the potential for redistributive policies increases. An exogenous upward shock to tax revenues would loosen the patron's grip on power. Intuitively, the reason is that taxes allow the challenger to offer larger transfers to voters, reducing the relative importance to voters of the monopolized good. Hence our patron-monopolists are anti-tax and anti-redistribution, not because we impose on them any particular ideological coloration, but because the likelihood that they will be reelected declines as taxes increase. Our model has the nice feature, then, of explaining the oft-noted conservatism of clientelist politics.

Our model contains the assumption that the productivity of applying one's endowments to non-monopolized, risky goods is greater for people with larger endowments of skill and human capital than for people with more modest endowments. Therefore the resource that gives the patron an advantage over the challenger matters less to high-skilled, high-income people, and they are less in his thrall. The well-paid engineer is less worried about the loss of public employment than is the low-skilled clerk. If poor people rely more heavily than do wealthy people on monopolized goods, then both the patron's and the challenger's offers are regressive – they transfer more to wealthier voters than to poor ones.

The regressive quality of clientelist politics would be magnified if poor people, in addition to being relatively less productive when they use risky goods, are especially risk-averse.

Our model assumes that tax levels are exogenous, and candidates simply offer different methods of dividing a given pie. But one could imagine patrons as the people whom a national party relies on to generate votes, a national party that sets tax policy. This patron-dependent party would be loathe to raise taxes if doing so would undermine the electoral prospects of its patrons around the country. Hence, again, clientelism as political monopoly implies anti-tax, anti-redistributive politics.

Monopoly and economic development

We noted at the outset that clientelism appears in societies that are poor. A list of places where researchers have uncovered clientelist political mobilization underscores its coincidence with poverty. Given the empirical link between clientelism and poverty, it is surprising how few studies explicitly try to explain why the two are linked. The reader is seldom told whether clientelism causes poverty, or poverty causes clientelism, or the two reinforce one another, and why. An exception is Judith Chubb's work on southern Italy. She describes a symbiosis between clientelism and poverty – clientelist mobilization works best on voters who are poor; therefore patron-politicians have an interest in perpetuating poverty. In a discussion of the failed efforts of the Cassa per il Mezzogiorno, an institution established in 1950 to stimulate economic development in the South, she writes, "The investment activity of the Cassa, while failing in its proclaimed objective of industrializing the South, did perform important political functions . . . it preserved in large part the traditional economic and social structure of the South upon which the DC's clientelist local power bases depended . . ." (1981: 110). Clientelism and poverty were thus mutually reinforcing.

But why exactly does clientelism work best when the clients are poor? The usual answer is that it focuses on diminishing marginal utility of income (see Dixit and Londregan 1996; Calvo and Murillo 2004; Stokes 2005) or on their risk aversion (Scott 1969; Chubb 1981; Kitschelt 2000; Wantchekon 2003; see also Hernández 2001).

Our explanation is different.[4] One way to think about economic development is as a rise in productivity; poor countries are ones in which productivity in a major economic sector, such as agriculture, is extremely low, whereas wealthy countries are ones where productivity is high (Lewis 1978). To the extent that the monopolized good in our model is public employment, it is reasonable to assume that economic development brings bigger leaps in productivity to sectors of the economy where

---

[4] Our model is not incompatible with Hernandez's risk-aversion approach – our mechanism linking poverty with clientelism would operate whether or not poor people are especially prone to risk-aversion. Ours is in this sense the more general model.

monopolized goods are less relevant. Hence development erodes the value of the monopolized goods to voters. It is intuitive that, as the productivity of non-monopolized or competitive goods increases, voters suffer less when the patron denies them access to the monopolized good. Hence economic development can loosen the patron's grip on clients.

As the productivity of non-monopolized goods grows, voters also allocate more of their endowments to activities involving non-monopolized goods; hence, for this reason as well, development reduces the political bite of monopoly. Development may have the effect, furthermore, of breaking up economic monopolies. The risk-reducing credit arrangements that the local patron makes available to clients, for instance, are replaced by private credit institutions that maximize their profits by considering all customers, independent of their political loyalties.

In sum, if an incumbent politician exercises monopoly control over a political or economic good, one that voters could use to increase their income or reduce their risk or both, and if the incumbent can monitor voters (in a sense that we enlarge on below), then (a) the incumbent may deploy the threat of denied access to this good to block the entry into electoral competition of challengers, even ones whose programs have higher payoffs (in terms of tax transfers) for a majority of voters; (b) exogenous upward shocks to tax revenues undermine the importance of the monopolized good and hence encourage electoral competition; and (c) economic development erodes the political strength of the patron. If the patron is aware of (b) and (c), he will have an interest in low taxes and underdevelopment. Inequality and poverty favor clientelism; therefore clientelists favor inequality and poverty.

What does our model tell us about the settings in which we should *not* expect clientelism? We do not expect it in settings where the political and economic monopolies we described above are absent. But when monopolies do exist, when would we expect them to fail to create electoral advantages for the monopolist? We do not expect the advantage to appear in places where tax revenues are high and hence the potential for redistribution is great. We do not expect it in wealthy polities where risk-reducing goods and other monopolized goods are easily replaced by goods available to all takers in the private economy. And we do not expect it, as we shall see in the next section, in political systems where no politician can monitor – even with error – how voters vote and reward or punish them for their vote choice; or where monopolies are strictly political (e.g., control over public sector jobs) and all competitors are equally capable of monitoring.

Clientelism and monitoring

Many approaches to clientelism, ours among them, rely on the idea that patrons concede rewards to voters who support them and punish those who don't. Yet this idea sparks the question: how can patrons enforce clientelism if the vote is secret? In the words of an Argentine politician, what keeps people from "receiving with one hand and voting with the other?" (Fernández Meijide, quoted in Szwarcberg 2001: 4). In the discussion that follows we hope to show that electoral monitoring is not an eccentric idea, and to develop some propositions about the kinds of political institutions and voting technologies that encourage such monitoring.

The term *monitoring* as we use it in this chapter actually involves two abilities: the ability to know something *ex post* about how voters voted, and the ability to reward or punish voters in response to the votes they cast. The first ability intuitively appears unlikely to those of us used to voting in advanced industrial democracies, and it is on this ability that our discussion focuses. But note that the second ability does not follow automatically from the first. A politician who can, *ex post*, identify voters with vote choices may still face legal obstacles that keep him from rewarding or punishing voters. A politician in France or Australia who threatened retribution against a community where his favored candidate did not win a majority of votes might very well get in trouble with the press and the courts.[5]

In considering the monitoring of voters, two things must be kept in mind. First, what's crucial for clientelism as political monopoly (and, we think, for many other models of clientelism) is not that voters believe that the patron will know with certainty how they individually voted. What's crucial instead is that voters perceive that the expected value of future flows of their utility income will rise or fall significantly, depending on how they as individuals vote. Second, patrons don't have to know how each individual voted. They merely need to know how groups of voters voted at some sufficiently disaggregated level such that they can induce the belief that voters' future flow of utility incomes is positively correlated with their electoral choices.

We begin with a grim example. In the 2002 campaign for presidential elections in Colombia, the leading candidate was Alvaro Uribe. Uribe attracted much attention in the campaign by adopting a hawkish stance *vis-à-vis* leftist insurgents, and he was alleged to have ties to right-wing paramilitary groups. Some leaders of these paramilitary

---

[5] Efforts to reward and punish *ex post* can raise tricky legal questions. See our discussion of Hillary Clinton's possible vote buying below.

groups threatened to "take reprisals against entire communities if Uribe fails to carry them" (Guillermoprieto 2002: 54).[6] (Uribe went on to win the elections decisively, in the first round of voting.) Hearing about the threat, a voter in a community where paramilitaries were active might well use a thumbnail version of expected-value reasoning to think about how to vote. She might say to herself, if Uribe doesn't win in my community, the paramilitaries might kill me or a family member. To avoid such an outcome a majority of people in this community must vote for Uribe. The probability of his carrying my community goes up (by a very small amount) if I vote for Uribe. Even though the increment by which my vote increases the probability of Uribe's victory in my community is small, when I multiply this increment by the utility to me of avoiding being killed or having a family member killed, it becomes worth it to me to vote for Uribe.

This example suggests that monitoring works better the greater the cost of punishment (or benefit of the reward) that voters anticipate. If the voters think that paramilitaries are likely to provoke tavern brawls in towns that Uribe failed to carry, the voter who was inclined to vote for another candidate would be unlikely to be deterred by this threat.

The Colombian example also suggests that the smaller the constituency, the greater the ease of monitoring.[7] Some indirect support for a link between clientelism and small constituencies comes from Wantchekon's experimental work in Benin (2003). He shows that candidates who used "clientelistic" appeals (promises of jobs, local public works) mobilized more support than those who made "programmatic" appeals (poverty alleviation, agricultural development, eradication of corruption). Clientelistic appeals boosted a candidate's support in races for local office more than it did in races for national office. Our model suggests an explanation. It may be that voters view local candidates with small constituencies as able to discern voting patterns *ex post* more accurately than are national candidates with large constituencies, and hence as better able to channel benefits to supporters. In this sense politicians with large constituencies cannot credibly commit to helping those who vote for them (or to hurting those who don't), whereas politicians with small constituencies can.

---

[6] Of course an election in which people had to vote under such threats stretches the limits of the concepts of "free and fair" elections, a point which many Colombians made at the time. But less dire consequences may still induce voters to support a patron, as we show in a later example. Note, also, that in this case the threat of reprisal comes not from someone with monopoly power over an economic resource (although some paramilitary families did hold such monopolies), but from someone who deployed a coercive resource.

[7] The empirical implication, testable cross-nationally, is that, all else being equal, the smaller the constituency that an electoral system provides for, the smaller the number of effective parties competing.

We detect an irony here. Small constituencies are thought to enhance the accountability of political representatives, making it easier for voters to obtain information about their actions in office and to vote them out if their actions are bad (Rehfeld 2000). But if small constituencies coexist with political monopolies, patrons can also better monitor voters and use this ability to stifle competition. The same feature that makes politicians accountable to voters may also make voters "accountable," in a perverse sense of the term, to politicians (see Stokes 2005).

Small constituencies may foster clientelism for another reason as well. It is well known that monopolies thrive in small markets – given that firms have fixed costs, a small market will efficiently support fewer firms than a large market. Consider the sparsely populated rural communities which are also small political constituencies. In light of the discussion about constituency size, these places have no chance; they are small markets where monopolies are more likely to exist, and they are small constituencies where such monitoring is easier. They are fertile ground for clientelism.

Monitoring is also easier, as suggested in the Introduction to this volume, when constituencies are relatively homogeneous (in ethnic or religious terms) and tend to vote en bloc. Bloc voting may reflect a demographic or cultural homogeneity that spontaneously leads people to the same electoral choice, or it may allow a community to coordinate its vote more easily. An example comes from US electoral politics. In 2000, the First Lady, Hillary Clinton, was elected to the US Senate from New York. Among her supporters were almost all the voters in New Square, an upstate community of Hassidic Jews (she received 1,359 votes there; her opponent, Rick Lazio, received 10). After Clinton was elected, then-president Bill Clinton reduced the sentences of four New Square residents. (They were in prison for stealing federal and state funds and channeling them toward yeshiva schools and other institutions in the community.) The case conveys three important points. First, it is a nice example of a monopoly resource: Clinton's position as First Lady would have allowed her to credibly offer clemency whereas her opponent could not (she claimed later to have made no such offer). Second, it shows how constituency homogeneity eases the problem of monitoring votes and channeling rewards to supporters.[8] New Square regularly votes en bloc for politicians, from both major political parties; it's not so much that

---

[8] Federal prosecutors explored the possibility that candidate Clinton's actions amounted to vote buying, but eventually they decided not to prosecute. The crucial question was whether she had offered to press for clemency when she made a campaign visit to New Square, or whether the community was merely rewarded after-the-fact for delivering a large bloc of votes to her. Prosecutors found insufficient evidence of an *ex ante* deal. For a detailed analysis, see *The Jerusalem Post*, 2001.

people's party preferences there are homogeneous, but that the community's (in this case, religious) homogeneity allows it to strategically coordinate votes in order to extract goods from candidates. And this leads us to the third point. This case shows, in contrast to our Colombian example, that "accountability" of voters to politicians can benefit voters. Just as voter accountability allows spurned monopolists to inflict punishment on voters, it also allows successful monopolists to channel rewards to them.

Clientelism conceptualized as political monopoly should also work better the more disaggregated the information on voting returns available to the patron. Imagine that the Colombian paramilitaries' threat had been to take reprisals against people in parts of the capital city, Bogotá, that didn't provide majority support for Uribe. If returns were only reported for the city as a whole (a city with more than a million voters), then our hypothetical voter would reason that her vote will increase the probability of a majority supporting Uribe by an increasingly small increment, and the threat would play little role in her voting decision. If, in contrast, returns were reported by precincts and the threat was to retaliate precinct by precinct, she might well see her vote as meaningfully positively correlated with the outcome of the election in her precinct and hence with her own probability of suffering reprisals. And even though her vote would probably still contribute little to Uribe's fate in her precinct, with so much at stake in the outcome she might well be induced to support him.

The extreme of disaggregation is the individual voter, and certain electoral technologies enable politicians to monitor individual voters. Suppose that party operatives accompany voters into the voting booth and watch them vote, or ballots are color-coded and observable by the patron, or the patron's lieutenants know which party's pre-prepared ballot was stuffed into a voter's pocket as she approaches the polling place, and suppose that the voter were certain that the patron would use this information about how she voted to reward or punish her in ways that would make a substantial difference to her welfare. In such limiting cases the voter would believe that the correlation between how she voted and her probability of receiving a reward or punishment as a consequence of her vote is almost perfect. Absent any strong countervailing considerations, she supports the patron.

Certain technologies of voting also help politicians exert some control over how people vote. Among Latin American countries, Argentina, Panama, and Uruguay have never instituted the Australian ballot. In Argentina, instead "ballots" (*boletas*) are slips of paper that parties and candidates produce, which *punteros* slip into the hands of voters, or under their doors, and which are also available for voters in the *cuarto oscuro*. Alvarez (1999), who studies local politics in the same northeastern province (Misiones) where Urquizo works, quotes a *puntero* explaining how they mobilize votes:

[On election day] we have to keep them [*retenerlos*]. In the early morning, or the night before, we bring them down from the mountains . . . Then we bring them down and send them to Pedro. That night they drink, eat steak, dance, and the next day they vote; but we keep them there because otherwise they get taken away [*nos sacan*]. You have to have them tied down [*sujetos*]. We put the ballot straight in their pocket.

In addition to small constituencies, homogeneous constituencies, disaggregated reporting of election returns, and party-controlled voting technologies, some electoral rules may facilitate monitoring. Chubb's work on southern Italy links clientelism to the open-list proportional representation system used in national and in municipal elections. Italian voters at the time cast two ballots, one for a party and another for their preferred candidate on the party's list (see also Sartori 1976: 93). As we saw in the opening quotation, Chubb identifies the preference vote as the key institution enforcing the clientelist "contract." The more preference votes cast for a politician running on a list for the national chamber of deputies or for a city council, the more heavily that politician's *raccomandazione* (recommendation, backing) was weighed in the distribution of government jobs. If you were a Palermo resident who held a recommendation from city councilor Gioia, you were likely to see your future welfare as affected by the number of preference votes he received. Chubb views as an overstatement that in Palermo "'a job signifies a vote, and vice versa'" but the phrase's "common acceptance conveys the political climate of a city where politics is perceived as the only road to obtaining secure employment" (Chubb 1982: 91; she quotes *L'Ora* of Palermo).

The preference vote basically has the effect of reducing the size of the constituency and of disaggregating the level at which returns are reported. Whereas one person's vote would contribute infinitesimally to how the Christian Democratic Party's list for the national chamber of deputies does in a particular election, it contributes more significantly to the number of preference votes a candidate receives and how that number compares with those of other politicians on the list. Furthermore, here the question a voter might ask herself is not, "how probable is it that my vote breaks a tie between, say, the Christian Democrats and the Communist Party?" but, "how probable is it that my vote makes a difference in whether my patron does well or not so well in the election, and therefore the number of jobs that he will be able to give away?"

In this case, because the number of jobs allotted to a party boss depends on his electoral strength, the usual argument that victory is an all-or-nothing event is invalid. Stated technically, the employment-for-preference-vote exchange has the effect of turning the relation of the votes to outcomes from a discontinuous to a linear function. In the usual election the margin of victory makes no difference, and voters may have little incentive to vote, let alone to vote for one candidate over another. But in the Italian case, where preference votes can be parlayed into jobs, this is no longer true. Even if your candidate is sure to win by 1,000 votes, it still makes sense for you to vote so as to make that advantage larger and, hence, more fertile in yielding jobs.

In our model, when a patron's monopoly is economic – when his control over the monopolized resource is not contingent on his retaining office – he can induce voters to enter into a sort of exclusive-dealing contract and bar the entrance of competitors as long as he can monitor the vote (in the loose sense that we hope to have conveyed in this discussion). We needed no additional assumptions about the challenger's ability to monitor. But when the patron's monopoly is political, he loses his power to deploy the monopoly against challengers unless his ability to monitor is superior to the challenger's. If the patron's and the challenger's ability to monitor is symmetrical, and if the patron's monopoly depends on his retaining office, then whoever wins can punish and whoever loses can't. Consider a challenger facing an incumbent who gives his supporters public-sector jobs. The challenger with equal monitoring abilities could simply promise voters that, if they support her and she wins, she will keep these employees in their jobs. Stated positively, if all politicians have the same monitoring capabilities, the office-holders can't use public employment (or other political monopolies) to forestall the entry of challengers, and politics is competitive.

This is good news. Incumbency in every democracy comes with some (traditional or legal) rights to distribute patronage. Therefore, if asymmetrical monitoring were not a necessary condition for patrons to exploit their power, clientelism would be endemic to democracy. And our model would be weakened – it would over-predict clientelism.

Is it ever the case that patrons can monitor voters better than challengers can? It is if patrons command richer organizational resources than their opponents, and can deploy this organizational advantage to monitoring. For instance, their organizational resources might allow them to send operatives to accompany voters to the voting booth, or to keep track of turnout and voting patterns, or to stuff pre-prepared ballots into pockets.

In our model, patrons are able to mobilize electoral support by influencing voters' expected utility calculations. But in reviewing the evidence we are also struck by a less rationalistic way in which local notables in small constituencies, or even powerful political organizations in big cities, were able to influence voters. This was the influence that came from intimidation. Powerful patrons were sometimes able to intimidate voters, and to induce a sense in them, among other things, that their votes were more closely monitored than they actually probably were. We therefore close our discussion with two examples from Argentina of "monitoring" by intimidation.

In the small city in northeastern Argentina cited in the opening of this chapter, the local magnate's economic interests are so extensive that an anthropologist who studies politics in the city refers to him jokingly as the "*dueño del pueblo*," or owner of the town. In her descriptions he sounds like a kind of a local J. R. from the TV series *Dallas*. His family is not shy about displaying its wealth, and townspeople are very aware of it. The family owns private electricity generators, for instance, and when the rest of the town suffers power outages the *dueño*'s family's houses alone glow through the dark. If the *dueño* wants to impose an economic loss on a fellow resident he can easily do so, by firing him from his job if he is one of the *dueño*'s many local employees, or by denying him various services. In the mayoral race of 1999, the incumbent – once the *dueño*'s protégé, now his nemesis – faced a new candidate whom the *dueño* supported. The election polarized the city. Urquizo reports that voters thought of themselves as at risk of suffering reprisals, including losing their jobs, if the *dueño*'s candidate lost, and they didn't want to take chances (personal communication). This perception ran especially deep among those most closely dependent on the *dueño*.

Economic threats, as we have seen, would be the more effective the closer the patron was able to come to observing each individual voter's vote. Party operatives couldn't accompany voters into the voting booth (known in Argentina as the *cuarto oscuro* or dark room); since the Saenz Peña reforms of 1912 Argentines have been guaranteed the secret ballot. But they could come pretty close. In heated elections like this one, Urquizo reports, "the *puntero* is the last person the voter sees before entering the *cuarto oscuro* and the first person he sees after leaving it" (personal communication). Whatever the limitations of the patron's ability to monitor voters, this sort of intimidating presence seems designed to convey the message: *we're watching you.*

Clients' sense of being watched comes through clearly in Szwarcberg's (2001) study of community organizations in a poor neighborhood of

Buenos Aires. In one interview Szwarcberg conducted, the head of an organization talked about the organization's relation to parties and electoral politics. Their official stance was apolitical; but the food their soup kitchen relied on came from a program founded by Hilda "Chiche" Duhalde. Chiche Duhalde was a Peronist running for office at the time, and was also the wife of the then-governor of the Province of Buenos Aires. The community leader told Szwarcberg that in a meeting with recipients of free meals,

we would ask as if it was a poll who people were going to vote for. And I'm telling you, of all the people we asked, only one said they weren't voting for Chiche, but then again maybe because they were getting things, they felt forced to say so *thinking they would be watching.* (2001: 24, our emphasis)

To summarize our discussion of monitoring, our (and other clientelism theorists') reliance on politicians' being able to monitor voters does not mean that politicians need to know exactly how everyone voted. They just need to cause it to be the case that voters' expected welfare is contingent on their electoral choices. Politicians can monitor effectively by some combination of raising the stakes for voters of the outcome of the election and increasing the probability that each voter's vote will influence the outcome. This way of thinking about monitoring brings to the fore electoral practices, technologies, and institutions that make voters more "accountable" to politicians – more transparent and punishable (not a form of accountability many democratic theorists would endorse). These included small constituencies, homogeneous constituencies, disaggregated reporting of returns, balloting systems enhancing a party's control of voters, preference voting, and voting practices and technologies that make people's votes more transparent. We explored situations in which incumbents would enjoy superior abilities to monitor (necessary to block competition unless they monopolize some non-incumbency-dependent good).

Clientelism as political monopoly and programmatic politics

In a civics textbook caricature of democracy, political parties compete by presenting alternative programs to citizens, citizens endorse one of these programs by giving a majority of votes to one party, the party empowered by the election implements its program, and at the end of the term the process starts anew. The program consists of generally worded proposals aimed at mobilizing support from categorically defined constituencies: military personnel, people worried about the environment, families with million-dollar estates. A change in the tax code will help you not because you are John Smith or Corporation X, but because you are a low-income taxpayer or a steel company that has cleaned up its productive technologies. And you receive a state pension not because you know someone in the governing party who can secure a check for you but because you contributed to the pension system. The presumed fairness of this democracy lies not in its treating everyone the same; every party program implicitly announces who the winners will be and silently identifies losers, too. Its fairness is not substantive but procedural – programs are debated openly and voted on.

Of course this caricature fully describes no democracy on earth. Our guess is that the difference between systems where programmatic debate matters in voters' choices and systems where clientelism dominates is one of degree. The difference is not whether but how often public-sector jobs are given as rewards for party loyalty rather than for a high score on a civil service exam or a good place in line the day the ministry was hiring clericals; or how often one has to make personal appeals (for "constituent service") to secure a pension check; or how often incumbents channel benefits to "marginal" districts, ones that the incumbent barely won or lost in the last election, rather than to districts that fall into some abstract category of need or merit.

That "programmatic" and "clientelist" countries occupy different places on a series of continua, rather than separate political universes, does not invalidate efforts to draw sharp conceptual distinctions between these methods of political mobilization. Like many other contributors to this volume and others who study clientelism, we are drawn to the topic in part because it tarnishes the quality of democracy in many developing countries and new democracies around the world, a fact that is not lost on citizens in these countries. But understanding what clientelism is and how it works can help us to understand the limitations of democratic politics in poor, new democracies and in wealthy, old democracies alike.

4   Counting heads: a theory of voter and elite behavior in patronage democracies

Kanchan Chandra

The observation that patronage politics and expectations of ethnic favoritism go together is supported by a well-documented consensus among scholars of patronage democracies. According to Kearney, a student of Sri Lanka: "A common expectation seems to be that a person holding a public office or other position of power will use his position for the near-exclusive benefit of his 'own' people, defined by kinship, community or personal loyalty" (1973: 8). According to Haroun Adamu, a student of Nigerian politics: "It is strongly believed in this country that if you do not have one of your own kin in the local, state and/or national decision-making bodies, nobody would care to take your troubles before the decision makers, much less find solutions to them" (quoted in Joseph 1987: 67). Kenneth Post's description of elections in Nigeria emphasizes much the same point: "It was rare for a man to stand for election in a constituency which did not contain the community in which he was born. It did not matter if he had been educated elsewhere and had his business interests outside the community in which he was born, so long as he regarded it as his home. He would still be a better representative for it than someone who came from outside, who could not even speak in the same tongue" (1963: 391). According to Chabal, speaking of Africa in general: "All politicians, whether elected locally or nationally, are expected to act as the spokespeople and torchbearers of their community" (Chabal and Daloz 1999: 99). And Posner's investigation of voter expectations in Zambia in the 1990s found that the assumption that politicians in power will favor their own ethnic group was practically "an axiom of politics" (Posner 1998: 118).

This chapter proposes a theory of individual voter and elite behavior in "patronage democracies" which explains expectations of ethnic favoritism as an outcome of the information constraints that characterize patronage transactions in such democracies. Situations in which

This chapter is excerpted from Kanchan Chandra, *Why Ethnic Parties Succeed: Patronage and Ethnic Headcounts in India* (Cambridge University Press, 2004), chs. 1 and 2.

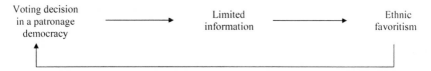

Figure 4.1 Self-reinforcing equilibrium of ethnic favoritism

observers have to distinguish between individuals under severe information constraints, I argue, bias them toward schemes of ethnic
categorization. The voting decision in a patronage democracy is such
a limited information situation. Consequently, voters are biased toward
ethnic categorizations of the beneficiaries of patronage transactions. Confronted with voter biases, I show why elites are forced to favor voters from
their "own" categories in their search for office. And voters, observing in
turn that politicians help their "own," but unaware that their own perceptual biases drive elites to adopt such a strategy, place their trust primarily
in co-ethnic politicians, leading to a self-enforcing and reinforcing equilibrium of ethnic favoritism in patronage democracies. This theory is
summarized in Figure 4.1 above.

The remainder of this chapter is as follows. The next section elaborates
upon the concept of a "patronage democracy." I then lay out the theory
identifying the link between limited information, patronage democracy,
and a politics of ethnic favoritism. The final section identifies factors
that mitigate the information constraints under which the voting decision is made in patronage democracies and therefore reduce the likelihood of ethnic favoritism. Throughout, my focus is on the behavior of
individual voters and elites. In the broader project of which this chapter is a part, I relate the individual micro-foundations developed here
to the behavior of aggregates such as political parties and organizations
(Chandra 2004). I use the terms politician or political entrepreneur to
mean any individual seeking to obtain or retain elected office. Among
politicians, I distinguish between candidates (those who seek to obtain
office) and incumbents (those who seek to retain office). In patronage
democracies, those who have the capital to launch a political career tend
to be "elites," i.e., upwardly mobile middle-class individuals, better educated and better off than the voters whom they seek to mobilize. I use
the term "elite" interchangeably, therefore, with the terms "politician,"
"candidate," "incumbent," and "entrepreneur" in this chapter.

The concept of "patronage democracy"

I use the term "democracy" here in a minimal sense to mean simply a
system in which the political leadership is chosen through competitive

elections (Huntington 1993: 7). By the term "patronage democracy," I mean democracies in which the state has a relative monopoly on jobs and services, and in which elected officials enjoy significant discretion in the implementation of laws allocating the jobs and services at the disposal of the state. The term "patronage democracy" may apply to a political system as a whole, or to a subsystem within it.

The key aspect of a patronage democracy is not simply the size of the state but the power of elected officials to distribute the vast resources controlled by the state to voters on an *individualized* basis through their discretion in the implementation of state policy. This individualized distribution of resources, in conjunction with a dominant state, I will argue, makes patronage democracies a distinct family of democracies with distinct types of voter and elite behavior. A democracy is not patronage based if the private sector is larger than the public sector as a source of jobs and provider of services, or if those who control the distribution of state resources and services cannot exercise discretion in the implementation of policy concerning their distribution.

Before going further, let me clarify the relationship between the term "patronage politics" as used in this chapter and other terms which have slightly different meanings but are often used interchangeably: "rent-seeking," "corruption," "clientelism," and "pork-barrel politics."

The terms "rent-seeking" and "corruption" typically refer to the sale of public goods for private gain, without specifying whether that private gain takes the form of wealth or political support. I use the term "patronage politics" here to refer to that form of rent-seeking and corruption in which the returns to politicians take the form of votes rather than bribes.

The term "clientelism" is often used, especially in anthropological studies, to refer to a dyadic transaction between traditional notables and their dependents bound by ties of reciprocity. While "patronage politics" as used here certainly describes dyadic transactions between voters and politicians, the definition does not require voters and politicians to be connected by traditional status roles or traditional ties of social and economic dependence. In fact, as I will show later, voters and politicians can end up in a relationship of mutual obligation to each other without such pre-existing ties. The use of the term "patronage politics," thus, is distinct from the traditional anthropological usage of the term "clientelism." However, in the Introduction to this book, the term clientelism is differently defined to mean "a particular mode of exchange between electoral constituencies as principals and politicians as agents in democratic systems." This definition of clientelism is consistent with my use of the term "patronage politics." Indeed, Kitschelt and Wilkinson use the terms patronage and clientelism interchangeably.

Finally, the term "pork-barrel politics" refers primarily to the practice of courting voter support through policy legislation (especially budgetary allocations). The term "patronage politics" as used here refers to an attempt to court support not by promising some group of voters favorable *legislation* but assuring them of favorable *implementation*. For instance, an attempt to obtain the support of farmers by enacting a law providing them with subsidies on inputs would fall into the category of pork-barrel politics. The term "patronage politics" as used here does not describe the enactment of such legislation. However, let us imagine that in order to procure such a subsidy, farmers have first to obtain a certificate of eligibility from some politician with discretionary power over the distribution of such certificates. If such a politician courts the support of some farmers rather than others by promising to selectively employ his discretionary power in their favor, the transaction would be classified as a "patronage" transaction according to this chapter. Although the term "patronage politics" is often used interchangeably with "pork-barrel" politics (see, e.g., Ames 1987; Geddes 1994; or Benton 2001), this distinction between the two terms is important. The collective transfer of goods to citizens through policy legislation produces different political outcomes from the individualized transfer of goods through policy implementation.

Theory of voter and elite behavior in patronage democracies

In a patronage democracy, obtaining control of the state is the principal means of obtaining both a better livelihood and higher status. Elected office or government jobs, rather than the private sector, become the principal sources of employment. And because individuals who control the state are in a position of power over the lives of others, working in government brings with it higher status. Those who have the capital to launch a political career in patronage democracies, therefore, seek political office. And for those who do not, obtaining access to those who control the state becomes the principal source of both material and psychic benefits. Proximity to a state official increases a voter's chances of obtaining valued state resources and services. At the same time, it affords the voter the chance to bask in the reflected glory of his patron's power. Patronage democracies, therefore, produce an overwhelming preoccupation with politics on the part of both elites and voters seeking both material and psychic goods (Joseph 1987; Riordon 1994).

The propositions in this section explain when and why these overwhelmingly politicized populations are likely to organize their struggle along ethnic lines. Propositions 1–8 explain why voters in patronage democracies should expect elites to favor co-ethnic elites rather than others in the distribution of material benefits. Proposition 9 explains why voters expect to obtain psychic benefits also from elites from their "own" ethnic group rather than elites with whom they share other bases of group affiliation. Proposition 10 shows how these expectations result in a self-enforcing and reinforcing equilibrium of ethnic favoritism in patronage democracies.

(1)   Politicians in patronage democracies have an incentive to collect rents on policy implementation

In any society in which the state has monopolistic or near monopolistic control over valued benefits, and elected officials have discretionary power in the implementation of policy concerning the distribution of benefits, these officials have incentives to market these benefits for above their actual value.[1] Basic goods and services, which all citizens should have automatic access to, become commodities on which officials can collect rents. Officials who decide whose village gets a road, who gets the houses financed by a government housing scheme, whose areas get priority in providing drinking water, whose son gets a government job, whose wife gets access to a bed in a government hospital, and who gets a government loan, are in a position to extract rents from beneficiaries for favoring them over other applicants. I have used here examples of the opportunities for rent-seeking by elected officials in their dealings with the poor, who seek basic necessities. However, similar opportunities also exist in dealings with the rich. Industrialists, for example, who need access to land, permits for building, or licenses for marketing their products, are similarly subject to the discretionary power of state officials, and so offer them similar opportunities for rent-seeking.

In patronage-driven states that are not democratic, the rents that elected officials seek are likely to take the form of private wealth such as money, assets, and land. In patronage democracies, although rents are also sought in these forms, votes are the most lucrative form of rent, since they provide the opportunity for continued control of the state. Wherever "patronage democracies" exist, therefore, we should also see a black market for state resources where the currency is votes and the clients are voters. Incumbent and aspiring candidates in such democracies should court voter support by making selective promises about whom they will favor in policy implementation if they win.

---

[1] This section draws on the extensive literature on rent-seeking and corruption, including particularly Scott (1972), Bates (1981), and North (1990).

This black market, it is important to note, comprises *retail* transactions in which customers are individuals, rather than *wholesale* transactions, in which customers are entire blocs of voters. Wholesale transactions can only take place through policy legislation, which applies simultaneously to large groups of individuals at one stroke. Policy implementation, however, is of necessity a retail enterprise that applies piecemeal to individuals who come forward to claim the resources and services made available to some collective through policy legislation. Throughout the chapter, I will refer to this retail black-marketing of promises to implement policy in return for votes as "patronage politics."

One immediate objection needs to be addressed before describing the features of this black market and its implications for the character of politics in patronage democracies. Does a secret ballot not prevent the operation of such a black market? Under a secret ballot, there is nothing to deter voters from cheating, by promising their votes to one candidate while casting them in favor of another. Knowing that they cannot enforce their contract, why should elected officials sell state resources on the electoral market?

Voting procedures in patronage democracies, however, are unlikely to be secret, or perceived to be secret, for reasons I elaborate on below. First, given the strong incentives that candidates in patronage democracies have to obtain information about how voters vote, we should see regular attempts to subvert the secrecy of the ballot by exploiting loopholes in the design of the voting procedure. Such subversion is made possible by the difficulty of designing and implementing a "fool-proof" secret ballot. Consider the following examples. In municipal elections in the city of New Haven, a voter who voted for the party ticket for all fifteen municipal offices could do so simply by pulling a lever. Those who chose to split their votes between the two parties for individual candidates could do so only through a time-consuming procedure. Even though the ballot was officially "secret," the method of casting the ballot provided a clear signal about how the individual voted. As Wolfinger points out: "To observers in the polling place, the length of time the voter spent in the booth revealed the strength of his devotion to the party ticket, particularly since a bell would ring when either party lever was pulled. This arrangement . . . was an important inducement to straight-ticket voting" (1974: 23).

A second example comes from the procedure through which votes are counted. According to Schaffer's description of the 1993 elections in Senegal, each polling station accommodated an average of about two hundred voters. The ballots were then counted at each station and posted publicly. As Schaffer notes of this procedure: "Where the electoral choice of each individual elector remained secret, the aggregate results for each (larger) village or group of (smaller) villages did not. Consequently, local level political patrons were still able to gauge the effectiveness of their efforts and the overall compliance of relatively small groups of voters" (1998: 136). In India, the procedure of counting votes by polling stations revealed voting patterns by locality until it was eliminated recently. In each of these cases, the secret ballot was implemented to the letter. However, in each case, politicians with an incentive to know how voters voted were able to subvert the secrecy of the ballot by exploiting loopholes in its implementation. Newer and more effective methods of secret balloting, furthermore, are likely to be met only with newer and more effective methods of subversion. For instance, as Schaffer points out of the introduction of the Ballot Act of 1872 in England: "[It] put an end to most flagrant forms of vote buying. More subtle forms of bribery were then invented" (Schaffer: 135). Similarly, electoral reform in Senegal in 1993 "simply forced patrons to devise new methods of surveillance" (135).

Second, even in cases in which the secret ballot is somehow insulated from subversion, voters in patronage democracies are unlikely to *believe* that their vote is secret. In a democracy in which elected officials enjoy discretion in the implementation of most laws and procedures, why should voters trust that voting procedures are somehow an exception? The *perception* that voting procedures are subject to the same type of discretion as other policies should deter cheating and encourage the sale of goods and services in return for votes in the same way as if the ballot were actually secret. Rather than seeing the secret ballot and trust in the secret ballot as exogenous constraints on the functioning of such a black market, therefore, we should see them as among the early endogenous casualties of a patronage democracy.

(2)   Voters in patronage democracies have an incentive to use their votes as instruments to extract material benefits

Since Mancur Olson (1965) published *The Logic of Collective Action*, we have presumed that there are few instrumental reasons to vote.[2] This presumption rests upon two propositions: Proposition 1: The benefit from voting is typically in the form of policy legislation, which all individuals would benefit from, regardless of whether or not they vote. Proposition 2: Any single vote is not likely to affect the electoral outcome. Since her vote is not likely to affect the outcome, and since she will benefit if his preferred candidate wins whether or not she votes, it always makes sense for a rational individual to abstain from voting. Consequently,

---

[2] For attempts to explain the decision to vote within a rational choice framework, see Fiorina (1976) and Aldrich (1993).

we expect that those who vote do so for expressive reasons: perhaps because they think it is what good citizens should do; perhaps because their parents did; perhaps because they want to stand up and be counted for what they believe in; or perhaps because of the satisfaction of going to the polling booth with friends and companions. In each of these examples, it is the *act* of voting rather than the *outcome* that gives them satisfaction.

For most voters in patronage democracies, however, a single motivation overrides the rest: the need to secure some of the vast material benefits at the disposal of those who implement policy. Such material benefits are highly valued, scarce, and most importantly, private; as the examples above illustrate, they are distributed in retail transactions to individuals (e.g., jobs, medical care, university admissions, housing loans, land grants) and the micro-communities that they represent (e.g., roads, schools, electricity, water). And the vote is the currency through which individuals secure such goods for themselves or their micro-communities. The "expressive benefits" provided by the act of voting are ephemeral. The pleasure of doing the right thing, or performing a traditional act, or registering an opinion, or participating in shared group activity does not last beyond the brief moment of casting the vote. The ephemeral expressive benefits provided by the act of voting are overshadowed by its utility as an instrument through which to secure the protection, services, and opportunities at the disposal of elected officials. While we might certainly find "expressive voters" in patronage democracies, they are likely to be composed mainly of that minority of voters who, within these societies, are relatively independent of the state. Most voters in patronage democracies, however, should be instrumental actors, who use their vote as a means through which to extract material benefits from competing candidates.

Voting in patronage democracies, therefore, should not be viewed as a variant of the collective action problem. The collective action applies to voting only in cases in which the payoff from voting accrues to all individuals collectively, or to large groups. In patronage democracies, however, the act of voting carries with it substantial individualized benefits, and the act of not voting substantial, individualized, costs.

(3)   Benefit-seeking voters have an incentive to organize collectively in the pursuit of individually distributed goods

The retail and informal nature of the patronage transaction poses a problem for voters – how to maximize the value of their investment and how to ensure delivery. Any individual voter knows that her capacity to purchase a job, a housing loan, or a university slot with her solitary vote is negligible. Any individual vote makes no difference to the overall outcome and so gives the candidate little incentive to provide goods and services in return. The voter, therefore, must find a way to magnify the purchasing power of her vote. Second, she must find a way to ensure that the goods her votes purchased are delivered. Once the vote is cast, why should the candidate feel compelled to deliver on his promise?

Both problems are solved for the voter by organizing collectively. In throwing in her lot with a group, an individual agrees to vote for some politician even if she does not benefit herself as long as the politician favors *some* group member over non-members. By joining a group, the voter magnifies the value of her vote. Because a bloc of votes can make a difference to the outcome, a number of individuals organized as a group can bargain more effectively with candidates than the same number of individuals voting individually. The price for this greater bargaining power is the possibility that some other member of the collective might obtain scarce benefits in place of the voter. However, it gives those members who are denied these benefits some expectation that their turn will come in the future. And, to the extent that the politician favors her group over other groups and individuals, the voter is still better off than she would have been by voting individually. Further, organizing as a group makes it easier for voters to ensure delivery. A candidate who does not deliver on his promise can be punished by the defection of the group as a whole, with a corresponding negative effect on his future electoral prospects.

While voters have an incentive to organize collectively in patronage democracies, it is worth reiterating that the goods that they seek are individually, not collectively, distributed. Joining a group allows individual members to increase the odds that they or the micro-communities that they represent will receive greater priority in the allocation of these benefits than individuals who are outside the group. However, all group members do not receive benefits simultaneously. In this sense, joining a group in order to obtain access to an individual benefit is analogous to buying a lottery ticket. Just as each individual must pay for her lottery ticket in order to be eligible for the prize, each group member must actually turn out to vote in order to be eligible for a benefit. But just as the prize is individually allotted to only a small number of those who buy lottery tickets, benefits are also individually distributed to only a small number of group members. When an individual voter chooses to join one group rather than another, therefore, she is choosing one lottery rather than another. Given a choice, she will choose that group which promises her the best odds of obtaining benefits. However, joining some group, any group, is always better than voting on her own.

(4)   Benefit-selling candidates have an incentive to target the distribution of individual benefits to group members rather than free-floating individuals

Just as the voter's problem is how to magnify the value of her vote and ensure delivery, the candidate's problem is how to magnify the purchasing power of the benefits at his disposal, and how to monitor compliance. No matter how large the supply of jobs, licenses, loans, roads, and wells at his disposal, each job, license, well, or road can only be given to a single individual or a single community represented by the individual. A procedure where each favor buys the vote of only the direct beneficiary would never produce the broad base of support required to win an election. How can the candidate multiply the value of his investment, so that each favor brings with it the support of others besides the direct recipient? And even if he were to purchase a large number of votes with a small number of favors, how might he ensure that voters pay him as promised?

Both problems are solved for the candidate by targeting favors to group members rather than free-floating individuals. Distributing a favor to one group member sends a signal to others in the group that they can count on him in the future. Dealing with groups, therefore, converts a zero-sum game into a positive-sum game. If he had been dealing with individuals, a favor given to one individual would be a favor denied to another. It would cost him as much as it would gain. In dealings with group members, however, a favor given to one member sends a signal to others that they too can count on him in the future. It also sends the signal to all group members that he will favor individuals in their group over others. As such, it wins him support even from those denied favors in the present. Second, dealing with groups makes it easy for the politician to monitor compliance. Obtaining information about individual voting behavior, which requires personalized knowledge of individual decisions and behavior, is costly and often impossible. However, groups can be infiltrated more easily and group voting behavior can be monitored through collective institutions.

Electoral politics in patronage democracies, therefore, should take the form of a self-enforcing equilibrium of "group voting," maintained by the incentives voters have to organize in groups, and the incentives candidates have to encourage the organization of voters as groups. In principle, such groups might be organized on any basis: by place of residence, by class identity, by organizational affiliation, by ideology, and so on. In the remainder of this chapter, I will show why patronage politics privileges ethnic group mobilization in particular.

(5)   Voters in patronage democracies evaluate the promises of can-
        didates about the distribution of benefits in the present by look-
        ing at the record of past patronage transactions by incumbents.
        Consequently, incumbents seek to develop records of patronage
        transactions that will help them most in the future

In any system in which there is a gap between legislation and implementation, voters have little reason to take the promises of candidates on faith.
Candidates may openly declare their support for some category of voters. However, voters in patronage democracies should believe only those
promises that they can verify by surveying the record of past transactions.
Where discretionary power in the implementation of state policy lies in
the hands of elected officials, promises to enact policy legislation in favor
of an individual or group are worthless unless they are also accompanied by a verified record of implementation in favor of that individual or
group.

Voters in patronage democracies, therefore, will make their decision
about whom to support by looking retrospectively at the pattern of past
patronage transactions. By probing for broad patterns in the history of
previous patronage transactions by incumbents, they identify the principle on which patronage benefits were distributed in the past, which is
their best guide to how they will allot benefits in the future.

Incumbents in patronage democracies, therefore, will distribute
patronage with an eye to future support, seeking to build that record
which will help them most in obtaining votes in the future. And the
credibility of promises that first-time candidates make will depend on
the record established by incumbents in the past. In this sense, previous
incumbents have an agenda-setting power, determining which types of
promises are more credible in the present and which less credible. If those
who have controlled the state in the past have consistently distributed
patronage according to one principle, the credibility of politicians who
promise to distribute patronage benefits in the future according to the
same principle will be higher than the credibility of politicians who seek
to introduce a new principle altogether.

(6)   Voters surveying the record of past patronage transactions are
        typically forced to distinguish between individuals under severe
        information constraints

Patronage transactions cannot be conducted openly in modern democracies. Any attempt by candidates to trade policy implementation for votes
in the open market would constitute a serious violation of the norms of

modern government and in all likelihood collide with the laws of most modern democracies. As an illustration, take the instance of public health facilities. A bed in a public hospital is a scarce commodity, and politicians in many developing countries are routinely called upon by favor seekers to secure beds for their friends and relatives. However, no politician could openly promise to favor some voters in the allocation of hospital beds over others. Selective allocation of basic services such as public health, to which all citizens should have equal access in principle, would be indefensible on both normative and legal grounds. The normative and legal constraints of modern democratic government ensure that politicians can only send surreptitious signals about whom they intend to favor in the implementation of policy, signaling their intent by unofficial action but not by open declaration in the official political sphere.

As a result, voters typically have very little background information about the beneficiaries of patronage transactions. Their main sources of data about the beneficiaries of past transactions are reports in the newspapers or on television or on the radio about new appointments and promotions; rumors about who got rich under which government and who did not, whose sons got jobs and whose did not, whose villages got roads and electricity, and whose did not; or physical observation of the personnel staffing a government office on television or in person. Even though politicians have an incentive to provide voters with as much data as possible on their past patronage transactions, the normative and legal constraints on such transactions prevent them from sending open messages; and even though voters have an incentive to acquire as much data as possible, the quality of the data sources available to them limits the information that they receive.

(7)   Consequently, voters are biased towards schemes of ethnic categorization in interpreting how past patronage benefits were distributed

The severe information constraints characteristic of patronage politics, I argue here, mean that voters concerned with assessing who benefited under which regime will always code beneficiaries on the basis of one of their many ethnic identities, whether or not these identities were actually relevant in securing benefits. The argument here is built upon the insight by Frederik Barth that ethnic groups are defined, not by internal homogeneity, but by the possession of a limited set of "cultural differentia" which separate insiders from outsiders (1969: 15–16). Although all individuals possess ethnic and non-ethnic identities, only their ethnic identities are marked by these "cultural differentia." These "differentia" allow the outside observer to sort individuals into ethnic categories in a relatively superficial interaction.[3]

Note that the possession of these markers does not yield any single or objectively correct classification. Different observers could code the same person differently, depending upon the information they could bring to bear on the interpretation of the markers. Second, even if all observers used the same information, considerable uncertainty might remain. It is often difficult, for example, for even the most sophisticated observers to distinguish between individuals from India, Pakistan, and Bangladesh simply by looking at physical features or names. Third, regardless, or even because of, her level of sophistication, the observer might simply get it wrong. Fourth, the categories in which the observer places an individual need have no relationship to the categories with which an individual identifies. The key point here is that notwithstanding the considerable heterogeneity within any single category, the different perspectives of different observers, the considerable room for ambiguity and error, and the individual's degree of identification with any of these categories, these physical and cultural markers convey enough information for most observers to classify the individual in some category or another. Just as importantly, observers can also identify the categories in which the individual is not eligible for membership. And depending upon how they categorize themselves, they can make a judgment about whether the individual is one of them or not.

An individual's non-ethnic identities do not come with these "differentiae" attached. Take class, for example, which we might think is also signaled by similar cues, including accent, dress, and manner. "There is an elite look in this country," notes Paul Fussell. "It requires women to be thin, with a hairstyle dating back eighteen or twenty years or so . . . They wear superbly fitting dresses and expensive but always understated shoes and handbags, with very little jewelry. They wear scarves – these instantly betoken class, because they are useless except as a caste mark. Men should be thin. No jewelry at all. No cigarette case. Moderate-length hair, never dyed or tinted, which is a middle-class or high-prole sign . . ." (1984: 54). Fussell's tongue-in-cheek account underlines the existence of a number of cues that give away class identity. The story of upwardly mobile individuals seeking entry into a higher class stratum, in fact, is precisely the story of an attempt to drop "giveaways" associated with the lower stratum and acquire those of the upper stratum. If we look closely at the cues associated with class identity, however, it quickly becomes clear that they are few, and that the information they convey is

---

[3] For a more detailed discussion of this argument, see Chandra (2004), ch. 2.

sparse. First, and perhaps most important, information about class identity is typically not contained in the name. When class and ethnic distinctions coincide, observers might infer class from name, substituting
ethnic for class markers. Where class and ethnic identity do not coincide, however, it is typically impossible to code an individual's class identity from her name. Prominent exceptions (e.g., Rockefeller) prove the
rule. Second, the remaining cues permit the observer to draw distinctions
only when the signals are particularly dramatic. A prominently patrician
accent, or ostentatiously big hair might send out signals to the observer
about the individual's class identity. However, unless these cues are dramatic, it is difficult to classify individuals. Third, even when dramatically
displayed, class cues enable the observer to draw only broad distinctions at the extremes. They might tell the observer whether the observed
comes from an upper-class or working-class background. However, they
do not convey sufficient information to categorize the large amorphous
mass in between. More precise class distinctions can be revealed only by
obtaining additional information on the personal background of each
individual (income, occupation, address, level of education, parents'
occupation).

Consider another example. Imagine a society in which all individuals can be objectively classified as either "rich" or "poor." We could
get at this objective reality simply by looking at the income distribution of a population and categorizing those above a given income level
as rich and those below as poor. It may even have a subjective reality
for those included in these categories. Political mobilization, for example, may have made people aware of the categories in which they have
been placed, so that those who are categorized as "rich" perceive themselves as being members of an imagined community of the rich while
those who are poor experience themselves as being "poor" and part of
an imagined community of the poor. However, how would individuals
from either category sort others into insiders and outsiders in impersonal interactions? As in the case of class, it is normally impossible to
infer income from the name, unless income and ethnic categories coincide. And, as in the case of class, cues of dress and manner make it
easy to classify individuals only when they are dramatic and only at the
extremes. Someone dressed in rags might be coded as "poor" without difficulty, while someone with ostentatious diamond jewelry might be coded
as "rich." But barring these dramatic signals, the only way to code the
"rich" and "poor" would be to procure personalized information on their
economic background and lifestyle. In superficial interactions, observers
who belong to the "rich" and "poor" categories would simply not be able
to "recognize" whether an individual belonged to their category or not.

Other non-ethnic categorizations (urban *vs.* rural; landed *vs.* landless; farmer *vs.* peasant *vs.* worker) come with a similar lack of differentiating markers.

The lack of differentiating markers attached to non-ethnic identities means that in any individualized interaction with limited information, observers concerned with classification will of necessity sort individuals based on their ethnic rather than non-ethnic identities. This has critical implications for patronage politics. It means that voters concerned with assessing who benefited under which regime will always code beneficiaries on the basis of one of their many ethnic identities, whether or not these identities were actually relevant in securing benefits. Consider the following two examples:

"When in the middle of the nineteenth century," writes Wolfinger of politics in New Haven, "the first Irishman was nominated for public office, this was recognition by the party of the statesmanlike qualities of the Irish, seen and appreciated by many Irishmen" (1974: 36). Apart from being Irish, the nominee was presumably many other things. Imagine, for instance, that he was a worker, or possessed particular professional qualifications for the office, or was known to be an influential neighborhood leader. Those who knew him personally might interpret the nomination as an act that recognized his identity as a worker, or his qualifications, or his influence among his peers, or a variety of other considerations. However, those who did not know him but encountered him in a government office or read his name in the newspaper or heard him speak on the radio would have identified him purely on the basis of one of his ethnic identities, helped along by name, accent, manner, or any of the cultural differentiae that he happened to carry. It is not surprising then, that the nomination was widely "seen and appreciated" as an act recognizing the Irish. Even if it had not been intended as such, it would be impossible for most voters to interpret it in any other way.

Consider another example, from Posner's study of patronage politics in Zambia. A newspaper column, concerned with describing the extent of in-group favoritism in Zambia noted: "There are organizations in this country, even foreign-owned for that matter, where almost every name, from the manager down to the office orderly, belongs to one region . . . In this country, professionally qualified youngsters never find jobs if they belong to the 'wrong' tribes. When you enter certain . . . offices, you get the impression they are tribal establishments."[4] How did the author of this article know that certain tribes were being favored and others were not? The article identifies two sources of information: names, and superficial

---

[4] *The Post*, January 24, 1996, cited in Posner (1998: 116).

observation of the staff in certain offices. Both these cues, as I argued above, provide clues to the ethnic identity of the individuals concerned but say little or nothing about non-ethnic identities. Even had he or she wanted to, the author of this article could not have coded the beneficiaries on a non-ethnic basis based on these sources of information. Imagine that those given jobs in any one office, for example, were only coincidentally from the same ethnic group. Perhaps the real tie that got them their jobs was that they all went to the same school. Although the "true" criterion for distributing benefits in this case would have been membership in an old boy network rather than ethnic affinity, this criterion would be invisible to the outside observer.

In these and other examples, those who are intimately acquainted with the beneficiaries might code them in complex ways. However, most outside observers would only be able to sort them into ethnic categories. Such sorting need not be standardized; as I pointed out earlier, different observers might allot the same beneficiary to different ethnic categories, or misidentify the individual to one category when they really belong to another. Political entrepreneurs, I will argue later, will attempt to manipulate this ambiguity, encouraging voters to code beneficiaries in categories that give them a political advantage. However, the key point here is that information about patronage transactions is processed and transmitted through a process that amplifies signals revealing the ethnic identities of the beneficiary and suppresses his non-ethnic identities.

(8)   When voters are biased towards an ethnic categorization of beneficiaries, politicians will favor co-ethnics in their distribution of material benefits although they may also channel leftover benefits to voters from other ethnic categories

Consider now what this means for the strategy of politicians in patronage democracies. In an environment in which voters at time $t + 1$ formulate expectations of benefits based on the history of patronage transactions at time t, and can only interpret these past transactions using schemes of ethnic categorization, incumbents at time t have no choice but to employ ethnic principles in the way in which they choose to distribute benefits. They may want, for whatever reason, to distribute benefits based on other principles, such as loyalty, or ideological affinity, or income. And candidates may also want, for whatever reason, to use these other principles in making their promises. However, these non-ethnic principles, for the reasons mentioned above, are *unverifiable* on the ground. Watchful voters used to the gap between rhetoric and implementation in patronage-based systems will treat these unverifiable treatments as mere noise.

Consequently, incumbents have no choice but to send ethnic signals in their distribution of benefits.

Incumbents constrained by voter biases to distribute benefits on an ethnic basis have to decide how to distribute favors across ethnic categories. Should they distribute benefits equally across all ethnic categories? Or should they be selective, allotting a larger proportion of benefits to some categories rather than others? And if they are selective, how do they decide which ethnic category or categories to favor? I show below why, paradoxically, incumbents in patronage democracies should always elect to allot the lion's share of benefits to members of their "own" ethnic category, regardless of its size. They may also send leftover benefits in the direction of other ethnic categories, especially when their "own" is too small to be efficacious. However, the proportion of benefits they distribute to members of their "own" should always be larger.

In order to acquire a following, politicians need not only to promise to favor some distinct category of voters, but also to establish greater credibility among this category of voters than other politicians. A strategy of distributing favors equally across individuals from all ethnic categories does not give any candidate a comparative advantage. If an incumbent distributes favors equally to individuals from various ethnic categories at time t, voters will believe that other candidates are also likely to distribute benefits in the future according to egalitarian principles. Since supporting any one candidate produces the same odds of obtaining benefits as supporting another, voters should be indifferent across candidates. Consequently, candidates should always avoid the strategy of equal distribution across ethnic categories in favor of selective targeting.

Consider now the strategy of selective targeting. At first glance, we might imagine that an incumbent should distribute the lion's share of the benefits at his disposal to any ethnic category (or combination of categories) that is sufficiently numerous to take him to a winning position, whether or not this is his own. Such a strategy, however, is inadvisable because it does not allow the incumbent to establish a comparative advantage. If incumbents distribute benefits at time *t* primarily to members of ethnic groups other than their own, voters surveying these past transactions will believe that a politician from one ethnic category can be trusted to deliver benefits to voters from another. In a competitive environment in which elites from one ethnic category can be trusted to deliver benefits to members of another, we should expect politicians of all hues to enter the race for support from the numerically dominant ethnic categories. The result would be a whittling down of the support that any one politician is likely to receive. This is not an optimal outcome from any politician's point of view.

But if incumbents distribute benefits primarily to members of their "own" ethnic category at time t, voters at time $t + 1$ will believe that those in power will help their "own" first and discount promises to distribute support on a cross-ethnic basis. In a field in which the only credible promises are those made by co-ethnics, all politicians from one ethnic category acquire a comparative advantage over others. Politicians from an "outside" category, because they do not have the right markers, will not be viable contenders for support. Playing ethnic favorites, therefore, gives politicians a "core" base of support, insulated from incursions by all but fellow co-ethnic competitors.

The attraction of this core base of support should lead incumbents in patronage democracies to allot the lion's share of benefits to their "own" category regardless of its size. However, the magnitude of the benefits they distribute to "others" might well vary, depending upon the size of their "own" ethnic category. If their own ethnic category is large enough to be independently efficacious, they will have no incentive to distribute any benefits to members of other ethnic categories. However, if their "own" category is relatively small, they should be willing to spare a larger proportion of benefits for members of other ethnic categories in order to attract their support. Voters witnessing such behavior will conclude that while politicians may help members of other ethnic categories at particular times under unfavorable competitive configurations, they are most consistent in helping their own. Consequently, voters should place greatest trust in co-ethnics in their struggle for the delivery of patronage benefits.

At the same time that they have an incentive to favor their "own" ethnic category in an attempt to establish a comparative advantage over others, however, all politicians have an incentive to define their "own" category as large enough to take them past the threshold of winning or influence. The multiplicity of interpretations that can be attached to ethnic markers gives them this freedom in defining the boundaries and membership of this category. The correspondence between the "markers" any individual possesses and the ethnic category that these markers correspond to is not given but changeable according to the context, knowledge, and interpretive frameworks of the observer. Consequently, a politician whose "own" category is initially too small to confer an electoral advantage has an incentive to manipulate the correspondence between markers and categories to produce a more advantageous definition of who his "own" people are. He may do this by reinterpreting his own markers to qualify him for membership in a larger ethnic category than before, so that he can claim some larger section of the population as his "own"; by redefining the membership criteria for his "own" category to encourage more voters to identify with him than before; or by attempting to transform the prevailing system of categorization itself, changing the dimension on which voters attempt to categorize politicians in a way that gives him an advantage.

(9)   The superior visibility of ethnic identities in limited information environments also drives voters to obtain psychic benefits from co-ethnic elites rather than others

So far, I have discussed how the severe information constraints in a patronage democracy should lead voters to expect greater access to material benefits from co-ethnic elites. Here, I discuss why the same mechanism should also lead them to expect psychic benefits from co-ethnics.

I build here upon the insights introduced by the social psychological approach that individual self-esteem is a product of the socially recognized position of the groups of which one is a member, and that in patronage democracies the principal source of collective social recognition is the state. Those groups whose elites control the state are likely to confer greater self-esteem upon voters who are their members than on groups whose elites are less well represented in state institutions. In a world of multiple group affiliations, however, when and why does ethnic group membership in particular become a source of self-esteem? I propose here that voters seeking self-esteem identify with their ethnic categories when information constraints make it difficult for third parties to detect other types of group affiliation.

This proposition rests on the observation that in order to bask in the reflected glory of an elite who has obtained control of the state, a voter must be "seen" by others to be a member of the same group as the elite. In the absence of such third-party acknowledgment, the demonstrated superiority of the elite as an individual will not be interpreted as the demonstrated superiority of the group to which both elite and voter belong. In a personalized, information-rich setting, third parties would possess the background data to sort voters and elites according to their non-ethnic group affiliations. In the more typical impersonal environment of mass politics, however, the ethnic identity of each becomes the principal means that external observers have of ascertaining group affiliation. Voters should obtain greater self-esteem, therefore, principally from groups in which membership is signaled by their widely observable ethnic identities, rather than their concealed non-ethnic identities. Politicians in patronage democracies, therefore, have an incentive not only to distribute material benefits to co-ethnic voters but also to portray their political successes as successes for their "own" ethnic category.

(10)   Consequently, we should see a self-enforcing equilibrium of eth-
         nic favoritism in patronage democracies

Once politicians, constrained by limited information conditions, bid for
the support of co-ethnics, voters should follow suit by sorting themselves
into ethnic blocs.

In patronage democracies, therefore, we should see a self-enforcing
equilibrium of ethnic favoritism, in which voters mainly target co-ethnic
politicians for favors, and politicians mainly target co-ethnic voters for
votes. New politicians, faced with a playing field in which all others appear
to be helping voters from their "own" ethnic category, are forced to court
the support of co-ethnics if they want to remain in the game. At the
same time, however, they should attempt to propose as advantageous
a definition of their "own" ethnic category as possible. Those who do
not have a following among their "own" are likely to be winnowed out.
Similarly, new voters, faced with a playing field in which all other voters
appear to be best served by politicians from their "own" category, are
forced to throw their support behind co-ethnics.

Once this equilibrium of ethnic favoritism is in place, we should also
see a feedback loop, with ethnic politics strengthening the conditions of
patronage politics that gave it birth. Once politicians have established
the principle of ethnic favoritism, new voters entering the political arena
should also mobilize on an ethnic basis and demand state largesse for
their ethnic categories. We should expect the pressure from these newly
mobilized ethnic categories to motivate politicians not only to jealously
guard the discretionary power that they have but to seek an expansion
of state services and their discretionary power over the allocation of such
services in order to maintain and expand their bases of support. Patronage
politics and ethnic politics therefore should be locked into a stranglehold,
with the one reinforcing the other.

Over time this equilibrium should also generate additional reinforcing mechanisms that allow it to persist even after the initial information constraints that gave it birth are lifted.[5] For instance, both voters
and politicians have an incentive to create and maintain networks and
institutions in order to reduce the transaction costs of communicating
demands and delivering benefits. Neither voter nor politician has a similar incentive to create or maintain non-ethnic networks and institutions.
Further, over repeated elections voters should acquire a store of fairly

[5] For a distinction between self-enforcing and self-reinforcing institutions, see Greif,
forthcoming).

precise information about the ethnic identities of political entrepreneurs and those whom they favored in the past to assist them in predicting the behavior of these entrepreneurs in the future. Similarly, politicians should acquire a store of information about the relative numerical strength of different ethnic blocs, defined on different dimensions, to assist them in formulating profitable strategies. Neither voter nor politician has any incentive to collect and store comparable information on non-ethnic categories. As a result, ethnic identities become progressively more "real" and non-ethnic identities progressively more invisible, over repeated interactions. Finally, the cycle of expectations built around patronage transactions during elections is likely also to spill over into the broader political arena, turning the notion that politicians favor their own, and voters vote for their own, into a "basic axiom of politics" (Posner 1998).

Under what conditions might such an equilibrium break down? This equilibrium, I have argued above, is driven by information constraints, which are in themselves a product of the structural conditions defining a patronage democracy. It is likely to break down only when the structural conditions that sustain these information constraints are altered. For instance, a downsizing of the state sector would eliminate the root of the cycle of ethnic favoritism by removing the necessity for voters to use their vote as the means to secure their livelihoods. The reduction of discretionary power over implementation of state policy, by legislating precise guidelines or introducing procedures for oversight, would have a similar effect. And, as I will argue below, even within the constraints of patronage democracy, the vesting of control over the distribution of resources in politicians at micro rather than macro levels of politics should erode the foundations of this equilibrium by replacing a limited information environment with an information-rich one. The effect of such structural changes may be impeded by the continued existence of ethnic networks, institutions, ethnically based statistics, and other reinforcing mechanisms that emerge as by-products of the equilibrium of ethnic favoritism. Over time, however, changes in the underlying structure should dismantle these reinforcing mechanisms and so gradually erode this equilibrium.

Before proceeding further, therefore, let me address the possibility of endogeneity. Might not the politics of ethnic favoritism itself produce patronage democracy, rather than the other way round?

The argument here predicts that once the politics of ethnic favoritism is activated by the introduction of patronage democracy, it should generate a feedback loop, strengthening and expanding the conditions that gave rise to it. In this sense, the discovery of reverse causal arrows after the introduction of patronage democracy would confirm rather than disprove the argument. However, we should be less confident of the argument in relation to the alternative if we found that the initial establishment of patronage democracy was systematically correlated with a pre-existing politics of ethnic favoritism. A systematic test of this argument awaits the collection of data tracking the establishment, expansion, and contraction of patronage democracies over time. Here, let me note simply that there is no reason to expect that the two defining conditions of a patronage democracy – large states, and discretionary control over the implementation of state policy – are the systematic product of the politics of ethnic favoritism. The size of the public sector or the degree of regulation over the private sector might increase for a variety of reasons: as a consequence of ideology (e.g., communist or socialist regimes); a desire for accelerated economic development (e.g., the "developmentalist" state in India); or a concern for social welfare (e.g., welfare states in Sweden and Finland). And discretion over the distribution of jobs and services controlled by these large public sectors or regulated private sectors might be acquired by elected officials when the procedures for implementation are not well codified; or under conditions of widespread illiteracy or large-scale immigration, where an inadequate understanding of the letter of the law among citizens gives state officials discretionary power in practice; or under conditions of extreme scarcity, where an excess supply of identically qualified applicants gives state officials the power to select from among them arbitrarily in allocating jobs and services.

Factors mitigating the likelihood of ethnic favoritism in patronage democracies

I have argued so far that the propensity of patronage democracies to produce the politics of ethnic favoritism is a product of the degree to which the voting decision in patronage democracies approximates a setting in which observers have to distinguish between individuals under severe information constraints. When the voting decision does not approximate this type of setting, other things being equal, we should not see patronage democracy produce the politics of ethnic favoritism. Here, I identify four conditions that, by altering the information environment, can lower the likelihood of ethnic favoritism in patronage democracies.

Vesting of control over the distribution of patronage at the micro level

Micro levels of politics (e.g., family, village, ward, neighborhood, and municipality) are information-rich environments, in which individuals know each other personally and have engaged in repeated interactions over a long period of time. Macro levels of politics (state, province, region, nation, large district) are information-poor environments, in which individuals do not have personal knowledge about each other and do not have a history of repeated interactions. The level at which control over the delivery of benefits is vested varies across political systems. In some systems, it is politicians at the macro levels of politics (e.g., national legislators, provincial legislators) who pull the strings by which benefits are released at lower levels of politics. In others, control over these benefits is vested directly in elected officials at these lower levels (e.g., with municipal councilors or village headmen).

When control over patronage transactions is vested in politicians at the micro level, voters surveying a politician's record of past patronage transactions are faced with the task of classifying only a small number of individuals about whom they typically have additional sources of information based on previous interactions. This allows them to supplement the limited data that usually accompanies patronage transactions. Simply by hearing the name of some individual who has been denied a favor, for instance, voters may be able to ascertain, by drawing upon the store of information collected through previous interactions, whether this person was denied a favor because of her personal rivalries with a politician, or her character, or economic circumstances, or family feuds. As a result, they can code beneficiaries of previous patronage transactions in complex ways. When patronage is distributed at the macro level of politics, however, voters are called upon to classify larger numbers of individuals of whom they have no personal knowledge and with whom they do not have any history of prior interactions. Consequently, they are more likely to code them on an ethnic basis. Other things being equal, therefore, we should be more likely to see ethnic favoritism in patronage democracies in which control over patronage is vested in politicians at the macro rather than the micro level. Further, if institutional reforms in patronage democracies transfer control over the distribution of patronage from the macro to the micro level of politics, we should see a decline in the likelihood of ethnic favoritism, other things being equal; and if institutional reforms transfer control over patronage from the micro to the macro level, we should see an increase in the likelihood of ethnic favoritism, other things being equal.

Mediated democracy

"Mediated democracies," in which only a small number of voters are autonomous, also reduce the likelihood of ethnic favoritism in patronage democracies by increasing the sources of information available to voters about the beneficiaries of patronage transactions. When only some voters are autonomous and control the votes of the rest, politicians can target benefits to a small and select pool of beneficiaries. With a small number of beneficiaries, the cost of obtaining information about each is also reduced. As a result, voters can formulate hypotheses that do not rely solely on ethnic characteristics. Examples of mediated democracies include "traditional" polities in which landed or other powerful classes are the autonomous voters and control the votes of subordinate groups through ties of deference and coercion. As these ties of deference and subordination are eroded, however, and political participation increases, we should see the likelihood of ethnic favoritism increase in patronage democracies.

Aggregate beneficiaries

The likelihood of ethnic favoritism is also reduced when the customers in patronage transactions are aggregates rather than individuals. Observers are likely to be biased toward ethnic categorization under limited information constraints only when they are concerned with distinguishing between individuals (see Chandra 2004: chapter 3). When called upon to distinguish between groups, observers should not be biased toward ethnic categorization even under severe information constraints, since groups do not sport ethnic markers, as individuals do. Consequently, regimes in which voters are required to code aggregate rather than individual beneficiaries should not necessarily be characterized by expectations of ethnic favoritism.

Examples of cases in which the principal beneficiaries of patronage benefits are aggregates rather than individuals abound, particularly in Latin America, which exhibits a distinct pattern of "corporate" or "collective" clientelism (Auyero 2000; Burgwal 1993; Martz 1997). According to Robert Gay's (1994) ethnographic study of patronage politics in two *favelas* in Brazil, for instance, candidates sought voter support by paying off the entire neighborhood of Vila Brasil – providing collective goods such as paved roads, uniforms for the neighborhood soccer team, and public bathrooms in the neighborhood association building. With some exceptions, the candidates did not barter with individuals. Susan Stokes's (1995) study of shantytown politics in Peru reveals the same pattern – residents of the shantytown of Independencia bargained with politicians not as individuals but as communities, and sought from these politicians not individual goods – such as jobs, university slots, and loans – but community goods – such as water, electricity, and land titles conferred collectively to the shantytown as a whole. Jonathan Fox's (1994) study of patronage politics in Mexico, similarly, identifies collectives rather than individuals as the beneficiaries of patronage transactions – food was made available to entire villages in the form of food stores, or to collectively organized region-wide community food councils; Regional Solidarity funds were provided not to individuals but to "project proposals submitted from the organizations of the region"; and public works programs were provided to local committees.

Perfect homogeneity and perfect heterogeneity

When a population is perfectly homogeneous (i.e., all individuals have identical ethnic markers) or perfectly heterogeneous (i.e., all individuals have unique ethnic markers), voters surveying the beneficiaries of past patronage transactions will be unable to detect any pattern in the distribution of patronage. In such situations, politicians will be hampered in their attempt to use their discretionary control over state jobs and services as a strategy for obtaining votes. Even though they have an incentive to market these jobs and services in return for votes, they will be unable to send meaningful signals to their target voters. We might expect politicians in such situations to transfer control of patronage from the macro to the micro level of politics and so enable themselves to send non-ethnic signals about the distribution of patronage. Alternatively, we might expect them to switch to a different method of courting votes and to divert their discretionary control of state resources in order to seek rents in forms other than votes. In either case, we should be less likely to see the politics of ethnic favoritism.

Conclusion

I have argued here that severe information constraints are an important and neglected variable explaining the politics of ethnic favoritism. Although the argument has been developed specifically with reference to patronage democracies, it should also be applicable to other settings in which voting decisions are made under comparable information constraints, such as "founding elections" or elections in unstable party systems.

The argument that the perceptual biases inherent in the patronage transaction are responsible for generating self-fulfilling expectations of ethnic favoritism among voters and politicians constitutes a departure from the theoretical literature on ethnic mobilization, which locates the cause of the association in other variables such as the presumed functional superiority of ethnic networks, institutional legacies that privilege ethnic identities, a presumed cultural similarity which makes patronage transactions between co-ethnics easier than transactions with non-coethnics, and pre-existing patterns of identity salience. These alternatives are discussed at some length in the book from which this chapter is excerpted (Chandra 2004). Here it is sufficient to note simply that these other variables are not necessary to bring about the outcome of ethnic favoritism. Indeed, variables such as institutional legacies and ethnic networks may well be endogenous to the conditions of limited information and should reinforce the politics of ethnic favoritism only as long as the underlying information constraints persist.

Let me highlight in conclusion some testable implications that result from the argument: first, to the extent that politicians are able to manipulate the interpretation of ethnic markers, we should expect them to propose interpretations that produce ethnic categories of optimal size, given their electoral objectives. If the politics of ethnic favoritism is produced by information constraints, therefore, we should expect a systematic correlation between the size of an ethnic category and its degree of political salience. On the other hand, if the politics of ethnic favoritism is produced by preexisting networks and institutions, then there should be no systematic correlation between the size of an ethnic category and its political salience. In this case, the ethnic categories that are salient should be a straightforward reflection of preexisting structural and historical patterns, regardless of size. Second, if the politics of ethnic favoritism is produced by information constraints, then, given a choice between ethnic categories of equivalent size, politicians should mobilize voters around those ethnic categories that are most *visible*.[6] On the other hand, if the politics of ethnic favoritism is produced by networks or institutions independent of information constraints, then there should be no systematic correlation between visibility and the political salience of an ethnic category. Finally, if the politics of ethnic favoritism is produced by information constraints, then administrative reforms such as decentralization, by shifting the locus of patronage to information-rich environments such as the neighborhood and village, should result in a deactivation of ethnic identities. Conversely, if the politics of ethnic favoritism is independently produced by networks or institutions, then decentralization should not result in any change in the salience of ethnic identifications unless it also simultaneously transforms the character of networks or institutional legacies.

---

[6] I owe this point to a discussion with Susan Stokes.

5 Explaining changing patterns of party–voter linkages in India

Steven I. Wilkinson

When India attained independence in 1947, it was already in many respects a clientelistic polity. The British had strengthened their own colonial rule by providing land and other goods to important social groups and their leaders, and they also institutionalized ascriptive criteria such as caste and religion as authoritative ways for the state to allocate jobs, positions in state-funded educational establishments, and seats in parliamentary and provincial assemblies (Wilkinson 2004). The Congress Party, far from being an "external party" of the type characterized by Martin Shefter – one bent on cleaning up the mill of patronage – had itself been transformed by more than twenty years in control of the various provincial and local assemblies set up by the British after 1919 to quiet demands for independence. Congress's control of these assemblies, characterized by one historian as "enormous pools of patronage" (Washbrook 1973), meant that the party acted more like one of Shefter's *internally mobilized* parties – using the state administration and state patronage to build support and reward allies – than an external programmatic party. In Calcutta, the Congress used its control of the municipal corporation after 1923 to strengthen its position, so that by independence perhaps 70 percent of the corporation's staff were party workers or their family members (Weiner 1967: 328). The considerable spending power the local and provincial assemblies eventually controlled, combined with the prospect of even greater power when the British left, also attracted many members to Congress in the decade before independence whose primary concern was less ideological than material. After the party's unexpected victory in five major provinces in the 1936 provincial elections, Congress membership increased rapidly from half a million to 4.5 million, and senior party officials worried about the motivation of many of these new members (Brown 2003: 130). Congress leader Jawaharlal Nehru wrote to Mahatma Gandhi in April 1938 complaining about the rise of "Tammany Hall" politics in the party and the descent of Congressmen "to the level of ordinary politicians who have no principles

110

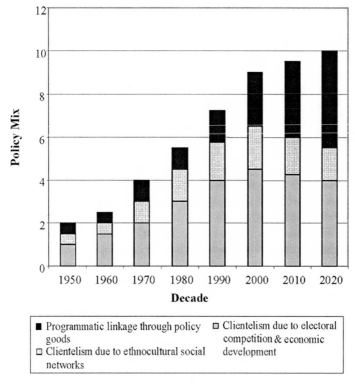

Figure 5.1 The policy mix in India at different levels of competition and economic development

to stand by and whose work is governed by a day to day opportunism" (Brown 2003: 131).

Since independence, different levels of economic development and electoral competition have led at various times to very different levels of both the supply and demand for clientelistic goods, as I show in Figure 5.1. In the first period of "Congress dominance," from 1950 to 1967, low levels of economic development interacted with low levels of political competition to lead to relatively low levels of clientelist provision, not much different from those provided under the British. In the second period, however, lasting roughly from 1967 to 2000, substantially increased electoral competition at all levels of the polity (national, state, and local *panchayat* institutions) interacted with substantially increasing demands from a growing number of educated and literate voters to force politicians to promise and deliver ever greater amounts of clientelistic goods to voters: subsidies, jobs, higher education, loans, housing, and even clothing.

This chapter argues, however, that we are currently at the beginning of a third era, in which the costs of clientelism in India are increasing and unsustainable, and the political constituency in favor of political reform of the existing patron–client structures is growing in size and political importance. Since the 1991 economic reforms, it is possible to identify several broad developments that seem likely to limit the future growth of clientelistic linkages in Indian politics. First, overall levels of economic development and education have ratcheted up voters' demands to the level where it is now increasingly difficult for politicians to meet them at a time of very large annual central and state budget deficits, now around 10 percent of GDP. Second, the substantial growth of the private sector and the corresponding growth of a large middle and upper middle class has reduced the relative dependence of the Indian electorate on the state, and increased the constituency for reform. This class's demands for reform have both influenced and been influenced by a massive expansion in the Indian mass media over the past decade, which has given wide coverage of the extent of corruption within the system as well as helped publicize efforts at reform. Some politicians, taking their cue from the emergence of a larger pro-reform constituency, have increasingly tried to position themselves and their parties as pro-reform and have passed several laws that in the long run seem likely to increase the pressure to reduce clientelism.

The three eras of clientelistic politics in post-independence India

Low demand and low supply: 1950–1967

In the two decades after 1947, the fact that levels of economic development and levels of electoral competition were both low meant that there was a limited demand from and a limited supply of clientelistic goods to the overwhelmingly rural electorate. Low levels of education and literacy in rural India, and experience with a colonial state that had done little in terms of development in most rural areas had created very low expectations of government among most rural voters. The most important demand of rural voters, land reform of the large *zamindar* estates, was relatively cheap both politically and economically for Congress to provide, since it involved the expropriation of land (with only partial compensation) from a relatively small number of unpopular upper-caste Hindu and Muslim landlords, some of whom had formerly been allied with the

British Raj or the Muslim League.[1] A succession of *zamindari* reform acts were quickly passed in the 1950s throughout northern India. Other than that, Congress's overwhelming electoral dominance after 1950 at both the central and state level in the face of a divided political opposition created very little political incentive for the party to channel large amounts of goods to rural India. The bulk of development spending, therefore, went to major initiatives in "modern sectors" such as industry, higher education, and power.

At the local level, Congress politicians in the 1950s and 1960s typically contracted for votes through upper-caste local intermediaries, who used their social status and control of land, credit, and muscle power to contract to deliver local upper as well as lower-caste votes to the Congress candidate. This did not necessarily involve the direct exchange of goods in return for votes or the monitoring of individual votes. Patrons instead invoked norms of reciprocity and obligation, and stressed the necessity for villagers to have continued access to the power of the Congress-dominated state. One 1966 survey of voters in Andhra Pradesh found, "The voters themselves are told and convinced that there would be no use choosing the candidate who does not have access to the minister concerned since he cannot get any benefits to the village" (Reddy and Seshadri 1972: 13). One survey of 500 voters in a village in Gujarat during the 1957 state and national elections found that many voters viewed the Congress and state as indistinguishable, and took the view that as the "sarkar" (government) had given them their land they were obligated to vote for the incumbent Congress. Many villagers interviewed in the survey spoke of their vote in terms of feudal obligation: "we are going to vote for the Sarkar (the ruling party) because we have eaten its salt" Somjee (1959: 12).

Behind these norm-based appeals there were also threats, usually implied but sometimes real. Political scientists working in rural India consistently found that "it was practically universally believed that the village leaders had their ways of finding out how people voted" (Brown 1988: 152). Though it is hard to assess how often this was true in practice, it was certainly the case that ballots prior to 1971 were counted at the local polling stations, making it easy to determine if particular polling stations had voted against the ruling party or not. Election surveys in Gujarat and elsewhere in the 1950s and 1960s found evidence of voters being threatened by rural notables with loss of credit and land tenancies if they did not vote for the government. Sometimes the threats came directly

---

[1] Though after the 1936–37 elections, some of these landlords joined Congress and were able to later use their political influence to subvert the 1950s land reforms.

Table 5.1 *Volatility and party fractionalization in the Indian states, 1950–1996*

Decade	Average volatility across states (%)
1950–59	41
1960–69	28
1970–79	37
1980–89	43
1990–96	42

Source: Raw data from Wilkinson State Elections Database 2003

from the politicians who controlled the state; the Congress government in Rajasthan, for example, circulated a letter in the 1960s implying that teachers would be fired if they did not vote for the party.

India 1967–2000: electoral competition, economic development and increasing clientelism

The late 1960s marks a watershed in India's post-independence politics, the dividing line between the dominance of a relatively coherent "Congress system" on one side, and a new era of intense and increasing party competition, on the other. This competition was both intra-party (with a major split in Congress in 1969 between Mrs. Gandhi's faction and the "syndicate" of established leaders in the states) and inter-party, with Congress facing major electoral challenges in the late 1960s from parties representing business, landlords, regional linguistic groups, and farmers, as well as the communists. In the February 1967 state elections these opposition parties won a majority of the seats in eight out of fourteen states and, since 1967, Congress has always faced intense competition at the state level. Politicians have responded to this increase in competition by increasing the supply of clientelist resources they command and clientelist goods they can offer.

One way of measuring the extent of this increase in political competition since 1967 is by calculating the aggregate level of party volatility in Indian states through time. Party volatility measures the sum of net party changes in seat totals from one election to another: systems with high levels of incumbency such as in the USA or some countries in Western Europe might have volatility of only 5–10 percent while Latin American volatility was closer to 20 percent in the 1980s and even higher in the 1990s (Roberts and Wibbels 1999). In Table 5.1 and Figure 5.2, I show

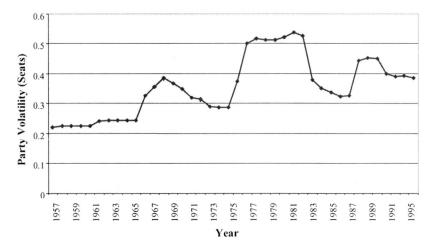

Figure 5.2 Average party volatility in India's states since independence, 1950–96

the decade-by-decade and yearly average party volatility in Indian states from 1950 to 1996, calculated using data from Election Commission of India returns. Indian states, as we can see from the table and graph, were close to Latin American levels of net electoral volatility even in the 1950s and 1960s. Since the 1967 state elections, however, Indian levels of state electoral volatility have become much higher, with the data showing that more than 40 percent of seats changed hands in an average state election in the 1980s and 1990s.[2]

The rise in electoral competition since 1967 has dramatically increased the scope and magnitude of clientelism in India. The mere presence of stronger opposition parties after the late 1960s had an immediate effect in increasing the supply of goods delivered to voters. A multivillage survey of elections in Andhra Pradesh in 1970 makes this point clear. In villages where the Congress candidates now faced strong competition from the communists or Jana Sangh, the very low-cost gifts or threats of retaliation that had been used in the past no longer worked. Candidates realized that threats to have people evicted if they did not vote the right way or to recall a villager's cooperative loans would only be counter-productive and

---

[2] Volatility is of course only one way of measuring the intensity of political competition. Some political systems could be highly competitive even if only a small net number of voters or seats changed sides from one election to the other. So the average margin of victory at the seat level in states might in some situations be a superior indicator of the level of political competition than the volatility measure I use here.

drive voters into the arms of the opposition (Reddy and Seshadri 1972: 50). Instead, candidates had to promise more in terms of cash, food, and promises of economic development for the village. The study found that:

Reports from all nine villages were unanimous with regard to the role of money in the elections. Every leader and candidate frankly said that without adequate money they could not think of winning the election. In several instances it was the case of giving cash either to voters themselves or to group or caste leaders. In this respect it did not vary from party to party and every party had to resort to this at some stage or the other. In a village where the Congress and the CP(M) were considered powerful, it was observed that the Congress candidate spent three nights in [a hamlet] and spent the money lavishly, supplied food and drinks abundantly to them and the Communist candidate who was a rich man, also lavishly spent money. (Reddy and Seshadri 1972: 50)

The most direct way in which increased intra-party and inter-party competition increased the supply of state clientelism was during the premiership of Indira Gandhi in the late 1960s and early 1970s. In the early 1970s, after her crushing national electoral victory following India's military defeat of Pakistan, she created massive new sources of central government patronage with which to outflank the state-level patronage machines controlled by her Congress rivals or by opposition parties. As part of her broader campaign to "abolish poverty" (her slogan in the 1971 election campaign) and cultivate new groups of voters for her party she created a large number of Centrally Sponsored Schemes (CSS) to channel central government resources directly to key segments of the electorate. These programs – such as the Accelerated Rural and Urban Water Supply Programs begun in 1972–73, the Rural Land Guarantee Employment Program, 1971, the Small Farmers' Development Agency, 1971, and the Marginal Farmers and Agricultural Laborers Programme, 1971 – came to represent the major portion of the Indian state's development spending.

Mrs. Gandhi also created massive new sources of patronage for her party by nationalizing (1969–73) most of the country's major banks and insurance companies. These nationalizations created a huge new reservoir of campaign funds and money with which she could appeal to voters. Congress required the newly nationalized banks to switch 40 percent of loans to the "priority" rural and small-scale industry sectors, and Congress politicians then naturally helped determine which cases were priorities and which were not. Although most of these transactions were discreet, involving supporting notes or phone-calls, some senior politicians in the 1970s instituted public loan *melas* (fairs), at which bank officials and attending politicians gave out loans *en masse* to political allies or voters. One head of the national anti-corruption bureau pointed out, with admirable understatement, that such *melas* "have probably sent a message that if you get a loan from a nationalised bank, you need not return it." The facts bear him out. Public sector banks' non-performing loans now amount to around Rs. 470,000 million (*c.* $10 billion), or 16 percent of total loans outstanding, and in the late 1990s three of major nationalized banks had to be bailed out by the central government to prevent them going bankrupt.[3]

While increasing her own sources of patronage in the early 1970s, Congress also struck at the capacity of rival parties to conduct election campaigns. To meet the threat posed by Swatantra and other parties such as the Jana Sangh, Mrs. Gandhi cut off the opposition parties' main source of income by introducing reforms to "clean up" India's political financing laws (Kochanek 1987). In 1969 she banned company donations to political parties, and she also greatly extended the industrial licensing system, which enabled her to both retaliate against companies that were political enemies and reward those who gave the Congress illegal donations or other favors (Desai 1999). Industrial licensing decisions were henceforth made on a "case by case basis," which was believed to refer to the suitcases of money necessary to secure Congress approval. In addition, the Congress Party dealt a huge financial blow to the patronage enjoyed by the former feudal princes who had backed the Swatantra and other opposition parties in 1967 in states such as Rajasthan, Orissa, and Madhya Pradesh, by taking away the sizeable yearly pensions that the princes had negotiated with the government prior to the partition of India in 1947.

The new CSS programs initiated by Indira Gandhi's faction of Congress in the early 1970s were highly successful in bypassing the traditional patronage networks controlled by her Congress rivals. At the local level, the availability of many new centrally sponsored programs allowed many voters to escape the hold of the dominant local castes on which they had previously been forced to rely for loans, seeds, and access to political power. Marguerite Brown describes how in the village of Mallannapalle in Andhra Pradesh, for example, the established village leaders tried to persuade their clients not to take advantage of the new programs, recognizing that their political and economic control would suffer. However, one villager, despite the risk of retaliation, applied for the government loans for fertilizer, and his success (despite retaliation by the traditional village leaders) led to a broader movement by poorer members of the village over the next few years to apply for government help to politicians outside the

[3] Speech by N. Vittal, Central Vigilance commissioner, on "Expenditure Control in Government," April 6, 1999. Available at http://cvc.nic.in/vscvc/cvcspeeches/99april6.html.

village. The villagers Brown interviewed were bolstered in their defiance of the traditional patrons by the fact that Congress had passed land ceiling and debt laws that now prevented the dominant castes in their village from calling in their loans or evicting them from their land (Brown 1988: 261–62). Over the following decade, Brown describes how villagers were able to use other central programs for housing, loans, and seeds to gain a measure of independence from the traditional power structure of the village, and also to begin to educate their children.

Although in the short term Indira Gandhi's programs were successful in winning voters over to Congress, over time increasing economic development in the villages, combined with a larger number of parties competing for villagers' votes has led to a gradual ratcheting up of voter demands. Brown, visiting her village in the 1980s after a gap of a decade, remarked on how "People who never dreamed of rights to clean drinking water, a site for a house, credit for agricultural inputs, or subsistence wages now demand them." And politicians who went to the village, having observed the decline in the influence of the traditional local patrons, now preferred to make promises directly to the voters (Brown 1988: p. 265).

In the decades since the 1967 state elections political parties of all stripes have competed with each other by creating an ever-wider array of social spending programs that they can use to pay off voters in return for their political support. State parties such as the Telegu Desam in Andhra Pradesh have tried to combat the influence of centrally sponsored schemes by creating welfare schemes that are identified with their own party: a free midday meal scheme for schoolchildren, for example. In turn the parties in control of the national government (successively the Congress, Janata Dal, and BJP) have created their own schemes to channel goods to voters in order to increase support for their own parties in the states. For instance in 1984–85 the national Congress government initiated a federal loan program that it used to try to undercut support for non-Congress governments in the states. Bank officials in Karnataka who protested at the loan *melas*, at which Congress Party workers handed out loans to prospective supporters were threatened by Congress Union Minister of State for Finance Janardhan Poojary (an MP for Karnataka's South Kanara seat) with transfer to Assam or Chandigarh, which at the time were the sites of major separatist campaigns in which civil servants were frequently targeted by militants.[4]

Various studies have shown that many of these central and state development programs (usually announced just before an election) have been mainly ways of securing votes, and that, with the exception of a few

---

[4] *India Today*, November 30, 1986, pp. 119–20.

programs that disburse such small benefits that they do not attract the attention of politicians and corrupt officials, they have often achieved little in terms of their stated development goals (Nayak, Saxena, and Farrington 2002). One study has estimated that only 25 percent of the money allocated to CSS employment schemes ever reaches the intended beneficiaries (2002: 6). A 1998 World Bank study of the Integrated Rural Development Program, a scheme to give loans to people to lift them out of poverty, was reported to have found that "almost no IRDP beneficiary in the sample survey satisfied the eligibility criteria: their participation in the program came through political interference and decisions by some bank officials to ignore repayment records" (2002: 44). The Gujarat auditor general likewise found that the Accelerated Rural and Urban Water Supply Programs recipients are seldom from the poorest groups that are supposed to receive the water, and that beneficiaries are chosen largely by state and national representatives. Because the program is so highly politicized, few beneficiaries have repaid loans through the program. By February 2000 the Gujarat water program alone had failed to collect Rs. 460,000,000 (c.$10,026,000) in loans.[5]

In the 1990s the Congress, in what we might think of as a repeat of Indira Gandhi's strategy in the early 1970s, once again tried to bypass clientelist machines in the states. The Congress central government passed a constitutional amendment in 1991 (ratified in December 1992) to create new village level institutions that would draw support away from the opposition parties who now controlled many legislative assemblies and would benefit Congress activists at the village level (Nayak, Saxena, and Farrington 2002). The 73rd and 74th amendments to the constitution forced states to establish elected village and town-level councils – panchayati raj institutions (PRIs) – through which to implement and select development projects.

However, this effort was much less successful than efforts in the 1970s to channel benefits directly to voters who could therefore be won over to Congress. State-level politicians (MLAs) quickly realized that these PRIs could develop into a threat to their own power and influence, especially if they were allowed to disburse a large share of the state development budget (Nayak et al. 2002). So the state acts that created these institutions were carefully drafted to ensure that MLAs would be in a position to co-opt and control the PRIs that were created. In Karnataka, for example, the 1993 Act that established the PRIs gave most of the discretion to decide which programs should be funded and how these

[5] 2001 Report of the Gujarat Auditor General. http://cagofindia.delhi. nic.in/cag/reports/gujarat/rep_2001/gujarat_civil_01_tc.htm

funds should be distributed to the state government, rather than to the PRIs themselves.[6] Moreover the 1993 Act also allows MLAs and MPs to attend the local PRI meetings as ex-officio members, which in practice enables these politicians to monitor and control the PRI representatives (Oversees Development Institute 2002). An audit of an allegedly PRI-administered housing program in several districts of Punjab, for instance, found that most of the house beneficiaries were in fact selected by members of the state assembly or ministers rather than by members of the panchayat.[7] There is some evidence that the local officials who are meant to transfer funds to the PRIs do not even bother to turn up to the local PRI meetings unless the state MLA is going to attend.[8] State politicians have included similar provisions that allowed them to monitor and control the PRIs in other states as well, for example in the Andhra Pradesh (1994) and Rajasthan (1994 and 1995) Panchayati Raj Acts.[9]

As a result of the dominance of the MLAs the center's plan for the panchayats to emerge as a separate power base has been thwarted and they have operated largely as an extension of existing patronage networks. In practice, all local representatives need to be tied to MLAs and (to a lesser extent) MPs in order to secure resources for their local areas. Every independent study that has been done of the panchayati raj elections has found that they are party elections in which MLAs take a clear interest and put up candidates from their own faction and party (Overseas Development Institute 2002). Some states, such as AP, have created parallel development institutions run by MLAs – the Andhra Pradesh District Planning Committees set up in 1999 – that essentially make the PRIs redundant (World Bank 2000b: 11). In other states such as Maharashtra state politicians have formed boards to "recommend" who the beneficiaries of development programs should be to PRIs (World Bank 2000b: 145).

State politicians have also ensured that newly created development schemes have rules that allow MLAs rather than village councils to decide

---

[6] I attended a meeting of PRI members in Raipur (then in Madhya Pradesh, now in Chhattisgarh) in 1995 at which PRI members complained bitterly about the fact that the Madhya Pradesh government was not releasing funds to them in a timely manner, and that MLAs were interfering in the process.

[7] Report of the CAG of India for the year ended March 31, 2002, Report (Civil) Government of Punjab http://www.cagindia.org/states/punjab/civil/chapter6.htm

[8] The reason given for this is that the officials know the MLA can have them transferred, while the PRI members have no leverage over them (see World Bank 2000b).

[9] See e.g., the Andhra Pradesh Panchayati Raj Act 1994 (which allows MLAs and MPs to sit as ex-officio members in the PRIs, and also gives state governments discretion over what gets funded through the PRIs).

who gets water, land, jobs or whichever other goods are being distributed. In Andhra Pradesh, for example, new water management councils were set up by the Telegu Desam Party government in the late 1990s not so much for their stated reason of improving water management, but rather to marginalize the village councils' role in water management (the Congress was stronger at the village level) and create a new patronage organization that could be staffed entirely by TDP members to distribute water in return for votes (Nayak, Sakena, and Farrington 2002: 53). In Uttar Pradesh, the state government instituted (illegal) rules to ensure that its own MLAs got to select twenty-five hand pump beneficiaries each under a centrally funded water provision scheme (Nayak, Sakena, and Farrington 2002: 30).

In 1993, national-level politicians, worried about being frozen out of the local patronage loop by opposition-controlled state governments, forced the extremely weak Narasimha Rao government to establish a whole new government program that would give members of the national parliament personal control over a large portion of the centrally funded development pie. The MPs Local Area Development Scheme (MPLADS) was established so that each MP had a fund (originally Rs. 10,000,000/$220,000 per annum, increased to Rs. 20,000,000/$440,000 per annum in 1998) with which he or she could fund small capital projects in his or her constituency (each constituency has a population of c.1–2 million). From 1993 to 2003 the central government released a total of Rs. 12,140 crores ($2.639 billion) to MPs through the scheme., and there are currently proposals to raise the annual payout to MPs to as much as $870 million.[10] Because the auditing rules for MPLADS are lax and because funds not spent in any one year can be carried forward, MPs have used these resources extensively to pay off supporters just after elections and then to reward potential voters in the run up to elections.[11]

State politicians have been quick to increase their own direct pool of patronage by replicating the MPLADS at the state level (see Table 5.2), and throughout the 1990s states set up Local Area Development Schemes for members of state Legislative Assemblies. In major states such as Tamil Nadu and Uttar Pradesh each MLA now has around $1,000,000 in funds to distribute to supporters in his or her constituency in between one

[10] PUCL Bulletin, June 2003, available at www.pucl.org/Topics/Industries-envirn-resettlement/2003/funds-misuse.htm

[11] For a review of the frequent mis-utilization of MPLADS funds see the 2001 report of the Indian Comptroller and Auditor General's Office on the working of the scheme from 1997 to 2000, available at www.cagindia.org/reports/civil/2001_book3a/index.htm

Table 5.2 *State MLA Local Area Development Schemes as of 2002*

State	Year established	MLA Development Funds per constituency[a]	MLA Development Funds per constituency[b] $
Delhi		20,000,000	434,782
Tamil Nadu	1997–98	8,200,000	178,261
Uttar Pradesh	–	7,500,000	163,043
Rajasthan	–	6,000,000	130,435
Bihar	1981–82	5,000,000	108,696
Pondicherry	2001–02	2,500,000	54,348
Gujarat	1989–90	2,500,000	54,348
Haryana	1994–95	2,000,000	43,478
AP	1999–2000	2,000,000	43,478
Tripura	2001–02	500,000	10,870
Orissa	1997–98	500,000	10,870

[a]In Rs. per annum.
[b]In $US per annum.

election and the next. In addition, each MLA also has a great deal of influence over general government spending in his or her constituency; for example, many development projects have to be approved by District Rural Development Agencies (DRDAs), in which MLAs are usually the dominant figures, *de facto* if not *de jure*. The proportion that each MLA or MP has control of is consequently a very large portion of the overall development pie. In Tamil Nadu for example (see Table 5.2), my analysis of the rural development budget shows that over 80 percent of all local development spending is under the direct or indirect control of individual MLAs and MPs. Directly the MLAs and MPs control 32 percent of rural spending through the MP and MLA Local Area Development Schemes, and indirectly they control a further 49 percent through their positions on DRDAs or through other requirements that they be consulted in the selection of beneficiaries for government programs. The total amount of money spent annually through DRDAs in India was estimated at $2.17 billion in 1999–2000, and audits have shown that much of this money is spent with little oversight or control.[12] In addition, MLAs can also influence the small portion of rural spending

---

[12] Government of India, Advisory Panel on Legal Control of Fiscal and Monetary Policies; Public Audit Mechanism; Standards in Public Life, *National Commission to review the working of the constitution: A consultation paper on efficacy of public audit system in India: C and AG – Reforming the Institution* (January 2001). http://lawmin.nic.in/ncrwc/finalreport/v2b1–11.htm.

outside their direct control by holding up the flow of state funds and withholding other monies.[13]

How large is the scope of clientelism in India? It is virtually impossible to arrive at a total figure, but the Indian government probably spends around $10 billion alone on CSS schemes (*c.*25 percent of total government plan spending), and this excludes the large number of discretionary grants that can be given to the states, as well as the state financed schemes such as the Andhra Pradesh subsidized rice scheme. MPs and MLAs control well over half of this expenditure with virtually unchecked authority to select beneficiaries. One senior IAS official with three decades of experience in development, when discussing the IAY subsidized housing scheme that (in theory) is administered by village *gram sabhas*, has pointed out that, in reality, "the lists of IAY beneficiaries are often handed to the administrative machinery by MLAs" (Nayak, Saxena, and Farrington 2002: 25).

In Table 5.3, I have attempted to break one state budget down to provide a sense of just how much of one major budget category, rural development, in one major state now represents patronage resources. By reading through program rules for each of the schemes in the Tamil Nadu rural development budget for 1999–2000 – which represents a total of around $156 million at Rs. 46 to the dollar – we can see that 32 percent of all rural development spending in the state is now under the personal control of individual members of the state and national assemblies. Through their control of development councils through which other development funds must be channeled, as well as their (illegal) power to transfer officials who refuse to direct government grants and spending to their political supporters, the MLAs and MPs also have a great deal of influence over perhaps a further 49 percent of the development budget. Even allowing for corrupt officials skimming money from these grants and for some politicians using patronage resources to enrich themselves, these schemes (and the many other segments of the state budget that are also used for patronage but that I have not broken down here) represent a formidable electoral resource.

The struggle over who controls patronage at the local level is still ongoing; MLAs are clearly in the most powerful position because under the Indian constitution it is the state governments that must administer most of the development programs. But MPs have begun to fight back and make sure that they do not lose all their influence when the money originates from the central government: the major step in this is clearly the MPLADS scheme, for which there are currently proposals to

[13] Ibid.

Table 5.3 *How much of the overall development budget is patronage? An analysis of the Tamil Nadu State Rural Development Budget, 1999–2000*

Name of scheme (central/state % of funding)	Date scheme initiated	Stated purpose of scheme	Expenditure (Rs.)	Percent of total budget %	Who selects the beneficiaries?
Employment Assurance Scheme (75%/25%)	1993–94	Provide secondary employment in rural areas during lean season	1,213,001,000	17	MPs and MLAs in consultation with local elected bodies
MLA Constituency Development Scheme (0%/100%)	1997–98	MLA selects small capital projects for development of constituency	1,175,000,000	16	MLA
MPs Local Area Development Programme (100%/0%)	1993–94	MP selects small capital projects for development of constituency	1,140,000,000	16	MP
Jawahar Gram Samiridhi Yojana (75%/25%)		Improve infrastructure in rural areas while employing poor	1,098,732,000	15	Village panchayat
Indira Awaas Yojana (75%/25%)	1985–86	Provide dwellings to SCs/STs and others below poverty line	779,467,000	11	MPs and MLAs through their role in District Rural Development Agencies (DRDAs)
Anna Marumalarchi Thittam (0%/100%)		Provide all the following services to one village per constituency: drinking water, education, health, nutrition, housing and street lights, roads and fair price shops	726,417,000	10	MLA

Scheme	Purpose	Amount	No.	Decision-making authority
Tenth Finance Commission (100% Central Funds)	Provide minor irrigation, roads, school buildings, noon meal centres, sanitation facilities	718,300,000	10	Village panchayats but spending must be approved by MPs and MLAs through their role in DRDAs
Rural Housing – Credit cum subsidy Scheme	1997–98	50,025,000	1	MLA
Namakku Naame Thittam	Wide variety of village development projects	100,000,000	1	Village panchayats but spending must be approved by MPs and MLAs through their role in DRDAs
Restructured Central Rural Sanitation Programme (50%/50%)	Provide latrines for SCs/STs and rural poor	79,621,800	1	Village panchayats
State Finance Commission	Direct grants by state to facilitate working of local government	45,506,440	1	unclear
Equalization and Incentive Grant	"Bridge the resources and infrastructural gap existing between local bodies"	45,506,440	1	unclear
Improved Chullah (Stove) Scheme	Provide improved stoves to reduce pollution and deforestation	3,600,000	0	Village panchayats but spending must be approved by MPs and MLAs through their role in DRDAs
Bio-Gas		4,500,000	0	Local officials
Total		7,179,676,680		

Sources on rules for schemes:
www.tiruvallur.tn.nic.in/schemes/index.htm;
www.tn.gov.in/citizen/drda-new-e.htm

double the annual grant. But MPs have also ensured that they have ex-officio status on District Development Councils that approve local grants for centrally sponsored schemes. And MPs are lobbying for even larger shares of the patronage pie; for example, MPs have recently been pressing for a rule that each MP should be allowed to select a fixed number of house beneficiaries under the centrally financed Indira Awaas Yojana subsidized housing scheme, to prevent MLAs alone from selecting who gets houses (Nayak, Saxena, and Farrington 2002: 27).

How does clientelistic exchange work in practice?

The major way in which politicians transfer resources to their clients is through personal promises to local leaders or (in local elections) to individual voters. Public meetings are important as shows of strength and in national elections, but in state elections and at the village level personal meetings and door-to-door contact with individuals and groups are seen as the key methods of persuading voters. A Ford Foundation sponsored survey of 3,343 voters and 4,775 elected representatives in the 1995 Karnataka panchayat elections, for example, found that 87 percent of voters reported that they had received a door-to-door visit by candidates or campaign workers, while only 15 percent had attended any sort of public meeting (Subha 1997: 27).

In village elections – where the candidates are less able to make development promises because these resources are controlled by MLAs and MPs higher up the political ladder – the main thing that politicians can offer is ties to these higher-level politicians. So panchayat elections, while in theory non-party, are in practice struggles between competing parties or factions from the same party. However, beyond this basic connection with a machine, which may be enjoyed by several viable candidates for local elections, there are several more tangible things that candidates can offer voters: immediate gifts of money, food, and liquor. When asked to identify the main factors influencing their vote most villagers in a 1995 Karnataka survey (see Table 5.4, below) listed direct payment with cash (listed by 36 percent of respondents), and gifts of food (20 percent) and alcohol (58 percent) – with richer voters being given what in India is referred to as "foreign liquor" such as gin and whisky while poorer voters were given locally brewed arrack (Subha 1997: 27–28).

In more important elections for seats in the state legislature and national parliament we see direct payments of food, drink, and money much less often than in elections for the village-level posts, though there

Table 5.4 *Reported influence of various material inducements on 1995 Karnataka Panchayat elections*

Influencing factors	Number of respondents	Percentage
Money: to some extent	902	27.0
Money: to great extent	315	9.4
Alcohol	1,954	58.5
Foodgrains/clothes, etc.	270	8.1
Dinner	669	20.0
Others	160	4.8

Source: Subha (1997: 27–28).

are exceptions, if candidates are particularly desperate. For example, one MLA who was behind in the polls in Andhra Pradesh in 2002 promised local voters Rs. 25 each (*c.* 60 cents) to vote for him. In general, though, MLAs and MPs campaign on the basis of past performance and future promises to direct specific projects to their supporters as well as continued access to general government development projects, employment, and educational opportunities.

Tracing through these exchanges is not easy because most of the reported data on government expenditure are aggregated at the district or even the state level, but politicians reward or punish voters at even smaller geographical units (villages or municipal wards) or else they reward specific groups of voters within these units. However, in recent years several village-level studies conducted by development agencies – whose primary interest is in why development funds are not reaching the neediest clients – provide a clear picture of how these transfers work. The development agencies went to the considerable effort of establishing the ethnic and political composition of each village, party, and factional alignments, and exactly how much money each village received in development grants (Singh, Gehlot, Start, and Johnson 2003).[14]

These studies show that politicians direct state funds to reward groups of voters who have already helped get them elected, or to provide an incentive for voters who did not vote for them – but are seen as critical for their future electoral prospects – to switch their votes. Politicians are determined to give non-supporters and people whose votes are seen as not

[14] Each elected panchayat contains approximately three villages with 500 households.

pivotal as little as possible.[15] A fascinating study of the disbursement of development program funds at the village level in Madhya Pradesh from 2000 to 2002 by Singh, Gehlot, Start, and Johnson (2003) found that members of the State Legislative Assembly (MLAs), and elected block (ward) representatives both disbursed the funds they controlled mainly to core supporters or to key marginal constituencies, and tried to give as little as possible to everyone else. In Table 5.5, for instance, which looks at the funds disbursed by MLAs under the Local Area Development Scheme funds in one sub-district, we can see that 72 percent of all the MLA funds spent in these three years (Rs. 560,000) went to the three panchayats (out of ten) that had strongly supported the MLA in her reelection campaign.

These grants followed a clear electoral cycle, with immediate payoffs being made after an election to reward core supporters for their support, and then a wider number of grants being approved for pivotal groups of voters as the next election grew nearer. Parties seem to reward *both* core and marginal groups of voters, despite what Dixit and Londregan say about the conditions under which rewards to either "core" or "marginal" voters predominate (Dixit and Londregan 1986). But the timing of such rewards for different groups will vary: marginal voters will have to receive some firm promises or actual transfers of goods before an election to take the risk of defecting to a new candidate, whereas established supporters will be prepared to wait. In Table 5.5, for example, we can see that 58 percent of the total MLA money spent between 1999 and 2002 was spent on the three "staunch supporter" panchayats in the fiscal year (1999–2000) immediately following the election – a clear payback for promised electoral support (though within these panchayats one particular small village that had voted for the opposition received nothing). Then, two years after the election, the MLA began to broaden the number of grants she gave to try to attract support from pivotal panchayats whose support seemed critical in the forthcoming elections. In Table 5.6, which shows the disbursement of Employment Assurance Funds by elected block panchayat leaders, we can see the effects of electoral cycles even more clearly. Panchayat 9 had opposed the winning block leader, and was penalized for it during the two years immediately after his election, receiving no money at all in employment funds. But then prior to the 2002 grant cycle the powerful castes in control of panchayat had a public ceremony (attended by leaders from the dominant block faction) at which they publicly

---

[15] As Singh, Gehlot, Start, and Johnson (2003: 5) put it, "flexible funds are distributed almost entirely to buy votes; by rewarding successful or potentially successful *Panchayats* or factions, particularly floaters who can change the balance."

Table 5.5 *Patron–client exchange: the distribution of MLA development funds (in rupees) in one subdistrict of Madhya Pradesh*

Panchayat	Supported or opposed Congress MLA in election?	Dominant caste composition of village	Other relevant political information	1999–2001	2001–02	Total	Percent of total
Panchayat 1	Opposed	Middle		0	0	0	0
Panchayat 2	Opposed	Middle		0	50,000	50,000	9
Panchayat 3	Divided support	Lower (SC)		0	0	0	0
Panchayat 4	Strongly supported	Upper	Staunch supporters of winning MLA candidate	100,000	0	100,000	18
Panchayat 5	Divided support	Lower (SC)		0	0	0	0
Panchayat 6	Strongly supported (except for one small opposition village)	Middle	Staunch supporters of winning MLA candidate (One small part of panchayat opposed MLA and got no projects approved)	100,000	0	100,000	18
Panchayat 7	Opposed	Middle		25,000	0	25,000	4
Panchayat 8	Opposed	Upper		0	50,000	50,000	9
Panchayat 9	Divided	Upper		0	33,000	33,000	6
Panchayat 10	Strongly supported	Lower (SC)	Staunch supporters of winning MLA candidate, though being aggressively courted by rival INC faction	120,000	82,000	202,000	36
					Total	Rs. 560,000	

Source: Singh, Gehlot, Start, and Johnson (2003: 19–22).

Table 5.6 *Patron–client exchange: block-level distribution of employment assurance funds in one subdistrict of Madhya Pradesh (funds not given by MLA are excluded)*

Panchayat	Supported or opposed block official in election?	Dominant caste composition of village	Other relevant political information	2000–02	2001–02	2002–03	Total	per cent of total
Panchayat 1	Weak support	Middle		0	68,000	20,000	88,000	7
Panchayat 2	Supported	Middle		0	82,000	63,000	145,000	11
Panchayat 3	Supported	Lower (SC)		53,000	0	48,000	101,000	8
Panchayat 4	Supported	Upper		0	140,000	0	140,000	10
Panchayat 5	Opposed	Lower (SC)	Block representative wants to attract SC support to help gain MLA ticket	0	0	75,000	75,000	6
Panchayat 6	Supported	Middle		100,000	70,000	0	170,000	13
BLOCK 2								
Panchayat 7	Supported	Middle		0	125,000	50,000	175,000	13
Panchayat 8	Supported	Upper		0	75,000	0	75,000	6
Panchayat 9	Opposed	Upper	Initially got nothing, then powerful castes in control of village converted to "right" INC faction before Fiscal Year 2002–03	0	0	225,000	225,000	17
Panchayat 10	Strongly supported	Lower (SC)		70,000	75,000	0	145,000	11
						Total Rs.	1,339,000	

Source: Information in Singh, Gehlot, Start, and Johnson (2003: 19–22).

changed their allegiance to the dominant faction. As a direct reward for this public shift, and also presumably to encourage other defectors from rival factions, this panchayat received the largest single grant (Rs. 225,000) of any panchayat in the following year (Singh, Gehlot, Start, and Johnson 2003: 29).

This basic political logic – to reward core supporters and pivotal voters and punish known opponents – is subject to some modification. For one thing, lower castes generally receive less patronage than we would expect given their share of the electorate because they are generally seen as a less valuable voting bloc by the middle and upper castes that control the major parties. Part of this is prejudice, and part of this is recognition that lower castes generally have less influence and clout in rural India than middle and upper castes. In Table 5.5, for example, we can see that the MLA gave several small grants to try to attract support in the upcoming elections from middle and upper caste dominated panchayats (nos. 2, 7, 8, 9) that had previously given her weak support or been openly opposed. However, lower-caste panchayats that had been divided in their support (panchayats 3 and 5) received no funds at all. Only one lower caste panchayat (no. 10) which had an especially skillful *sarpanch* (leader) – who played off different Congress factions and had strongly supported the MLA in her reelection campaign – received substantial funds under the MLA program – in fact 36 percent of total spending, the largest of any panchayat.

One factor that complicates our efforts to trace the clientelist logic of transfers is that there may be some cases where a local village may not have previously supported a candidate but may nonetheless attract funds because it is important to a party's wider effort to cultivate new groups of voters. Payoffs that appear irrational in the context of a single shot game in a local election make sense once we realize that politicians are thinking about how gaining support among particular groups will affect their prospects when they begin to compete on a wider political stage.[16] For example, in the Singh, Gehlot, Start, and Johnson (2003) study of Madhya Pradesh just cited, one local leader gave funds to a predominantly Scheduled Caste (ex untouchable) village that had previously voted for his opponent. This seemingly irrational decision begins to make sense, however, when we learn that the leader wanted to secure his party's nomination for a Legislative Assembly seat in which SCs were a significant proportion of the voters, so he therefore needed to prove to the party leaders that he was a proven vote getter among the Scheduled Caste community.

---

[16] On this issue more generally, see Tsebelis (1990).

India 2000–2020: high demands, high competition, and growing pressure for reform?

Several economic and social developments over the past decade have, I believe, created a growing constituency for economic reform that will in time restrict the growth of clientelistic politics and lead to more programmatic appeals in Indian politics. The most obvious and important of these developments has been the rapid expansion of the Indian economy since the 1991 economic reforms.[17] The reforms and the growing prosperity they have engendered for at least some of the population have created a sizeable and growing constituency for political reform. Most estimates are that the overall proportion of upper-income households in India has at least doubled since 1991, and there is unanimity that the growth in the middle and upper middle class has been driven by growth in private employment rather than in the state-controlled sector.[18] Increasing numbers of voters are therefore not reliant on state jobs, subsidies, or state education or state licenses for the economy. And in the larger boom cities such as Bangalore and Hyderabad, businessmen have taken the lead in pressing for improvements in the delivery of government services and a lessening of corruption.

There is also a new level of concern and information about the extent of political patronage and corruption, spread by a rapidly expanding mass media. As this chapter was being completed in December 2005 a major expose of the corruption in the MPs development scheme project broke in the Indian media, with hidden camera footage showing MPs and their agents bargaining for commissions on projects they approved, and justifying these demands for kickbacks on the grounds that they needed the commissions in order to finance their election campaigns.[19] According to the 2002 National Readership Survey the total newspaper readership in India is now approaching 180 million people, or 23 percent of the adult

---

[17] These reforms might never have happened without a major balance of payments crisis that allowed domestic proponents of reform to claim that there was no other option than to accept the IMF's medicine.

[18] Looking at the relative share of public and private employment in the organized sector of the economy provides only an imperfect measure of this shift. This is because private industry tries to add workers through contract labor to avoid the labor regulations in the organized sector. T. C. A. Anant reports that contract labor's share as a percentage of all private employment has therefore shot up in the past decade, from 11.9 percent in 1989 to 29.1 percent in 1998. "Labour Market Reform in India: An Overview," ppt presentation available on Global Development Network (Feb 2003) ctool.gdnet.org/conf_docs/Anant_presentation.ppt.

[19] This case demonstrates that much of what we think of as simple corruption is in fact politically motivated, the result of politicians trying to generate cash for their election campaigns rather than simply to enrich themselves.

population. Much of the recent explosive growth in newspapers (there was a 20 percent rise in readers from 1999 to 2002 alone) has come from people in rural areas and from those who are not members of the English-speaking elite, for example speakers of Hindi, Marathi, Kannada, Assamese, and Bengali (Bunsha 2002). The expansion of the press and mass media into rural areas, in part due to greatly improved distribution networks and printing technologies, has had important effects in creating both wider knowledge and concern about the extent of local patronage. Many of the new regional language newspapers employ dozens of stringers in small towns and villages who pass on information about local patronage and abuses through phone booths, faxes, and buses, to regional and state newspapers.[20] The press also creates a wider sense among voters of the levers they can pull in order to challenge local patronage networks.

Adding to this media pressure is the work of numerous domestic NGOs, some of which work in cooperation with, or get funding from, international organizations such as the World Bank, the Ford Foundation and Transparency International, that have been founded over the past two decades to draw attention to the extent of patronage networks and the scope and damage caused by political corruption. In the western state of Rajasthan, for instance, the Mazdoor Kisan Shakti Sangathan (MKSS) has used open government laws and public sit-ins (one lasting fifty-two days in the state capital) to uncover evidence of the substantial diversion of government funds to local political networks – Rs. 800,000 in one village alone went to non-existent local projects (Roy and Dey 2001).

State governments, in part to gain access to World Bank loans and in part to show investors and voters that they are doing something about corruption, have also begun to pass freedom of information laws and introduce computerization of records that will, over time, provide fewer opportunities for politicians to extract rents and deliver patronage to their clients. Karnataka for instance, passed several bills that in theory allow public access to government financial documents (the Transparency in Public Procurement Act, the Fiscal Responsibility Bill, and the Right to Information Act in the early 2000s), in part because it was negotiating for major World Bank loans and the bank had made "governance" and transparency a major element of loan conditionality. Similar acts have been passed in other states such as Delhi and Rajasthan. Once established, even if only as a sop to financial institutions, these acts can be used by NGOs and reform organizations to find out the extent to which political

---

[20] For coverage of this revolution in the reach of papers and news networks in rural India, see Senati Nian (2002).

patronage networks are diverting resources – contracts, ration cards, etc. – and to make efforts to reduce it. In Delhi, for instance, an NGO called *Parivartan* (change) has used the Right to Information Act to investigate the diversion of subsidized food and non-completion of local public works such as sewers.[21]

Finally, supporters of cleaning up politics within several government agencies (e.g., the Election Commission of India, the Comptroller and Auditor General's office, the Central Bureau of Investigation, and the Planning Commission) have over the past decade issued reports designed to create political pressure for reform by demonstrating the extent of criminality, patronage, and inefficiency within the current political system. These reports have been well publicized in the Indian press and are often used as evidence by those who want to change the system. The Election Commission, for example, put out a 1997 reform that demonstrated the extent to which people with criminal records were participating in politics. More importantly from the perspective of clientelism, reformers such as N. C. Saxena and Montek Ahluwalia used their tenure at the Planning Commission in the late 1990s and early 2000s to sponsor large-scale reviews of many areas of government spending, demonstrating the way in which their alleged goals of reducing poverty were being subverted by corruption and the need to pay off political clients.[22] Just to give one example from the many surveys they commissioned, a 1999 Planning Commission survey of 514 participants in nine central government sponsored welfare schemes in a backward district of Uttar Pradesh found that a large percentage of beneficiaries (36 percent) came from groups whose income level ought to have made them ineligible for the scheme.[23] The evidence is that at least 50 percent of these beneficiaries were nominated by local politicians, with a further 20 percent being nominated by local welfare officials and the remainder unwilling to disclose who had nominated them. Perhaps the most highly publicized reports have been the 1998 and 2001 comptroller and auditor general's reports on the MPs

---

[21] http://indiatogether.org/2003/apr/gov-rtidelhi.htm.

[22] N. C. Saxena, a former high-ranking bureaucrat, was secretary of the Planning Commission from June 1999 to March 2002. Montek Singh Ahulwalia, a prominent pro-reform economist who had been an aide to Manmohan Singh during the reforms in the early 1990s, was a member of the commission from August 1998 to March 2001. These surveys are available on the web at http://planningcommission.nic.in/.

[23] Planning Commission of India, "Evaluation of Rural Development Schemes in Gonda District," http://planningcommission.nic.in/reportsf.htm. In similar surveys in Bihar and Karnataka the proportion of ineligible recipients was 24 percent and 50–56 percent respectively. "An Empirical Study of Poverty Alleviation Programmes in Bihar," Mathura Krishna Foundation for Economic and Social Opportunity and Human Resource Management http://planningcommission.nic.in/maker/epilogue.pdf.

Local Area Development Schemes, which revealed widespread corruption, political selection of beneficiaries, and inefficiencies.[24] Numerous articles in the Indian press gleefully revealed the extent to which MPs were using these funds as their private campaign chests.

There is evidence that the constituency among voters for reform and more performance-oriented policies in India is growing. There is an obvious problem of course in getting good time series data on this, because different polling samples have been used over time. But even if we only restrict ourselves to the very largest polls (4,000+ respondents) there does seem to be a pattern of increasing public concern about corruption in public life. In 1996 a Gallup Survey of 5,122 Indians asked "What do you think is the country's most important current problem?" The leading answer was "poverty" (46 percent), followed by "unemployment" with 14 percent. Corruption was only the third most frequently mentioned issue, mentioned by 14 percent of the sample (followed by "illiteracy" 5 percent, "electricity" 4 percent, "casteism" 3 percent, and "communalism" 2 percent). An India-Marg poll of nearly 13,000 voters the same year came up with very similar results when it asked a question about the most important issue that had to be tackled by the country: 42 percent said poverty, followed by "employment" at 22 percent, and "corruption" was again in third place, mentioned by 16 percent of respondents.[25] Compare this with the recent massive 2004 pre-election poll conducted by NDTV/AC Nielson and a major Indian newspaper. In the 2004 poll, "reducing corruption" was the leading answer to a similar question about the most important issues facing the country, mentioned by 30 percent of respondents, with "prices," "poverty," and "jobs" being mentioned by 24 percent, 22 percent, and 17 percent of respondents.[26]

Politicians of course have to balance the demands of a reform-oriented constituency with more pragmatic concerns about delivering patronage to key constituencies in order to stay in power. Several parties – most notably the TDP in Andhra Pradesh and the Congress in Karnataka – seemed to lean too far in the direction of programmatic politics in the early 2000s and not enough in the direction of providing basic goods such as electricity and water to farmers and they paid the price at the polls in the 2004 elections. It is at least arguable that it is only through delivering patronage to poorer voters that reformers can hold their economically

---

[24] www.cagindia.org/reports/civil/2001_book3a/index.htm

[25] "India-Marg Post-Election Survey: BJP-Gaining More," *India Today*, June 30, 1996, pp. 28–31.

[26] March 5–18 *Indian Express*/NDTV/AC Nielson Poll of 45,478 voters in 207/543 parliamentary constituencies. http://www.aghilham.com/news/india-election/20040327b.html

and socially heterogeneous coalitions together in the first place. The BJP and Congress both play to multiple constituencies at once, delivering subsidies and jobs to some groups of voters and programmatic messages to others. The many losers from economic reforms might have brought the whole reform process to a halt long before now without access to government subsidies, loans, jobs, and food.

But there are clear signs that the push for reforming clientelist structures will not go away. Within each of the main national parties there are influential politicians arguing that their party should position itself as the party of reform and clean government. The BJP-NDA, for example, has made the presence of several criminal and corrupt legislators within the Congress coalition that took office in May 2004 a major issue. Senior spokesman Arun Jaitley has demanded the removal of four ministers "in the larger interest of Parliamentary democracy, public interest, national security and norms of probity in public life."[27] Jaitley and others obviously hope not just to break up the coalition by playing on public unease with the presence of several criminals in the Cabinet, but also to position their party as *the* reform party and benefit from growing public concern with political corruption. If the experience of other countries is typical, we can expect many other parties (though not all) to adopt similar postures when they begin to lose large numbers of votes over the issue. Once such positions have been staked out, parties find it very difficult to avoid taking action against those in their own parties who are shown by the media to be corrupt; several parties were forced to suspend their own MPs in December 2005 when they were caught in media stings.

The odds are that, over the next decade, growing political economic pressures on the capacity of state and central governments to support the costs of the existing clientelist system will also force reforms. There is no doubt that the present clientelist system, with hundreds of inefficient public sector units, overmanned government departments, and massive subsidies for food, power, transport, housing, and power are very expensive. Public sector units are supposed to make money, but in fact their inefficiencies have led to massive annual losses that now total 1.4 percent of GDP. Power sector losses and subsidies now total 1.3 percent of GDP, with unpaid electricity board liabilities now estimated at a further 1.1 percent of GDP. Other subsidies include food and fertilizer (1.25 percent of GDP), kerosene (0.4 percent), and railway travel (0.2 percent of GDP) (International Monetary Fund

---

[27] www.outlookindia.com/pti_news.asp?id=225972.

2001: 3). One confidential but widely leaked May 1997 report estimated the cost of overall government subsidies at 14.4 percent of GDP, more than two-third of which is generated in the states (Sachs and Bajpai 1999: 3–12).

Many states have been unable to take the politically unpopular step of increasing tax revenues to cover their spending and they have been forced to rely on either central government transfers or else raids on their capital and pension reserve funds to cover the resulting finance gaps. Uttar Pradesh, for example, is now financing 40 percent of its total $10 billion budget through borrowing, mainly from the central government, with 8 percent of its annual budget now coming from transfers from its pension and reserve funds, which the state government promises to pay back at some undetermined point in the future.[28]

It is clear that neither the center's ability to continue such large transfers to the states nor the states' abilities to raid their pension and reserve funds can continue indefinitely. The General Government Deficit in India reached 58 percent of GDP in March 1986 and is now 85 percent of GDP (107 percent of GDP if we add the debt and liabilities of the various Public Sector Units) (World Bank 2003: 3). There is now widespread agreement in policy circles in India – among bankers and industrialists, academics, senior members of the Planning Commission, and even the leaders of many of the national parties – that the current system's large budget deficits and inefficiencies are simply unsustainable and that fiscal crisis will eventually lead to some change in the present clientelist system.[29] The states and central government are under growing pressure from the World Bank and the IMF to reform their existing subsidies and clientelist electricity boards, cooperatives, and public sector corporations.

These political economic pressures are mobilizing several diverse constituencies to press for reforms of the current structure. Voters as well as Indian companies and international financial institutions want general improvements in infrastructure, and they recognize that politicians' clientelist transfers to their clients are crowding out capital spending on things like water, roads, sewers, and hospitals. States' capital spending declined from 3.6 percent of national GDP in 1981–82 to only 1.7 percent

---

[28] Calculated from data in Kumar Singh (2000: 1512–13).

[29] See the central Planning Commission's annual reports, which contain extensive evidence of the scale of the current deficit spending as well as pleas for a reduction in subsidies and the support of inefficient programs and PSUs that benefit only narrow groups of voters: www.planningcommission.gov.in. For industry's views see the paper "The State of State Finances," a Confederation of Indian Industry discussion paper available at www.ciionline.org/common/91/images/stateofstatefinances.org.

in 2001–02 while their annual interest payments rose from 0.8 percent of GDP to 2.8 percent.[30] All the major Indian business groups have publicly called for a reduction in the scale of subsidies and regulations, as have the major international financial institutions on whose loans several large state governments (e.g., Uttar Pradesh, Andhra Pradesh, Tamil Nadu) rely. The business groups recognize that high state deficits and government dominance of several sectors of the economy increase their input costs, especially for power, where private businesses are charged more to allow cross-subsidies to farmers, as well as their cost of capital, because the central government has had to sharply increase the interest rates it pays to finance its ever-growing deficit spending and transfers to the states (Government of India Planning Commission 2001: 48). And the finance ministry wants reform of the highly inefficient public sector units because, as one recent Planning Commission report recognizes, an overall improvement in the center's budget receipts is only possible if a larger percentage of PSUs start making profits and therefore become net contributors to the budget.[31]

The pressure for reform of clientelism in India will not of course be equal all over the country. Given overall high levels of political competition, we can expect states with (1) above average levels of per capita state domestic product (SDP) (2) literacy and (3) media penetration, to experience an earlier push for reform than other states. In Table 5.7, below, I categorize states very roughly according to their levels of these three variables. We would expect states such as Kerala, Gujarat, Punjab, and Maharashtra with relatively high SDPs, literacy above the Indian average of 67 percent, and large mass media audiences (the Indian state average is 24 percent newspaper penetration) to be earlier reformers, while we would expect little near-term change in states such as Uttar Pradesh, Bihar, Madhya Pradesh, and Orissa. In some cases, such as Bihar, where levels of economic growth are very low or negative and middle-class out-migration is high, it is hard to see any real push for reform succeeding except in the very long term, absent an intervention from the central government.

Conclusion

My view that programmatic party competition will increase and that clientelistic competition will diminish over the coming decades may

---

[30] See ibid.

[31] "improvement in the Non Tax Revenue of the Centre would be possible only if efficiency of the Public Sector Undertakings improves across the board." Government of India Planning Commission (2001: 46).

Table 5.7 *Which states do economic and social development indicators suggest will reform first?*

State	Per capita net state domestic product 2000–2001 (Rs.)	Literacy (2001) %	Estimated newspaper penetration among adult speakers of dominant local language (2001)[a] %
High Likelihood			
Delhi	38,864	82	–
Punjab	25,048	70	15[b]
Haryana	23,742	69	19[b]
Maharashtra	23,726	77	35
Tamil Nadu	19,889	73	32
Kerala	19,463	91	67
Gujarat	19,228	70	32
Himachal Pradesh	18,920	77	–
Medium Pressure			
Karnataka	18,041	67	29
Andhra Pradesh	16,373	61	21
West Bengal	16,072	69	21
Rajasthan	11,986	61	23
Assam	10,198	64	26
Low Pressure			
Madhya Pradesh	10,803	64	17
Uttar Pradesh	9,721	57	14
Orissa	8,547	64	15
Bihar	5,108	48	15
Chhattisgarh	NA	65	NA
Jharkhand	NA	54	NA

[a] Press Readership from 2001 National Readership Survey extracts reported by B. S. Chandrasekhar, "Analysing Indian Language Newspaper Readership."
[b] Punjab and Haryana newspaper readership is a substantial underestimate because many Punjabis are bilingual and read Hindi newspapers.
Source: Literacy 2001 *Census of India.*

strike some readers as unduly optimistic. It rests of course on some assumptions about the continued economic growth and expansion of the middle class in India, on the one hand, and the continuing relative independence of the private sector from further government regulation on the other. The main uncertainty, I think, is whether reformers can resist renewed pressure for a repeat of the state-regulatory initiatives undertaken by Mrs. Gandhi in the early 1970s. If existing political patronage programs are extended into the private sector, as many lower and middle-caste politicians worried about the relatively declining share of the state sector are currently advocating, then it is conceivable that both overall levels of economic growth and the decline of patronage policies will slow down.

6 Politics in the middle: mediating relationships between the citizens and the state in rural North India

Anirudh Krishna

Caste and patron–client links have been regarded most often as the build-ing blocks of political organization in India, especially in its rural parts (Migdal 1988; Weiner 1989), and caste associations have been thought to be the pre-eminent mode of interest formation and interest articulation for ordinary villagers (Bailey 1957; Morris-Jones 1967; Panini 1997). Caste has changed over the last twenty-five years, however, and the links between caste and occupation and caste and wealth are no longer as close as they used to be (Mayer 1997; Sheth 1999). Many observers continue to stress caste and patron–client linkages as important factors explain-ing political mobilization in rural India (Karanth 1997; Kothari 1997; Manor 1997). The relation of caste to political organization is medi-ated, however, by the nature of state policies. Changes produced by state policies over the last twenty-five years have had the result of dimin-ishing the utility for villagers of older caste- and patronage-based con-duits. In sixty-nine villages where I studied these features, located in the northern Indian states of Rajasthan and Madhya Pradesh, different forms of political association have arisen and gained ground, and the salience of older patronage-based associations has waned considerably in comparison.

Varying stimuli produced by the state at different times have resulted in reconfiguring caste and political association, the historical account shows (Bayly 1988; Dirks 2001). As the nature and the rules of the political game have changed once again over the past twenty-five years, caste and other forms of social aggregation have changed further in response. New imperatives and new opportunities for influence with the state have given rise to newer and more open political networks in the villages where I worked.

Democracy has become more widespread as a result, and more peo-ple participate in democratic politics than ever before. The literature on strengthening democracy has identified a variety of factors that help improve the quality of democracy in different circumstances.[1] A sub-group of these factors – including economic modernization and education together with increased party competition and government provision of goods and services – is relevant to the account of change in these villages of India.

Changes in democratic practice over two decades

Between 1997 and 2002, I spent a total period of about 24 months conducting field research in a group of sixty-nine dissimilar villages located in five districts of Rajasthan and three districts of Madhya Pradesh.[2] Democracy has come to be more widely dispersed and more equally distributed in these central Indian villages over the past twenty-five years. No considerable industrialization is associated with these changes; more than 70 percent of the workforce continues to remain rural and agriculture-based. Nor have programmatic parties emerged in central India that can help account for these changes (Dreze and Sen 1997; Kuhn 1998). Participation in politics and in the everyday tasks of influencing government has become much more widespread, however, and many more poorer and lower-caste persons are engaging with democracy than ever before.

"Things are different now," claims Bhuraram Prajapat, a hereditary potter of Sema village, "Today, people are much freer. Previously, the *samants* [powerful men in the village] commanded us like servants . . . and we could do nothing except to tolerate their abuse. But now we are more equal."

New conduits of participation and influence have been opened up, which provide ordinary villagers with useful linkages to the state machinery. Non-caste-based political entrepreneurs – popularly known as *naya netas* (literally, new leaders) – have emerged in villages in this region, and they enable other villagers to participate more effectively in the activities of democracy and to share more equitably in its benefits.[3]

---

[1] Including economic development (Haggard and Kaufman 1992; Lipset 1960, 1994; Przeworski 1991), education (Almond and Verba 1965; Dreze and Sen 1995; Sen 1999), institutionalized parties (Huntington 1968; Kohli 1987, 1990), institutional arrangements and electoral procedures (Carey and Shugart 1995; Linz 1994; Mainwaring 1999), expanding markets (Apter 1965; Inkeles and Smith 1974; Lerner 1958), a professional civil service (Shefter 1994), and social capital (Fukuyama 1995; Krishna 2002a, 2002b; Putnam 1993).

[2] The five Rajasthan districts are Ajmer, Bhilwara, Rajsamand, Udaipur, and Dungarpur, and the three Madhya Pradesh districts are Neemuch, Mandsaur, and Ujjain.

[3] Early indications of these changes were provided by Bailey (1960), Reddy and Hargopal (1985), and Mitra (1991, 1992). Indication that similar changes have also become manifest in parts of southern India is provided by Manor (2000).

Having emerged mostly within the past twenty-five years, these *naya netas* provide other villagers with their most effective means of making contact with politicians, with the government bureaucracy, and with market operations of different kinds. Their authority and respect in the village derives not from any ritual or economic status but from the information and connections that they make available to other villagers.

After living in a smaller group of sixteen villages for an initial period of eighteen months and observing trends and patterns closely in these villages, I conducted sample surveys in the larger group of sixty-nine villages with the help of eight male and eight female investigators, who are themselves local residents. We interviewed a random sample of 2,232 villagers between 1998 and 2000. Individuals to interview were selected through random sampling from the most recently compiled electoral roll for that village.[4]

Different types of leaders are available to villagers, including political party officials, traditional village patrons (*jajmaan*), elected local council (*panchayat*) leaders, caste leaders, and *naya netas*. The interviews revealed that compared to leaders of any other type, many more villagers choose to rely upon *naya netas* for diverse purposes requiring mediation with the state. More than 60 percent of villagers in each case prefer to deal with *naya netas*. Far fewer villagers, no more than 20 percent in any case, seek assistance from any other type of political actor in their village (see Table 6.1).

Caste leaders and traditional patrons play a smaller role insofar as political exchange and economic transactions are concerned in these villages, and the new non-caste-based political entrepreneurs, the *naya netas*, play a far larger role. Apart from political party officials, all of the other types of leaders examined here are resident locally within these villages, so it is not merely a question of relative access influencing which leaders are consulted in each case. Relative *effectiveness* more than ease of access determines why villagers prefer to consult one type of local leader in far greater numbers.

The new village leaders have neither formal nor ritual authority nor, in most cases, do they have any significant economic power. Their landholdings are smaller compared to the traditional village patrons', as Table 6.2 shows. What they do have to a comparatively greater degree, however, are higher educational ability, more information about the world outside the village, and better contacts among people who run things in this external world. These assets, mostly self-acquired, enable *naya netas*

---

[4] Because of frequent competitive elections, these voters lists are quite complete in their coverage, I rarely came upon an instance of someone's name missing from this list.

Table 6.1 *New village leaders and other intermediaries*

Number of villagers who said they would approach each type of leader for help related to:[a]	Types of agency (leadership)				
	Political party official	Traditional village patrons	Elected village council officials	Leaders of caste groups	*Naya netas*
(a) Dealing with the police or the *tahsil*	114	72	101	372	1,172
(b) Getting a bank loan or an insurance policy	92	317	166	146	1,118
(c) Learning about agricultural technology	107	49	313	203	1,149
(d) Replacing a non-performing school teacher	84	25	332	215	1,218
(e) Getting wage employment	87	64	274	156	1,431

[a] Numbers in the table reflect the preferences expressed by a random sample of 2,232 villagers. Row totals may not add up to this total as some villagers did not respond to a particular question or selected a residual "other" category.
Source: adapted from Krishna (2002a).

Table 6.2 *Characteristics on average of old and new leaders in 60 villages*

	Traditional village patrons and caste leaders (N=197)	*Naya netas* (new village leaders) (N=211)
Age	54.5	38.3
Education (number of years)	3.5	9.6
Caste rank (0 to 4)	2.9	1.7
Land per capita (hectares)	0.84	0.48
Information sources (out of 7)	3.2	6.1
External contacts (out of 10)	3.6	7.9

Source: adapted from Krishna (2002a).

to obtain positions of considerable political influence in their native villages. They cannot coerce or compel other villagers to follow their lead. But since they enable other villagers to obtain larger benefits from democracy and from the market, most ordinary villagers choose to stay by their side.

Most villagers – more than 85 percent – ranked economic development higher than any other type of individual or collective benefit from the state. Leaders who can help villagers acquire such economic benefits have consequently gained in popularity and esteem:

People's attitudes have changed . . . [and their] concern for development has increased enormously; *vishwas* [faith alone] has no meaning and no worth any more. Even the smallest village wants electricity, a road, a school, a health center – these basic minimum requirements are wanted by all villagers. Leaders are judged by what they can achieve . . . Youth have come up in large numbers in politics since 1977. Old leaders who were not able to get villagers' work done are now in the corner [they have been sidelined].[5]

Traditional caste leaders and village patrons are not as capable of addressing these new demands. Because they lack education and contacts with the outside world, as shown in Table 6.2, these types of local leaders are less capable of delivering the benefits that villagers most often want. They have been displaced within the course of the past twenty-five years by a new group of first-generation village leaders.

These new village leaders, the *naya netas*, are "usually between twenty-five and forty years of age . . . [and] educated to about middle school [level]. They read newspapers, have contacts in government offices, and are experienced [in dealing] with the government bureaucracy and with banks, insurance companies, and such like . . . Their caste does not matter . . . [they] can be of any caste, but they must have knowledge, perseverance and ability."[6]

Naya netas come from a variety of backgrounds. Some are upper caste, though a proportionately larger number of these new leaders belong to the middle and lower castes of villagers; 14 percent of 211 new leaders in sixty-nine villages belong to the upper and middle castes; however, 49 percent belong to backward castes, and 26 percent are from the formerly untouchable castes.

Family background has relatively little to do with who becomes a new leader. Functional literacy and certain personal qualities are much more important, including a willingness to work hard on behalf of ordinary villagers:

When people come to me with some work, I have to attend to it at once. Even at night, if someone has a medical emergency or a police matter is involved I have

---

[5] Interview with Bhanwarlal Garg, Congress Party worker for twenty-five years, presently the chairman of its Block Committee for Suvana Block of Bhilwara District, and also *Pradhan* (president) of *Panchayat Samiti*, Bhilwara, July 25, 1998.
[6] Interview with Chunnilal Garasiya, long-time Congress Party leader and minister in the Rajasthan state government during the 1980s (Udaipur, March 19, 1999).

to go at once on my motorcycle . . . Yes, my family members do complain quite often: "What do you get out of all of this [work and inconvenience]," they ask. But what can I do? I have stepped into [this role of] *netagiri* [leadership], and I have to do what it takes . . . No, it is not a full-time occupation. It does not take more than a couple of hours on average every day, and the rest of the time I can do my own personal work. But when someone comes to me [with a request for assistance] I must go [with them] forthwith.[7]

People's needs have changed and different leaders have arisen to fulfill these needs. Older leaders who are less educated and less capable of dealing on a day-to-day basis with the clerical bureaucracy of a post-colonial state have had to make way for a new generation of self-made village leaders. Consequently, caste has become a less important factor of political organization in these Indian villages, as we will see below.

The new village leaders have also brought with them a new mode of political exchange. Traditional upper-caste patrons pressured other villagers to act politically at their direction. Their inherited and largely unquestioned authority was met with fear and subservience on the part of ordinary villagers. But interactions between villagers and the new leaders constitute a very different manner of political transaction, more equal and voluntary on both sides. No villager is bound to act to the directions of any *naya neta*. Rather, villagers select of their own accord to take advice and assistance from some new leader in their village – and they can choose to pay no attention to any *naya neta* if they please.

Significant change has occurred in these contexts over the past two decades. The locus of an explanation is found at the middle level of political institutions.

Middle level institutions

Political scientists expect that parties will function as a middle-level institution of democracy, mediating between citizens and public officials and assisting with the purposes of both. But parties are notoriously poorly organized in rural Rajasthan and Madhya Pradesh and in most other parts of India.[8] And hardly any villager expects to find much assistance from party officials, as the figures in Table 6.1 show. The nearest party office is usually at district headquarters, a journey of 100 kilometers or

---

[7] Interview with Narulal Dangi, new leader of Ramâ village, Udaipur district (Badgaon, Udaipur, May 30, 2002)

[8] The clearest case about dysfunctional or even non-existent district-level party organizations in India is made by Kohli (1990). One exception is provided by the state of Kerala, where the Congress Party and the Communist Party (Marxist) have for long been engaged in mobilization and counter-mobilization, with party offices reaching down to the village and ward levels. See in this regard, Heller (2002) and Herring (1983).

more for many villagers. Neither well staffed nor adequately motivated, district-level party officials can hardly deal adequately with the myriad tasks of political mediation (Kohli 1990; Krishna 2002a).

Because party channels are weak, politicians have usually relied upon some pre-existing form of social organization. Caste-based and traditional patron–client organizations were important for this purpose twenty-five years ago. Various accounts show how politicians of different parties commonly relied upon upper-caste village strongmen for bringing in the vote (Frankel and Rao 1989; Migdal 1988; Narain 1976; Saxena and Charan 1973; Singh 1988; Weiner 1967).

The nature of these substitute middle-level organizations has changed considerably over the past twenty-five years, however. Alternative modes of middle-level linkage have emerged to fill the vacuum of upward representation that exists in much of the Indian countryside. Politicians can no longer rely primarily or even substantially upon big landlords and caste leaders.

"The nature of influence has changed," declared Mangilal Joshi, president of the Bharatiya Janata Party (BJP) for Udaipur district of Rajasthan state, "Those individuals are gaining most influence in villages who are able to get villagers' day-to-day work done in government offices . . . these are the people who matter in the village today [and not those who have more land or higher caste rank]."[9]

Sheshmal Pagariya, president of the Congress Party, the other major party in this district, pronounced a similar view. "The criterion for voting was earlier *jati* (caste), now it is *vikaas* (development). Development work done in a village has the most effect on voting . . . We cannot watch over these activities in every village, so we support and rely upon the local worker. We catch hold of these worker-type persons in every village, and we know that the other party will also do the same, so we try to get to them first at election time," he stated.[10]

Modes of political linkage between villagers and the democratic regime have changed considerably over the past two decades. A different set of roles has emerged, associated with different forms of political exchange (Uphoff and Ilchmann 1972).

Although it is based upon individualistic and personalized relationships – where an individual casts her vote based on favors granted (or promised) to herself or her village community – the new mode of political exchange differs in significant respects from the model of clientelism as usually construed. Successful clientelistic parties usually build "political machines that reach from the summits of national politics down to

[9] Interviewed in Udaipur (July 9, 1998).   [10] Interviewed in Udaipur (July 12, 1998).

the municipal level" (Kitschelt 2000b: 849). Resources for patronage are generated and made available to lower levels by people at the top, and each successive link downward has power only to the extent it receives patronage resources from above. Control within this hierarchical chain of favors and fealty is maintained by a credible threat of withholding resources from the top.

The central Indian examples discussed below differ from this model in two important respects. First, the interactions that new village leaders have with politicians at higher levels are hardly those of a client locked into a hierarchical relation with a patron. *Naya netas* are not bound to any particular political party. Rather, they look around for whichever politician can provide them credibly with most resources to finance development works in their village, and they switch allegiance easily from one set of politicians to another. Parties chase after *naya netas* as much as or more than *naya netas* chase after parties; consequently, the top half of the clientelistic pyramid is inverted to some extent.

The bottom half of the clientelistic pyramid is also partly skewed. Akin to a standard patron–client relationship, *naya netas* perform diverse services on behalf of ordinary villagers, and they expect to be repaid for these services at election time.

Naya netas have hardly any means available to monitor precisely how different villagers cast their votes on election day. They cannot, therefore, hold villagers to account in this respect (any more than caste leaders could do so in their day).

One *naya neta* informed me that "it is a matter of keeping faith. People can obviously vote as they wish. But most people remember well who has helped them in times of need. And it is only a rare person who is faithless."[11]

Faith must be kept on both sides, however. Individual villagers are not bound to any particular *naya neta*, and new leaders who are effective and honest in their dealings attract a sizeable following among their fellow villagers. But villagers are watchful and wary. Alternative *naya netas* are available in most villages, and any hint of cheating or diminished effectiveness can result in a transfer of allegiance by a majority of villagers.[12]

---

[11] Interview with Mothulal Vaishnava, *naya neta* of Kailashpuri village, Udaipur district (May 22, 2002).

[12] Such large-scale transfers of allegiance are not unknown. Villagers cast their lot with some *naya neta* depending upon how well he serves their needs, i.e., how honestly, dedicatedly, effectively, and efficiently he conducts transactions on their behalf. Reputation plays an important part in determining how much villagers respect some new leader. Most new leaders, in particular, politically ambitious ones, are keen to present an image of selfless duty to villagers. The truth, however, may be quite different from the image.

Rather than being pyramid shaped, the structure of political exchange in this context is more akin to an hourglass. The man in the middle constitutes a critical central point, and chains of influence emanate both upward and downward.

What accounts for these quite significant changes of the past two decades? How have otherwise ordinary villagers managed to seize a greater share of benefits from democracy for themselves? How has the stranglehold of rich and powerful villagers been displaced? And what has given rise to the new modes of political exchange?

The rise of new leaders in central Indian villages

Three factors help account, in my view, for the relative decline of caste leaders' and village strongmen's political influence and for the concurrent rise of *naya netas* in these villages. As discussed in the Introduction to this volume, education, state expansion, and intensified party competition are important for understanding change in the mode of political exchange. All three factors have played an important role in the transition of the past twenty-five years.

Education: In the context of central India, Sisson (1972: 323) had anticipated that education would produce democratizing effects such that "new and more assertive leadership from among [Scheduled Castes and Scheduled Tribes] will arise," who because of their higher education levels "will be less responsive to the paternal cues that have customarily emanated from well-intentioned, high-caste patrons." Other, more recent, analyses have shown how educational attainments influence the quality of democracy (Dreze and Sen 1997). It is not coincidental, thus, that a rapid rise in educational attainment has proceeded alongside considerable deepening and widening of democratic practices.

In terms of functional literacy – defined here as attending school for at least five years – younger villagers are considerably further ahead of their older counterparts. Only 18 percent of villagers aged 55 years and older are functionally literate, but nearly 70 percent of villagers in the age group 18 to 25 years have gone to school for five years or longer.[13] Within the space of a single generation there has been a fourfold increase in functional literacy.

A vast network of government-run schools has been spread out over the last three decades, and although the quality of education provided in

---

[13] These figures are based on a random sample of 1,898 villagers in sixty Rajasthan villages interviewed between 1999 and 2000. Krishna (2002a) provides more details in this regard.

these schools is far from perfect (Dreze and Sen 1995), it does enable all village children, even those of the comparatively poorer villagers, to attend school and to learn the basics of reading, writing, and arithmetic. Nearly every village in Rajasthan and Madhya Pradesh now has a primary school located within its boundaries. At the time of independence from colonial rule educational facilities were almost non-existent in rural areas.

A rapid expansion of functional literacy among villagers – from under 20 percent to over 70 percent within the space of a single generation – has been accompanied by a very considerable narrowing of difference between upper and lower castes. Among villagers aged over 55 years, 41 percent of upper castes but only 6 percent of Scheduled Castes are functionally literate. Among the younger generation of villagers, however, this difference is much smaller; 81 percent of upper castes aged 18–25 years are functionally literate – but so are 72 percent of backward and Scheduled Castes of this age group. The size of the caste gap has narrowed to 9 percent, and it is narrowing further as more and more younger villagers go to school.

The advantages that upper castes possessed in terms of functional literacy have tended to erode over time. Caste differentials in terms of educational ability are no longer very salient for explaining differences in political efficacy.

Rising educational ability has helped equip poorer and lower-caste villagers with an independent capacity for dealing with the bureaucratic state. They are no longer as much in need of interpreters and scribes from among upper-caste village elites (Robinson 1988). Many more *naya netas* have arisen from among backward castes and the former untouchables than might have been possible without this expansion of state-run rural schools.

Expanding state programs in rural areas constitute the second part of the explanation for the rise of *naya netas*. While an expansion of education has increased the supply of potential *naya netas*, the rapid enlargement of state programs has enhanced the demand for their services. Government funding for rural development schemes increased sevenfold (in inflation-adjusted terms) in the period between 1980 and 1995 (GOI 1998), and it has increased further in more recent years. While expenditure on the sixteen schemes classified together as Rural Development was about 1 billion rupees in Rajasthan in fiscal year 1992–93, it was more than double this amount just four years later.[14]

---

[14] Rather than reducing its programs and budgetary expenses, as the logic of liberalization might have required, the government in India has selected through the 1990s to expand its presence in rural areas.

Utilized mostly on public works programs intended to construct community assets, such as school buildings, approach roads, and health centers, funds expended on rural development projects are also intended to provide employment and wages to large numbers of village residents. In the five-year period 1992–97, upward of 4 billion rupees were allocated for various rural employment schemes in Rajasthan, and 104 million person-days of employment were generated, i.e., approximately ten days of wage employment for every adult who lives in rural areas.[15]

Sustained and expanded continuously for over twenty years, these employment generation programs have become critical to the everyday lives of ordinary villagers. As many as 45 percent, almost half, of more than 2,000 villagers whom we interviewed mentioned that the wages they made working on such government projects constituted a critical component of their expected annual incomes. Without earning these wages on a regular basis, they would lose the ability to pay for basic household expenses, such as food. The creation of such dependence on government programs among a substantial constituency of voters provides momentum for the growth that has been witnessed in these programs' funding.

A huge effort is required for implementing the vast numbers of small projects that constitute the portfolio of rural development work. Full-time government staffs are not able to cope by themselves with the demands of overseeing large numbers of small and scattered projects in distant and often quite remote villages. Officials look to find suitable villagers who can work informally on their behalf.

Several lower- and middle-level officials of different implementing departments testified to their increased reliance on unofficial cadres of "mates" and *mistris,* educated villagers who undertake site supervision on their behalf:

I have been in this [Soil Conservation] Department for 21 years. First there were mostly large works. Four or five engineers used to work on the same site. Now there are many more local sites . . . My unit has work sites in 24 villages, located many kilometers away from each other. It is not easy to get around. I cannot visit any site more than once every month or two months . . . and my official assistants cannot go more than once a week. In between our visits, local persons supervise the work . . . Without their help we cannot achieve our targets . . . Everyone in a village knows who has supervised [labor-generating] works in the past . . . We had such "mates" earlier also in our large sites, but they worked

---

[15] Similar employment-generating schemes were being implemented at the same time in other Indian states. In the state of Maharashtra, approximately "nine days of employment for each worker in the rural labor force" were provided by government-run schemes in the late 1980s (Echeverri-Gent 1993: 94).

under our direct supervision. Now we must rely on these persons much more. They measure and record the work; they take the attendance of laborers; they handle local payments.[16]

It is not just employment-generating government departments that look to local intermediaries for achieving their annual targets of work. Officials in numerous other departments also rely increasingly upon the services provided by such village intermediaries. A government doctor testified how "[we] cannot achieve our targets [for family planning] unless . . . [some] important villager helps us. We look after these fellows when they bring patients to us at the hospital, and we go to them when we need help for achieving our family planning targets." A senior banker recounted how bank managers in rural areas need local persons who can fill out loan application forms on behalf of other villagers and who can help them recover the loaned amounts. Several other officials I interviewed, including police officers, veterinary surgeons, and agriculture extension agents commonly mentioned how, because of a vast and scattered work program, they rely – unofficially, but quite centrally – upon intermediaries at the village level.

The increased demand for intermediaries on the part of diverse government officials has arisen at about the same time that expanding education has worked to supply a near-ideal set of potential intermediaries. Several educated village youths have become supervisors of government-run projects. They are educated, so they can be relied upon to maintain records and accounts. They are unemployed, so they can work long hours, supervising construction on public works.[17] They will continue to live within the village, so they cannot hope to get away with it if they conspire with officials to cheat, exploit, or under-pay villagers.

Caste and ritual status are not relevant to these transactions. Personal ability and trust are far more important. Villagers trust a local leader who ensures that wages are paid fairly and on time. Officials trust a village intermediary who is able to keep complete and accurate records and on whose assurance large numbers of villagers will turn out to work. Neither side is particularly concerned with the caste of the village intermediary.[18]

---

[16] Interview with M. K. Singh, assistant engineer, Soil Conservation Department, Udaipur (July 10, 1998). Name disguised at the request of the respondent.

[17] Comparatively few educated village youths have succeeded in finding regular jobs in the private or public sectors in urban areas.

[18] Some particularly finicky high-caste officials may not eat at the same table as a lower-caste "mate," but in the process of selecting who will be "mate," competence usually counts higher than caste rank. Caste continues to be important for personal and social relations, but in the economic and political realms it is considerably less salient.

Many *naya netas* have put together multicaste village networks that help distribute available work opportunities fairly among different caste groups. Logar Lal Dangi, an influential new leader of Nauwa village, Udaipur district, had the following to say about his relationships with other villagers and government officials:

We have a team now . . . Tekaram among the Bhils, Sangram Singh among Rebaris, and others; we all work together. I convince the villagers that the project is sound and that they will be paid fairly, even if the payment is a little delayed. On my guarantee, the village shopkeeper gives *atta* [flour] and other goods to them against future wages. To government officials and NGO supervisors, I promise a loyal and hardworking labor force. We protect these officials against complaints and inquiries – but they must pay the laborers fully and on time.[19]

Another *naya neta*, Mothuram Vaishnav, reported a similar view:

Officials come to us when they want some work implemented. They know we can get it done . . . and no one else in the village. We also [take the initiative and] go to government officials ourselves. We want employment for our fellow villagers, and they want to achieve their work targets . . . Within the village, we rotate whatever employment is available, so that all who need wages are able to get a fair share.[20]

Neither Logar nor Mothuram belongs to a high caste, but each has a relationship of equality with government officials. Each of them also plays a critical leadership role in his village.

People's aspirations have changed, and leaders who are not able to help achieve these aspirations have been replaced by others who can do better in this regard. In some villages that I visited, older and less educated village leaders have accepted mostly gracefully and peaceably this ascent of *naya netas*.[21] But in many other villages power has not passed over easily or without struggle. Khivaram, a Scheduled Caste, is a *naya neta* of Sangawas village. Together with Sawai Singh, a Rajput, and other villagers from different castes, Khivaram has successfully struggled against the dominance of a group led by Girdhari Singh, the traditional strongman and hereditary patron of this village.

They registered false police cases against us when we started agitating against their corrupt practices in the panchayat [elected village council]. Girdhari Singh would use his political connections to pressurize the police and the local administration. But Sawai Singh and I are educated. We went and met the Collector [the head of the district administration] and we told him that we had been falsely implicated.

[19] Interviewed in Nauwa village, Udaipur district (June 25–26, 1998).
[20] Interviewed in Udaipur (May 13, 2002).
[21] "We are not able to do what the youngsters can achieve . . . *samai badalta hai* [times change] and we must change with it" (interview with Chaturbhuj Gujar, Balesariya village, Bhilwara district, July 25, 1998).

I produced *written* proof that panchayat funds had been stolen. I told him there was only hearsay evidence against us, the police had nothing firm to go on. We went many times . . . [until finally] the cases against us were closed . . . We kept up our work in the village. We collected funds among our group, and I went back to the Collector to ask for a matching grant under [a government] scheme for constructing an additional building for our village school . . . We invited the Collector and the Superintendent of Police to inspect the new building . . . I have got to know many government officials now. Our group has taken up other development projects with funding from other government departments. Nearly all villagers are with us now, and not even five percent are with the other group. Many political leaders meet us first when they come looking for votes in our village.[22]

An educated youngster belonging to a Scheduled Caste took on the upper-caste patriarch of his village, and – because of superior education and better knowledge about the rules and processes of the state bureaucracy – the younger leader prevailed. The rules of the game have changed, and the nature of power and influence in villages has changed as a result. The old upper-caste patrons are no longer able to exercise authority unchallenged. As Bailey (1960) and Sisson (1972) had expected, relationships established *outside* the village have enabled a new group of village leaders to acquire status and authority *within* the village community.

Politicians have been quick to seize upon the growing influence of *naya netas* and turn it to their own advantage. Intensified party competition over the last twenty-five years has provided a sharper edge to this contest for local influence.

Intensified party competition: For the first time, after 25 years of uninterrupted rule by the Congress Party, a different party came to power in Rajasthan (and in Madhya Pradesh) in 1977. Parties have alternated in power since then, with the Congress Party returning to power in Rajasthan in 1980, 1985, and 1998, and the Bharatiya Janata Party (or BJP) returning as the majority party in 1990 and 1993. Because each party is now more realistically a contender for power at the state level, competition for votes has become more intense in the countryside.

Neither the BJP nor the Congress (nor any other political party for that matter) has any stable or deep-rooted organization that can help it compete for votes. So each party strikes temporary alliances with pre-existing social formations. Caste-based and traditional patronage-based local organizations were important earlier in politicians' calculations of electoral influence (Brass 1994; Kothari 1988; Manor 1997; Weiner

---

[22] Interviewed in Sangawas village, Rajsamand district (August 1, 1998).

1986). But politicians of all hues have been quick to realize that alternative networks and different leaders have taken root in these villages, and they have fashioned new devices to attract *naya netas* within their fold.

Starting in 1993, members of parliament have voted to allocate substantial budgetary provisions to themselves, which they use to finance infrastructure building and employment-generating activities in villages. Budgetary provision for the Members of Parliament Local Area Development Scheme has increased year after year since this scheme was introduced. In fiscal year 1998–99, a sum of Rs. 10 million was allocated for this purpose to every MP. In 1999–2000, this allocation was doubled.

Members of Legislative Assemblies (MLAs) have also voted similar budgetary subventions for themselves. In fiscal year 1998–99, each MLA in the state of Rajasthan was provided with Rs. 500,000 which he or she could use to fund development works in villages. For 1999–2000, each MLA was allocated a sum of Rs. 2.5 million, a fivefold increase over the previous year. More recently, this allocation has been further enhanced.

Naya netas play a prominent role in negotiations between politicians and villagers related to how these funds are spent. Which village will get what part of an MP's or MLA's discretionary fund is determined in large part by which village has the more effective negotiator. More effective *naya netas*, such as Goverdhan Gayari of Sema village and Gangaram of Dantisar village, have been able to harness larger amounts of funds for projects located in their villages.[23]

Political leaders have also provided comparatively large allocations to Ramâ village, where Narulal Dangi has played the role of negotiator. It is interesting to note that even though Narulal Dangi is a self-proclaimed BJP supporter, the local Congress Party MLA is wooing him with funds.

Party alliances are a matter of expediency in these villages. One never knows when a *naya neta* might not be willing to cross party lines. Many of them do so with considerable regularity. Politicians are only too glad to deal with effective leaders, with large numbers of followers in their village. New leaders who have acquired a considerable following among fellow villagers constitute very attractive targets for politicians.

---

[23] *Naya netas* also play large roles in negotiating the locations of other types of development programs. Officials have considerable discretion in determining where these funds are spent. They usually prefer to find local projects in villages where reliable and experienced intermediaries are available.

Parties, patrons, and clients

Who is the patron and who the client is not entirely clear within these transactions. To some extent, since MPs and MLAs control the purse strings, they should be regarded as patrons. But *naya netas* are hardly client-like in the traditional sense of the term. For instance, I can hardly imagine them tipping their hats to politicians or behaving subserviently in any other manner. These overt and symbolic manifestations apart, *naya netas* also have a real choice in terms of which politician they will select as patron and for how long. Politicians chase after *naya netas* for support as much or more than *naya netas* chase after politicians.

Parties rely upon *naya netas*, and *naya netas* expect that parties will, in return, channel additional development benefits to their village. If there is any patron–client relationship in this case, it is a horizontal one, based on equality of status on both sides and easy entry and exit for all parties; it is not a vertical or a closed relationship.

Logar Lal Dangi, *naya neta* of Nauwa village, narrated the following story related to senior politicians:

> We voted for the Congress first. Then Shanti Lal Chaplot [BJP member from the Udaipur constituency and Speaker of the Rajasthan State Assembly] came to our village. We prepared a ceremony to receive him, and we had him lay the foundation stone for a new community center. Just as he was about to do so, he asked "Where is the money coming from for this project?" We said "Don't you know? It is coming from you. You came here so you should do some good for this village" . . . Chaplot Saheb got us funds from DRDA [the District Rural Development Agency of the government]. Before the next election, he got us funding for a new drinking water scheme. 90 percent of villagers voted for him.[24]

Naya netas are not bound to any particular party politician. And ordinary villagers are similarly not bound to any particular *naya neta*. They can choose to utilize the services and join the bandwagon of one *naya neta*, and they may choose alternatively to remain aloof or join with another *naya neta*. Usually (but not always) there is more than one *naya neta* in a village, and villagers have no particular reason, other than personal advantage, for remaining loyal to a particular individual.

Caste does not form any important part of the new leadership; neither does religion. Jabbar Khan, a Muslim, is a prominent new leader in Chitakhera village of Ajmer district, whom I have known for the past ten years. His two lieutenants are both Hindus, and their followers in the village are drawn equally from Muslims and Hindus. These are the leaders who have the best record of gaining benefits from the state and from

---

[24] Interview with Logar Lal Dangi, Nauwa village, Udaipur district (June 25–26, 1998).

market operations, and they have widespread support in their village, regardless of caste or religion.

This is not to say that a different dynamic, more caste- or religion-based, cannot displace the one that is currently dominant in these villages. Incentives sent down by the state – in the form of expanding educational infrastructure, widespread construction and employment programs, and fiercer inter-party competition for votes – have generated impetus for a particular form of political exchange. As these incentives change, perhaps helped along by canny political entrepreneurs, newer modes of political transaction might develop in these villages.

What might the future hold?

The advent of *naya netas* represents a welcome new development, in my view. Participation and contestation have both increased, thereby deepening democracy on both of Dahl's (1971) dimensions. Barriers to entry that existed twenty-five years ago have been lowered substantially, and many more ordinary villagers have gained access to the benefits of democracy.

Naya netas do not, however, constitute a sustainable solution to the vacuum of upward representation that separates villagers from the Indian state. Parties continue to be weakly organized, and villagers still cannot resort to party channels – or to any other institutionalized channels for making connections with the state. When they need to communicate upward, with government officials or party functionaries, villagers seek assistance from particular individuals instead of institutions. The nature of these individuals has changed, no doubt. Upper-caste and landed individuals have been replaced to a significant extent by *naya netas*. Traditional bonds of servitude and loyalty have given way to newer and more equal relationships in villages of this region. But there are still no institutionalized venues that villagers can easily access.

Naya netas represent at best a temporary and makeshift solution to the problem of the missing middle. They are not a permanent and institutionalized force that can stand in place of well-organized political parties. Some *naya netas* get jobs in urban areas, and they leave the village. Others give up their leadership position to spend more time with their families.

It might be possible to build new parties that draw in recruits from among *naya netas*. But I am not sanguine about this possibility. Referring to political parties in India, Yadav (1996: 100) observes that "Most of these political formations, which serve as instruments of democratization of society . . . are themselves completely undemocratic in their organizational set-up as well as style of functioning." Party nominations are not usually awarded in any democratic or transparent manner, and family connections often count as much as or more than ability or service to the constituency.

It becomes hard, thus, to imagine that a group of people will arise who will have the incentive and the resources to build well-organized political parties. Until such parties get built, however, *naya netas* will continue to provide the best alternative available to ordinary villagers in these rural Indian settings.

7 Rethinking economics and institutions: the voter's dilemma and democratic accountability

Mona M. Lyne

What are the key features of delegation and accountability that structure the relationship between voters and their elected representatives? Can we construct a general theory that can account for variation in patterns of linkage and levels of accountability across democracies? In this chapter I take a step toward such a general theory by considering how the collective nature of electoral accountability confronts voters with a critical collective action problem, what I call "the voter's dilemma." A close examination of the delegation relationship between voters and their elected representative reveals that voters face a collective action problem akin to a prisoner's dilemma in delegating to politicians to provide collective goods. I argue that this voter's dilemma is the central causal factor driving voters' choice for either clientelistic or programmatic goods. The voter's dilemma highlights how the strategic context created by collective accountability can compel voters of all income levels to relinquish their statutory authority to pass judgment on overall policy in return for a quid pro quo. The theory thus provides a parsimonious general explanation for the widely varying efficacy of the electoral connection across democracies.

In the second half of the chapter, I integrate the voter's dilemma with the new institutionalism. The voter's dilemma explains whether direct, clientelistic linkages, or indirect linkages based on the delivery of some package of national and local collective goods will predominate in a given polity. New institutional theory as currently construed treats direct and indirect exchange as equivalent for the purposes of understanding how institutions shape politicians' strategies. As I will demonstrate below, however, the direct or indirect nature of links between voters and politicians radically alters the requirements for credit-claiming with voters, and thus also dramatically alters how institutional variation shapes credit-claiming strategies. I integrate the voter's dilemma and institutional analysis to generate a new set of hypotheses for party behavior aimed at credit-claiming with voters for the case when voters opt for a direct, clientelistic relationship to politicians. The result transforms what is currently a dichotomous typology into a fourfold typology that can resolve important anomalies confronting institutional analysis.

Finally, I test the theory of the voter's dilemma directly against institutional theory in explaining important changes in patterns of credit-claiming behavior in Brazil. Despite constancy in all key institutions across the two most recent periods of democracy in Brazil (1945–64 and 1989–present), an examination of both intra-party unity as well as inter-party divisiveness demonstrates that contemporary Brazilian parties exhibit considerably more programmatic behavior than in the prior period. I develop a new measure of clientelism based on the degree to which politicians' bases of electoral support are built upon blocs of delivered votes, and I demonstrate that direct linkages have given way to indirect exchange by showing that bloc vote delivery has declined both cross-sectionally across periods as well as longitudinally within the current period. This shift in the dominant linkage pattern in turn explains changes in parties' credit-claiming behavior across the two periods.

Current theories of democratic accountability and the failure of political entrepreneurship

Poverty-based theories of clientelism, as well as formal institutional theories share a preference for a micro-foundational explanation for political actors' choices and the resulting relationships of delegation and accountability. Yet both of these approaches fail to take their essentially rational-choice understanding of delegation and accountability to its logical conclusion. Developmentalist scholars emphasize the short time horizons of low-income voters, whereas institutionalists emphasize the constraints of disaggregative institutions, but neither approach provides a convincing explanation for why competitive elections fail to drive a competition to resolve these obstacles to more effective policy.

The original formulation of new institutional arguments suggested that restricting voters' choices to higher levels of aggregation should better align politicians' incentives with the promulgation of broad national public policy. The more institutions drive voters to choose the national executive and their legislator on the basis of the direction of national public policy, the more electoral accountability will produce broad collective goods.[1] Douglass North (1990) argues forcefully, however, that

---

[1] See for example, Cain, Ferejohn, and Fiorina (1987); Ramsayer and Rosenbluth (1993); Cox and Rosenbluth (1995); and Carey and Shugart (1995). A revisionist view can be found in Shugart (2003). For a discussion of why the revision does not resolve key anomalies for the theory, see Lyne (2005).

institutions are endogenous to electoral politics. If this is correct, how can politicians who maintain the institutions that produce such disastrous outcomes in many developing democracies survive, and even thrive? If institutions are the key variable driving the abysmal public policy outcomes commonly observed in many developing democracies, then we would expect abundant electoral gains to accrue to those political entrepreneurs who found a way to mitigate their effects. In short, institutional theories cannot convincingly account for the vast gap in the efficiency of choices in what is purportedly the same political market across developed and developing democracies.

Similarly, poverty-based explanations do not provide a convincing explanation for failures of welfare-enhancing entrepreneurship in many developing countries. According to this school, low-income voters' short time horizons, typically driven by substantive need, compel them to accept an immediate material reward in direct exchange for their vote. Yet if clientelism is driven by constraints faced by *individual* voters, then the problem is akin to any other side-payment problem for achieving Pareto-improving policy change. Why couldn't welfare-enhancing politicians/parties provide side payments to low-income voters in the form of soup kitchens, group-based insurance schemes, and other forms of assistance? There is no theoretical reason why this type of side payment, coupled with welfare-enhancing policy reform, would not be an attractive solution to these voters' individual constraints. Thus, a poverty-based explanation, just as with an institutional explanation, leads us back to similar questions about why political entrepreneurship fails in some democracies but not in others.[2] I argue that a general theory of delegation and accountability must provide an account of the failure of political entrepreneurship in many competitive democracies. It must also explain the failures of modernization theory raised by O'Donnell (1979): why does more effective accountability often fail to take hold even in the context of rising per capita income and considerable socioeconomic modernization?

---

[2] In the Introduction the editors allude to the high organizational costs associated with organizing to solve individual voter time horizon problems as well as the collective action problems associated with providing collective goods. But this begs the question of why this took place in some democracies (arguably, the United States, Great Britain, Scandinavia) but not in others that were apparently on a similar upward political and economic development trajectory, such as Argentina (1912–30) and Brazil (1945–64). This is precisely the puzzle raised by O'Donnell (1979): why weren't several decades of apparent progress in democratic reform and economic development sufficient to lay the foundation for this kind of evolution in political organization?

Democratic accountability as collective accountability: the voter's dilemma

I argue that the electoral appeal of clientelism stems not from the specific characteristics of some voters, but from a universal feature of electoral delegation. The view that clientelism prevails primarily at low levels of income rests heavily on the assumption that individual voters have the power to choose and receive either clientelistic or programmatic goods. This conception of the link between voters and politicians overlooks a key feature of electoral delegation. An individual voter cannot elect or vote out a given politician – electoral accountability is inherently a problem of collective accountability. The individual voter's ability to reward a good agent with reelection, or punish a bad agent with electoral defeat depends on the actions of many other voters in the district. In short, electoral sanctioning is a problem of social, not individual, choice.[3]

If we combine asymmetry of excludability with collective accountability, we gain a more accurate picture of the obstacles the individual voter confronts in successfully delegating to an elected representative to provide collective goods. Successful delegation to procure collective goods requires that a winning coalition of voters opt for some collective goods candidate. Yet each individual voter has no guarantee that other voters will in fact choose a collective goods candidate. Moreover, the difference in excludability that defines clientelistic versus collective goods means that voters have powerful incentives to doubt the collective goods commitments of other voters. The voter who opts for a collective goods candidate while a winning coalition chooses a clientelistic candidate receives neither collective nor clientelistic goods. At the same time, those in the clientelistic coalition have used their vote to secure their place in a system of exclusionary politics. Conversely, a voter who votes for a clientelistic candidate while a winning coalition elects a collective goods candidate still receives the collective goods.

The difference in excludability, combined with collective accountability, means a clientelistic vote provides the individual voter with an "insurance policy" that potentially protects him from the vagaries of other voters' choices. A clientelistic vote has the potential of providing protection against being excluded from political benefits should the voter's clientelistic candidate win. A collective goods vote does not. The upshot is clear:

---

[3] In the language of principal–agent theory, voters are a collective principal, not a single principal (Kiewiet and McCubbins 1991). Other scholars have recognized the problem of collective accountability inherent in electoral sanctioning (see Ferejohn 1986, 1999; Lohmann 1998), but none have coupled this with the asymmetry of excludability between collective and clientelistic goods.

due to the fact that clientelistic goods are excludable goods tied directly to the delivery of their votes, voters attempting to use elections to procure collective goods will find themselves in an n-person prisoner's dilemma, with its well-known free-rider problems. Voters avoid the "sucker's pay-off" by opting for individually targeted benefits (clientelistic goods), *rather than* choosing on the basis of *any* mix of locally and nationally targeted non-excludable goods. The voter's dilemma thus implies that it is not a simple increase in income that makes it possible for voters to choose collective goods. The collective nature of the choice means that it is only when voters can ignore the effects of free-riding on their own welfare that they will find it possible to use elections to hold politicians accountable for collective goods.

In order to translate this individual calculus to the aggregate level and determine when clientelistic or collective goods strategies will prevail in a given electoral contest, we must specify five types of players, and define their individual prices and the aggregate price of a given election. Producers can either extract under inefficient property rights (*rent-seekers*), or compete under efficient property rights that impose market discipline on most producers most of the time (*profit-seekers*).[4] Each producer has a reservation income (I), at or above which he prefers extractive property rights because the marginal return on his time investment is higher.[5] Below this threshold I, the producer will trade leisure for effort in order to increase his income. Voters either sell their vote in a direct exchange for some excludable political good and become *clients*, or make their choice based on some weighting of local and national collective goods and become *citizens*. Finally, we have *politicians*, who may be the agents of either the general citizenry (which includes voters and profit-seekers), or of rent-seekers.

We can define a voter's reservation price as the price at or above which she will trade her vote for an excludable benefit and become a client. Because individual voters cannot exercise the option for programmatic

---

[4] Rent-seekers are typically socioeconomic elites whose dominance provides them with the means to buy off clients. The classic example is the feudal lord or the latifundista, whose dominance is based on access to land in an agricultural economy. Clientelistic exchange, however, can be built on any scarce valuable resource such as an industrial job under import substitution industrialization. In most developing countries, producers who were socioeconomic elites initially bought off clients and delegated to politicians to maintain the property rights and policies that allowed them to do so. As development proceeds, this relationship may shift, as politicians, through control of resources such as bureaucratic jobs, become the actors able to deliver votes *and* design policy.

[5] Extraction requires simply utilizing resources to create output, whereas profit-seeking requires the much more difficult task of utilizing resources to create output *more efficiently* than current practice.

goods, a voter will vote for a programmatic party, and ignore the possibility that others will free-ride, only when the proffered clientelistic benefit has insignificant value to the voter. How voters value clientelistic goods is in turn driven by the degree to which he is dependent on clientelistic exchange to maintain his standard of living. A voter's reservation price will be set at a level that is at or above what he can easily procure through his own efforts in the private market. Thus, middle-class voters will not trade their vote for the minimal reward offered to voters in the informal economy (shoes, building materials, food) or even for a working-class job, because their level of skill and education makes it relatively easy to maintain a higher standard of living in the private market. And a middle-class voter who controls assets or has secure employment outside of the clientelistic system that allows him to maintain his standard of living, may even refuse the relatively high remuneration and very generous benefits associated with a white-collar position in the government bureaucracy. But a middle-class voter who does not own such wealth or have such opportunities in the private market will find such a good highly valuable. In other words, since collective accountability means voters cannot choose and receive collective goods, their best choice is to weigh whether the proffered clientelistic good will maintain or improve their standard of living relative to what their skills and education will allow them to obtain in the private market. Finally, we can define the reservation price of a given election as the sum of the reservation prices of the voters that make up a given winning coalition. The election for any given office has a reservation price which is equal to the *lowest-priced possible winning coalition* of voters.[6]

Clientelistic linkages will dominate as long as politicians can maintain rent-seekers' threshold income and pay the reservation price of the election.[7] Under these conditions rent-seekers become the *de facto* democratic principals and delegate to politicians to maintain property rights and adopt policies that allow them to extract from clients.[8] Under these

---

[6] The size of the winning coalition of voters depends on electoral law, and may also be constrained by other institutional or organizational factors. As I will argue below, in clientelistic systems voters are typically organized into blocs that deliver their votes in mass. To the extent that brokers can control the members of these blocs, it may not be possible to bid away a single voter. Any deal that includes one voter of the bloc may have to include all voters in the bloc. Thus, winning coalitions may be constrained by the way voters are organized into blocs. Such blocs may, but do not necessarily, correspond to political parties.

[7] A fully general argument about when direct or indirect linkages will dominate must also discuss supply of resources for striking clientelistic bargains. Due to space considerations I do not discuss supply here. For the full argument, see Lyne (2005b).

[8] Resources for direct exchange are available from a variety of sources, including rent-seeking producers, control of the government apparatus, and authority to design property

same conditions voters relinquish their ability to influence public policy and sell their votes for an excludable benefit, and become clients.

Programmatic strategies will become electorally viable *only* once politicians cannot maintain rent-seekers' threshold income *and* pay the reservation price of the election. At this point, available resources cannot meet the reservation price of any possible winning coalition of voters. If politicians can no longer pay the reservation price of the election (which implies rent-seekers' income is already at threshold and no new resources can be found), this means that there is no longer any viable winning coalition of voters that will risk something of value in eschewing clientelistic goods. Under these conditions, voters can ignore free-riders and delegate to politicians to provide collective goods, and politicians thus enforce a mix of efficient property rights and rents/pork which force most economic agents to profit-seek in the market most of the time.

Programmatic strategies become more competitive once politicians can no longer pay the reservation price of the election because the benefits producers and voters receive with programmatic politics are not zero-sum. There is a finite limit to what can be extracted from a given endowment of resources, and what one producer receives from preferential production rights another producer loses.[9] In contrast, the profits available from innovation are technically unlimited. One producer's gain from innovation does not preclude another producer's gain based on distinct innovations. Similarly, when jobs are created by direct subsidy and delivered to voters in direct exchange, the job one voter receives another voter necessarily loses. In comparison, when votes are won with the provision of collective goods such as economic growth based on innovation, this zero-sum problem is avoided. The job one voter receives based on entrepreneurial success does not preclude the job another voter receives based on some other profit-seeking investment. At the point at which the reservation price can no longer be met, a programmatic politician can campaign on the promise of replacing extractive

---

rights. Thus, as alluded to in n. 4 above, politicians can come to compete with or complement rent-seekers in their control and distribution of resources for building clientelistic networks.

[9] This is not meant to imply that clientelistic economies are static and producers simply extract as much as possible from initial endowments. Even when property rights do not reward investment in more efficient use of available resources, clientelistic economies are not static because the endowment itself and what can be extracted from it is dynamic. For example, the value placed on a given natural resource can change over time, domestic producers' bargaining position with international investors can improve such that they can demand more of the surplus, etc. The point is that the politics of direct exchange means clientelistic economies are organized around extraction, rather than around investment in innovation, even if the basis of extraction is dynamic over time.

property rights with market-driven property rights, providing profit-seeking opportunities for former rent-seekers now willing to trade leisure for income. Simultaneously, market-driven property rights will generate jobs for former clients who are no longer receiving at least their reservation price.

To summarize, the voter's dilemma provides a theory to explain why competitive elections often fail completely as a mechanism for driving politicians to welfare-enhancing entrepreneurship. When voters opt for a quid pro quo, they necessarily forgo their ability to pass judgment on overall policy, and thus, improvements in overall outcomes that follow from welfare-enhancing policy change are not registered in voters' choices. Under these conditions, elections' ability to discipline the welfare effects of politicians' policy choices is lost. It is important to emphasize how this differs when voters and politicians are linked through indirect exchange. Even when voters heavily weight the delivery of non-excludable *locally targeted goods* (often labeled pork or particularism), they do not relinquish the possibility of also looking at overall outcomes in making their choice. As long as the voter is not trading her vote directly, she can weight local and overall results in any way she chooses. Thus, with indirect exchange, acceptable overall outcomes always remain a background condition constraining the distribution of locally targeted goods, and elections serve as an important brake on politicians' ability to serve the few at the expense of the many.

This causal theory of clientelism differs from that presented in the Introduction and in other chapters in a couple of important ways. First, it views voters as price-makers rather than price-takers. This means that the structural factors cited in the Introduction as causes of clientelism are endogenous to how supply and demand cash out for the majority of voters. Thus, structural factors such as the timing of introduction of mass politics versus professionalization of the bureaucracy, the politicization of the political economy, and ethnocultural division will not be exploited to construct large-scale clientelist networks if supply and demand cash out to minimal risk for voters to reject clientelism. Of course, some small-scale clientelistic networks might fly under the radar of rationally ignorant voters in an otherwise collective-goods oriented polity. The point is that voters are not passive vessels that accept whatever prevailing structural conditions make possible in the way of direct or indirect exchange. Instead, voters are typically *either* trying to maximize the value of a quid pro quo good, *or* are weighing some combination of overall outcomes and locally targeted goods, and politicians compete fiercely to provide the clientelistic goods or find the right combination of non-excludable goods that draws the greatest voter support.

A second important difference stems from the definition and effects of clientelism. In contrast to other authors, I view the critical feature of clientelism to be true direct exchange (rather than implicit bargains, rewards and punishments to party members (as opposed to voters)) which forces voters to forgo their ability to pass judgment on overall outcomes. Any other kind of relationship that does not force voters to exchange their vote directly (this includes group monitoring that successfully rewards and punishes) means that overall outcomes always have the potential to play a deciding role in voters' choices, and thus to discipline politicians' policy choices.

If the level and type of provision of basic collective goods are acceptable to voters, then this factor apparently disappears as a causal force in voting choices, as voters use their vote to then drive politicians to compete in the distribution of more specialized benefits. But if overall outcomes deteriorate to the point that they become unacceptable to voters (take for example the levels of inflation that accompanied the substantial, but short-lived growth in Latin America post-war), as long as voters are not monitored in a quid pro quo, they can always alter the weighting they place on basic collective goods from almost zero to something much higher. As long as there is no quid pro quo, even quite heavy emphasis on the delivery of highly specialized goods has roughly similar effects on the electoral connection and thus policy outcome as do other forms of emphasis on localized non-excludable goods (pork-barreling). Thus, the voter-politician relationships depicted in other chapters in countries such as Japan, Belgium, and Austria, for example, do not seem to debilitate democratic accountability any more than do highly candidate-centered systems such as the United States. The background threat of high weighting of overall outcomes in voting choices forces politicians to maintain specialized benefits within certain bounds.

In short, for the important questions impinging on the effectiveness of democratic accountability, all three of these are linked. Clientelism means forgoing passing judgment on overall policy, clientelism severs the link between electoral success and economic performance, and thus, unlike polities exhibiting apparently massive specialized benefit provision but not quid pro quo, deteriorating overall outcomes will not lead to electoral sanctions that drive politicians back to welfare-enhancing improvements. The dividing line in terms of where democratic accountability essentially succeeds and essentially fails is drawn by whether a sufficient number of voters can eschew direct exchange with minimal risk and vote for politicians providing *and claiming electoral credit for* some mix of non-excludable goods.

The role of economic development

The voter's dilemma demonstrates that changes at the macro level do not impinge directly on individual voter choices, but are mediated through how they affect supply and demand, and thus how they affect the risk voters face in rejecting clientelism. This formulation allows us to resolve some of the key anomalies that plagued poverty-based and developmentalist theories of linkage. Economic development can increase the available extractable wealth, increase the number of rent-seekers or their threshold income, or increase the reservation price of an election. The manner in which these different possible effects of development cash out to change the nexus of supply and demand determine their effect on linkage.

There are many different ways in which economic development can increase available extractable wealth. Discovery of new resources, introduction of new technology or new types of production can all increase the level of extractable wealth. This is one way to think about the shift from export agriculture to import substitution industrialization (ISI) in Latin America. The property rights which underpinned ISI, including market reserves and preferential access to subsidized foreign exchange, provided a whole new range of policies for extracting from the majority of consumers and delivering to the emerging urban groups of the period.

Economic development can also increase the number of rent-seekers or their threshold income. The shift to industrialization in most developing countries did not entail an elimination of landed elites, but instead the layering on of a new set of rent-seekers chosen to produce manufactured goods for the domestic market. Finally, economic development can raise voters' average income level and skill set and thus raise the costs of providing voters with goods of non-negligible value. This in turn will raise the reservation price of the election.

The effect of economic development on linkages depends on the interaction of these different factors. *Ceteris paribus*, if economic development increases extractable wealth it will prolong the viability of clientelistic politics. But if economic development increases the number (and thus the aggregate threshold income) of rent-seekers, or increases the reservation price of a given election, *ceteris paribus*, it will hasten the demise of clientelism. It should be emphasized, however, that *only* when aggregate threshold income and reservation price outstrip available resources will we see a shift in the dominant linkage patterns. It is only at this point that voters can choose collective goods without facing high risks due to the possibility of other voters free-riding. To conclude, there is no one-to-one correspondence between economic development and a reduction

Table 7.1 *Synthesis of the voter's dilemma and institutions*

	The voter's dilemma	
Institutions	I. Clientelism Direct exchange link	II. Policy-based sanctioning Indirect link
A. Candidate-centered institutions	Decentralized direct exchange networks	Party–personal indirect link
	Observable implications: Lack of intra-party unity and lack of inter-party divisiveness	Observable implications: Moderate intra-party unity and moderate inter-party divisiveness
B. Party-centered institutions	Centralized direct exchange networks	Party-based indirect link
	Observable implications: High intra-party unity but lack of inter-party divisiveness	Observable implications: High intra-party unity and high inter-party divisiveness

in the risks voters face in rejecting clientelism. This explains why political development does not necessarily follow in lock step with economic development, as modernization theory had it.

The voter's dilemma and institutions: a synthesis

In this section I integrate the voter's dilemma and institutional arguments and I develop observable implications for party behavior aimed at credit claiming with voters. If the theory presented here is correct, the effect of institutions on politicians' incentives is endogenous to the outcome of voter delegation in elections. If macro variables dictate that voters cannot ignore free-riding in using elections to procure collective goods, then politics will be organized around clientelistic exchanges. Under these macro conditions, institutions will shape the organization of clientelistic linkages. Party-centered versus candidate-centered electoral laws will alter the level of centralization, and who has "ownership" of distribution networks. But institutional variation will not alter the basic direct clientelistic link between voters and politicians. On the other hand, once macro variables dictate that voters can ignore free-riders in using elections to procure collective goods, electoral competition will reward the forging of indirect links, and institutions will condition politicians' choices between different mixes of national and locally targeted public goods as currently argued by new institutionalists. The synthesis of the voter's dilemma and institutional theory is presented in Table 7.1.

The distinct observable implications for each combination of linkage type and institutional rule stem from the fact that building each of the four different types of links creates different problems of credit-claiming with voters. When electoral competition favors indirect links to voters, politicians win votes by delivering some mix of national and locally targeted non-excludable goods as driven primarily by institutional rules. By definition, non-excludable goods are not delivered directly to voters, but are available to all members of the relevant political unit. Thus, the only way voters can be sure whom to reward for general policies is if the party regularly takes positions in favor of, and votes for, such policies, while other parties regularly oppose them. Intra-party unity in legislative voting is necessary for demonstrating issue position and for passing a legislative program, whereas inter-party difference in voting is necessary for claiming responsibility for passing certain types of legislation. If all parties vote to pass the same legislation, no particular party will be able to credibly claim they are distinct from the others in securing certain policies.

Thus, both intra-party discipline and inter-party divisiveness are crucial to surmounting the credit claiming problems associated with the indirect delivery of collective goods. This holds even when executive-legislative relations and electoral law promote candidate-centered voting. Candidate-centered voting will lead individual politicians to buck the party line more often and focus on providing locally targeted goods. This will certainly dilute the party label, and will be exhibited in less intra-party cohesion and inter-party divisiveness. But if politicians are to claim credit for *any* collective goods, a moderate degree of intra-party cohesion and intra-party divisiveness is necessary in order for voters to identify an agent responsible for passing such legislation. To the degree executive-legislative relations and electoral law create incentives for voters to cast a party vote, intra-party cohesion and inter-party divisiveness will rise. Under these institutions, party behavior is not diluted by legislators seeking to compete with copartisans by cultivating a personal link to voters.

When electoral competition rewards direct links, the tasks of demonstrating issue position and political responsibility are transformed into those of demonstrating access to political power and resources. Demonstrating this access and obtaining resources for delivering excludable goods is what makes claims in clientelistic systems credible. This is the root of the absence of inter-party divisiveness in such systems. As long as the legislative arena is the primary locus of decisions regarding the distribution of most government resources, we should expect low inter-party divisiveness because legislators or parties will be eager to join any legislative deals that can provide them with direct benefits.[10] By the same token, when goods are exchanged directly for votes, there is no need for parties to differentiate themselves in terms of issue position in the legislative arena. When voters cast their vote based on the receipt of a direct benefit, rather than based on issue position, principled legislative votes (the opposition voting against government legislation, for example) have no electoral value. In clientelistic systems, voters are not looking to a party's public record on legislation to determine their vote, but instead to whether the party has delivered. Under these conditions, any legislative vote that increases a party's ability to deliver is pure electoral gain.

The impact of institutional rules on parties' credit-claiming behavior in clientelist systems can be seen in differences in inter-party behavior. Institutional variation determines who "owns" the clientelist networks and maintains the reputation for delivering. With party-centered rules in which voters are allowed only a choice between different parties (cell IB), the party will "own" the clientelist networks and will be the agent with the reputation for delivering. Individual legislators become delegates assigned the task of maintaining these networks in the name of the party. Party leaders jealously guard the ownership of the clientelist networks, and must ensure that rank and file behavior maintains and enhances the party's reputation and ownership. Unpunished votes against the party might damage the party's reputation and, perhaps more importantly, create an opening for an individual deputy to demonstrate an independent ability to deliver. By punishing any transgression with a withdrawal of the party imprimatur, the party maintains the upper hand in reputation building. These parties have often been erroneously identified as collective goods parties because of the resulting high internal unity.[11]

When institutions permit voters to choose among politicians of the same party (cell IA), individual politicians become the carrier of the reputation for delivering, and individual politicians develop the direct exchange links to voters. Under these conditions, the most effective

[10] Rules that take decisions about resource distribution out of elected representatives' hands will alter this prediction. An example is Costa Rica, where the Constitution of 1949 created a range of autonomous administrative agencies, which in some cases designed, implemented, and raised revenues for their own budgets, and in others were protected from legislative reductions in their budgets below a specified level. See Mijeski (1977: 61–63).

[11] Venezuela is a prominent case in which monographic studies documented widespread clientelistic practices, yet stability and intra-party voting unity led many to argue these were nationally integrative programmatic parties. An exception to this characterization is Coppedge (1994), who notes that Venezuelan parties are an aberration in the extreme degree to which the leadership controls the rank and file.

electoral strategy will be to free those individual politicians to make their own decisions about legislative voting. Individual members who are responsible for creating their own reputations will have both the incentive and the best information for correctly determining how a particular vote will affect his ability to effect direct exchanges with voters. Since party reputation for delivering collective goods has no influence on voting choices, party vote totals are simply aggregations of individual politicians' vote totals, and thus a strategy that maximizes individual politicians' vote totals also maximizes the party vote. Paradoxically, then, the best electoral strategy for the party results in a pattern of low internal unity that many scholars have argued renders these institutions not parties at all.

An empirical test

Despite employing the same formal tools of accountability, democracies across the globe display widely varying levels of efficacy of the electoral connection. In particular, there seems to be an important divide between advanced industrial and developing democracies. Yet it is often difficult to design a test that can isolate the effects of a given independent variable while holding all others constant. The two most recent periods of democracy in Brazil (1945–64 and 1989–present) provide a rare opportunity to test one of the most prominent leading contenders: the new institutionalism. Many institutionalists have cited Brazil as a textbook case of the detrimental effects of highly disaggregative candidate-centered electoral law that decimates parties' ability to organize around issues of national scope (Ames 2001; Geddes 1994; Geddes and Ribeiro Neto 1992; Mainwaring 1992, 1995, 1999; Mainwaring and Perez-Liñán 1997; Shugart and Carey 1992). By examining the degree to which parties organize to provide voters with clear programmatic alternatives across the two periods that were governed by nearly identical institutional rules, including presidentialism, bicameralism (a Chamber of Deputies and a Senate), federalism, and open-list proportional representation, we can conduct a controlled test of the institutional argument.

Before examining the data some brief background is useful. The period of 1945–64 was characterized by a multiparty legislature with three large parties: the PSD (Social Democratic Party), the UDN (National Democratic Union), and the PTB (Brazilian Workers' Party); and the three small parties: the PSP (the Progressive Socialist Party), the PR (the Republican Party) and the PDC (the Christian Democratic Party). The party system that took shape in the late 1980s in Brazil had many similarities with the earlier period. It is once again a multiparty regime, with four large parties: the PMDB (the Party of the Brazilian Democratic

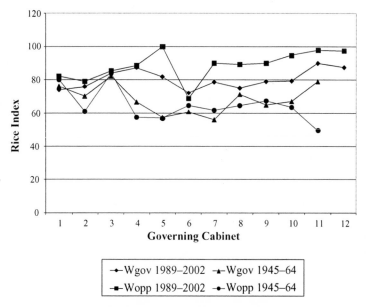

Figure 7.1   Roll call voting in the Brazilian Chamber of Deputies Rice Indexes (weighted averages)

Movement), the PFL (the Liberal Front Party), the PSDB (the Brazilian Social Democratic Party), and the PT (the Workers' Party); and two smaller parties: the PDT (the Democratic Labor Party) and the PDS/PPR/PPB (Democratic Social Party/Reformist Progressive Party/Brazilian Progressive Party).

Figure 7.1 above provides plots of average levels of intra-coalition unity (weighted Rice Index) on all roll calls for both the governing and the opposition coalitions across the two periods. The unit of observation is the governing cabinet, and I define the government coalition as the parties holding cabinet positions, and the opposition coalition is defined as the largest contiguous coalition to the left or the right of the government coalition. Figure 7.2 plots a measure of inter-coalition difference between governing and opposition coalitions on all roll calls and all coalition votes across both periods.[12] The standard measure of inter-party difference,

[12] Following Cooper et al. (1977) and Cox and McCubbins (1993), the level of divisiveness that defines a party vote is that at least 50 percent of one party opposes at least 50 percent of the other party. I adapt the measure to multiparty coalitions by defining a coalition vote as a vote in which at least 50 percent of the members of all of the parties in the governing coalition oppose at least 50 percent of the members of all of the parties in the opposition coalition.

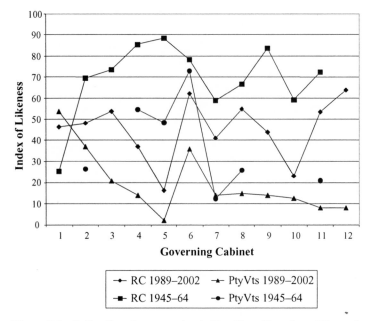

Figure 7.2   Roll call and party voting in Brazilian Chamber of Deputies (index of likeness)

the index of likeness, is a measure of the degree to which members of two groups (in this case, government and opposition coalition) vote the same way on a bill; the higher the index of likeness, the less inter-party divisiveness in legislative voting.[13]

As can be seen from the figures, both intra-party unity as well as inter-party divisiveness have risen considerably across the two periods. Figure 7.1 shows that increases in intra-party unity previously documented for individual parties also hold for both government and opposition on all roll calls.[14] Figure 7.2 also clearly highlights an important decrease in the index of likeness for all roll calls and all party votes (with the exception of

[13] The index of likeness is obtained by calculating the percentage of members from two separate parties or blocs that vote in the same direction and subtracting the difference from 100.

[14] Amorim-Neto and Santos (2001) demonstrated that the average Rice Index for the period from 1946–64 was 57, indicating that, on average, 78.5 percent of the members of a given party voted the same way on any given roll call. Limongi and Figueiredo (1995; see also Figueiredo and Limongi 2000), however, have shown that the average Rice Index for the current period (1989–98) has risen to 80, meaning that the "average floor discipline in the Lower House is 90 percent, that is, for any roll call 9 in 10 representatives voted according to their party leader recommendation" (2000: 158–59).

the second and seventh cabinets) across the two periods. The weighted average index of likeness on all roll calls is nearly twice as high in the earlier period as in the current period, and on party votes, the weighted average in the earlier period is almost three times what it is currently.[15]

The data are consistent with what we would expect if Brazil has moved from cell IA to cell IIA in Table 7.1 above. While in the earlier period both intra-party cohesion and inter-party divisiveness were low, in the current period both of these have risen to moderate levels comparable to other programmatic, candidate-centered presidential systems such as the United States.[16] Since the institutional context of both regimes is nearly identical, institutional theory sheds little light on these very important changes in party behavior.

These changes in Brazilian party behavior observed between the two periods are what we would expect if voters can now ignore free-riders in delegating to politicians to provide collective goods. Unfortunately, the theory of electoral sanctioning based on the voter's dilemma does not allow us to identify neat variables that can be directly measured to indicate which type of linkage prevails. The factors determining the predominance of direct or indirect linkages are aggregates of individual utility functions on the demand side, and combinations of structural and policy variables on the supply side, which cannot be measured and summed in any meaningful way. Moreover, as the concluding chapter discusses in great detail, the problems associated with gathering information directly from voters or politicians are legion. Despite these difficulties, I follow King, Koehane, and Verba (1994: 10) and argue that the availability of simple direct measures should not drive social science inquiry. As these authors argue, we must elaborate as many observable implications of our models as possible and develop more subtle, indirect tests of our theories.

We can develop an indirect measure of the type of linkage that predominates based on the most efficient strategy for maximizing votes for each linkage type. Exchanges that require direct distribution of benefits and monitoring can be carried out most efficiently by carving up the district into smaller discrete units or blocs and delegating the delivery and monitoring to brokers. Organizing to win most of the votes in a few

---

[15] The discontinuities in the graph of index of likeness from 1945 to 1964 reflect the fact that there were no party votes for five out of the twelve cabinets of the period. For more detailed data and figures, and a demonstration that a weighting of roll calls according to Carey's (2005) index of closeness enhances the conclusion of more programmatic behavior in the current period, see Lyne (2005a).

[16] Carey (2005) provides evidence from sixteen countries that indicates that Rice Indices in contemporary Brazil are only slightly lower than in Chile, and higher than in the US House and Senate.

blocs, rather than a few votes across many blocs will minimize the physical and knowledge resources required per vote delivered. In other words, the competitors most likely to prevail in clientelistic systems will be those who discern the basis on which the district can be carved up in order to deliver votes efficiently as a unit.

In contrast, when votes are won based on non-excludable programs, we should not expect such a "carving up" of the district and we should not expect the distribution of electoral support to reflect such bloc delivery. When votes are won based on collective goods, the vote spread of leading candidates will be more evenly distributed across the same units or blocs. Here there is no requirement for monitoring and exchange, and all else equal, we would expect that programmatic preferences will be evenly distributed across the units or blocs. Thus, as voters shift from clientelistic to collective goods, we should see a "deconcentration" of vote distribution across the district, as politicians attempt to appeal to all those with amenable preferences across the district. The analysis requires knowledge of the unit across which delivery takes place, and this may not always be a territorial unit. It could also be an occupational unit, such as a corporatist interest organization. But all clientelistic systems should exhibit this "carving up" of the electorate on some dimension that minimizes the costs to monitoring and delivering excludable goods.

Considerable monographic work indicates that in Brazil the unit of delivery of the vote was the municipality (Bezerra 1999; Leal 1977). Building on the pioneering work of Ames (2001), I use a measure of dominance across municipalities as an indicator of the kind of vote that is being cast in the two periods in Brazil. We can create a composite dominance score for any candidate by calculating the weighted average of each candidate's dominance in each individual municipality. Dominance in each municipality is simply the percentage of the total vote received by the given candidate in that municipality. Dominance scores for each municipality are then weighted by the percentage of the deputy's total vote received in that municipality and averaged. Candidates for federal deputy compete across all municipalities within the district of the federal state. Presidential candidates compete across all municipalities in the country.

Ideally, one should be able to control for socioeconomic factors that may render a municipality highly homogeneous in programmatic preference. But if we assume that such contamination of the data is random across candidates and across periods, then straight dominance scores should give a reasonable, albeit crude, measure of whether voters are choosing excludable or non-excludable goods. In general, when clientelism dominates, we should expect to see higher dominance scores for winning candidates in comparison to a system in which programmatic strategies dominate. We should also expect to see differences in the dominance scores of winning and losing candidates. If clientelism is predominant, what will differentiate winning and losing candidates will be overall vote totals, not level of dominance. Winning candidates will be those able to string together enough dominated municipalities such that their total exceeds the electoral threshold. Losing candidates will have similar dominance scores across individual municipalities, but will dominate fewer municipalities overall, giving them smaller overall vote totals. If programmatic politics is predominant, winning candidates will be those that enjoy widespread programmatic preference, and thus they may take a large percentage of the vote in many municipalities, particularly if they take a large percentage of the overall vote. Losing candidates, however, do not enjoy widespread programmatic preference, and thus we would expect that they would gain a few votes in each municipality, but dominate few municipalities.

The data on presidential candidates for both periods are displayed in Table 7.2 below. The number in parentheses is the percentage of vote won, and the first bold number gives the raw dominance score. Since there will be a systematic relationship between percentage of the vote won and dominance, the larger italic number, at the bottom of each cell gives the ratio of dominance to percentage of the vote won. This number thus gives a measure of dominance that controls for vote percentage. This is useful for comparing similarly placed candidates across elections.

As the raw dominance scores indicate, in the vast majority of cases, dominance scores are considerably higher in the earlier period for similarly placed candidates. In the cases in which dominance scores are similar for the same-placed candidates across the two periods (1st placed: Kubitschek and Quadros versus Cardoso I and II; 3rd placed: Fiuza and Barros versus Garotinho; 4th placed: Salgado versus Brizola and Gomes), there is only one case in which the ratio of dominance to vote percent is higher in the later period, which is that of Salgado versus Brizola.

Differences in dominance scores between winning and losing candidates in the same presidential elections are also consistent with a switch from clientelistic to collective goods competition. In the current period the winner's dominance score is almost twice that of the second-placed candidate, whereas in the earlier period this difference is only about 20 percent, despite the fact that the winner in the current period took a higher percentage of the vote than in the earlier period. Differences between winners and third-placed candidates are even more dramatic, with the exception of Garotinho. In the earlier period the third runner up has a dominance score somewhere between 40 and 89 percent of the winning

Table 7.2 *Municipal dominance of presidential candidates in Brazil by election year*

	placed 1st	placed 2nd	placed 3rd	placed 4th
1945	Dutra	Gomes (I)	Fiuza	Telles
	(52%)	(42%)	(5.3%)	(1.4%)
	0.59	*0.50*	*0.24*	*0.21*
	1.13	*1.19*	*6.86*	*15*
1955[a]	Kubtischek	Tavora	Barros	Salgado
	(36.2%)	(31.0%)	(24.5%)	(8.6%)
	0.47	*0.38*	*0.38*	*0.18*
	1.30	*1.23*	*1.55*	*2.09*
1960	Quadros	Lott	Barros	
	(48.8%)	(33%)	(18.2%)	
	0.51	*0.40*	*0.26*	
	1.05	*1.21*	*1.43*	
1994[a]	Cardoso I	Lula	Quercia	Brizola
	(61.1%)	(30.4%)	(4.9%)	(3.6%)
	0.47	*0.25*	*0.06*	*0.1*
	0.77	*0.82*	*1.22*	*2.78*
1998	Cardoso II	Lula	Gomes (II)	Carneiro
	(55.3%)	(31.0%)	(11.7%)	(2.1%)
	0.47	*0.29*	*0.13*	*0.02*
	0.84	*0.93*	*1.11*	*0.95*
2002	Lula	Serra	Garotinho	Gomes (II)
(1st Round)	(46.4%)	(23.2%)	(17.9%)	(12.0%)
	0.44	*0.26*	*0.22*	*0.16*
	0.94	*1.12*	*1.23*	*1.33*

[a] Data broken down by municipality were not available for the 1950 and 1989 elections.

candidate, whereas in the current period this difference is between 12 and 28 percent.

Data on federal deputies show similar trends. Table 7.3 reports the very incomplete results from the earlier period. The most complete data came from the 1946 election, in which eleven out of twenty-one states reported data (Alagoas, Bahia, Ceará, Goiás, Minas Gerais, Mato Grosso, Pará, Pernambuco, Rio de Janeiro, Rio Grande do Sul, Santa Catarina). In 1950, data exist only for three states: Bahia, Pernambuco, and Rio Grande do Sul. The data in 1954 are the same as 1950, with the addition of Sergipe. In 1958, data are available from Acre, Bahia, Mato Grosso, Rio Grande do Sul, and Sergipe. Finally, in 1962, we have data from Espírito Santo, Goiás, Mato Grosso, Piauí, Rio Grande do Sul, and Sergipe.

Table 7.3 *Percentage of deputies in lower Chamber with given level of dominance, 1946–1962*

	1946[a]	1950	1954	1958	1962
Dom > .1	80.0	68.0	74.3	72.6	85.7
Dom > .2	45.2	29.3	28.6	42.1	44.0
Dom > .3	25.2	5.3	6.7	11.6	8.8
Dom > .4	10.5	2.6	0.0	1.1	0.0
Dom > .5	4.3	0.0	0.0	0.0	2.2
Avg. Dom. In Leg.	0.223	0.162	0.163	0.173	0.193

[a]These data were gathered by the author, with the help of able research assistants in Brazil, by searching the stacks of the Brazilian National Elections Archive for the individual state reports sent to the National Election Commission. As the data indicate, I was unable to find reports for many of the states. To my knowledge this is the only centralized and the most complete database of municipal level vote distributions for legislative candidates for the period.

Source: Brazilian National Electoral Court Archives.

The data from 1946 are most complete and therefore most representative of the country as a whole, with two or more states reporting from four out of the five most important regions of the country, and one state from the fifth, northern region. In all other years, the data are seriously incomplete and not very representative of the country as a whole. If we compare 1946, the most complete set of data from the period, we see that it looks very much like 1986. Even with this limited data, however, we can note that in the latter three elections, average dominance scores increase, rather than decrease over time.

Turning to the current period, the evidence presented in Table 7.4 shows a declining trend of dominance in the current period up through 2002, with a small blip in 1998. And although the dominance scores for 1998 show an increase over 1994 and 1990 at the 0.1 and 0.2 levels, the average level of dominance in 1998 remains lower than in 1986. Overall, there is a clear decline in dominance over time in the current period.

The exception of the spike in 1998 and the maintenance of high percentages at the 0.1 dominance level deserve comment. Two factors made the 1998 elections unusual. First, the 1998 numbers may look artificially high because the 1994 numbers may have dropped more than the "normal" trend. This possibly resulted from the impeachment of the president in 1992 before the scheduled end of the term in 1994. Thus, it may be that networks of exchange were in more disarray than "normal" in 1994, and thus there was a greater drop that reflects disorganization

Table 7.4 *Percentage of deputies in lower chamber with given level of dominance, 1986–2002*

	1986[a]	1990	1994	1998	2002
Dom > .1	63.4	58.2	51.1	69.2	61.8
Dom > .2	46.4	38.6	16.8	44.2	34.3
Dom > .3	29.2	23.9	2.9	17.7	9.2
Dom > .4	15.2	10.5	0.4	4.7	2.3
Dom > .5	4.7	2.2	0.0	1.2	0.0
Avg. Dom. In Leg.	0.229	0.181	0.118	0.185	0.158

[a]In 1986 and 1990, some states are missing. The calculations of percentages are thus taken based on the total number of deputies for which dominance scores are available, rather than the total number of deputies in the Chamber for that legislature
Source: 1986–90, Barry Ames. 1994–2002 official web site of the Brazilian Electoral Tribunal.

rather than elimination of clientelistic exchange. Second, 1998 was the first re-election of a sitting president. This may have led to an unusual ability to build and maintain clientelistic networks across elections, and thus may be the cause of the spike. In other words, extreme discontinuity or unusual continuity of the chief executive (for this series) could well have introduced noise in the trend. Despite the spike in 1998, however, the data from 2002 show a continuing downward trend.

The maintenance of high percentages at the 0.1 level of dominance may well reflect Brazil's personalist electoral laws. Despite the decline in the viability of clientelism, legislators still have a strong incentive to cultivate personal votes, as cell IIA in Table 7.1 illustrates. Moreover, legislators no doubt continue to rely on municipal organization to build their personal reputation, and thus we can expect some dominance at the municipal level to remain. But since the personal reputation is based on indirect exchange and locally targeted public goods, and is tempered by collective goods preferences, we don't expect to see the high concentration of vote delivery by municipality that appears under clientelism.

Conclusion

The theory presented here provides a parsimonious general explanation for the variation in relationships of delegation and accountability that in turn drive variation in the efficacy of the electoral connection. Democracies with competitive elections fail to converge on roughly similar levels of political entrepreneurship due to factors inherent in electoral delegation to provide collective goods. This theory provides a reformulation of the poverty-based theory of variation in linkage, and its integration with institutional theory provides a more fine-grained theory of variation within the two linkage types. It was shown that this theory can explain changes in Brazilian party behavior that institutional theory alone cannot address.

8 Clientelism and portfolio diversification: a model of electoral investment with applications to Mexico

Beatriz Magaloni, Alberto Diaz-Cayeros, and Federico Estévez

Interest in the study of clientelism has reawakened in recent years. While the sociological and anthropological frameworks developed in the 1960s and 1970s still provide important insights into the logic of patron–client exchanges, a reckoning with the underlying political process that makes those forms of political linkage so prevalent is in order.[1] Clientelism was then viewed as a phenomenon typical of underdeveloped political systems, usually at early phases of institutionalization, often under authoritarian or colonial regimes. Indeed, the literature suggested that clientelism was the most characteristic form of political exchange occurring in backward agrarian societies. Presumably, as societies became more developed, social structures more differentiated, and political systems more institutionalized, clientelism was bound to disappear. Yet it has not. Throughout most of the developing world and even in many parts of the developed one, clientelism remains a political and electoral fact of life.

The defining trait of clientelism is that it involves direct exchanges between patrons and clients in which political support is traded for excludable benefits and services. Under what conditions do politicians attempt to buy votes through the provision of particularistic, excludable private goods, rather than through universalistic, non-excludable public goods? To answer this question, this chapter develops a portfolio theory of electoral investment and demonstrates its usefulness in the context of the erosion of hegemonic party rule in Mexico.

Research for this chapter was partially funded by the World Bank and the Academic Senate at UCLA. Superb research assistance was provided by Lorena Becerra and Arianna Sánchez. The electoral database was compiled by Jacqueline Martínez. The database on Pronasol spending was compiled by Marcela Gómez and Sandra Pineda. We thank Robert Bates, Herbert Kitschelt, John Londregan, Mona Lyne, Aaron Tornell, and participants in workshops at Stanford, Duke, and Berkeley for insightful comments. The views expressed, as well as errors remaining, are solely the responsibility of the authors.

[1] For some classic contributions see Lemarchand and Legg (1972), Scott (1972), and Lemarchand (1972).

Our theory proposes that the relative importance of clientelism *vis-à-vis* public goods provision depends upon the extent of poverty, political competition, and the level of electoral risk. We suggest that clientelism is a political investment strategy designed to deter voter exit and, simultaneously, to hedge electoral risks when more investment in public goods is required to win elections. While previous studies of clientelism have been unable to disentangle the effects of party system configuration and electoral risk from those of socioeconomic development, since they tend to be correlated through time in the course of the modernization process, our dataset allows us to separate the effect of socioeconomic modernization from those generated by electoral dynamics. In terms of modernization, we find that clientelism is most prevalent at intermediate ranges of development. Our findings also suggest that, controlling for levels of development, clientelism is less prevalent where there is more political competition. Nonetheless, consistent with the logic of the model, an incumbent party hedges electoral risks by investing disproportionately in clientelistic transfers in places where higher electoral risk reflects the defection of core supporters at rates faster than in the rest of the country.

The chapter is organized as follows. Clientelism is discussed next in the context of party hegemony in Mexico, reviewing the literature on clientelism and its insights about the distribution of public funds to political supporters. The following part presents the portfolio model of political investment, in which the logic of clientelism is clearly distinguished from that of the provision of public goods. Later, evidence is provided for the model, drawn from the case of the *Programa Nacional de Solidaridad* (Pronasol) in Mexico.

Sustaining hegemony through clientelism: deterring exit by targeting

Clientelism is characterized by dyadic personal relationships that are asymmetric but reciprocal. In electoral politics, this form of linkage translates into a direct exchange of private benefits and favors for votes. James Scott (1972: 125) argues that patron–client links are based on inequality, which arises from the fact that the "patron is in a position to supply unilaterally goods and services which the potential client and his family need for their survival and well-being." As a monopolist with control over critical resources, the patron is in a position to exploit his market power and demand compliance from those who wish a share of those goods. If the client did not need these goods, or if she had savings and alternative sources of income, or if she had the resources to move to another jurisdiction in order to secure needed services, she might not succumb to the patron's domination. The patron–client relationship is also asymmetrical because there is normally just one patron and a multiplicity of clients. Clientelism, however, is a form of reciprocal exchange. Politicians must deliver in order to sustain the support of their clienteles, and clients must support their patron with votes. Potential shirking from either side to the contract creates an inevitable problem of commitment, the solution to which makes clientelism advantageous for electioneering but inefficient for social welfare.

In our view, clientelism pervades monopolistic political markets because it allows politicians to *deter* exit (Diaz-Cayeros, Magaloni, and Weingast 2002; Medina and Stokes this volume; and Magaloni forthcoming). To understand how clientelism serves to sustain a political monopoly, imagine a voter who faces the following choice: support the incumbent party and receive transfers in the form of jobs, income supplements, credit and the like, or opt for the opposition and receive none of these desirable benefits. Unless the voter possesses alternative sources of income and is indifferent to those benefits, her rational strategy is to support the incumbent, even if reluctantly. If most voters reason likewise, the political monopolist will remain in power. The dilemma voters face is one of coordination. If all could agree simultaneously to vote against the incumbent, they could defeat it; but if voters can't coordinate, each will fear to be the first to defect and face punishment in the form of lack of access to vital resources. In equilibrium, the incumbent party maintains its monopoly at the local level, not because voters prefer it to the alternatives, but because a credible threat of punishment inhibits exit.

This type of hegemonic equilibrium is maintained through a clientelistic form of political exchange. In Mexico, clientelistic exchange was based, first, on the monopoly over fiscal resources in the hands of the national PRI (*Partido Revolucionario Institucional*), and second, on the PRI's ability to target transfers by screening between supporters and opponents. Defecting to the opposition entailed a credible threat of exclusion from the stream of benefits that the PRI *qua* political monopolist controlled.

What is the difference between clientelism and other forms of democratic exchange in which politicians trade policies for votes? As in Medina and Stokes, we believe that the main difference lies in that the discretional nature of particularistic transfers always implies a credible threat of exclusion, should the client renege on her political commitments to the patron.[2] Thus, we invariably associate clientelism with the trade of

---

[2] In a somewhat different argument, but where credibility figures prominently, Phil Keefer (2003) suggests that clientelism emerges because politicians fail to credibly commit to a promise of delivering goods equally to all voters.

excludable benefits for political support. Public goods that are not divisible imply that a voter can support whichever politician she chooses, and still benefit from such policies.

Robinson and Verdier (2002: 1) provide a model in which clientelism represents a solution to this commitment problem. "By its very nature, since the law cannot be used to enforce [clientelistic] political exchanges, they must be self-enforcing. The problem of credibility is two-sided. Citizens/voters must indeed deliver their support, and politicians, once in power, must pay for their support with the policies they promised." In their model, the solution to the commitment problem is given by trading employment in the public sector for political support. We agree with Robinson and Verdier that the commitment problem is central to understanding clientelistic ties. We believe, however, that public jobs are only one of many possible instruments that politicians use to deal with this problem. In the analysis that follows, we implicitly assume that the more a party can target transfers, the better it can solve the commitment problem.

The PRI in Mexico could choose to target transfers to the individual, the local jurisdiction, or not to target at all, by investing in public goods extending beyond the locality. Public goods cannot solve the commitment problem, because they generate non-excludable and irreversible benefits. Local public works, however, are less risky than public goods spanning beyond a single political jurisdiction. Local or small-scale public goods allow the ruling party to employ *geographic targeting* according to the landscape of political units as in Diaz-Cayeros, Magaloni, and Weingast (2002). Nonetheless, in contrast to particularistic transfers, public works do not fully solve the commitment problem – once the party transfers a public good to a locality, it cannot be certain that *all* voters, especially those who prefer the opposition on ideological grounds, will comply with their part of the exchange. And once delivered, a public good cannot be withdrawn, as is clearly the case with private resource transfers.[3] This is the reason why we believe public goods are always riskier than private outlays.

Private benefits such as jobs and other transfers better solve the commitment problem. A party can identify voters individually, screen between supporters and opponents, and invest only in those core constituencies that will support it with certainty. A party requires a dense organizational network to successfully deliver these transfers and identify loyal partisans from all non-partisans who have incentives to misrepresent their type. Historically, the organizational network that the PRI employed to

---

[3] Diaz-Cayeros, Magaloni, and Weingast (2002) do not discuss the commitment problem since they assume that the locality coordinates in some way to reelect the PRI.

deliver private transfers ranged from party-affiliated unions and local party bosses, to schoolteachers, *caciques* (local bosses) and *presidentes eji-dales* (the heads of the *ejidos*, a form of communal landholding). The goods that the party distributed through these networks ranged from land and water rights, cheap credit and fertilizers, to subsidized food, scholarships, and government-built housing, among many others.

The PRI did not coerce voters into choosing the ruling party over the opposition; it did not need to do so. In smaller and isolated localities there was often not even a menu of electoral choices. Even in the presence of some opposition, often all that the PRI really needed to do to get peasants to cast a vote for the party was to pay for their transportation, because peasants' "sincere" preference was the PRI. Peasants freely chose the PRI, although their choice was constrained. On the one hand, the PRI could use its monopolistic control over key resources to buy their support; and on the other, its network of party organizations and government agencies permitted it to monitor the political behavior of its clients in the countryside and in small cities. By threatening, whether explicitly or not, to suspend or withdraw the transfers that peasants needed, the PRI thus managed to deter rural voters from supporting another party or engaging in any form of open confrontation with the regime.

The story of the larger and wealthier localities is different. Since the early 1950s, the opposition had an important presence in the larger cities. Mexico City, for example, was the earliest opposition bastion (Ames 1970; Klesner 1996; Molinar Horcasitas 1991). Until the 1980s, the PRI enjoyed political support among the working class affiliated with the official unions. It also attempted to build clientelistic links among the migrant poor in the city slums and among informal sector workers (Cornelius 1975). To these groups, the party offered property titles, subsidized housing and food, work opportunities, and licenses for selling merchandise in the numerous flea markets of the cities, among other inducements. However, with the onset of the debt crisis, the urban poor were not loyal to the PRI, as became clear in the 1988 presidential elections when they defected *en masse* to Cuauhtémoc Cárdenas. Even some sectors of organized labor, traditionally unconditional in their support for the party, including the powerful oil workers' union, supported Cárdenas in that election.

Why was the PRI much weaker in the larger and wealthier localities? One key difference between the city and the countryside, we argue, is voter heterogeneity. The overwhelming majority of the urban poor that abandoned the PRI in 1988, for example, came from the low-skilled service sector of the economy – taxi and other public transportation drivers, domestic employees, low-level bureaucrats, nurses, etc. There was no functional party organization that could encompass such dissimilar groups largely because these groups had few goals in common. Without efficient party organization, shirking from the clientelist contract became pervasive. The second difference between city and country is related to income levels. Richer voters are much less susceptible to vote-buying (Dixit and Londregan 1996). Modernization helps to undermine party hegemony because it makes clientelism less effective, as it is much more expensive to deter wealthier localities from voting for the opposition. The model below seeks to provide an understanding of how a political monopoly under threat might respond to electoral competition.

A strategy of portfolio diversification

The choice of clientelistic strategies is driven by both demand and supply factors. The most important demand factor stressed by the literature is the economic status of citizens, which permits them to accept or reject this type of exchange. If voters have an income elasticity of public good demand larger than one, they will prefer less clientelism delivered by government as they become richer. Other factors on the demand side are correlated with economic status: cognitive capabilities that depend on literacy rates, and organizational capabilities that depend on membership in voluntary and independent associations. Thus, a socioeconomic theory of clientelism is primarily a demand-side account.

Although explaining the demand for clientelism is important, our framework takes that demand as given and focuses on clientelist exchange as a strategic choice made by politicians.[4] The existing literature stresses the lack of a professional bureaucracy and the motivations that historically led politicians and parties to mobilize voters through clientelist inducements. In formal models of clientelism, its supply is constrained by monopoly over the control of valuable resources (Medina and Stokes this volume; Robinson and Verdier 2002). This chapter models the supply side as a budgetary decision by a risk-averse politician seeking to achieve a desired level of electoral support.

The gist of the model is the following: an incumbent party seeking reelection must decide how to allocate a basket of discretionary transfers to voters. These transfers range from private, excludable outlays that can be individually targeted, to non-excludable public goods that are targeted to a jurisdiction or consumed by all voter groups across several

---

[4] We thank Bob Bates for clarifying the supply and demand aspects of clientelism. For a discussion of clientelism as supply and demand based, see Shefter, Martin (1994), and Piattoni (2001).

jurisdictions. As instruments of electoral investment, these transfers differ in (a) their relative budgetary cost; (b) their expected electoral return, defined as the expected number of votes from a unit of transfer; and (c) their level of electoral risk. The model assumes a positive correlation between expected yields and risks – risky investments yield higher expected electoral returns.

Risk varies according to the "publicness" of the electoral investment instrument. Private, excludable transfers that can only be consumed by a party's core supporters are risk-free, while public, non-excludable goods that can be consumed by all voters, regardless of partisan ties, are the riskiest. Risk-free private goods do not, however, yield the highest electoral return, since fewer voters can normally be targeted through clientelism and governments face budget constraints. Private transfers can be extremely expensive due to the transaction costs that must be overcome for effective targeting and to the amount of vote-buying needed to ensure election victories. In contrast, public goods reduce transaction costs and are more cost-effective per beneficiary. But they are much riskier than private goods, because the incumbent can invest in them without receiving any *ex post* electoral pay-off.

The model is derived from a portfolio diversification approach to electoral investment. Incumbent politicians buy votes in order to stay in office, but are risk-averse. They would rather invest resources in private transfers targeted to loyal voters than spend on public goods consumed by all and with uncertain electoral yields. In their quest for a high electoral return, however, they shift their electoral investments into public goods that offer higher returns, notwithstanding the risks involved.

The diversification logic of "safety first" suggests that a party will never devote all of its financial resources to the provision of public goods. The electoral yield of public goods is potentially high, since they benefit a larger group of voters, but also highly uncertain. Private goods, in contrast, are safer bets; they assure, through the monitoring and compliance mechanisms entailed in clientelism, that beneficiaries will support the incumbent party. The problem of finding the politically optimal allocation of public funds from the incumbent's point of view can be conceived as a decision over the relative allocation of funds among particularistic and collective goods projects. Figure 8.1 depicts such a choice between a public good yielding an uncertain electoral return, described by the expected vote value $E[X]$ with known variance σ^2; and a private good with a smaller but certain electoral return, denoted $Y < E[X]$.[5] A crucial assumption in this framework is that the electoral return of clientelism does not match

[5] We thank Aaron Tornell for suggesting this depiction of the portfolio model.

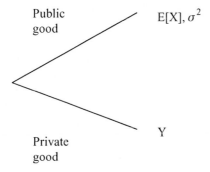

Figure 8.1 Incumbent choice set and expected payoffs

the expected return on public goods. But public goods do not embody monitoring and compliance mechanisms that ensure voters' support, the way clientelism does. Hence, while the vote return of public good investments is a random variable, with uncertain realizations (although with mean and variance known *ex ante*), the vote return from clientelism is assured. The two values are expressed in terms of the votes that an allocation of the entire budget (B) to each type of good would generate.

Hence, the electoral returns Y and E[X] incorporate both a budget constraint and the relative cost of public versus private good provision. Given a fixed budget B that can finance n_y private transfers with a unitary cost c_y for each beneficiary, if there are no transaction costs or commitment problems in the clientelist exchange, n_y voters would support the party for sure (when $B = n_y c_y$; $Y = n_y = B/c_y$). This means that the vote return of clientelism is given by the budget divided by a fixed unitary cost of each private transfer. For example, the unitary cost could represent the market price of a sack of grain, and the assumption in this framework is that the incumbent can be certain of receiving as many votes as the sacks of grains it distributes, given the size of its budget and the clientelistic networks already in place.

Of course, the effectiveness of private transfers depends on the relative propensity of voters to exchange their votes for money. For destitute voters, a small private transfer, such as a sack of grain, is likely to tilt their voting choice. With relatively rich voters, more generous private transfers will be needed. In either case, the size of the budget limits the provision of particularistic goods.

Alternatively, the budget could be allocated to a public good with total cost $C_x = B$. The number of voters that support the party with this strategy is uncertain (and might depend, for example, on a complex relationship given by heterogeneous public good demand functions). We depict a reduced-form expression of this relationship in Figure 8.1, which says simply that the electoral yield of public goods (X) is a random variable that depends on an aggregate propensity to support the party that provides such benefits, with a known variance.

When budgets are not divisible, the choice-theoretic problem is whether to provide public or private goods. This choice hinges on the degree of risk aversion characterizing an incumbent. Even if public good provision has an expected yield greater than that of private transfers, an acutely risk-averse incumbent will prefer the safety of private good provision. Of course, the return on private transfers must be large enough to satisfy the minimum vote share necessary to keep the incumbent in office. This condition in turn depends on how cheap it is to buy votes from core constituencies. Hence, the central feature of the socioeconomic theory of clientelism, namely the association between poverty and clientelism, is accounted for in this model by the demand-side assumption that it is cheap to buy votes from the poor.

Budgets, however, are rarely if ever indivisible. Consequently, incumbents can be better off combining both clientelism and public goods in their investment portfolios, provided they have a preference over risk. If incumbents were risk-neutral, they would obtain no advantage from diversification, because they would have no use for risk hedging.

We assume that incumbents seek to obtain a given vote level that ensures their permanence in power, with the least possible risk. Their optimal strategy is then to find a diversified allocation of funds between public and private goods, devoting a proportion α of the budget to public goods, and the remainder $(1 - \alpha)$ to private ones. This strategy yields a higher overall return, taking advantage of the electoral opportunities afforded by public good provision, while hedging risks through an optimal combination with the risk-free investment.[6]

The problem for the incumbent can then be reformulated into that of finding a combination of public and private goods that minimizes risk (the variance in vote returns), given the constraint of a desired level of expected electoral support. The vote constraint is given by:

$$V = \alpha E[X] + (1 - \alpha)Y \tag{1}$$

where V is the exogenously desired level of votes (which may be well above a bare majority). Risk is measured by the variance in the total vote:

$$S = \alpha^2 \sigma_y^2 + 2\alpha(1 - \alpha)\sigma_{xy} + (1 - \alpha)^2 \sigma_x^2 \tag{2}$$

---

[6] A mixed portfolio *always* involves less risk (except when the covariance of both goods is 1).

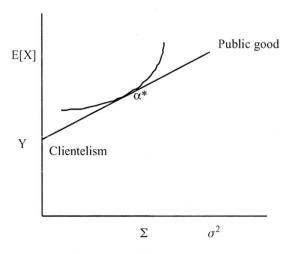

Figure 8.2 Closed form solution

Since private goods are assumed to provide a constant electoral return, the variance of private goods and its covariance with public ones is zero, $\sigma_x = \sigma_{xy} = 0$, which means that the variance in the total vote is only the first term in (2), the variance of public goods, discounted by its (squared) share in the portfolio.

A constrained maximization of (2) given (1) yields:

$$\alpha^* = \lambda(\text{E}\,[\text{X}] - \text{Y})/2\sigma^2 \tag{3}$$

where λ is a Lagrange multiplier, denoting the degree of risk that is acceptable to the incumbent. This expression signifies that the optimal portfolio of electoral investments depends on individual risk-aversion, the variance of public good returns, and the spread between the electoral returns of public versus private goods.

Hence, *ceteris paribus*, the comparative statics of this expression predict that the proportion of private good allocations or clientelism will be higher:

> The smaller the difference in yield between the two types of goods
> The greater the risk of the public good
> The higher the politician's risk-aversion

Figure 8.2 depicts the solution to the problem in a standard mean-variance space, showing a specific allocation of the electoral investment portfolio, given by an indifference curve.[7] The space depicts two goods,

---

[7] To simplify the exposition we have not introduced a utility function, which gives closure to the formal model. The mean-variance space and risk-aversion interpretation of the

labeled as clientelism and public good, according to their electoral yield and variance. The variance of clientelism is zero, but the votes it can provide are fewer than those of the risky investment in a public good. The difference between E[X] and Y on the vertical axis represents the first result in the comparative statics. As that gap grows, clientelism becomes less attractive. The variance on the horizontal axis represents the second result. As the level of risk increases, clientelism becomes more attractive as a "safety first" instrument. The line linking the public good and clientelism denotes all the possible combinations that produce intermediate risks and returns. Every point in the line yields a higher return in expected value than clientelism alone. In that sense, if politicians care about higher returns, diversification is always better than solely distributing private goods. Every point in the line also yields a lower risk than the public good, so diversification is attractive on the grounds of risk hedging. The specific solution to the composition of the investment portfolio depends on the curvature of the indifference curve (risk-acceptance, related to λ in the comparative statics), and the slope of the line (which depicts the relationship between risks and returns).

To sum up, the model suggests that the relative importance of clientelism depends upon the extensiveness of poverty, which makes it more prevalent; on political competition, which works at increasing public good provision; and electoral risk, which makes clientelism more attractive to incumbents. Were we able to measure politicians' attitudes towards electoral risk, our model suggests that more risk-averse politicians will maintain higher shares of clientelism in their portfolio mix. The next section provides some evidence on these predictions regarding the choice of clientelism as a response to electoral risk in the context of declining hegemonic control by the PRI in Mexico.

Clientelism and public goods in Mexico: the case of Pronasol

Launched in 1989 after one of the most contested and controversial presidential races in the history of the PRI, Pronasol's stated objective was poverty relief. Pronasol was the cornerstone of the Carlos Salinas government's war on poverty, with program expenditures averaging

---

utility function is a well-known result, dating back at least to Roy (1952). The simplest utility function that yields a mean-variance space like the one depicted in Figure 8.2 is a quadratic one. While economists dislike this functional form, in politics its properties are rather reasonable: at some point the marginal utility of some extra votes is negative, an assumption which is very reasonable for votes but not for money. See Hirschleifer and Riley (1992).

1.18 percent of GDP each year. This is a very significant amount. Had Pronasol resources been perfectly targeted as monetary transfers to the most desperately poor, about a third of Mexico's poverty could have been alleviated with those funds (World Bank 1999).

The program's true objective, however, was to halt the decline of the PRI's electoral hegemony.[8] Pronasol was organized around twenty programs, each of them geared toward various provisions of private or public goods. While earlier analyses of Pronasol's allocations have investigated the state- and municipal-level dynamics of the program, our work constitutes the first to present data on municipal-level allocations for the entire country and to provide an empirical assessment of the relative allocation of Pronasol funds between private goods targeted to core clienteles and public goods benefiting a wider range of voters, including opposition backers.

The coverage of Pronasol was so extensive that all municipalities in Mexico received some monies every year, although the composition by programs varied widely from year to year and among municipalities. By breaking down each program into the specific goods provided, we were able to classify the money spent according to two categories, consonant with the portfolio allocation model. The first are private goods, which we identify with clientelism and include strictly excludable goods delivered to individuals and organized groups of producers, Indians and women. For public goods we included both projects that were limited in their impact to local jurisdictions as well as projects that spanned the municipality and beyond. Clientelism in Pronasol expenditures is measured through the share of private goods in total spending and the per capita allocation of private goods. Table 8.6 in the Appendix provides a detailed description of the projects involved in each of the programs, and the way we classified them. The main indicator we used for the classification was information regarding the unit of measurement of the project, as reported in Table 8.6.

Throughout the life of the program, clientelism constituted 29 percent of the funds received by an average municipality. As the program became consolidated throughout the years, it became more clientelistic; when Pronasol was initiated in 1989, 25 percent of the funds distributed to the average municipality constituted private transfers; by 1994 the share had increased to 35 percent. The overwhelming majority of the municipalities were provided shares of private goods below 40 percent. This suggests that the PRI was providing public goods through Pronasol as a strategic

---

[8] The literature on Pronasol is extensive. Some references include articles in Cornelius *et al.* (1994), Bruhn (1996), Hiskey (1999), and Magaloni (forthcoming).

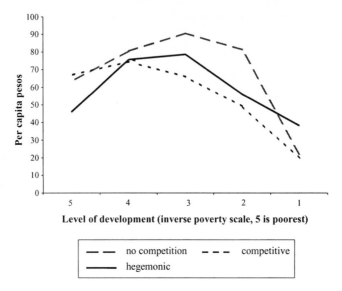

Figure 8.3 Pronasol spending on private goods per capita by municipality

effort to reach out to voters beyond its core clienteles. Most municipalities received combinations of goods, consonant with a portfolio diversification logic.

Diversification strategies can be distinguished according to two dimensions of interest: the poverty levels of municipalities as a measure of socioeconomic modernization, and the competitiveness of their party systems, as a measure of electoral considerations. Below we explore both of these issues.

Figure 8.3 shows the average per capita allocation of Pronasol in private goods (clientelism) disaggregated by socioeconomic development levels and partisan configurations. Development is measured through the deprivation index from the *Consejo Nacional de Población* (CONAPO), which is constructed with a factor analysis of census variables commonly associated with deprivation (illiteracy, no elementary school, dwellings lacking access to drinking water, sewage and electricity, quality of housing construction, population living in rural localities, and workers earning less than two minimum wages) (Consejo Nacional de la Población 1993). The figure reports how clientelism varies at different levels of development in municipalities characterized by various partisan configurations. We distinguish between municipalities without *any* electoral competition (the PRI received 100 percent of the vote); hegemonic municipalities, where there was some opposition presence, but the effective number of parties (using the Laakso-Taagepera (1979) index) was lower than 1.7; and competitive localities where there were two or more effective political parties (N above 1.7).

With regard to socioeconomic development, the graph shows that clientelism exhibits an inverted J-shape relationship, which is striking from the point of view of a modernization account. Regardless of party configurations, clientelism tends to be greatly eroded at the highest level of development (localities showing a deprivation index of 1, which represent only 5 percent of our observations). This suggests that, consonant with the socioeconomic theory of linkage-building, rich voters much prefer public goods provision over private transfers, which makes it too expensive for a party to attempt to buy them off through particularism. However, clientelism is most prevalent in middle-range levels of development (deprivation index of 4, 3, and 2, which represent close to 80 percent of our observations). In the poorest localities (14 percent of our observations at deprivation index 5) clientelism is higher than in the richest ones, but lower than in the intermediate ones. The figure thus suggests that voters in semi-urban localities and smaller cities are highly susceptible to vote buying, and that modernization does not erode clientelism until it surpasses a sufficiently high threshold.

The figure also shows how political competition impacts clientelism. As we expected, holding development levels constant, political competition induces politicians to invest more in public good provision in an attempt to cater to wider and more heterogeneous electorates. Note that at high levels of electoral competition, clientelism is abandoned very quickly; the inverted J almost becomes a downward sloping curve.

Electoral competition induces investment in public goods. However, a question remains as to whether electoral competition is responding to economic development, lacking an independent effect. Our dataset allows us to separate the socioeconomic from the political processes that influence clientelism. Development, of course, is correlated with political competition. However, the correlation between the deprivation index and the effective number of parties is negative, but moderate at best (-0.37), which means that there are poor localities with significant party competition and rich localities with none.

Table 8.1 shows how party system configurations are related to the CONAPO deprivation index. Among competitive configurations, the table distinguishes between bipartisan (N between 1.7 and 2.3) and multipartisan ones (N greater than 2.3). Indeed, the richest municipalities (with a CONAPO index of 1) tend to have more bipartisan and multipartisan configurations, but there are quite a few highly developed

Table 8.1 *Party system configurations and socioeconomic development (percentages)*

Marginality Index[a]	Non-competitive N = 1	Bipartisan		Multipartisan N > 2.3	Total
		Hegemonic 1 > N > 1.7	1.7 > N > 2.3		
Very high (5)	27	12	7	7	14
High (4)	44	37	26	15	34
Medium (3)	16	22	21	21	20
Low (2)	13	25	38	44	27
Very low (1)	1	3	8	14	5
Total	100	100	100	100	100

[a]CONAPO index measures marginality, so 5 is poorest, 1 is richest.

municipalities that are hegemonic. By the same token, the poorest municipalities (with a CONAPO index of 5) tend to have less competition, but there are many very poor localities that are competitive. Municipalities at middle-range levels of development exhibit almost an equal chance of being hegemonic or bipartisan. Multipartisan configurations are the least likely at all levels of development, but tend to concentrate in the richest municipalities.

Thus, electoral competition and development, while correlated, are clearly distinguishable variables. Holding political competition constant, there is more clientelism at middle-range levels of development; holding development constant, there is less recourse to clientelism as political competition increases.

An additional political variable that our portfolio model stresses is electoral risk. Our expectation is that political competition should lead politicians to diversify their portfolios, introducing more public good provision in an attempt to attract votes from a more heterogeneous electorate. Nonetheless, since public good provision is accompanied by higher risk, we expect politicians to attempt to hedge these risks by disproportionately investing in clientelism in the riskiest localities, holding levels of support constant.

Measuring risk in each municipality is not straightforward. One possibility is to measure the standard deviation of PRI support. This measure, however, is largest in those municipalities where PRI support has been highest. Given the general trend for convergence in levels of electoral support, a standard deviation measure would make the politically most backward municipalities seem to be the riskiest. The measure of risk we use instead, drawing from the finance literature, is the *systematic risk*

Table 8.2 *Beta coefficients according to party system and development*

Development index	No competition	Hegemonic	Two party	Multiparty	Total
Very high marginality	0.182	1.011	1.855	2.212	0.729
High marginality	0.336	1.096	1.854	2.193	1.038
Medium marginality	0.639	1.122	1.841	2.244	1.303
Low marginality	0.780	1.191	1.626	1.845	1.356
Very low marginality	0.393	1.081	1.216	1.497	1.178

for each municipality, controlling for electoral risk at the national level. Systematic risk is calculated through what the finance literature calls a *beta coefficient*[9] for each municipality, regressing the PRI's municipal vote share on its national vote share.

We measure risk as the coefficient of the independent variable in a linear regression of the form $Y = \alpha + \beta X$, where X is the national support for the PRI since 1970, and Y is the support in each municipality. Depending on the staggered electoral calendar of municipal elections, the number of observations is six or seven. National PRI support is calculated for each year according to the elections taking place in that particular year. This means that the national vote trend for the party depends on the specific states that held elections that year. This calculation allows for a comparison across municipalities that discounts the shocks that might occur to the national support for the party, isolating the risks that are specific to each locality. It also separates an idiosyncratic component of electoral volatility, the non-systematic risk (measured by the variance of the error term in the regression). Politicians cannot predict non-systematic risk, since it depends on random events that are, statistically speaking, mere "noise." Hence, they should not concentrate simply on how volatile vote shares are, but rather on their systematic behavior in comparison with national trends.

Table 8.2 reports the average beta coefficients calculated for Mexican municipalities according to the CONAPO classification of level of development and the partisan configuration given by the effective number of parties. Any coefficient above 1 implies that the municipality is riskier than national electoral trends. Places with risk below 1 compensate the national trends. Risky places, instead, would constitute attractive places

[9] For the seminal work introducing this concept see Sharpe (1964). A huge discussion emerged from the empirical work. See, in particular, Fama and French (1996). A good textbook discussion is Bodie *et al.* (2001). For one of the few applications of beta coefficients as risk measures in political science, see Crain, Messenheimer, and Tollison (1993). For an application to Mexico see Diaz-Cayeros, Magaloni, and Estevez (2003).

for electoral investment to the extent that they have high expected vote shares, or are pivotal for winning an election.

On average, municipalities are riskier than the nation as a whole for the PRI, since the average beta coefficient for all municipalities is slightly above 1 ($\beta = 1.15$). Furthermore, risk is linked to partisan configurations and more competitive municipalities entail higher risk for the PRI. Yet, as can be inferred from the table, risk and party configurations are different measures. There is large variance in the level of risk even among municipalities with the same partisan configuration. Starting from the last column, which shows the average risk regardless of party system, only the poorest municipalities show electoral behavior that can hedge against the national trends; in those places, given that PRI support has remained high, even as it falls elsewhere, the beta coefficient is less than one. Localities of high marginality show the same trend as the country as a whole. The next least risky municipalities are the richer areas of the country. This is probably due to the fact that competition there has stabilized or consolidated into two- and three-party systems, where the PRI is sometimes capable of reversing the national trend. The biggest collapses, and highest risks, were faced in bipartisan and multipartisan races, at intermediate and low levels of development.

Thus, electoral risk cannot be considered a consequence of economic development. Developed regions are riskier than the poorest areas, but when partisan configurations are taken into account, developed areas in the country with stable bipartisan and multiparty electoral configurations are less risky, from the incumbent's perspective, than poorer areas where electoral competition is just emerging. Hegemonic party configurations on average are slightly riskier than the nation; and it is only in non-competitive municipalities that electoral risk is less than in the country as a whole. The richest cities and the poorest rural municipalities are not the riskiest arenas of competition for the PRI. This provides a rationale for the greater emphasis on clientelism at intermediate levels of development.

To see that the beta coefficient as a measure of risk is not the consequence of political modernization, Table 8.3 groups municipalities according to whether their beta coefficient is above or below the municipal average. It also separates the outlier cases, namely, the coefficients that are outside one standard deviation on either side of the distribution. The average beta coefficient was 1.15, with a standard deviation of 1.30. Hence, we define as very low beta coefficients those that fall outside of the range on the mean minus one standard deviation ($b < -0.15$); as below average those that are within one standard deviation under the mean ($-0.15 < b < 1.15$); as above average, those within one standard

Table 8.3 *Risk distribution by level of development (percent)*

Beta coefficient	Very high marginality	High marginality	Medium marginality	Low marginality	Very low marginality
Very low	9	10	8	9	7
Below average	61	48	41	35	39
Above average	19	26	34	36	47
Very high	11	16	17	19	7
Total	100	100	100	100	100

Table 8.4 *Clientelism (private good provision) by risk and development (entries are the percentage of funds channeled to clientelism)*

Betacat	Very high marginality %	High marginality %	Medium marginality %	Low marginality %	Very low marginality %	Total %
min/−.15	22.8	24.5	24.1	20.2	15.1	22.6
−0.15/1.15	23.1	26.7	31.6	24.9	16.3	26.0
1.15/2.30	28.3	32.3	33.5	27.7	21.8	29.9
2.30/max	29.2	32.7	33.7	35.3	22.9	33.2
Total	25.0	29.0	32.1	27.6	19.3	28.6

deviation above the mean ($1.15 < b < 2.45$); and as very high, those that are above the one standard deviation range ($b > 2.45$).

The risk distribution is skewed to the left in very poor places, reflecting a modernization effect, in that poorer places are less risky. However, past an intermediate level of development the risk distributions are quite symmetric, and even slightly skewed to the right, suggesting greater-than-average risk in poorer areas. What this means in terms of the allocation of clientelism is that poor places might be given resources because they are poor, or because they are riskier places, where the PRI is losing support at faster rates than the national trend. If both poor and rich places are allocated more clientelism when they have high levels of risk, we can be relatively confident that the overriding consideration is electoral risk, rather than economic or social development.

Table 8.4 provides the final evidence that this is the case, by showing the average share of clientelism according to level of development and risk category. The final column in Table 8.4 reveals that clientelism increases with risk – while in low-risk areas clientelism constitutes about a fifth of Pronasol funds, in the highest-risk municipalities this share increases to one third. In places with very low marginality, clientelism is less prevalent, but the share still increases as risk increases. At intermediate levels of development clientelism is most prevalent, and still responds to risk. This general pattern is confirmed to be statistically significant in an unreported test of means as well as in a multivariate regression including controls for level of development.

In the remainder of this section, we explore the plausibility of our hypotheses more systematically. We employ a GLS maximum likelihood estimation of the share of private good provision in slightly less than 2,400 municipalities from 1989 to 1994. One lag of the dependent variable (*Lag*) is used to control for serial correlation. The independent variables are the level of development (*Develop*), using the deprivation index from CONAPO. The index was rescaled to take positive values ranging from 0 to 5. The rescaling also allows us to introduce a quadratic term (*Develop*^{2}), which tests whether development has a curvilinear relationship with the dependent variable. Our expectations are that, *ceteris paribus*, greater investment in clientelism should occur in poorer municipalities. The effect of the deprivation index should thus be positive. If development exercises a curvilinear effect and the quadratic term for the deprivation index is negative, it would signify that municipalities at middle levels of development receive larger shares of clientelist benefits.

We also employ the effective number of parties (*Effective N*) and the margin of victory (*Margin*) in the previous municipal race. Our argument is that clientelism is less efficient at vote buying in more heterogeneous and in more competitive municipalities. We thus expect these variables to have a negative sign. Due to the high correlation between *Effective N* and *Margin of victory*, we run these variables in separate models.

We also include our measure of systematic risk (*Beta/risk*), calculated through the *beta coefficient* that reflects how fast the PRI is losing votes in any municipality relative to the national trend for that party. Recall that this variable is calculated with municipal vote returns since the 1970s. Thus, our measure of risk reflects long-term electoral patterns that are missed when simply using the number of parties or margins of victory. The correlation between *risk* and effective number of parties is obviously positive, but not that strong (0.46). Similarly, our measure of risk is negatively correlated with margins of victory (0.40). Our expectation is that the PRI should hedge risks by investing more in clientelism in high-risk municipalities, those in which the PRI has been losing votes at a faster rate relative to the national trend. We thus expect systematic risk to show a positive sign. Because clientelism shares increased through the six years Pronasol operated, the analysis controls for the time trend (*Trend*). Our theory of political investment does not yield predictions regarding the particular combination of private versus public good provision in

Table 8.5 *Determinants of clientelism, 1989–1994*[a]

	Coef.	(SE)	z	Coef.	(SE)	z
Lag	0.32***	(0.01)	36.77	0.32***	(0.01)	37.50
Develop	0.11***	(0.01)	11.15	0.12***	(0.01)	11.64
Develop^2	−0.02***	(0.00)	−9.48	−0.02***	(0.00)	−9.87
Beta/risk	0.01***	(0.00)	5.23	0.01***	(0.00)	5.04
Effective N	−0.01**	(0.01)	−1.99			
Margin of victory				0.02*	(0.01)	1.73
No opposition	−0.04***	(0.01)	−6.17	−0.04***	(0.01)	−5.98
Trend	0.03***	(0.00)	18.51	0.03***	(0.00)	18.33
constant	−0.04**	(0.02)	−2.25	−0.07***	(0.02)	−5.01
N Observations	10171			10251		
N Groups	2363			2364		
Wald χ^2 (df=7)	2366.08***			2417.51***		
R^2 Between	0.58			0.58		
R^2 Overall	0.18			0.19		

$^*p < 0.10$ $^{**}p < 0.05$ $^{***}p < 0.001$

[a]Dependent variable is share of private good provision per municipality. Coefficients come from a random effects GLS regression. *Develop* is the rescaled CONAPO deprivation municipal-level index. *Develop*^{2} is the index squared. *Beta/risk* is our measure of systematic risk. Effective N is the effective number of parties and PRI margin is the PRI's margin of victory in the previous municipal race. *Election* is a dummy indicating if a municipal election took place that year.

municipalities where there is no opposition presence. To control for this particular political configuration, we add a dummy for municipal elections where the opposition did not even field candidates and the PRI got 100 percent of the vote (*No opposition*). Results are reported in Table 8.5 above.

All our expectations are confirmed. With respect to the socioeconomic theory of clientelism, we find strong evidence that there is more clientelism in poorer municipalities and that clientelism tends to shrink as municipalities develop. However, against the expectations of modernization theory, there is greater recourse to clientelism in municipalities at middle levels of development. The variables that put our approach to the test, with respect to the *political logic* driving clientelism, all perform as expected. Clientelism tends to be less prevalent in politically heterogeneous municipalities, as measured by the effective number of parties. When margins of victory are employed instead of effective N, the result is that there is *less* clientelism in municipalities that are won by smaller margins. Thus, political competition has a virtuous effect in generating incentives for politicians to shift their investments toward public good provision in such environments. However, consistent with our expectations, particularism is more prevalent in high-risk municipalities, as measured by our *beta coefficient*, which reveals a faster rate of vote loss by the PRI than it suffers in the nation as a whole. An intriguing finding is that there is less investment in particularistic transfers in municipalities where there is no opposition presence at all.

These results suggest that to defend its monopoly under threat, the long-lasting ruling party in Mexico diversified its portfolio of electoral investments, allocating more public goods to more heterogeneous and competitive municipalities in an attempt to cater to a wider voting audience. At the same time, the PRI intensified its clientelistic practices by allocating more private goods to high-risk municipalities, those where its core voters were defecting at a faster rate than the national trend. Consistent with our approach, clientelism is thus a political investment strategy designed to deter voter exit and, simultaneously, to hedge electoral risks when more uncertain investments in public goods are needed to win elections.

Conclusion

This chapter employs a portfolio diversification model to make predictions about politicians' choice of clientelism as an electoral investment strategy. Under the assumption that politicians seek both to obtain a certain electoral threshold *and* to minimize electoral risk, we argue that incumbents will diversify their portfolios between risk-free particularistic transfers and public good provision, for which an electoral return is more uncertain.

Clientelism, we have argued, minimizes electoral risk because politicians can employ preexisting clientelistic networks to target transfers to core constituencies and true partisans whose electoral support is certain. In addition, clientelism has the advantage of allowing incumbents to retain their electoral clienteles for the future because it allows them to deter exit with remarkable effectiveness. By targeting benefits to supporters and punishing opponents, politicians can deter an opposition-leaning voter from actually defecting. That voter is confronted with the choice of backing an incumbent with funds or the opposition without funds. Unless the voter can live without access to the incumbent's resources the logic compels her to support the incumbent, even if reluctantly. This deterrence logic applies as long as the incumbent possesses a monopolistic control of resources and can effectively target transfers according to the recipient's electoral behavior or political identity.

Budget constraints and transaction costs in targeting do not allow politicians to rely upon clientelism as their sole investment strategy, however. Only where voters are really poor, we have argued, is the exclusive reliance on clientelism optimal. As a country modernizes and the pivotal voter becomes wealthier, politicians will be compelled to rely less on clientelism and to introduce public good provision as a dominant form of political exchange.

From the incumbent's point of view, public goods have the advantage of lowering transaction costs and benefiting a larger and more heterogeneous electorate. In our view, the expected electoral return of public goods is higher than that of private goods, yet public goods have the disadvantage of greater risk precisely because all voter groups can consume them regardless of their expected voting behavior.

Clientelism thus differs from pork-barreling and other forms of vote buying in two main respects: first, it is targeted to individuals or clearly specified groups; and second, it is delivered through a party's clientelistic network such that screening between true loyalists and opponents takes place. Our approach yields three main empirical predictions, the first two related to the impact of development and the erosion of party hegemony over time and the last one with prevailing configurations of party competition and electoral risk. First, as a country develops and the pivotal voter becomes wealthier, clientelism should erode as a dominant form of political exchange simply because it becomes too costly. Second, as the size of the incumbent's electoral monopoly shrinks over time, the party should attempt to buy-off the increasingly more heterogeneous electorate through public good provision. This means that there should be less clientelism as political competition is consolidated. Third, consistent with the logic of portfolio diversification, the incumbent should attempt to hedge the higher risks involved in public good provision by devoting more resources to clientelistic transfers in the riskiest localities, those where its core base is eroding quickly, holding party system configurations and the incumbent's level of electoral support constant.

Appendix

In Table 8.6, we provide a detailed description of the projects involved in each of the programs, and the way we classified them. The main indicator we used for the classification was information regarding the unit of measurement of the project on which basis we contrast private goods and club goods with public goods.

Table 8.6 *Classification of pronasol expenditure by type of good, according to the unit of measure reported for each project*

		Clientelism		
Program name	Private good	Club good	Public good	
Drinking water and sewage (*agua potable y alcantarillado*)			Wells; systems; meters	
Food and distribution (*alimentación y abasto*)			Milk; market; slaughter-house; work	
Support for social services (*apoyo al servicio social*)	Scholarship			
Health (*atención a la salud*)			Lake; community; hospital	
Productive ecology (*ecología productiva*)		Work		
Rural and urban electrification (*electrificación rural y urbana*)			Colony; work; well; system	
Solidarity production funds (*fondos de solidaridad para la producción*)		Hectare		
Solidarity municipal funds (*fondos municipales de solidaridad*)			Unit; system; park; work; M2; garden; building center; workshop; factory; cooperative; warehouse	
Dignified hospital (*hospital digno*)			Center	
			Hospital	
(Mexican Social Security Institute)			Center	
(IMSS-Solidaridad)			Clinic	
Highway infrastructure (*infraestructura carretera*)			Kilometer	
			Bridge	
Infrastructure for productive support (*infraestructura de apoyo productivo*)		Group; apiary; wood mill; warehouse; dam (*Bordo*); cattle; cattle/year; canal; center; collector; hatchlings; packing; equipment establishment; stable; pond; factory; hectare		

Program	Unit
Sports infrastructure (*infraestructura deportiva*)	Court
Education infrastructure (*infraestructura educativa*)	Altas; annex; auditorium; classroom; center; school; laboratory; square; workshop
Women in solidarity (*mujeres en solidaridad*)	vegetable garden; research; kilometers; lot; luminaries; Meters2; Meters3; mine; mill; work; plant; plant/year; well; processor; terrace; ton; ton/year; Ton/catch; unit; vehicle; nursery; Lavatory; Action; team; mill; workshop; tortilleria; unit
Regional development programs (for the national indigenous institute) (*programas de desarrollo regional*)	Study; team
Solidarity for a dignified school (*solidaridad para una escuela digna*)	School
Urbanization (*urbanización*)	Kilometer; Meter; Meter2; Meter3; work; bridge; system; vehicle
Housing (*vivienda*)	Toilet; Dwelling
Drinking water (*agua potable*)	System
Children in solidarity (*niños en solidaridad*)	Scholarship

9   From populism to clientelism? The transformation of labor-based party linkages in Latin America

Steven Levitsky

Labor-based parties faced a dual challenge in the 1980s and 1990s.[1] On the one hand, fiscal crisis, increased capital mobility, and the resurgence of free market ideologies limited parties' capacity to implement pro-labor and welfare statist policies. On the other hand, industrial decline and the expansion of tertiary and informal sectors weakened labor movements, limiting their capacity to deliver the votes, resources, and social peace upon which party–union "exchanges" had traditionally been based. These changes created an incentive for labor-based parties to loosen their ties to unions and target new electoral constituencies (Kitschelt 1994; Koelble 1991, 1992). Such coalitional change often faced intense opposition from unions and party activists. However, non-adaptation risked long-term political decline.

This chapter examines the capacity of contemporary Latin American labor-based parties to "simultaneously manage working-class decline and the rise of new strata" (Esping-Anderson 1999: 315). It argues that unlike the advanced industrialized countries, where the primary electoral challenge lay in appealing to emerging "new middle classes," Latin American labor-based parties face a dualistic scenario: white-collarization was accompanied by the growth of an even larger stratum of urban informal poor. In this environment, clientelistic linkages often proved more successful than the media-based electoral professional strategies adopted by many European parties.

Parties' capacity to make the transition from labor-based populism to machine politics hinged on three factors: (1) access to a politicized state bureaucracy; (2) levels of electoral competition; and (3) the entrenchment of party–union linkages. Coalitional transformation was thus must likely

---

[1] Labor-based parties are those whose core constituency is *organized labor*. Such parties depend on trade union support (in the form of organizational resources, votes, and social peace) for their success, and in exchange, unions are granted influence in the party's decision-making and leadership and candidate selection processes.

where parties enjoyed access to a politicized state, faced strong electoral challenges, and possessed loosely structured ties to unions.

The majority of this chapter is an examination of the case of the Argentine (Peronist) Justicialista Party (PJ), a party that enjoyed widespread access to state patronage and possessed strong but weakly institutionalized ties to labor. After suffering a stunning electoral defeat in 1983, the PJ underwent a dramatic transformation, de-unionizing more rapidly – and thoroughly – than any other party in Latin America. PJ reformers removed old guard unionists from the party leadership, dismantled traditional mechanisms of labor participation, and replaced union linkages with informal patronage-based organizations.[2] These changes were critical to the party's political success during the 1990s. The erosion of union influence allowed PJ leaders to broaden the party's appeal to middle-class voters. At the same time, the consolidation of urban clientelistic networks helped the PJ maintain its traditional working- and lower-class base. The PJ's transformation also facilitated its programmatic shift to the right under the government of Carlos Menem (1989–99). The removal of unions from the party leadership eliminated a major source of opposition to neoliberal reform, and clientelistic networks helped dampen popular sector opposition to economic reform. Hence, this chapter demonstrates that clientelistic linkages not only proved compatible with neoliberal policies, but they were critical to the implementation of those policies by the PJ. The chapter then concludes with an examination of the fate of four other Latin American labor-based parties during the 1980s and 1990s – Democratic Action (AD) in Venezuela, the Institutional Revolutionary Party (PRI) in Mexico, and the Chilean Socialist (PSCh) and Communist (PCCh) parties – to place the Peronist experience in perspective.

The transformation of party–union linkages in Latin America

In Latin America, as elsewhere, established party–union linkages came under strain during the 1980s and 1990s.[3] Domestic economic crises

---

[2] It should be noted that the changes examined here are primarily relevant to urban Peronism. Peronism has historically been based on a dual electoral coalition of industrial workers (organized by unions) in urban areas and lower- and middle-class voters (organized into clientelistic networks) in the poorer, non-industrial provinces (Gibson 1997; Mora y Araujo and Llorente 1980).

[3] This pattern was not unique to Latin America, see Koelble (1991, 1992), Howell and Daley (1992), and Kitschelt (1994) on party–union tensions in Western Europe. More extensive discussions of party–union tensions in Latin America are provided by Murillo (2001), Levitsky (2003), and Burgess (2004).

and international economic change compelled governing labor-based parties to adopt market-oriented policies that were at odds with both their traditional platforms and the demands of union allies. Party–union linkages were also challenged by changes in class structure. As workers became less concentrated in factories and more heterogeneous in their skills, experiences, and interests, the capacity of labor organizations to mobilize or negotiate on behalf of members eroded. Consequently, unions had less to offer parties in terms of the traditional party–union exchange – they could deliver fewer votes, had fewer resources to invest in politics, and were less necessary to ensure social peace (Howell and Daley 1992). At the same time, industrial decline eroded labor-based parties' traditional electoral bases. In the advanced industrialized countries, labor-based parties confronted an increasingly educated white-collar, or "new middle-class," electorate characterized by weaker class identities and more volatile, issue-based voting patterns (Dalton, Flanagan, and Beck 1984; Inglehart 1977; Kitschelt 1994).

These changes created pressure for labor-based parties to loosen their ties to unions (Howell and Daley 1992; Koelble 1992; Burgess 2004). The persistence of strong union linkages hindered labor-based parties' efforts to adopt market-oriented policies (Koelble 1992). It also limited their capacity to appeal to new constituencies. In the advanced industrialized countries, these pressures reinforced tendencies to abandon mass linkages in favor of "electoral professional" organizations and media-based "catch-all" electoral strategies (Kirchheimer 1966; Panebianco 1988: 262–74).

The challenges facing Latin American labor-based parties differed in two ways. First, due to deeper economic crises, weaker national economies, and the influence of international financial institutions, the scope of policy-making autonomy in Latin America was more limited. Thus, whereas most northern European social democratic parties underwent gradual programmatic change, Latin American labor-based parties were often forced to make sudden and dramatic shifts to the right. Second, in the electoral arena, Latin American labor-based parties confronted a dualistic post-industrial scenario: whereas one segment of the workforce followed the advanced industrial path toward white-collarization, a second – usually larger – segment was pushed into the urban informal sector (Castells and Portes 1989). Due to urban migration, industrial restructuring, and state retrenchment, the informal sector grew rapidly in the 1980s and 1990s, accounting for nearly 50 percent of urban employment in the region at century's end (ILO 1999). The growth of the informal sector created a difficult challenge for labor-based parties. Like white-collarization, informalization weakens class-based organizations and erodes class identities (Roberts 1998a: 65–73). Informal sector workers are less likely than blue-collar workers to have contact with unions, understand their interests in traditional class terms, or hold stable class or partisan identities (Castells and Portes 1989: 31–32). Unlike European new middle classes, however, most Latin American informal sector workers are poorly educated and live in poverty. Hence, they are less likely to be drawn to abstract ideological or universalistic programmatic appeals.

The challenge for governing labor-based parties in Latin America was thus to combine neoliberal macro-economic policies with the delivery of concrete material benefits. A major strategy for achieving this mix was to replace class-based linkages with *clientelistic* linkages, or territorial networks that bind followers through "direct, personal, and typically material side payments" (Kitschelt 2000b: 849). In contemporary Latin America, clientelism may be preferable to class-based linkages for two reasons. First, clientelist linkages are more compatible with market-oriented economic reform. Because political machines are primarily concerned with local, particularistic needs, they tend to be more programmatically flexible than class-based organizations (Scott 1969). Second, clientelistic linkages are more effective in winning votes in a context of large informal economies, widespread unemployment, and low union membership. The disappearance of large factories and industrial unions eroded the social fabric of many working-class districts, producing fragmentation and social isolation. Because clientelistic linkages are based on face-to-face interaction and particularistic exchange, they are better equipped to operate in such an environment.

Clientelistic linkages may also be preferable to electoral professional strategies. Whereas mass membership organizations may serve only a "vestigial" function in wealthy, well-educated societies (Katz 1990), grassroots structures that permit direct contact with (and the delivery of concrete material benefits to) voters remain highly effective in a context of extensive poverty and low education. In the face of precarious income flows and unreliable access to state legal and social protection, the urban poor frequently discount the future in favor of short-term material benefits, and opt for concrete individual solutions over collective ones (Auyero 2000; Kitschelt and Wilkinson, Introduction to this volume). In such a context, abstract ideological or universalistic programmatic appeals tend to be less successful than particularistic exchanges rooted in direct, face-to-face appeals.

From the standpoint of much of the literature, the transition from labor-based populism to machine politics is surprising. First, as noted in the Introduction, modernization-based theories expect the reverse sequence – as societies modernize, clientelistic linkages are supposed to *give way to*, rather than replace, class-based linkages. Second, the transition from statist to market-oriented economies was widely expected to limit (or be limited by) the practice of political clientelism. Yet two decades of evidence from Latin America has shown that – at least in the short-to-medium run – neoliberalism and clientelism are quite compatible. Not only did clientelism survive the implementation of extensive market-oriented reforms throughout much of the region, but also, in many cases, it facilitated the implementation of those reforms (Dresser 1994; Gibson 1997; Gibson and Calvo 2000; Roberts 1995, 2002: 19). As Gibson and Calvo (2000) argue, clientelism offers parties a relatively low-cost means of maintaining traditional constituencies – especially among the poor – in a context of fiscal austerity and state retrenchment.[4] Not only does the distribution of clientelistic goods help secure votes, but networks of neighborhood brokers can also play a critical role in dampening or defusing social protest (Auyero 2000).

Third, much of the literature treats mass or class-based linkages as incompatible with machine politics.[5] Yet evidence from Latin America suggests that labor-based parties may, in fact, be especially well-equipped to build machines. As Kitschelt and Wilkinson note in the Introduction, clientelistic linkages are costly to build and maintain. Large-scale clientelistic distribution, monitoring, and enforcement require an "elaborate organizational infrastructure" (Kitschelt and Wilkinson: 23). Moreover, effective clientelistic appeals are usually not one-shot deals, but rather are rooted in "ongoing networks of social relations" that foster trust, lengthen time horizons, and conceal the uglier aspects (*quid pro quo* exchange, surveillance, and enforcement) of the relationship. The construction of such an infrastructure is an "arduous, slow, resource-intensive undertaking" (Kitschelt and Wilkinson: 22). The potential advantage of established labor-based parties is that they *already possess* such an infrastructure. Thus, their machine-building efforts can draw on existing grassroots organization and activist networks, many of which are already embedded in working- and lower-class neighborhoods (see Auyero 2000). Moreover, established mass party identities provide a source of cohesion and loyalty in a context of a fragmented and heterogeneous electorate.

Machine politics is not, of course, without electoral costs (Warner 1997). Because the (real or perceived) corruption and inefficiency

---

[4] Also see Dresser (1991, 1994), Roberts and Arce (1998), and Schady (2000). Indeed, due to the profound economic crisis and fiscal austerity and state retrenchment in Latin America during the 1980s and 1990s, the demand for selective material benefits may have increased (Auyero 2000).

[5] In particular, see Shefter (1977, 1994).

associated with machine politics tends to alienate middle-class voters, clientelistic parties are vulnerable to reformist challenges. Particularly in middle-income countries such as Argentina, Brazil, and Mexico, where there exist significant sized middle-class "constituencies for universal-ism" (Shefter 1994: 27–28), an optimal strategy may thus be to "diversify linkage mechanisms" (Kitschelt 2000b: 853) by combining clientelism in low-income areas with media-based programmatic appeals at the national level and in urban centers (Gibson 1997; Magaloni *et al.* this volume).

Explaining labor-based party transformation

Latin American labor-based parties varied considerably in terms of how – and to what extent – they reconfigured their working-class linkages dur-ing the 1980s and 1990s. Whereas some parties made relatively rapid and successful transitions to machine politics (Argentine Peronism, the Mex-ican PRI), others adapted slowly and ineffectively (AD in Venezuela, the Chilean communists). Still others (the Chilean socialists) de-unionized but opted for a more electoral-professional strategy.

Three factors are critical to explaining these diverging outcomes. First, parties can only restructure along clientelistic lines where they enjoy access to a politicized state bureaucracy. Following Shefter (1977, 1994), clientelistic party rebuilding requires that (1) parties have access to public office and (2) the state lacks "bureaucratic autonomy," or effective civil service legislation (1994: 27–28).

Second, the probability of labor-based party adaptation is heightened by electoral competition. Electoral challenges, particularly those that result in defeat, are a powerful catalyst for party change. Electoral set-backs – and the resulting loss of resources – generate internal pressure for leadership change, which, in turn, facilitates strategic and organizational change (Harmel and Janda 1994: 279–81; Panebianco 1988: 243–44).

Third, labor-based parties' adaptive capacity hinges on the degree to which the party–union linkage is institutionalized (Levitsky 2003). When rules and procedures are institutionalized, stable sets of expectations and interests form around them. Actors invest in skills, learn strategies, and create organizations that are appropriate to the existing rules of the game. These investments give actors a stake in the preservation of existing arrangements – and a greater capacity to defend them (North 1990: 364–65). Institutionalized rules become "taken-for-granted," in the sense that actors comply with them without constantly evaluating the immediate costs and benefits of such compliance (Zucker 1977: 728). Institution-alized structures thus tend to be "sticky," in that they do not change as quickly as underlying preferences and power distributions. By contrast, non-institutionalized structures tend to be more fluid, in that changes in the underlying distribution of power and preferences may translate more quickly into organizational change.

In sum, transitions from class-based to clientelistic linkages were most likely where parties faced strong electoral challenges, enjoyed access to a politicized state bureaucracy, and possessed loosely structured ties to labor. Where labor-based parties lacked access to a politicized state, they often had no alternative but to adopt an electoral-professional strategy and media-based, issue-oriented appeals along the lines of many European parties. Where parties faced weaker electoral challenges and/or possessed highly institutionalized ties to labor, they adapted more slowly and ineffectively.

The case of Peronism

Peronism is a case of dramatic transformation from labor-based populism to machine politics.[6] In the wake of Argentina's 1983 democratic transition, the PJ was dominated by industrial unions from the General Workers Confederation (CGT). Unions were the party's primary source of finance and mobilizational muscle, and they played a hegemonic role in the party leadership. In 1983, union bosses controlled the PJ presidency, imposed the party's presidential ticket and platform, and secured nearly a third of its seats in Congress (Levitsky 2003: 93–94).

The PJ faced a difficult electoral challenge during the 1980s. Argentina had experienced a dramatic de-industrialization since the 1970s, with manufacturing employment declining by more than a third (Smith 1989: 264) and leading industrial unions losing up to 50 percent of their members (Abos 1986: 189). Whereas industrial unions had historically encapsulated a large sector of the urban working class, de-industrialization created a growing urban informal sector that was "organically disconnected from union activities" and whose interests were "not easily articulated with those of wage workers" (Villarreal 1987: 85). White-collar sectors also expanded (Palomino 1987). Better educated, more socially mobile, and less attached to traditional party identities than lower-class voters, white-collar workers swelled the ranks of the independent electorate. In this new environment, the PJ's close ties to industrial labor had severe electoral consequences. In 1983, the PJ lost a presidential election – to the Radical Civic Union (URC) – for the first time in its history, and two years later it was decisively defeated in legislative elections. These defeats were widely attributed to the PJ's inward-oriented, working-class-based appeal, which limited its ability to capture independent and middle-class

---

[6] For a more extensive account of this transformation, see Levitsky (2003).

votes (Cantón 1986: 48–49, 164; Catterberg 1991: 81–82; Waisbord 1995: 30–32, 181).

The PJ's capacity to adapt to this challenge was rooted in several factors. First, the stunning 1983 electoral loss discredited the old guard union leadership and generated broad intra-party support for change, giving rise to a successful internal challenge by the Renovation, a faction composed of progressive urban politicians, provincial bosses, and the "Group of 25" (or "25") union faction. Second, the PJ enjoyed widespread access to patronage resources. The Argentine state lacks bureaucratic autonomy. The civil service is highly politicized, and public sector jobs are widely used for patronage purposes (Calvo and Murillo 2004; Gibson and Calvo 2000). Although Peronism did not win the presidency in 1983, it won twelve of Argentina's twenty-three governorships, hundreds of mayoralties, and thousands of city council seats. The PJ's ability to transform these state posts into patronage networks was facilitated by its extensive mass organization, which included a membership of more than 3 million, a dense infrastructure of local branches that were deeply rooted in working- and lower-class society (Levitsky 2003: 60–65).

Third, unlike many established labor-based parties, the Peronist party–union linkage was weakly institutionalized (Levitsky 2003). Although unions were fundamental to Perón's rise to power in the 1940s and remained prominent allies through the mid-1980s, the Peronist party never developed stable rules or procedures to govern union participation. Efforts to institutionalize the party–union linkage, such as the short-lived Labor Party in the 1940s and the party-building efforts of the metalworkers' union leader Augusto Vandor in the 1960s, were derailed by Perón (McGuire 1997).

Prior to 1983, the Peronist party–union linkage was based on two informal and loosely structured mechanisms: the "62 Organizations" (or "62") and the *tercio* (or one-third) system. The "62" functioned as labor's informal representative within the Peronist leadership. Its origins lay in the 62-union coalition that won control of the CGT in 1957. During the early 1960s, the "62" emerged as the unions' collective representative within Peronism, with the (informal) right to nominate unionists for party candidacies and leadership posts. Though broadly accepted as Peronism's "labor branch" in the 1960s and 1970s, the "62" was never mentioned in party statutes, had no formal position in the party leadership, held no regular meetings, and lacked a central office, budget, or stable rules and operating procedures (McGuire 1997: 98–99).

The *tercio* system was rooted in Peronism's corporatist tradition of granting its "political," "women's," and "labor" branches one-third of party candidacies and leadership posts. The *tercio*'s origins are disputed. Whereas some Peronists claim that it was respected "like a law" during

the first Perón government,[7] others describe it as a "retrospectively created myth" that was always "more folklore than reality."[8] Whatever its
origins, the *tercio* was never written into party statutes or systematically
enforced after 1955. Rather than a taken-for-granted procedure, it was
usually enforced only as a result of pressure by powerful unions.

The Peronist party–union linkage was thus weakly institutionalized in
the 1980s. Labor lacked formal representation or stable rules of participation in the party leadership. Instead, its influence hinged on a set of
loose informal norms that often required active union enforcement. Consequently, the party–union linkage was highly vulnerable to changes in
the distribution of power and preferences within the party.

The transformation of Peronism's party–union linkages, 1983–99

Beginning in the mid-1980s, the PJ dismantled its traditional party–
union linkages and replaced them with clientelistic linkages. The post-
1983 Renovation movement pursued two goals: (1) to democratize the
PJ by replacing the corporatist *tercio* system with primary elections; and
(2) to broaden the PJ's appeal to independent and middle-class voters.
Their ability to achieve these goals was rooted in a shift in the balance
of resources within the party. After 1983, Peronist public office-holders
began to replace union resources with state resources. Using government
jobs to cement alliances with neighborhood activists, or *punteros*, they
built patronage-based organizations, or *agrupaciones*, at the margins of
the unions. The *agrupaciones* provided Renovation leaders with the organizational resources to challenge the union-backed Orthodox party leadership. In 1985 and 1986, patronage-based Renovation factions wrested
control of party branches in the country's largest industrial districts, lay-
ing the foundation for a takeover of the national party leadership in 1987.

The PJ–union linkage collapsed quickly in the face of the Renovation
challenge. As soon as the unions lost the capacity to enforce the old
informal rules of the game, Renovation leaders began to challenge and
break them. Thus, when their effort to gain control of the "62" failed in
1985, the Renovators simply circumvented it, refusing to recognize the
"62's" traditional right to nominate unionists for party posts and awarding
that right to the "25" in branches they controlled. As a result, the "62's"
claim to be the encompassing representative of Peronist labor weakened,
and over the next few years, other Peronist labor organizations – such as

---

[7] Author's interview with textile workers' union leader Jorge Lobais, December 11, 1997.
[8] Author's interviews with congressional deputies Juan Carlos Maqueda (September 11,
1997) and Lorenzo Dominguez (September 25, 1997).

the Menem for President Labor Roundtable – emerged at the margins of the "62." By the early 1990s, the "62" had become an "empty name"[9] that "no one pays any attention to."[10]

The Renovators also assaulted the *tercio* system. In the mid-1980s, Renovation factions refused to employ the *tercio* in many of the branches they controlled. After the Renovators gained control of the PJ in 1987, the party congress buried the *tercio* by establishing a formal system of primaries to select leaders and candidates. Although the new party statutes reserved 17 of 110 seats in the National Council for union members, they did not specify who would choose these representatives. In the absence of a "62"-like body to represent labor, this authority fell to the territorial bosses who drew up the party leadership lists.

The rise of the Renovation thus left the unions without any (formal or informal) mechanisms of participation in the PJ. These reforms facilitated the consolidation of machine politics in two ways. First, the primary system placed increased importance on the delivery of votes, which created an incentive for leaders and activists to organize around patronage distribution. As urban machines consolidated, state resources became the primary linkage between the PJ and its activist base. Second, the Renovation reforms fragmented labor politically. Lacking an encompassing organization after the collapse of the "62," unions were forced to negotiate individually with local party bosses for leadership posts and candidacies. As they concentrated power, party bosses were able to play unions against one another, leaving them at the margins of the leadership and candidate selection process.

The consolidation of machine politics can be seen in the cases of Argentina's two largest districts: the Federal Capital and Buenos Aires. The Federal Capital machine was led by Renovator Carlos Grosso, who was elected president of the local PJ in 1985 and appointed mayor by President Menem in 1989. The Grosso machine emerged out of the city council. Taking advantage of a burgeoning payroll, city council members became "professionals of patronage," building *agrupaciones* through a system of "paid activism."[11] When Grosso became mayor, these *agrupaciones* divided up the city government. By the early 1990s, nearly all of the local party's roughly 400 neighborhood branches were run by activists with government jobs. As activists flocked to pro-Grosso *agrupaciones* in search of patronage, power concentrated in the mayor's office, and consequently, union influence declined. Whereas unionists gained two

---

[9] Author's interview with Lorenzo Minichielo, general secretary of the Quilmes section of the auto workers union (SMATA), May 15, 1997.

[10] Author's interview with former CGT general secretary Oscar Lescano, October 27, 1997.

[11] Author's interview with local PJ leader Juan Carlos Castro, September 30, 1997.

Table 9.1 *The erosion of Peronist union representation in the Chamber of Deputies, 1983–2001*

	1983	1985	1987	1989	1991	1993	1995	1997	1999	2001
Number of union members in PJ bloc	29	28	22	24	18	10	6	5	4	3
Overall size of PJ bloc	111	101	105	120	120	128	130	119	99	118
Percentage of PJ bloc belonging to union	26.1	27.7	21.0	20.0	15.0	7.8	4.6	4.2	4.0	2.5

positions on the PJ's parliamentary list in 1989, they received one candidacy in 1991 and 1993 and none thereafter.

In Buenos Aires, Eduardo Duhalde built a powerful machine after leaving the vice presidency to run for governor in 1991. The *Duhaldista* coalition was based on an alliance between Duhalde's Federal League and the Buenos Aires Peronist League (LIPEBO), which represented Renovators linked to former governor Antonio Cafiero. The coalition was cemented with patronage. Whereas the Federal League controlled the public works ministry and the presidency of the national Congress, LIPEBO controlled the provincial legislature. Duhalde also made political use of the Suburban Reparation Fund, an arrangement by which 10 percent of federal tax revenues were diverted to Greater Buenos Aires for public works. The Fund allocated resources according to a clear political logic, with *Duhaldista* mayors getting the largest share (López Echague 1996: 167–73). Control over patronage thus allowed Duhalde to consolidate power. In 1993, the Federal League–LIPEBO coalition won internal elections with 93 percent of the vote, and in 1995, the party congress canceled the primaries altogether, authorizing Duhalde to single-handedly draw up the party lists.[12] As power became concentrated in the governorship, union influence declined. For example, the number of unionists elected to Congress fell from six in 1987 to two in 1995.

The consolidation of machine politics brought a precipitous decline in labor influence in the PJ. Because local and provincial party bosses controlled powerful patronage-based organizations, they no longer needed union support in primaries or general elections. As a result, unionists were increasingly excluded from party leadership positions. The erosion

[12] *Clarín*, December 11, 1994, pp. 12–13.

of union influence can be seen in the dramatic reduction in the number of unionists elected to the Chamber of Deputies. As Table 9.1 shows, union representation in the PJ legislative bloc fell from 28 in 1985 to just 3 in 2001.

The effects of de-unionization: clientelism as a successful adaptive strategy?

Peronism's transition from labor-based party to urban political machine contributed in several ways to its political success during the 1990s. First, it helped the party reshape and preserve its electoral coalition. The Renovation-led PJ pursued a two-pronged electoral strategy, seeking to increase its share of the middle-class and independent vote in metropolitan centers while preserving its traditional base among the poor and in the periphery. De-unionization facilitated this strategy in two ways. First, it enhanced the autonomy of PJ political leaders, allowing them to broaden the party's appeal. After the Renovators gained control of the PJ in 1987, they distanced themselves from the unions and made unprecedented use of the mass media, professional polling, and other modern campaign techniques. This strategy was successful, as the PJ decisively won both the 1987 mid-term elections and the 1989 presidential election. Critical to this success was the PJ's improved performance among the middle sectors. Survey data suggest that whereas it lost the white-collar vote by a two-to-one margin in 1983, it split the white-collar vote in 1989 (Catterberg and Braun 1989: 372).

Second, the consolidation of clientelistic linkages helped the PJ maintain a stable base among low-income voters during the 1990s. Although working- and lower-class Argentines continued to vote Peronist for a variety of reasons, including established loyalties and the Menem government's successful stabilization of the economy, clientelistic linkages appear to have played an important role. The Peronist vote was both higher and more stable in provinces with dense party organization and extensive public employment (Calvo and Murillo 2004; Gibson and Calvo 2000; Levitsky 1999: 272–79).

The transition from labor politics to machine politics thus allowed the PJ to both appeal to a new constituency (the new middle class) and find a new basis with which to maintain its old constituency (the urban poor). This two-pronged strategy was not without contradictions and costs. In districts with wealthy and educated electorates, such as the Federal Capital, the PJ machine became widely associated with corruption and inefficiency, with severe electoral consequences. For example, the Peronist vote in the capital fell to an unprecedented low of 9 percent in 1999. However, Peronism's poor performance in metropolitan centers was offset by its success in peripheral provinces and urban poverty zones (Gibson 1997; Gibson and Calvo 2000). Overall, the PJ won five consecutive national elections between 1987 and 1995, and after losing the presidency in 1999, it came back to win three consecutive elections (including the 2003 presidential election) between 2001 and 2005. From an electoral standpoint, then, the PJ's transformation was clearly successful.

The reconfiguration of the PJ–union linkage also contributed to the success of the Menem government's (1989–99) neoliberal economic reforms. First, it eliminated a major source of intra-party opposition to the reforms. Peronist union leaders were far more critical of neoliberalism than were non-union party leaders (Levitsky 2003: 139–42). By the 1990s, however, most union leaders had been removed from the party leadership, and those who remained complained that "no one listened" to them.[13]

Second, clientelistic linkages helped dampen popular sector opposition to neoliberalism. In low-income areas, local PJ organizations served as "problem solving networks" (Auyero 2000), obtaining wheelchairs, disability pensions, scholarships, funeral expenses, and odd jobs, as well as street lights, road pavement, and other neighborhood-wide goods and services (Levitsky 2001: 55–56). A 1997 survey of 112 PJ base units (UBs) found that 96 percent engaged in some form of social assistance (Levitsky 2001: 53). More than two-thirds (69.6 percent) of the surveyed base units engaged in the direct distribution of food or medicine, and nearly a quarter (22.3 percent) of the UBs regularly provided jobs for their constituents.

Clientelistic networks also provided a degree of social control in urban poverty zones. During periods of crisis, such as the 1989–90 hyperinflation and the 2002 economic collapse, neighborhood brokers used a combination of persuasion and intimidation (including the expulsion of leftist activists from neighborhoods) to defuse potential protests. These efforts had a significant – albeit difficult to measure – impact. Unlike Radical governments in 1989 and 2001, Peronist administrations never confronted widespread urban rioting or looting.

Finally, research by Javier Auyero (1998, 2000) suggests that the consolidation of clientelistic linkages has fundamentally reshaped Peronist identities. Historically, trade unions had played a central role in the formation and reproduction of Peronist identities, infusing the movement

---

[13] Author's interview with pharmacy employees union leader José Azcurra, October 20, 1997.

with a class character (James 1988: 18; Torre 1983: 12). During the 1980s and 1990s, as unions weakened and class-based identities eroded, the PJ's clientelistic networks became the "most important webs of relations in which the remains of a strong Peronist identity are kept alive" (Auyero 2000: 204). Consequently, Peronist identities increasingly resembled those "clients" rather than workers (Auyero 2000). As one party activist put it, "Peronism is about helping poor people . . . The economic situation is terrible and people are needy. So we give them bags of food, medicine, maybe even a job. That's what Peronism is all about."[14] Such an identity is far more compatible with a neoliberal program than the "oppositionist" class-based identities that characterized urban Peronism in the past (Auyero 2000: 188–200; James 1988).

Comparative evidence from Latin America

The argument made here may be further illustrated through a comparison with other Latin American cases. This part briefly examines the response of four other established Latin American labor-based parties to the challenge of working-class decline: AD in Venezuela, the Mexican PRI, and the Chilean Socialist (PSCh) and Communist (PCCh) parties.

Mexico

Like Peronism, the Mexican PRI replaced corporatist linkages with new clientelist linkages – with some success – during the 1980s and 1990s.[15] After half a century of dominant party rule, the PRI's political hegemony came under serious challenge in the 1980s. Decades of economic development had shifted the weight of the electorate toward urban centers and increased the size of constituencies – such as the middle classes and the urban poor – that lay outside the PRI's traditional base (Klesner 1994: 167–75; Molinar Horcasitas 1991: 159–70). In this new context, the PRI's corporatist structure, which relied on union and peasant organizations to deliver votes and social control, "became less and less reliable" (Middlebrook 1995: 304). Particularly in urban centers such as the Federal District, the PRI vote plummeted during the 1980s (Collier 1992: 75, 118; Pacheco 1991).

Several factors shaped the PRI's response to this challenge. First, having governed Mexico – at the national level and in every state and nearly

---

[14] Author's interview, August 26, 1997.
[15] See Magaloni *et al.* (this volume). For a comparison of the Argentine and Mexican cases, see Gibson (1997).

every municipality – for decades, the party enjoyed virtually unlimited access to the state. Indeed, the absence of bureaucratic autonomy had long allowed the party to combine a corporatist structure with both urban and rural clientelistic linkages (Cornelius 1977; Fox 1994).

Second, although the PRI did not lose an election during the 1980s, it nevertheless faced a serious electoral challenge. In several northern states in the mid-1980s, and, most importantly, in the 1988 presidential election, the party was forced to resort to massive fraud to maintain its hegemony. The 1988 electoral shock – which ushered in an era of far more competitive politics – had a profound impact on the PRI elite (Molinar Horcasitas 1991: 221–25), arguably comparable to that caused by Peronism's 1983 defeat.

Third, although the PRI–labor linkage was better institutionalized than that of Peronism, the organization's adaptive capacity was at least moderate. The PRI's corporatist system of labor and peasant sectors dated back to its formation in 1938 (Garrido 1982: 239–51), and although the rules and procedures governing labor participation were always "informal and flexible" (Burgess 1998: 86), the sector system provided labor with stable representation in the party leadership and a steady quota of legislative candidacies (Middlebrook 1995: 101–04). Efforts to dismantle the sectors, such as a mid-1960s proposal to replace it with primary elections, were successfully resisted by labor (Hernández 1991: 225; Zamítiz 1991: 123). Nevertheless, two organizational features facilitated PRI adaptation. First, the PRI was highly centralized, with vast powers concentrated in the presidency (Weldon 1997), which facilitated reform from above. Second, Mexico's ban on presidential reelection led to significant leadership renewal every six years, which limited the degree to which old guard leaders became entrenched in the party hierarchy.

The PRI substantially reconfigured its mass linkages after 1988. Like the Peronist Renovators, newly elected President Carlos Salinas and his allies sought to "restructure the party along territorial rather than sectorial lines" (Burgess 2004: 80), with the goal of broadening the PRI's appeal among the middle classes and urban poor (Collier 1992: 120; Hernández 1991: 225). During the 1990 PRI congress, Salinas' allies pushed through reforms eliminating the sectors' automatic representation in the party leadership and strengthening mechanisms of territorial representation (Hernández 1991: 242). However, union leaders fiercely resisted these reforms and ultimately blocked efforts to dismantle the sectors entirely (Hernández 1991: 237). Three years later, the party congress re-established sector-based representation in the leadership, and by 1994, "the basic contours of the organizational and political bargains between [labor] and the PRI had been restored" (Burgess 2004:

86–87). Labor's representation in Congress declined somewhat during this period, but only to its 1960s levels (Alarcón-Olguín 1994: 18; Middlebrook 1995: 103).

Yet even if the sectors were not dismantled, PRI reformers built new territorial linkages at their margins. Arguing that the neighborhood was "the natural place for the PRI to connect with citizens" (Hernández 1991: 229), PRI president Luis Donaldo Colosio launched a Territorial Movement aimed at rebuilding the party's linkages to the urban poor (Calderón and Cazés 1996: 59). In an "unprecedented effort to reclaim the grassroots" that "could have been undertaken only with the support of government resources," the PRI mobilized hundreds of thousands of "vote promoters" and "block chiefs" into territorial networks (Klesner 1994: 186; Morris 1995: 97). These efforts were reinforced by the National Solidarity Program (Pronasol), a nearly $2 billion a year targeted spending program that financed 150,000 public works projects, reaching up to 25 million Mexicans (Bruhn 1997: 264; Cornelius 1996: 59; Dresser 1991; Magaloni et al. this volume). Through politically targeted spending and partisan propaganda, the program aimed to recapture votes among the urban poor (Molinar and Weldon 1994; Bruhn 1997). Through PRONASOL, the PRI was able to "construct new patronage networks with . . . low-income constituencies" (Dresser 1994: 140), which helped it "reshuffle its base of support from a corporatist to an increasingly territorial one" (Magaloni 2005: 135).

Together with Mexico's economic recovery, the PRI's restructuring helped it stage an impressive electoral comeback after 1988. The PRI decisively won the 1991 mid-term legislative elections and retained the presidency – without substantial fraud – in 1994. Although the PRI failed to maintain its urban support bases and eventually lost the presidency in 2000, it remained the largest party in Mexico, winning the 2003 mid-term elections and competing seriously for the presidency in 2006.

Venezuela

Democratic Action (AD) is a striking case of labor-based party failure. Like the PRI, AD enjoyed widespread access to the state after 1958, controlling the presidency for all but two terms. Moreover, Venezuela's large politicized state apparatus created an opportunity to restructure the party's mass linkages along clientelistic lines. Indeed, particularly since the 1970s oil boom, AD had become an increasingly patronage-based party (Coppedge 1994).

Nevertheless, AD possessed neither an incentive nor the capacity to dismantle its corporatist structure. Compared to Argentina and Mexico, the electoral challenge facing AD was weak. Although the growth of the urban informal sector posed a potential threat, this threat was not realized during the 1980s, as AD won the 1983 and 1988 presidential elections by comfortable margins. Unlike the PJ, then, AD did not experience an electoral setback or the emergence of a significant internal reform movement during the 1980s.

AD's organizational capacity to adapt was also low. The AD–labor linkage was highly institutionalized. AD's Labor Bureau maintained a formalized presence in the party leadership, and it operated according to elaborate and well-established rules and procedures (Coppedge 1988: 169–70). The Labor Bureau played a "pivotal role in the internal affairs of AD" (Ellner 1989: 103), automatically placing representatives on local, state, and national party leadership bodies and receiving a stable quota of candidacies and delegates to the party congress (Ellner 1993: 79; Burgess 2004: 124–25).

AD largely failed to reconfigure its social bases during the 1980s. Union influence – including the number of labor leaders elected to Congress – *increased* over the course of the decade (Coppedge 1988: 170; Ellner 1989: 98–104), raising fears in some quarters that AD was becoming a "labor party" (Ellner 1993: 79). Although AD reformed its nomination process in 1991 to strengthen territorial structures (Ellner 1996: 97), the Labor Bureau remained intact throughout the 1990s (Burgess 2004). At least partly as a result, AD failed to build effective new linkages to the urban poor (Ellner 1993: 89; 1996: 97; 1999: 82). This was made manifest by the urban riots of February 1989, which took the party and its union allies "completely . . . by surprise" (Ellner 1993: 89), as well as in substantial lower-class support for Hugo Chavez's 1992 coup attempt. Along with a range of other factors, particularly Venezuela's protracted economic crisis, AD's failure to establish new linkages to the urban poor contributed to a steep electoral decline. After winning 53 percent of the presidential vote in 1988, AD fell to just 23 percent in 1993, and in 1998 the party trailed so badly that it withdrew its presidential candidate. Soon thereafter, AD disappeared as a major political force.

Chile

Chile offers cases of successful and failed labor-based party adaptation. The challenges confronted by the Chilean socialist (PSCh) and communist (PCCh) parties differed from those facing the other parties considered here in at least two ways. First, because economic reform and recovery had occurred under military rule, Chilean parties faced neither economic crisis nor the need to undertake painful reform (although the consolidation of neoliberalism forced governing parties to shift programmatically to the right). Second, the Chilean parties did not have access to a highly politicized state. All left-of center parties were in opposition through the 1989 democratic transition, and the PCCh remained in opposition throughout the 1990s. Moreover, although the PSCh was part of the governing coalition after 1989, due to the military regime's reform of the state and a series of protections for Pinochet-era civil servants, patronage resources were not abundantly available during the 1990s. Hence, a clientelistic linkage strategy was less viable in Chile than in the other countries considered here.

Although the electoral incentives facing the Chilean left are difficult to gauge due to the absence of elections between 1973 and 1989, the PSCh and PCCh clearly confronted a problem of working-class decline. A combination of repression, de-industrialization, and restrictive labor laws reduced the level of unionization from 32 percent in the early 1970s to less than 10 percent in the mid-1980s (Barrett 2001: 569; Roberts 1998a: 115). These changes, plus the imperatives of governing a highly liberalized economy, created an incentive for left parties to loosen their ties to labor.

The PCCh and PSCh differed in their adaptive capacities. Whereas the PCCh was a "highly structured and institutionalized" party that was generally slow to adapt to environmental change (Roberts 1998a: 47–50), the PSCh's "loosely structured party organization" and "lax disciplinary norms" (*ibid.*: 48) made it a more "open, dynamic, and flexible party, with a high predisposition to change and adapt" (Roberts 1994: 22).

The PCCh and PSCh responded to the challenge of working-class decline in distinct ways. Neither party pursued a clientelistic strategy. The PCCh, which remained in opposition throughout the 1990s, opted to "bunker down with its core constituencies" (Roberts 1998a: 159), maintaining close ties to organized labor and making little effort to broaden its electoral appeal (McCarthy 1997). The result was electoral decline (Roberts 1998a: 134–45, 159). After peaking at 16.2 percent of the vote in 1973, the PCCh vote fell to just 3.2 percent in 1999.

The PSCh and its sister party, the Party for Democracy (PPD),[16] adapted more successfully. Beginning in the 1980s, the PSCh loosened its ties to organized labor (McCarthy 1997; Roberts 1998a). Although

---

[16] The PPD was created by the PSCh in 1988 (when the Socialists were banned) to campaign in the plebiscite that brought an end to authoritarian rule. Afterward, the PPD remained in existence as a distinct, but closely aligned, party.

the party gained access to the national executive beginning in 1989, it adopted a catchall electoral strategy, not a clientelistic one (McCarthy 1997; Roberts 1998a). According to Roberts, the PSCh "made a transition from a class-mass party to a . . . catch all professional-electoral party" that "largely ceased to encapsulate popular sectors within its ranks" (1998b: 10). The adaptive process was even more pronounced in the PPD. A centralized party without an extensive bureaucracy or base-level organization (Roberts 1998b: 10), the PPD adopted an issue-oriented, "post-materialist" electoral strategy during the 1990s (Plumb 1998: 95–99). Thus, the party "carved out an independent niche as a progressive but non-ideological catch-all party that appealed to a broad range of unaffiliated moderate leftists and secular centrists" (Roberts 1998a: 138). Among Latin American labor-based parties, then, the PSCh/PPD strategy most closely approximated the "left-libertarian" strategy adopted by many European social democratic parties (Kitschelt 1994). The strategies were relatively successful, as the PSCh and PPD maintained a stable electoral niche within Chile's multiparty system. The parties' combined 24 percent of the vote in the 1993 and the 1997 elections was more than twice the average Socialist vote during the 1957–73 period.

Comparing the cases

This brief comparison suggests some initial empirical support for the argument developed in this chapter. The PJ, which suffered a stunning electoral defeat and whose union linkages were weakly institutionalized, underwent a far-reaching transformation, replacing union linkages with clientelistic linkages. The PRI, which suffered an electoral scare in 1988, and whose union linkage was moderately institutionalized, partially dismantled its corporatist structure and used new clientelist linkages to make temporary inroads among the urban poor. The loosely structured PSCh/PPD also de-unionized, but due to the relative autonomy of the Chilean bureaucracy, the parties were forced to adopt more media-based electoral-professional strategies. AD and the PCCh, two highly institutionalized parties, adapted slowly and ineffectively. In both cases, party–union linkages remained intact through the early 1990s, which limited parties' capacity to appeal to new constituencies.

Table 9.2 compares the five parties' average electoral performance in the 1980s and 1990s. The PJ and PSCh/PPD, which underwent extensive adaptation, maintained relatively stable electoral bases during the 1990s. The PRI suffered a moderate electoral decline, although much of this decline can be attributed to the fact that elections in the 1990s were

Table 9.2 *Electoral performance of six Latin American labor-based parties in the 1980s and 1990s (Lower House legislative elections)*

Labor-Based/Populist Party	1980s[a]	1990s	Absolute change	Relative change
Justicialista Party (PJ)	40.7	39.2	−1.5	−3.7
Chilean Socialist Party (PSCh)	13.0	12.2	−0.8	−6.2
Institutional Revolutionary Party (PRI)	61.1	49.5	−11.6	−19.0
Democratic Action (AD)	46.7	22.7	−24.0	−51.4
Chilean Communist Party (PCCh)	14.0	6.0	−8.0	−57.1

[a]Because Chile was not a democracy in the 1980s, electoral data for the PSCh and PCCh are taken from legislative elections from during the 1960–73 period.

cleaner than in the 1980s. AD and the PCCh, which largely failed to adapt, suffered steep electoral decline.

Conclusion

Economic liberalization and working-class decline pose serious challenges to contemporary labor-based parties. In the advanced industrialized countries, labor-based parties responded to these challenges by undertaking gradual programmatic change and adopting electoral-professional strategies to appeal to growing "new middle-class" electorates. In Latin America, where economic crises were deeper, new middle classes smaller, and poverty and inequality far more extensive, such strategies were less viable. Instead, many labor-based parties opted for clientelistic linkage strategies. Indeed, recent research has shown that party systems based on clientelistic linkages were the *least affected* by the economic crisis and radical reforms that hit Latin America during the 1980s and 1990s (Roberts 2002).

Given widespread theoretical expectations that modernization and economic liberalization will erode the foundations of clientelism, the persistence of machine politics in Latin America is somewhat surprising. Many scholars, including the editors of this volume, view clientelism as being at odds with market-oriented reform. That may be true in the long run, or in the case of economic liberalization in the purest sense. Over the last two decades in Latin America, however, clientelism has proven compatible with fairly extensive neoliberal reforms. Indeed, evidence from Argentina, Brazil, Mexico, Peru, and other Latin American cases suggests that, by dampening popular protest and securing votes for market reforming parties, clientelistic politics may enhance the political feasibility of those reforms. As long as state bureaucracies remain politicized and the rule of law remains relatively weak, political clientelism may survive – and even thrive – in the absence of a heavily regulated economy or bloated public sector. In much of Latin America, neither thoroughgoing legal-bureaucratic reform nor the emergence of powerful constituencies for universalism is on the immediate horizon. Hence, clientelist linkages are likely to endure.

10 Correlates of clientelism: political economy, politicized ethnicity, and post-communist transition

Henry Hale

Why do some countries emerging from autocratic rule feature competition between strong programmatic parties while others become preserves of clientelism? The present chapter contributes to an answer in several ways. First, it urges social scientists to think of clientelistic electoral competition not only in terms of clientelistic parties but also in terms of important non-party forms of political organization (party substitutes) that can constitute extreme manifestations of clientelistic linkage between voters and politicians in some new democracies but that are typically overlooked in studies that focus on parties alone. Second, it stresses that the strength of clientelistic politics can vary widely within a single state and that we can learn much by studying such variation, holding constant country-level variables. Third, it combines these approaches to test key elements of the general theory of clientelism developed by Kitschelt and Wilkinson in this volume's Introduction. Specifically, it takes advantage of a quasi-experimental opportunity presented by the Russian Federation, applying statistical analysis to an original database so as to understand why highly clientelistic provincial political machines are more powerful in some of Russia's eighty-nine regions than in others.

With minor exceptions, the results broadly support the volume's theoretical approach, indicating that on the whole the strongest degrees of regional clientelism are found where the attributes of economic development and political competition are lowest, where the state can most easily monitor and single out for punishment particular economic sectors, and where ethnocultural networks are politicized. We further find that the broad pattern detected in Russia is characteristic of countries with a particular type of communist legacy, that of patrimonial communism, a

The author is grateful to Naomi Wachs for research assistance, the Russian and East European Institute of Indiana University for helping fund this project through its Andrew M. Mellon Foundation Endowment, the editors and George Breslauer for helpful feedback, and Bob Orttung and the EastWest Institute for generosity with data and institutional support.

227

claim suggested by preliminary consideration of some data on nearly all post-communist countries.

Regional economic clientelism: Russian cases

The importance of understanding electoral clientelism is clear with the case of Russia since its politics determine the fate of one-seventh of the world's land mass and the globe's second-largest nuclear arsenal. This chapter focuses on one particularly important locus of patronage politics in Russia, the political machines controlled by its elected regional leaders, or "governors,"[1] during the first decade after the USSR disintegrated.[2] Indeed, these governors are generally agreed to have relied heavily on clientelistic forms of linkage and to be some of the most powerful actors in Russian electoral politics during the 1990s (e.g., Golosov 1997; Stoner-Weiss 1999). The following paragraphs describe more precisely the ways in which this is true in terms of the vocabulary established in this volume's introductory chapter.

Generally speaking, Russia's governors indeed had the power to engage in contingent direct exchange with voters, especially in the second half of the 1990s. This was above all due to their wielding of a highly complex series of levers with which they could target powerful benefits and punishments to specific groups of people (and even to key individuals) and could monitor these people's loyalty so as to determine how to mete out the rewards and sanctions. Since the benefits and punishments could have a major impact on the lives of a region's citizens, these levers frequently proved highly effective in generating votes for governors' preferred candidates in elections.

To begin, Russia's regional patrons usually held important keys to the well being of their region's economic enterprises and were in a strong position to withhold these keys should they learn that these firms failed to deliver desired votes. In many provinces, the state was a major shareholder in important regional enterprises and could directly determine their fates. In other regions, the state maintained tight control over local economic activity through the regulation process, requiring large-scale economic activity to be officially approved by regional administration offices. Often, such influence was exercised through tax rates, subsidies, price regulations, production quotas, building permissions, and banking policies. Also of enormous importance was the governor's role in obtaining and channeling federal or regional subsidies that could be selectively

---

[1] While these posts have a variety of formal titles, this term is used for simplicity's sake.
[2] Gubernatorial elections in Russia were eliminated starting in 2005.

allocated to economic entities in his or her region (Afanas'ev 1997; Treisman 1999).

There can be a fine line between coercion and exchange, particularly in a society where law is little respected and often viewed as unreasonable and hence frequently broken. Regulatory and legal authority can thus be selectively employed, as with the selective enforcement of health, sanitation, ecological protection, and fire safety requirements to harass or punish those not supporting the machine. Typical governors in the 1990s also had at least informal control over critical organs like the tax police, the prosecutor's office, and the regular police. Frequently added to this list were local courts. Since regional judges and legal system employees usually received miserly salaries, governors were often in position to make them much more comfortable, providing them with such things as desirable apartments or salary supplements. To be sure, leases or residency permits could be easily granted or denied to individuals or entities for political purposes (Afanas'ev 1997: 195; Reddaway and Orttung 2004).

Governors also tended to be in a good position to monitor the compliance of particular groups of voters. Monitoring was simplest when voting precincts coincided with constituents' economic dependence on a single enterprise that was highly dependent on the state. This was most obviously the case in rural villages that corresponded to (former) collective or state farms of just a couple of thousand people. Such villages usually constituted a single precinct whose vote totals were easily observed during the counting process. Villages voting the right way could thus be rewarded with vital farm equipment or infrastructure investment while others could be denied such goods. Similar situations existed, for example, in prisons, hospitals, and certain university towns. Monitoring capacities were not uniform across Russia's regions, of course. In the most complex urban settings where workers from many enterprises lived dispersed throughout the city, the compliance of particular firms' employees could not be tracked through vote counting. But, even here, governors could threaten whole groups of enterprise leaders with punishment should the vote not go the "right" way and should the firms not be directly observed actively promoting the machine's candidates. Indeed, governors' administrations were typically enormous institutions that could deploy small armies of officials (often including local representatives) throughout the province to monitor the compliance of elites and, where possible, the masses.

These same powers were also often applied to quash potential rival claimants to provincial patron status. In order to hinder would-be rival bosses or programmatic candidates from communicating an alternative future, opponents might be denied the right to speak on the factory floor, company buildings might be plastered with the machine candidate's campaign material, and that candidate might appear publicly with the firm director in some favorable fashion (not necessarily explicitly campaign-related). Major regional firms in the most clientelistic regions could also be expected to "volunteer" large sums of money to the "right" office-seekers and to avoid donating to rivals, further facilitating the spread and reinforcing the credibility of the governor's candidate's promises and hindering those of his or her rivals. This served to reduce the political competition that could lead people to defect *en masse* and thereby produce a rival victory, undermining the credibility of governors' threats to punish defectors.

Typical governors' political machines in Russia, therefore, had the capacity to engage very strongly in contingent direct exchange through their control over vital parts of the economy and polity and their monitoring capacity. Due to the importance of these areas of gubernatorial control to people's lives and the governors' ability to deny political opposition the opportunity to advance rival claims to control the machine, voting could be highly responsive (elastic) to the exercise of this power and therefore quite predictable.

The fact that Russia's post-communist governors wielded such power is no coincidence. While some have regarded these regional machines as direct holdovers from the Soviet era, they are better seen as a much more recent phenomenon (Hale 2003). Indeed, they developed and reached their peak of power in the 1990s primarily because governors themselves were given a great deal of authority to influence their regions' economic structure and determine the local relationship between the economy and the state through control over the privatization process and regulatory levers. This process originated when the USSR was collapsing, when Russian President Boris Yeltsin sought to outbid his rival and then-superior, Soviet President Mikhail Gorbachev, by offering regional leaders more and more autonomy and power in return for their support.

Some governors found themselves in possession of an additional resource that could be translated into clientelistic power and that is anticipated in this volume's Introduction: ethnic networks cultivated under the Soviet system. The Russian federalism of the 1990s, largely a product of the Soviet period, is structured in part along ethnic lines. Its eighty-nine regions fell into three general categories: (1) *oblasts, krais,* and two major cities (Moscow and St. Petersburg), all of which had no particular ethnic designation; (2) *republics* that were officially designated as homelands for certain "titular" ethnic minorities; and (3) *autonomous oblasts* and *autonomous okrugs* (AOs), ethnically defined territorial administrative units that were formally part of an oblast or krai but that were confusingly also counted as "subjects of the federation" in their own right with direct and separate representation in Russia's upper chamber of parliament, the Federation Council.

The governors of the "ethnic regions" (republics and AOs) thus had an additional patronage opportunity, arranging an exchange by which titular ethnic group members would supply electoral support in return for preferential treatment in education, state employment, territorially concentrated investment, and status. Where ethnicity and geography coincided, it was possible for governors to monitor the "ethnic vote" and to allocate ethnic rewards and punishments accordingly. In most cases, however, the power of the clientelistic exchange was not based so much on explicit monitoring as on the kind of cognitive or motivational mechanisms described in this volume's Introduction. That is, since the Soviet Union had politicized ethnicity and cultivated widespread understandings that republic and AO governments would privilege their titular ethnic groups in concrete ways, the leaders of these regions knew that they could count on a significant degree of support from their titular constituencies merely by providing and publicizing some such privileges. These gubernatorial policies thus effectively constituted a clientelistic exchange of club goods (benefits targeted to an ethnic group) for votes and other manifestations of loyalty to the local regime.

An additional feature of Russia's regional political machines in the 1990s is also significant for the present volume's purposes: their tendency to be non-partisan. The Russia of this time thus recalls important periods in the early United States and in India immediately after independence, during which regionally based and effectively independent political machines dominated local politics in many territories (Aldrich 1995; Weiner 1967). Since they often directly recruited and supported their own candidates without displaying exclusive loyalty to any one party, Russia's regional political machines could usefully be seen as *party substitutes*, organizational forms that effectively competed with political parties for dominance in electoral markets (Hale 2005). This is significant because parties, through their labels and platforms, tend to adopt at least *some* programmatic language even when their primary appeal is patronage, since clientelism tends to have a public aura of illegality or immorality, as noted in this volume's Introduction. To the extent that at least some part of the public takes this programmatic rhetoric seriously, even clientelistic parties can involve some degree of programmatic linkage, especially if party leaders come to see some electoral benefit in not entirely disillusioning program-oriented voters. Party substitutes, on the other hand, often rule out even this limited form of programmatic linkage from the very beginning. They deal with the public stigma attached to clientelistic methods less by taking on clearly programmatic appeals than by adopting

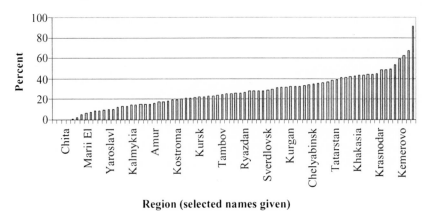

Region (selected names given)

Figure 10.1 Average share of SMD Duma vote won by governors'
candidates in Russia, 1999

one or a combination of the following strategies: "flying below the radar"
and restricting themselves to subnational scope; obscuring their real commitments by avoiding an advertised label or a unifying program; publicly
orienting themselves around the personality and pragmatic competence
of the governor; not pretending to constitute an institution that would
live on after the machine's boss leaves the political scene. Incorporating
largely non-party forms into our study of clientelism, therefore, can give
us new empirical leverage to understand clientelism's sources.

It is important to note that provincial political machines often augment
clientelistic behavior with purely coercive practices that amount to little
more than electoral "cheating" and that do not involve clientelistic content, such as falsifying a vote count. While fraud may be produced by
a clientelistic exchange between the governor and election commission
officials, the voters are not brought into the transaction and, indeed, are
intentionally being cut out of it. When we discuss gubernatorial machine
power in Russia, then, we are not capturing pure clientelistic exchange
between voters and politicians. But since electoral clientelism and coercive practices tend to go together and since electoral clientelism is such
an important part of machine strength, analyzing the determinants of
machine politics in Russia proves to be quite enlightening as to the sources
of electoral clientelism more specifically.

Subnational variation in the strength of clientelism

To say that Russia's governors exemplify machine politics is not to say
that the political machines are equally successful. Instead, they vary considerably in their power. Figure 10.1 reports a good measure of relative

gubernatorial machine strength, with each bar representing the average share of the vote obtained by governor-backed candidates in a given region in the 1999 single-member district voting for the Russian parliament, the Duma. We see that the strength of these provincial machines ranged from the 91 percent of the ballots won in remote Aga-Buriatiia to the low of 0.33 percent netted in Astrakhan. Four governors reportedly stayed above the fray, not backing any candidate, in which case their value on the machine politics scale was scored as 0. To illustrate what these differences mean in concrete terms, it is helpful to briefly contrast the experiences of two Duma candidates backed by two very different regional political machines.

An example of a strong machine in 1999 was Bashkortostan, one of Russia's largest ethnic republics. In the economic sphere, oil-related industry constituted some 40 percent of its GDP in 2000 and state-owned holding companies (BTK and Bashneftekhim) possessed major stakes in virtually all major firms in this sector.[3] The regional leader also controlled a *de facto* regional "central bank" (Bashkreditbank) in which all firms doing business in Bashkortostan were required to keep accounts – a critical lever for monitoring, regulating, rewarding, and punishing local businesses.[4] Clientelistic forms of linkage were the strongest in the republic's remote rural regions, often without gas, sometimes with just one telephone line, frequently full of small villages coinciding with both single farms and single election precincts, and almost always tightly under the thumbs of their collective farm directors. In the three Bashkortostan districts with the largest agrarian populations, the winning margins by the regional leader's favorite candidates in the 1999 Duma elections were quite impressive: 32 percent, 35 percent, and 37 percent. The region's boss also gained electoral support from his network of ethnic Bashkirs, for whom the region is named. In return, he privileged them in appointments and expanded education in their titular language, although he generally tried hard not to completely alienate other groups on which he also depended for electoral support. For example, he sometimes struck deals with leaders of the local ethnic Russian community.

Perm, on the other hand, featured much weaker electoral clientelism in 1999, enjoying a reputation as one of the most "democratic" regions in Russia.[5] Nevertheless, regional political analysts and politicians reported certain elements of clientelistic politics extant in the region. The

---

[3] *Vedomosti*, August 23, 2002, online version.
[4] Kh.B. Asylguzhin, "Banki," in R. Z. Shakurov, ed., *Bashkortostan: Kratkaia Entsiklopediia.* Ufa, Russia: Nauchnoe Izdatel'stvo "Bashkirskaia Entsiklopediia," 1996, pp. 145–46.
[5] *RFE/RL Newsline*, October 17, 2002.

governor, for example, retained a great deal of influence on the performance of key regional firms like the defense-industrial giant Perm Motors (highly dependent on federal orders) and Uralkalii (a leading Russian chemical concern). Observers also regarded these state-corporate ties as electorally important. But this did not prevent candidacies based outside the patronage system from seriously challenging incumbents who had both gubernatorial and corporate backing. For example, newspaper editor Sergei Levitan launched a spirited idea-based (though negative) campaign against incumbent Viktor Pokhmelkin in 1999 and came from far behind to within four percentage points of victory.[6]

The theoretical framework elaborated by Kitschelt and Wilkinson in the Introduction provides useful intellectual leverage for understanding why and when such variation will occur. Without repeating the logic itself, the following paragraphs discuss its major implications for Russia and how they can be operationalized and thus tested against Russia's empirical patterns. We then use these operationalized concepts in a statistical analysis of regional variations in levels of clientelism.

Development

Russia, with a per capita GDP of about $7,500 (purchasing power parity in US dollars[7]), was at a level of intermediate economic development in 1999. While a one-country study cannot test the impact of cross-national variation in average economic development levels, we can explore the impact of within-country variation in the attributes of development. For one thing, we would certainly expect the most rural regions of Russia, most distant from the effects of economic development, to display the greatest degree of gubernatorial success. Agricultural villages, generally poor, might be expected to prize immediate goods that facilitate survival over vaguer promises of long-term economic benefit. Geographically concentrated and isolated from other populations with other sources of income, farming communities are highly dependent on the supply of goods and services that the state can provide at the same time that their voting behavior is easy to monitor given that they tend to constitute single precincts (or just a few). We would thus expect the most electorally powerful gubernatorial machines to be in those regions with the greatest shares of their workforces employed in agriculture (the variable *Rural* in the statistical analysis that follows).

---

[6] *Kompan'on* (Perm), no. 32, September 14, 1999, pp. 1, 4.
[7] United Nations Development Programme Web site, www.undp.org/hdr2001/indicator/ cty_f_RUS.html, last accessed November 1, 2005.

Beyond the urban–rural divide, however, the effects of variation in regional wealth within a single country raise more complex issues. At the national level, higher levels of wealth should reduce clientelism, according to the Kitschelt/Wilkinson theory. Within a country at an intermediate level of development, however, the relationship between wealth and clientelism may not be linear. A leap from a low level of development (say, $1,000 per capita GDP PPP) to a high level (say, $30,000), can be expected under certain conditions to strongly undermine clientelism across all regions of a given country. At the same time, when one finds a smaller difference in wealth across regions within a country that is on average at an intermediate level of development and that already features strong clientelism, this may simply mean that wealthier regions have more resources with which to fuel the patronage machine. Thus while Russia's poorest regions were indeed quite poor, they did not approach the kind of squalor and isolation found in, say, Burkina Faso. Likewise, while Moscow was far richer, it too would rarely have been confused with a Western European capital in 1999 and thus even its level of development would not generally be expected to be sufficient to undermine entrenched clientelism. Furthermore, in such circumstances, higher popular incomes can be one sign that a political machine is doing well by its clients, delivering on promises to keep incomes high. This logic can be studied in the statistical analysis that follows through a measure of the average real per capita income in each region as of 1998 (*Income 1998*).

Independently of these effects, economic development is also expected to produce greater heterogeneity in politicians' constituencies. When people are employed by an increasingly diverse array of economic entities, it can become harder for patrons to monitor compliance and accurately mete out rewards to true supporters and punishments to true opponents. The variable *Concentration 1999* thus reports the share of a region's GDP comprised by its largest industry as of 1999. Since we would like to distinguish between the effects of sectoral concentration (*Concentration 1999*) that may have been influenced or created by governors themselves during the 1990s and the complexity of a regional economy independent of sectoral concentration, we employ a distinct measure (*Complexity 1990*) that captures the complexity of individual regional economies as of 1990, just before the end of the Soviet period and before the transformations of the 1990s.[8]

---

[8] The correlation between Concentration 1999 and Complexity 1990 is only −0.07. The latter index was provided by Ksenia Yudaeva, Maria Gorban, Vladimir Popov, and Natalia Volchkova. See their "Down and Up the Stairs: Paradoxes of Russian Economic Growth," www.gdnet.org/pdf/draft_country_studies/Russia_final.pdf, last accessed November 1, 2005.

Economic development can also be expected to work through several other channels that we explore here. Since modernity usually comes from a thriving center, the *Remoteness* of a region from Moscow (measured in kilometers) would be associated with higher levels of electoral clientelism if this theory is correct. Provinces that are the most penetrated by mass media (*Newspaper*, capturing total number of newspapers circulated, and *TV/radio*, indicating number of stations per capita) are also usually considered more modern and would thus be expected to display weaker regional political machines.

Political competition

Since political machine success is partly manifested in electoral success, one must be careful to avoid tautology in asserting that low levels of political competition produce machines' electoral success. There are several ways to test the logic behind this proposition while avoiding tautological reasoning. A core piece of this argument, as also elaborated in the chapter by Medina and Stokes, is that clients will be less responsive to their patrons' inducements when there is an increased chance that the patrons will not be around after the election to follow through on their threats and promises. Accordingly, when patrons themselves are up for reelection, more uncertainty is introduced as to whether the patron will in fact be in a position afterwards either to reward or punish voters in other simultaneous elections (such as parliamentary elections held on the same day as gubernatorial elections). Patronage networks can thus be expected to be strongest, and "subpatrons" (e.g., machine-backed parliamentary candidates) can be expected to win more votes, when elections of patrons and subpatrons do not occur simultaneously. This argument runs counter to common Russian wisdom, which tended during this time to expect a "coat-tails" effect by which a governor's victory would enhance the electoral prospects of gubernatorial allies. This makes for a strong test for this volume's logic. Operationally, then, we create a dummy variable *Gov/Duma Coincide* that is coded "1" for the nine regions that held their gubernatorial elections on the same day as the Duma voting in December 1999.

An additional way to operationalize competitiveness might be to consider whether the governor was likely to have been a figure consolidating regional interests. We thus include a variable (*Ex-Head Legislature*) indicating whether a regional leader's background included having served as chair of the province's first elected legislative assembly in 1990, when competitive elections to these bodies were introduced (and before governorships were instituted). These first regional legislatures were all elected in single-member district elections, meaning that to become speaker of the body, a leader had to possess strong coalition-building, log-rolling skills capable of connecting with representatives of a majority of that province's legislative election districts. Presumably, only the most effective speakers were later able to translate these posts into governorships, indicating that they were indeed capable of building broad-based regional coalitions of forces. While the indicator is far from perfect, we might still posit that governors with such backgrounds were best able to reduce or manage political competition in their regions, facilitating more effective patronage politics.

Public control of the political economy

As Kitschelt and Wilkinson argue, clientelistic exchange is facilitated by greater state involvement in the economy, especially when this involvement means direct administration. One of the most important state roles in the Russian economy has been the administration of pensions. While retirees are not geographically concentrated or characterized by other traits that make them easy to monitor, they are highly risk-averse since many of them often live in poverty and even on the brink of starvation. Pensions have been miserly indeed in the post-Soviet era. Their risk aversion can increase their responsiveness to patrons' promises to raise pensions in return for their votes even though governors actually have difficulty monitoring their voting activity outside of hospitals and nursing homes. Furthermore, pensioners' long experience with totalitarian rule arguably disposes many of them to look primarily to incumbent state leaders for support. Russia's pensioners are also like their American counterparts in their high turnout levels on election day, further encouraging patrons to appeal to them through promises of club goods even though their election day behavior is frequently hard to monitor. A variable labeled *Pension* is thus included in the analysis, indicating the percentage of a given region's population that receives pensions.

Of course, it is also important for governors to be seen as able to deliver on their promises of economic benefit for those who vote for them. One such indicator, as noted above in the discussion of economic development, might be averages in real income. Another indicator of performance would measure not the overall level of economic well being in the governor's region but the rate of improvement in key economic problems facing important blocs of voters, as citizens were most likely to perceive them. Since one of the major economic problems of the 1990s was wage arrears, we consider here the percentage of 1998's unpaid wages that remained unpaid in 1999 (*Arrears 1999*). Higher values of this measure, then, mean higher levels of arrears, poorer economic performance, and hence less effective political machines.

If we suppose that bosses with backgrounds in business or Soviet politics might be better than others at exercising control over the economy for the purpose of delivering private or club goods for political reasons, it makes sense to include a series of dummy variables based on governors' biographies so as to see if they are correlated with effective clientelism. These are coded "1" for a given region if its incumbent governor during the 1999 Duma elections was ever: the first secretary of a Communist Party of the Soviet Union organization at the regional, city, or district level (the variable *Ex-CPSU*); the director of an industrial enterprise prior to the first major economic reform, which took place in 1988 (*USSR Manager*); the director of an industrial enterprise during the Soviet-era reform period of 1988–91 (*Perestroika Manager*); the director of a state or collective farm (*Ex-Farm Director*); the head of a region's executive branch of government prior to 1988 (*USSR Executive Branch*); the head of a region's executive branch of government during the reform period of 1988–91 (*Perestroika Executive Branch*); or a leader in the Communist Youth League (*Young Communist*).

Additionally, we consider whether governors with roots in the "new" political economy tended to be more effective clientelists. These dummy variables are coded "1" if the governor of a given region was an industrial director in the post-communist era (*New Manager*) or a businessman in the private sector prior to becoming governor (*New Businessman*). Governors born in their own regions might also be posited to have had deeper ties to important social networks facilitating the effective delivery of promised goods and extraction of demanded votes (*Native of Region*). Those coming out of military careers might be expected to have had the special organizational abilities and personal authority necessary to build strong political machines (*Military*). Finally, we include a variable simply indicating a governor's relative *Youth*, measured by the year of his or her birth; younger governors might be expected to have been quicker to learn how to exercise economic power in the new transitional environment.

Finally, we might posit that the economies of the most populous regions are the most difficult for patrons to control. We thus include the variable *Population 1998*, defined as the number of residents in a given region.

Ethnicity

We can systematically consider the importance of ethnocultural networks, posited by Kitschelt and Wilkinson to be important, using three variables.

Two dummy variables capture whether a given region is officially designated as an ethnic homeland: *Republic* and *AO*. Republics not only feature ethnic networks institutionalized through decades of Soviet rule, but also possess certain additional institutional resources (such as academies of science) meant to promote the development and cultures of the titular groups. AOs, while formally subjects of the federation in their own right, are also formally parts of other regions that do not themselves have an ethnic designation (that is, krais and oblasts). This implies that while AOs are expected to feature ethnic networks, they have fewer institutional resources than republics since they are officially subordinate to another region. Thus we expect republics and AOs to display greater degrees of clientelism than non-ethnic regions, although AOs' ambiguous status might moderate their effects. If ethnic networks are important, we should also find evidence that those republics and AOs led by a member of the titular ethnic group (as indicated in a dummy variable *Titular Ethnicity*) tended to have the strongest political machines. Of course, titular ethnic networks might still be mobilized by non-titulars, though we would expect this to be less consistently effective.

Iteration

Finally, since the theory developed in the introductory chapter posits that clientelism can be reinforced by learning on the part of both patrons and clients, it is interesting to consider if regions that had previously held the greatest number of elections tended to experience stronger electoral clientelism. The variable *# Governor Elections* is thus created, counting the number of gubernatorial elections that a region had experienced prior to the 1999 Duma race.[9]

Institutions

The present volume adopts a very narrow understanding of the term "institution," referring primarily here to election system law.[10] National-level institutions are of course held constant across regions and their importance for clientelism cannot be tested here. At the regional level, only two Russian provinces had parliamentary systems as of the end of 1999 (Udmurtiia and Dagestan) and only four had introduced

---

[9] Gubernatorial races were held in different regions on different days throughout the year and some regions held their first such elections long before others.

[10] Hale (2003) posits a much broader definition, finding that institutions in the more general sense are very important. Some of these institutions in the broader sense are correlated with development levels, linking the argument in Hale (2003) with the present chapter.

proportional representation (PR) systems for some of their legislative seats by the end of 2000. Figure 10.1 makes clear that there is plenty of variation in the power of governors' political machines that is not due to a difference between parliamentary and presidential systems or that between PR and other forms of legislative representation.

The quasi-experiment: cross-regional variation

A multicase single-country study will enable us to hold country-level variables (such as national electoral institutions) constant in order to draw a bead on other factors posited to be at work. As was discussed in the preceding section, there are reasonable cross-regional tests for nearly all of the major hypotheses generated in Kitschelt's and Wilkinson's chapter.

Russia is attractive as a quasi-experiment for several methodological reasons. For one thing, its immense size and tremendous cross-regional diversity give the researcher significant variation on key factors of interest. Equally importantly, the Russian case offers an excellent measure of the strength of governors' political machines: the average percentage of the vote won by candidates backed by a region's governor in the 224 single-member district (SMD) contests for election to the lower house of the Russian parliament, the Duma, held in 1999.[11] The vote share received by these "subpatrons" reflects what we are interested in when we talk about the strength of political machines that rely heavily on clientelistic forms of linkage – the ability of these machines to secure votes in elections.[12]

Very importantly, data for the 1999 SMD Duma elections are available and have been compiled by the author. Along with the variables discussed above, the dataset used here contains the average percentage of the vote won by candidates backed by each governor in 197 of the 224 districts carved out of the country's 89 regions. Assessments of gubernatorial support were based on extensive and often overlapping reports from three sources: *Radio Svoboda* provincial correspondents, the Russian regional observer network of the EastWest Institute (EWI), and the internal SMD campaign database of a major Russian political party that was provided to the author.[13] Since some measures of

---

[11] No election was held in the Chechnya district due to the military operation taking place there in 1999.

[12] It is not important here whether this vote-winning involves simply finding candidates that already possess high ballot-getting potential or making winners out of candidates who would otherwise be sure losers. It is assumed that one indicator of governor machine strength is the ability to incorporate strong candidates no matter whether they are co-opted or "created."

[13] *Radio Svoboda* transcripts can be obtained at http://www.svoboda.org/archive/elections99, last accessed on October 29, 2005.

important variables are missing for a small number of regions (in ways not expected to be systematically correlated with independent and dependent variables), we conduct a full statistical analysis on 67 of Russia's 89 regions.

The variation in Russian regional machine strength, as measured here, is illustrated above in Figure 10.1. The gradation between the extremes is remarkably smooth, suggesting that regions do not simply fall into one or two categories determined by stark differences on one or two variables. This augments our confidence that a variety of factors might be at work, that there is no single "Russian level" of regional machine strength that is uniform across the country, and hence that its eighty-nine regions are likely to be fruitful as a quasi-experimental laboratory for exploring the determinants of clientelistic power. This smooth gradation also means that the data do not include significant "outliers" that could potentially skew results.

The *Tobit* statistical technique is used for the quantitative analysis because it is designed for datasets in which the dependent variable (in this case, the average SMD vote share for a regional governor's candidates) is bounded either from above or below (King 1998). In data used in this analysis, there are four cases where the governor did not actively intervene in the elections, in which case the strength of gubernatorial clientelism is coded at the minimum value of zero.

Correlates of regional machine strength

Table 10.1 summarizes broad patterns identified in the strength of governors' political machines by the multivariate analysis. In order to most effectively communicate which sets of variables are supplying the greatest causal power to the equation, we report the average percentage change in gubernatorial candidates' votes that is estimated to be brought about by a one-standard-deviation change in each listed independent variable.[14]

Economic development

The statistical analysis broadly supports the claim that a logic of development can help us understand clientelism. A change of one standard deviation in the share of a region's population employed in agriculture tends to correlate with a 6.5 percent jump in the vote-winning ability of a governor-backed candidate in the 1999 SMD Duma competition. We have over 99 percent confidence that the observed relationship between

[14] The constant is estimated as 30.1 (SE = 4.2); N = 66; Pseudo R^2 = 0.09.

Table 10.1 *Change in percentage of governors' candidates' vote totals associated with one-standard-deviation change in the following factors in Russia's 1999 SMD Duma election*

	Theory predicts	Magnitude of effect from 1 SD change	(SE)
Economic development			
Income 1998	+	+ 8.6**	(4.2)
Rural	+	+ 6.5***	(2.3)
Remoteness	+	+ 5.8**	(2.5)
TV/radio	−	+ 9.2	(16.0)
Newspaper	−	−4.3	(3.2)
Concentration 1999	+	+ 2.1	(2.1)
Complexity 1990	−	−1.5	(1.8)
Competitiveness			
Governor was head of legislature	+	+ 3.4**	(1.7)
Gubernatorial, Duma elections simultaneous	−	−3.0*	(1.6)
Control over political economy			
Pension	+	+ 6.9**	(2.8)
Population 1998	−	+ 6.0***	(2.1)
Governor was farm director	+	+ 3.6*	(1.8)
Wage arrears	−	−3.6*	(2.1)
Governor was USSR manager	+	−2.4	(1.6)
Governor was Young Communist	+	−2.3	(1.6)
Governor youth	+	+ 2.3	(2.3)
Governor was CPSU boss	+	−1.9	(1.8)
Governor was career military	+	−1.8	(2.0)
Governor is native of region	+	−1.6	(2.0)
Governor was in USSR Executive Branch	+	−1.1	(2.0)
Governor was new businessman	+	−0.9	(1.5)
Governor was Perestroika manager	+	+ 0.8	(2.3)
Governor was in Perestroika Executive Branch	+	+ 0.8	(2.0)
Governor was new manager	+	−0.05	(2.0)
Ethnicity			
AO	+	+12.0***	(4.1)
Governor is of titular ethnicity	+	+ 5.0*	(2.9)
Republic	+	+ 3.5	(2.8)
Iteration			
# Gubernatorial Elections held	+	−1.8	(2.1)

*p < 0.10   **p < 0.05   ***p < 0.001

agricultural employment and these candidates' performances is not random. Similarly, we have over 99 percent confidence that the greater the distance a region is from the developmental center, Moscow, the more powerful are governors' political machines. One standard deviation change in this distance goes along with a 5.8 percent improvement in the electoral performance of governor-endorsed Duma candidates.

While theory expects that a major increase in income would reduce clientelism nationwide, for countries at middle levels of development a more moderate increase in income concentrated in a few regions might not be enough to undermine entrenched clientelistic relationships. Indeed, as Lyne argues in her chapter and as Kitschelt and Wilkinson reiterate in theirs, it is only at a very high level of income that people generally lose any incentive to accept clientelistically targeted goods. Thus in countries like Russia, where even the richest region falls far short of this very high level, a moderate increase in regional income means mainly that there is more patronage for the governor to distribute and that clients are likely to be happier with the clientelistic arrangement. We thus see that a one-standard-deviation rise in real provincial income correlates with an 8.6 percent improvement in the electoral success of regional machine candidates.

Three other economic development variables are found to be associated with gubernatorial clientelism in the expected manner: economic concentration as of 1999 is linked to stronger clientelism while greater numbers of newspapers and greater economic complexity as of 1990 are connected with weaker clientelism. At the same time, however, the statistical analysis cannot rule out with at least 90 percent confidence the null hypothesis, that these factors in fact have no effect on subpatrons' electoral performance.

Only one variable appears to contradict the economic development hypothesis as elaborated in this volume: the number of television and radio stations per capita in a region is not significantly correlated with our measure of electoral clientelism and, if anything, points in the opposite direction. Closer consideration of what this variable is actually measuring in Russia, however, strongly suggests that this negative finding is more a problem of theory operationalization than a problem of the theory itself. This is because Russia's regional political machines typically gained control of television during the transition from totalitarian rule and have since maintained or even strengthened their grips on local channels. More often than not, then, local television is captured by clientelistic networks and serves as a mouthpiece for them. If television is to have an effect, then, we should expect it to strengthen regional political machines until it starts to gain a modicum of true independence.

Competitiveness

The quantitative analysis also supports the hypothesis that clientelistic exchange is less effective for politicians when they face competition for their positions as patrons. For one thing, governors' Duma candidates received significantly fewer votes when the governors themselves were up for reelection against an opponent and were hence vulnerable to replacement after the election. We have over 90 percent confidence that this relationship is not a random one. Russian governors have negative coat-tails, it appears, contrary to the expectations of many Russian observers. Moreover, governors who had been the first heads of their regions' legislatures – and who were thereby likely to be highly dominant coalition-building figures in their provinces – tended to generate stronger Duma election performances by their endorsees than did otherwise identical governors. Our confidence in this relationship is over 95 percent.

Control over the political economy

The statistical analysis also broadly corroborates the theoretical claim that greater effective state control over key economic resources facilitates stronger clientelistic relationships between politicians and voters. The clearest result involves Russia's retirees, a large population that is highly dependent on pensions administered by the state. A one-standard-deviation change in the share of a province's population that receives state pensions is associated with a 6.9 percent higher vote for regional subpatrons in the 1999 SMD Duma competition. While it is hard for governors to explicitly monitor the voting patterns of pensioners, they are highly risk-averse and live on the brink of poverty or starvation. They thus tend to share with governors a widespread expectation that they will vote for incumbents who promise to hike pensions and provide other goods and services this population demands, such as subsidized health care. We have over 95 percent confidence that this statistical result is not random. Likewise, we find that former collective or state farm directors, who we posit know well how to maximally control the rural economy for political purposes, tend to generate significantly more votes for their Duma candidates than do otherwise identical governors. This finding is statistically significant at the 90 percent level.

Those governors who proved most capable of delivering goods to their populations, improving the degree to which wages were paid on time between 1998 and 1999, also generated better votes for their subpatrons running in parliamentary elections in 1999 – a finding in which we have over 90 percent confidence. For every standard deviation by which a provincial leader was able to reduce wage arrears between 1998 and 1999, that leader's favorite candidates could count on an average bump of 3.6 percent of the vote in the 1999 election.

The only statistically significant finding contradicting theoretical expectations involved the variable Population 1998. While we posited that Russia's patrons might find it most difficult to control the economy of the most populous regions, we found to the contrary that those provinces with the largest numbers of residents also had the strongest political machines. A Russia-specific explanation suggests itself for this phenomenon. In a widely cited piece, Treisman (1997) argues that Russian federalism in the 1990s featured a critical process whereby regions bargained with the central government for resource transfers. Accordingly, regions with the most bargaining power tended to get rewarded with the greatest volume of transfers, and a large population was one factor he argued could give a region bargaining power. One interpretation of the present finding, then, is that the most populous provinces were able to extract disproportionately large resource transfers from the central government and that these transfers were used to make the patronage machine more effective.

Except for the former farm directors and ex-speakers of regional legislatures discussed above, the regression analysis finds no support for the notion that bosses with different kinds of experience in the (old) political system or (old) political economy were any more effective than others in winning votes for their Duma candidates. While the signs on a few of the coefficients for these variables are in the expected direction, many are not, and not one relationship is found with at least 90 percent confidence to be something other than zero.[15]

Ethnicity

We find very strong support for the claim that ethnic networks tended to be associated with strong clientelism in Russia in 1999. To begin, ethnically defined regions ruled by bosses who themselves belonged to the titular ethnic group (*Titular Ethnicity*) tended to have more powerful political machines than otherwise identical regions. We have over 90 percent confidence in this result. Moreover, while the relationship between ethnic *Republic* status and machine candidate strength is statistically insignificant, it is in the predicted direction. While this might seem less than impressive at first glance, it is crucial to point out that the *Republic* variable is highly correlated (0.79) with the *Titular Ethnicity*

---

[15] This basic result holds using a wide variety of categorizations of many of these variables.

of governors. This tells us two things. First, the fact that there is little independent information to distinguish the effects of these two variables means that the estimates of statistical significance for each are likely to be underestimates. Indeed, dropping either one produces a finding of strong significance for the other. Second, this tells us that what mattered about republics in 1999 was less their institutional make-up or resources (such as what Treisman 1997 suggests they gain through bargaining with the central government) than their ethnic content. Ethnic regions mattered most clearly when led by a member of the titular ethnicity, which is precisely what we would expect if ethnic networks themselves mattered independently of the resources they wielded.

While the finding that the ethnically defined AOs are characterized by higher levels of clientelism confirms theoretical expectations, it is still surprising that this effect is estimated to be *stupendously* strong – stronger even than that associated with the more institutionally powerful republics. We might conjecture that the variable AO is picking up not only "ethnic" effects, but also another factor with which it is tightly correlated: the population of Duma districts. Whereas virtually all other electoral districts for the 1999 elections were roughly the same size (between 400,000 – 600,000 people) as was required by Russian law, this law also required that each subject of the federation have at least one Duma district. Since most AOs were far smaller than the target district size, they wound up with some very tiny districts. For example, Evenkiia's district contained a total of just 12,759 registered voters in 1999. Four others had fewer than 50,000.[16] It is not difficult to suspect that such districts are far more easily monitored and that their economies are far more easily "administered" than those of regions containing ten times the number of people. This finding, of course, is in accordance with the theoretical claim that greater control over the political economy facilitates clientelism.

Iteration

The statistical analysis cannot rule out that there is no relationship between the strength of Russia's regional political machines and the number of times Russian voters have had a chance to cast ballots in a gubernatorial election. If anything, voters appear to be less receptive to their

---

[16] Central Election Commission of the Russian Federation, *Vybory Deputatov Gosudarstvennoi Dumy Federal'nogo Sobraniia Rossiiskoi Federatsii 1999*. Moscow: Ves' Mir, 2000, pp. 25, 38.

patrons' endorsees in Duma elections the more times they have voted in gubernatorial elections.

The post-communist world beyond Russia

While this study has sought to demonstrate that the strength of clientelism can vary greatly within a single country and that much can be gained from studying this variation, it is interesting to speculate as to whether the patterns we find within Russia are likely to resemble those found elsewhere in the post-communist world. In terms of economic development levels, the post-communist countries all still remain in a broad intermediate category. Thus while countries like Poland and Estonia that are now developing most rapidly might be starting to see a gradual erosion in clientelistic forms of linkage, we are unlikely to see pronounced effects owing specifically to development until these countries reach significantly higher development levels.

The greatest divergence among post-communist countries in the shorter run is likely to involve variation in levels of political competitiveness and control over the political economy. For example, while pensions are associated with strong clientelism in Russia, this is because pensions were state-administered there as of 1999 and this is not currently the case in all post-communist countries. Similarly, differences in the political reform process have generated more competitive political outcomes in some countries than in others.

A useful approach in coping with such complexity is the *indirect legacy* approach developed by Kitschelt, Mansfeldova, Markowski, and Toka (1999). The basic idea is that clusters of old-regime characteristics constitute distinctive types of communist legacy that tend to produce predictable patterns of post-communist politics by "weighting the dice" toward certain outcomes. One such type is *patrimonial communism*, characterized by vertical chains of dependence, extensive patronage and clientelistic networks, personality cults, low rational-bureaucratic institutionalization, and low tolerance for opposition outside of the regime. This is distinct from bureaucratic-authoritarian communism, the most totalitarian and bureaucratically stratified form, and national-accommodative communism, a moderately bureaucratized but relatively liberal type of system.

This typology, when applied to the Russian evidence presented here, helps us venture several generalizations regarding other post-communist countries. For one thing, Kitschelt *et al.* (1999) have argued that patrimonial communist regimes tended to adopt political institutions that favored incumbents. To the extent such reforms were successful, we might expect that countries with patrimonial communist legacies would feature less competitiveness and hence stronger clientelism.

In addition, patrimonial communist regimes, with weak opposition and a strong state, tended to have less interest than did the other two kinds of communist countries in adopting more radical economic reforms during the transition. Such reforms were often aimed at separating the state from the economy, thereby reducing opportunities for clientelistic exchange. Patrimonial communist regimes thus have had a tendency to preserve state-dependent populations that the Russian case shows are very important facilitators of electoral clientelism. Pensioners and (former) collective farms are two examples. Countries emerging from bureaucratic-authoritarian and national-accommodative communism, through their greater propensity to adopt radical market-oriented reforms, are more likely to dismantle these fonts of clientelism at the point of transition. The Russian case, however, suggests that clientelism can still develop in countries that adopt the mantle of radical reform since the reform process might give power to local politicians who, if sufficiently skilled and ambitious, could use this power to build up their own political machines even in highly complex and industrialized economies. The city of Moscow stands as an example, where a talented mayor built something resembling a "one-company town" out of Russia's most advanced and diverse economy (Hale 2003; Orttung 2002).

While Kitschelt *et al.* (1999) have shown in a study of four countries that patrimonial communist legacies tend to produce higher levels of patronage-based as opposed to programmatic party competition, the present chapter suggests an additional (if preliminary) test considering nearly all post-communist countries. If non-party electoral competition reflects an extreme type of clientelism, as was argued above is the case with key party substitutes in Russia, then variation in the degree to which a country's parliamentarians are elected as independents rather than party nominees should give us at least a rough idea of the relative prevalence of clientelistic politics across countries. Table 10.2 thus shows that of the twenty-five post-communist countries considered, all of those whose parliaments contained at least some independent members had patrimonial communist legacies.[17] While a more thorough test will have to await future work, this preliminary test does suggest that the general patterns

---

[17] Counting in this category Lithuania, which Kitschelt *et al.* (1999) describe as having a mixed legacy of national-accommodative and patrimonial communism. Russia's measure is relatively low because Kremlin authorities in 2003 applied an unprecedented effort to unify regional political machines under a party label for reasons described in Hale (2006).

Table 10.2 *Communist legacy type and independent representation in Parliament in post-communist countries in most recent election as of mid-2004*

Country	Type of communist legacy	Year of election	Percent of parliamentary seats won by independents
Belarus	Patrimonial	2000	73.6
Kyrgyzstan	Patrimonial	2000	69.5
Uzbekistan	Patrimonial	1999	50.4
Kazakhstan	Patrimonial	1999	44.2
Armenia	Patrimonial	2003	28.2
Azerbaijan	Patrimonial	2000	20.8
Ukraine	Patrimonial	2002	20.7
Tajikistan	Patrimonial	2000	15.9
Russia	Patrimonial	2003	14.9
Georgia[a]	Patrimonial	2004	9.3
Lithuania	National-Accommodative/ Patrimonial	2000	2.1
Albania	Patrimonial	2001	1.4
Bulgaria	Patrimonial	2001	0
Croatia	National-Accommodative	2003	0
Czech Rep.	Bureaucratic-Authoritarian	2002	0
Estonia	National-Accommodative/ Patrimonial	2003	0
Hungary	National-Accommodative	2002	0
Latvia	National-Accommodative/ Patrimonial	2002	0
Macedonia	Patrimonial	2002	0
Moldova	Patrimonial	2001	0
Poland	Bureaucratic-Authoritarian/National-Accommodative	2001	0
Romania	Patrimonial	2000	0
Slovakia	National-Accommodative/ Patrimonial	2002	0
Slovenia	National-Accommodative	2000	0
Turkmenistan	Patrimonial	1999	0

[a]Excludes 11 seats set aside for Abkhazia representatives elected in 1992.
Sources: Hale 2006, Kitschelt *et al.* 1999.

detected in Russia are to be found in at least as strong a measure in other countries with patrimonial communist legacies.

Conclusion

Overall, a qualitative study of Russia and a quantitative analysis of patterns across its regions illustrates the usefulness of the general developmental perspective laid out by the editors of the present volume. Elections tend to revolve most strongly around clientelistic forms of exchange when economic development and political competitiveness are low, when state control over the economy is high, and when ethnocultural networks have been politicized by the state. Even more broadly, there is evidence that relatively low political competition and high state control over the economy are characteristic of countries with one particular kind of communist legacy, the legacy of patrimonial communism.

This chapter has also argued for the importance of studying non-partisan forms of electoral organization that can be important parts of politics in some countries. Since such forms frequently eschew almost any programmatic component in seeking office, they often represent extreme forms of clientelistic politics. While governors' political machines did frequently flirt with party labels during the 1990s, they generally behaved in a non-partisan manner in 1999 and their political machines' success in electing candidates to the national parliament hinged on the kinds of factors emphasized in this volume: development, competitiveness, control over the economy, and ethnicity. Moreover, we found that the greatest levels of non-party representation in parliaments across the post-communist world were in those countries with patrimonial communist legacies. Future studies will do well to flesh out the cross-national analysis of clientelism in the post-communist world as well as to study the degree to which patterns of cross-regional variation in levels of patronage politics within these countries resemble those in Russia that were detected here.

11 Political institutions and linkage strategies

Wolfgang C. Müller

Individual politicians and political parties can be linked to their (prospective) voters by various means (Lawson 1980; Müller 1989; Kitschelt 2000b). The three most commonly referred to in the literature, beginning with Max Weber (1976), are policy, clientelism, and charisma. As charisma is a rare gift and hardly any Western party nowadays builds exclusively or overwhelmingly on the charisma of its leader I will not address it here. It is sufficient to note that charisma can be combined with any of the other linkage strategies. Likewise, policy and clientelism can go together. Moreover, I take it that policy linkage nowadays is the rule in Western democracies. Although this is probably more true at the normative level – the self-presentation of the relevant actors – than empirically, electoral politics are mostly policy-driven even in the countries that are labeled "high in clientelism" below. If anything, clientelism is nowadays less important for tying voters to political parties than two decades or more ago. Hence, the chapter is interested in the question of which institutional features make it more or less likely that linkages based on policies are *accompanied* by clientelistic appeals (and potentially provide for clientelism as the main linkage mechanism).

This chapter employs the definition of clientelism used throughout the volume as *particularistic* and *direct* exchange between clients and politicians. Directness means that in contrast to programmatic linkages the politicians/parties are able to identify their clients individually and engage in a contract-like exchange relationship in which politicians provide goods and services in exchange for electoral and other support.

In the political science literature "clientelism" sometimes has a broader meaning and involves pork-barrel legislation, i.e., legislation that only benefits constituencies targeted by *political* criteria, and policies that benefit specific social classes. While the latter does not conform to both criteria employed here, pork-barrel legislation shares particularism with patronage, but not directness. This means that bridges, roads, cultural centers, or whatever goes to a specific district, benefit *all* citizens living there. However, pork-barrel legislation produces a second beneficial effect: contracts for the construction and maintenance of these buildings. These contracts are club goods and therefore a patronage resource. Hence, geographically targeted pork-barrel legislation is likely to impact on the availability of patronage resources. When engaging in pork-barrel politics politicians often value both the collective goods that directly appeal to the voters and the club goods that can be used for exercising patronage.

Given that patronage to a large extent is "cover politics," its measurement is a notorious problem. While the country-specific literature provides many insights, comparative assessments of its scope and relevance are difficult, particularly given the great variation of direct and indirect patronage forms (see below). Manow (2002: 25) therefore has taken the international Corruption Perception Index (CPI) of Transparency International as a proxy for party patronage and has found it highly correlated with a judgmental rank order of countries according to patronage by national governments as derived from Blondel and Cotta (1996). The CPI measures the images of the relative level of corruption in various countries as held by international businessmen and is based on their contacts with business firms and government officials in the respective countries. The tying of voters or activists to political parties by the means of mass patronage at best indirectly impacts on the index. The same is true for the judgmental evidence of patronage that focuses at the apex of political power, the national government (Blondel and Cotta 1996; Müller 2000). Therefore the following grouping of Western democracies according to their levels of party patronage in the post-war period in four categories, worked out by Herbert Kitschelt and the author on the basis of a qualitative assessment of the literature, does not fully conform to these earlier attempts and, of course, remains debatable. To be sure, there are relevant differences between the countries in each group, nevertheless the ordering is alphabetical and not an attempt to rank order.

- No or virtually no party patronage: Denmark, Finland, Norway, and Sweden.
- Low level of party patronage: the Netherlands, Switzerland, and UK.
- Medium level of party patronage: France, Germany, Iceland, Ireland, Luxembourg, and Portugal, Spain, and the USA.
- High level of party patronage: Austria, Belgium, Greece, and Italy.

As time changes, party patronage does so both in scope and form. Although the chapter will identify some trends, it must leave finer distinctions for more specialized literature. Occasionally I will refer also to other systems that share specific institutions with countries included here, but generally this set of countries is the reference point of the present chapter.

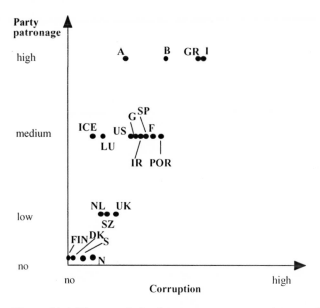

Figure 11.1 The association between patronage and corruption

Figure 11.1 places the CPI for 2000 relative to this four-fold categorization of the relative importance of patronage. The CPI ranges from 0 (highly corrupt) to 10 (highly clean) and covers more than 100 states. The Western countries covered in this chapter together with the other OECD nations plus a few relatively prosperous Asian, African, and Latin American countries occupy the top (clean) third and, with the exceptions of Italy (4.6) and Greece (4.9) score in the upper half of the ten-point scale. A worldwide attempt at measuring patronage without doubt would similarly compress the spread of countries in the vertical dimension of Figure 11.1. Nevertheless, Figure 11.1 suggests that countries placed in the same patronage category show considerable variation in terms of perceived corruption and countries with similar levels of perceived corruption are classified as displaying quite different levels of corruption. The greatest mismatch between patronage and corruption is Austria which is classified in the highest patronage category but is considered cleaner than most countries with a medium amount of party patronage. As mentioned above, mass party patronage is not a phenomenon that is likely to impinge directly on the perception of foreign businessmen. To provide one example, although nationalized industries traditionally were party-colonized, that did not mean that bribes had to be paid to the managers in order to do business with them and the same applies to the bureaucracy that is still under party tutelage.

The study of clientelism and patronage so far has almost exclusively focused on the demand and supply sides (clients and patrons, respectively), but has largely ignored the institutional environment in which the transactions between them take place. While individual institutions occasionally have been mentioned as relevant, there is no attempt at a more systematic discussion. Hence, this chapter focuses on political institutions as the neglected side of linkage politics. In the following section I briefly discuss the determinants of linkage strategies and focus on the general role institutions play. I also provide an overview of the varieties of clientelism. Finally, I identify three problems of linkage politics that political actors face: controlling the means for policy and/or patronage, credibly claiming credit for political actions, and enforcing contracts with both policy- and patronage-motivated voters. The subsequent sections take up the first two of these themes. A brief conclusion follows.

On the relevance of institutions and varieties of clientelism

Determinants of linkage strategies

Generally, three factors influence the nature of linkages between political actors and their followers: (1) the strategies of the actors who compete for political support (which are shaped, in turn, by their opportunity structures); (2) the characteristics of the potential clients; and (3) the institutional framework in which the interactions between politicians and citizens take place. Specific types of linkages, to be observed by political scientists and others, hence result from deliberate decisions of professional political actors (parties, factions, or individual politicians) to build or maintain them. Their cost-benefit analysis will be affected by the behavior of their competitors. On the supply side several authors have suggested a negative relationship between classic political competition and clientelism (Stigler 1972; Persson, Tabellini, and Trebbi 2001). However, when testing for the general level of competition Manow (2002) did not find that systems with a higher level of political competition are less plagued by (perceived) corruption (the author's shortcut for patronage). Why may this be the case? If patronage is expected to produce *positive* electoral effects, we should not expect rational and self-interested political actors to refrain from using it. Typically, the parties will vary in their relative position to exercise patronage at a given time (e.g., because they are holding or not holding government office) and abandoning it would undermine their competitiveness (Müller 1989: 349). As Geddes (1999: 207) has put it, "no party leader could afford unilaterally for his party to cease distributing patronage." If one party refrained from exercising patronage when in office, this would not bind the other parties. Yet, once clientelism is established, abandoning it may be difficult even if it is highly doubtful that it produces positive electoral net effects. Such inertia can result from path-dependency. Indeed, parties abandoning patronage may find themselves between two stools. On the one hand, they may frustrate clients who consider themselves as having vested rights for (more) returns. On the other hand, the claim not to exercise patronage any longer must be credible in order to attract voters who were disgusted by such a practice. Given that most parties have always publicly denied their use of clientelism, it is difficult for them to publicly signal that they are giving it up.

On the demand side, clientelism generally is associated with low levels of socioeconomic development and organization of the civil society, that is few and weakly autonomous (not party controlled) societal organizations (see e.g., Banfield 1958). Under such conditions society is more vulnerable "to the clientelistic bid from party politicians" (Hopkin and Mastropaolo 2001: 152). Similarly, Burstein (1976: 1026) identifies Israel's "large immigrant population unfamiliar with democratic politics at the time of arrival and in need of all kinds of services" as "one of the most likely to be the site of widespread machine activity." According to many accounts, these were indeed the conditions under which the political machines in major cities of the USA flourished.[1] However, Wolfinger (1972) has convincingly argued that these conditions were neither sufficient nor necessary for the existence of political machines in the major cities of the United States. The case of the USA also suggests that a system of democratic patronage is not necessarily the outflow of a history of pre-democratic clientelism – old notables being replaced by political parties or political entrepreneurs. All this suggests that demands from the citizens alone cannot explain the existence and maintenance of clientelism, though they certainly enter the cost-benefit calculations of political actors.

What institutions do

As useful as the supply and demand side explanations of clientelistic linkages are, this chapter is exclusively concerned with the relevance of

---

[1] See Gosnell (1968: 100–03), Lowi (1964), Callow (1976: 91–138), Erie (1988), and Shefter (1994); see Finegold (1995) for a qualification of this argument.

political institutions. In the most general terms, political institutions affect political actors by constraining their range of strategic options. Institutions rule out some types of behavior and make others more or less likely by influencing the *costs* and *benefits* that an actor can expect when following a certain course of action.[2] In short, the behavior of political actors is guided by their preferences, but constrained by the institutional framework. Following Kenneth Shepsle, the outcomes of party competition can therefore be considered structure-induced equilibria. A structure-induced equilibrium is an alternative "that is *invulnerable* in the sense that no other alternative, allowed by the rules of procedure [the institutional framework], is preferred by all the individuals, structural units, and coalitions that possess distinctive veto or voting power" (1989: 137). Formal theory has proven that structure-induced equilibria are rarely unique (Shepsle 1986: 75). In other words, while the institutional framework constrains the behavior of political actors it does not determine it, and while it limits the set of feasible outcomes of their interaction, it is not possible to infer precise outcomes from the rules of the game.

In this chapter, political institutions are the independent variables, whilst party strategies and linkages are the dependent ones. The relevance of institutions will be discussed in the form of *ceteris paribus* arguments. I will first identify potential linkage problems. With regard to all of them political institutions can create but also resolve problems. In this chapter I review the micro-logic of various institutional mechanisms, asking what types of institutions would encourage clientelistic linkages. I then look at the institutions employed by the countries covered, focusing specifically on the highly clientelistic countries (and among those emphasis will be on the three that share about the same level of socioeconomic development – Austria, Belgium, and Italy[3]). The relevant questions are: First, do these countries have institutions that are expected to encourage clientelistic linkages? Second, do institutional features systematically distinguish the most clientelistic countries from the others? Yet, strictly speaking all the institutional logics arguments are *ceteris paribus*, i.e., they are meant to be valid under otherwise identical conditions. Alas, otherwise identical conditions are rare in comparative politics when the units of observation are countries. Wherever possible, the chapter therefore refers to specific studies that show how the relevant institutions in the most clientelistic countries work in practice and whether they conform to the abstract institutional logic or not.

---

[2] See, e.g., Riker (1980: 444), Weingast (1996: 169), Scharpf (1997: 38), Lane and Ersson (1999: 27), Shepsle and Bonchek (1997: 302).

[3] In the Italian case, there are, of course, great differences between the North and South.

Variations of clientelism/patronage

Patronage is not all the same. We can identify the variety of patronage relations by asking the mutation of a classic political science question: *Who gives what to whom with what effect?* Before running through the different parts of this question I would like to stress that while some combinations of the answers are typical, there is ample room for local variation which can make a system unique. As will be argued below in more detail, institutions impact on most elements of this question.

Who . . . The professional political actors who deal in patronage are parties, factions, and individual politicians. Institutions impact on actor design, thus provide incentives for collective or individual action.

Gives what . . . While almost everything can become a patronage good, some analytical categories can be helpful. A first distinction is that between one-off transactions and a continuous flow of patronage, as it may be useful in a public sector career. Yet, the distinction is not always clear. What initially may look like a one-off trade may turn out to be only the first exchange in a longer row of such deals. For instance, if political parties provide local council housing for their clients, this in itself is a one-off thing, but modifications in demand may require the client to go back to the patron and ask to exchange one flat for another (for instance, for a larger one when the family grows, for one in a better environment, when quality of life considerations become more important, or one with no stairs to climb in old age).

To whom . . . The recipients of patronage are individuals or firms. Individuals count either in numbers or through their control of scare resources. In the former case mass patronage establishes a direct link between a political actor and the rank-and-file. In the latter case patronage either goes to local notables acting as brokers between the provider of patronage and the rank-and-file or it goes to individuals who command resources other than mass loyalties (money, policy-making capacity).

With what effect? In the last consequence the expected returns of political actors are either votes or policy-making capacity. If the payoffs are electoral, they can be the direct return from clients, who dutifully or gracefully vote for their patrons. However, establishing direct clientelistic links may not always be possible or may be very inefficient, so they may be substituted (or augmented) by indirect forms. Then patronage does not aim to provide sufficient numbers of voters but rather to provide the political actor with resources that allow for effective campaigning. These resources can be either labor or money, which, to some extent, can substitute each other (Strøm 1990). If party activists are tied to their party by being the recipients of patronage, the party's main return will be their labor (though they may also contribute small amounts to the party's campaign funds). However, if the party's patronage goes to "resource-rich" (Kitschelt 2000b: 849) individuals (or firms), the expected returns are monetary. These funds, in turn, are to be used for buying professional services such as opinion polls, political consulting, television spots, etc. on the market in order to boost the party's electoral performance (Wolfinger 1972: 393). While most patronage at least bears some features of corruption, here it is full-scale systemic corruption.[4] Finally, the party can also use patronage to increase its policy-making capacity. By planting their trustees in the administration and the public sector more generally, political parties can make their policies better informed and smooth their implementation.

Problems in linkage politics

We can understand policy or patronage linkages as implicit contracts between professional political actors and citizens. This belief I share with Herbert Kitschelt, who, however, seems to consider contracts based on patronage largely unproblematic, as the following quotation suggests: "It is very clear what politicians and constituents have to bring to the table to make the deals work" (Kitschelt 2000b: 852). While implicit contracts about patronage indeed work in many instances, they are nevertheless fraught with problems. These problems are more severe than those resulting from policy-based contracts. In this chapter I discuss two of the problems that political actors face in their attempts to establish linkages with voters. These problems are particularly important and likely to impact on the actors' choice of strategy, i.e., will they deal in policy, patronage, or both?

The first problem is that of *controlling the required means*. Does the political actor have the means to provide what the voters want? The second problem is that of *credit claiming*. Will the political actor be able to get credit for what is delivered to the voters? Can the actor effectively claim to be the causal factor of developments or decisions that benefit the relevant target group?

---

[4] In addition, we are likely to find individual corruption, where the money does not go to the party coffers but to the private bank accounts of individual politicians. This form of corruption, however, is not directly relevant for linkage politics.

Even if the political actor delivers what the voters want and even if the voters are aware of the causality, they may still withhold their compensation and hence not honor their part of the implicit contract. So the question is: Does the political actor have the means to enforce the contract, or, at least, to observe who is delivering and who is not? However, *contract enforcement* is beyond the scope of this chapter. Here institutions are largely a constraint on politicians and the question is how to get around the rules when opting for a clientelistic strategy.

Political institutions impact on all three aspects of linkage politics. In the remainder of this chapter I discuss whether they provide incentives or disincentives to "go clientelistic." In so doing I look at four layers of institutions: electoral institutions, legislative institutions, executive institutions, and external institutional constraints. While the first three of these layers are self-explanatory, external institutional constraints are institutions (largely) external to the democratic delegation regime that constrain the behavior of elected representatives (see Strøm, Müller, and Bergman 2003). In discussing these layers I will be selective and concentrate on those that have the greatest impact.

Controlling the means required for linkage politics

Policy-making capacity

As argued above, political parties offer their voters an implicit contract in which they promise to deliver policy and/or patronage. The question is whether they indeed have (or will have) the means to deliver. Here is not the place to summarize this literature in any detail. Yet, the question is whether policy-making capacity and clientelism are inversely related. In other words, do political parties turn to patronage if they cannot deliver policies to their voters? If this were the case, systems with few partisan veto players should be least pulled to use patronage, as Gordin (2002) has argued with regard to Latin America. Conversely, systems with many veto players that generally force the individual government parties to dilute their policies and to hammer out compromises with other actors should see more patronage. Indeed, there seems to be hardly any party patronage in Sweden and Norway, which for most of the post-war period have seen highly effective Social Democratic governments, and there is only a modest amount of patronage in the archetypical Westminster system, the UK (Blondel 1996). However, the policy-making capacities of Irish, Spanish, and Greek governments are also strong, but party patronage is flourishing. Likewise, among the countries in which policy-making powers are more dispersed among parties, we find the best-known cases of mass patronage (Italy, Belgium, Austria) but policy-making powers are also dispersed in countries where party patronage is virtually absent (Finland, the Netherlands).

The temporal dimension is also useful in investigating the relevance of the policy-making capacity thesis. Indeed, several countries have gone back and forth between different patterns of governing, endowing the government party or parties with quite distinct policy-making capacities: Norway and Sweden have alternated between Social Democratic single-party (minority) rule and bourgeois coalitions, Ireland between Fianna Fáil single-party governments and coalitions of the Fine Gael and other parties (though Fianna Fáil has formed coalitions more recently), and Austria between coalitions and single-party governments, to mention only the most prominent cases. Of those, the Austrian case is the most inter-esting one since the governments were almost exclusively majority-based and the periods were substantial: roughly two decades of grand coali-tion government were followed by sixteen years of mostly majority-based single-party governments, and (after a brief interlude of an almost mini-mum winning coalition government) another period of thirteen years of grand coalition government (until 2000). While fine-grained distinctions between these types of government exist with regard to party patronage, Austria has remained in the top (i.e., most clientelistic) category for the whole period. Likewise, I am not aware of relevant changes in the impor-tance of clientelism in the other countries mentioned above varying with government composition.

In conclusion, a clear pattern linking clientelism to different policy-making capacities does not emerge in the diachronic or in the synchronic comparison. Hence, party patronage cannot be seen as a strategy to which government parties that cannot deliver policy turn because they are severely constrained by the lack of a parliamentary majority or by coalition partners.

Federalism and decentralization

What are the conditions that provide political parties with patronage resources? Obviously, government status is critical. However, the bulk of patronage resources are not necessarily to be found at the national level. In Germany, for instance, the Lände governments have more resources available that are relevant to, and indeed used for, party patronage than the national government. Moreover, many potential mass patron-age resources are to be found at the local level (council housing, jobs, etc.). So government *vs.* opposition status at the national level may not be all that crucial for the endowment of political parties with patronage resources. Lane and Ersson's (1999: 188) account for eighteen Western European countries, for instance, demonstrates that in almost half of them (eight) the central government controlled less than half of final government consumption in 1992. Except Portugal, in no country did the central government controlled more than two-thirds of it. Of the countries with most party patronage the subnational level has considerably more spending power than the national one in Austria, a federal state. In Italy, the record was balanced, while in Belgium and Greece the coffers of the national government were much better filled. Of the countries with a relevant amount of party patronage, Germany, Spain, and the USA clearly privilege the spending power of subnational units, while the division of resources is very balanced in France and Ireland.

To be sure, the distribution of resources between different levels of government is not fixed once and forever. Italy has devolved powers and resources to its regions since the 1970s (Putnam 1993: ch. 2). Belgium has become fully federalized since 1992 and a long-term shift of spending powers to the regions has been introduced. In both cases a comprehensive patronage system was in place before devolution. In Italy regionalization was delayed by the parties in control of the central government because it meant sharing (patronage) resources with the communists (dominating Italy's "red belt"). In Belgium, the regional strength of the Christian Democrats (in Flanders) and Socialists (in Wallonia) means that these parties are likely to remain in charge of substantial patronage resources even if they are out of office at the national level (Deschouwer 1999; Swenden 2002). In systems with weak federalism it can work the other way round; a parliamentary majority may be able to alter unilaterally the allocation of tax funds between the various levels of government, and thereby increase its spending power and decrease that of the opposition (as happened in Austria in the inter-war years).

Even in systems of strong federalism, national government status remains critical as political parties may use it to transfer public funds with a partisan bias to the subnational levels where they become converted into policy or patronage. Conversely, there are cases in which national government spoils are shared with opposition parties, as was the case with the Austrian nationalized industries from the 1960s through the 1980s.

To conclude this discussion, the control of patronage resources varies considerably between political parties in government at the national level in various countries. Opposition parties in federal and decentralized systems generally can draw on more resources than their equivalents in centralized systems (provided that they have regional or local strongholds). Having resources available, of course, also increases the relevant parties' policy-making powers. However, the constitutional division of labor between the different layers of government will often avoid a direct confrontation between different approaches to policy. Hence, running local services (such as litter collection) is not much of a challenge to the national government's economic policy. As concerns patronage, there may be relevant differences with regard to the *quality* of the resources available at the national and subnational levels. Yet, in *quantitative* terms, political parties in opposition at the national level are likely to have more patronage than policy-making capacity.

Yet, federalism may not only influence the division of resources among different levels of government but also their use. Weingast (1995) has identified five conditions that provide for *market-preserving federalism*. This type of federalism can also be found in systems not formally federal; conversely, constitutionally federal systems do not always share its defining characteristics. These are (1) the existence of a hierarchy of governments with a delineated scope of authority; (2) subnational autonomy over the local economy; (3) a common market; (4) hard budget constraints; and (5) the institutionalization of political authority (i.e., the central authority cannot unilaterally change the decentralized governance structure). Once these conditions are satisfied the use of government resources for clientelism is severely constrained as economically inefficient government behavior is punished. Under market-preserving federalism the central government is limited because some share of the public resources is placed in the hands of subnational governments. At the same time the subnational governments are constrained in the use of these resources by checks from the central government and by competition among the subnational units (Weingast 2000). Weingast's theory so far is supported by historic and contemporary case studies. The quantitative comparative study of Treisman (2000: 430–33) seems to hint in the opposite direction. It demonstrates that (legal) federalism induces corruption, particularly in less developed countries. Yet, this analysis does not differentiate between different types of federalism. In contrast, the research of Rodden and Wibbels (2002) suggests that federalism that is based on the subnational units' raising their own taxes and fees rather than relying on transfers from the central government leads to better economic outcomes and, by implication, more efficient policies. Assuming a positive relationship between corruption and patronage and a negative one between patronage and economic efficiency, market-preserving federalism (or something close to that) hence is likely to constrain patronage.

Of the countries covered in this chapter, six can be considered federal (Austria, Belgium, Germany, Spain, Switzerland, and the USA). In Belgium, federalism is of recent origin and post-dates the establishment of the patronage system. Of the remaining countries, Switzerland and the USA come closest to the ideal of market-preserving federalism and both have less patronage and/or perceived corruption than the remaining federal states. As can be seen from Figure 11.1, countries with merely legal federalism tend to have more patronage than unitary ones. These observations are partly in line with the theoretical expectations: if anything, legal federalism is likely to encourage clientelism, market-preserving federalism works against it.

Electoral institutions

There is wide consensus in the literature that clientelism is expensive (because it inflates demands) and economically inefficient (because it leads to overinvestment). Moreover, clientelism is said to inflate demands and hence in order to keep its effects constant its costs increase over time (see, e.g., Belloni, Caciagli, and Liborio 1979). Tying voters to parties by the means of clientelism requires considerable public resources at the disposal of the parties and is the more expensive (1) the more votes need to be purchased and (2) the more expensive these votes are. While the second condition depends on the citizen's opportunity costs (Hechter 1987) the first one can be significantly influenced by the electoral system; the cheaper seat shares are in terms of vote shares (because of the effects of the electoral system) the more likely clientelism should be. Recall Buchanan and Tullock (1962) who, pushing the point to the extreme, maintain that under first-past-the-post majority rule slightly more than 25 percent of the voters can command a parliamentary majority (and technically the percentage could be even lower with more than two parties participating in the elections[5]). Hence, everything else being equal, clientelism should be more likely under majoritarian systems than under proportional systems (or, at least, clientelistic politics should have a longer life under majority systems). Along these lines of reasoning, malapportionment can change the seats–votes ratio under any electoral system and allow the parties to use their patronage resources most efficiently. For Japan, Scheiner (2001) shows that malapportionment is a relevant precondition for the vitality of clientelistic policies by the LDP. Voters in rural electoral districts are on the average much more in favor of clientelism and malapportionment grossly increases their weight on the electoral result.

Yet, three of the most clientelistic systems in Western Europe – Italy, Belgium, and Austria – employ PR systems or, in the case of Italy, have used them during the building-up of the post-war mass patronage system.

---

[5] This, of course, should not happen in the long run; see Cox (1997).

(Greece's "enforced proportionality" system *de facto* provides single-party majorities in parliament under normal circumstances.) A first attempt to measure malapportionment (Samuels and Snyder 2001: 660–61) sees the most clientelistic systems randomly placed among the Western democracies.[6] Indeed, malapportionment can be attractive to political parties for quite different reasons. However, the case of electoral reform in Iceland suggests that the argument made here has relevance beyond the borders of Japan. Looking at one single country, and, institutional change within it, of course, holds the other variables constant and hence allows singling-out the relevance of a particular one. In Iceland the move from a mixed system, partly based on single-member constituencies, to multimember PR in 1959 greatly equalized the relative value of votes and made clientelism less attractive (Kristinsson 2001: 185). Nevertheless, the overall conclusion is that inferences about linkage mechanisms cannot easily be drawn from the electoral institutions.

Legislative organization

If patronage is mainly driven by the interests of individual legislators, legislative organization can impact on the mobilization of the required resources. Specifically, Cox and McCubbins (2001: 39) argue that legislative decentralization helps individual legislators to extract resources from the executive. If various legislative actors have the *de facto* power to veto or significantly delay government policy, they have bargaining power and can extract pork from the executive. Pork-barrel politics, in turn, is understood as a resource to be employed for boosting the personal vote of those representatives who deliver it. Cox and McCubbins (2001: 52–53) cite the USA, Japan, and Italy as supporting cases. Indeed the USA is characterized by committee government (Shepsle and Weingast 1987; Weingast and Marshall 1988). Likewise, the power of the Italian committees to make "little laws" (*leggini*) that do not require a final vote in the plenary meeting (provided that a broad consensus can be achieved) has often been cited as serving clientelism and as a cause of making policy concessions to the opposition (Giuliani 1997).

In a broader perspective, however, the evidence is mixed. In their survey of committee power in Western European parliaments, Mattson and Strøm (1995) construct a two-dimensional index of committee power, measuring legislative drafting and agenda control powers. Of the countries that rank high in patronage only Austria ranks high in both

---

[6] Austria ranks high, but the calculation does not take into account the complex electoral system with three tiers that eventually allow for an almost perfect votes–seats ratio.

dimensions, while Italian and Greek committees are ranked relatively low on both. Clearly, with regard to the Italian case the index is more appropriate for measuring committee power in major legislation that will go to the floor than *leggini* that are considered relevant by country experts to produce the effect Cox and McCubbins suggest (Hine 1993: 174–80). Belgium ranks high only in the drafting authority dimension. The countries with some party patronage are scattered around as are those with little or no party patronage.

Although Austria ranks relatively high in both dimensions, country experts would probably not agree that the causal mechanism described above is indeed working here. If patronage flows generously, it is not because committees and other parliamentary actors exercise blackmail power *vis-à-vis* the government. Belgium ranks higher than Austria in the drafting authority dimension. Also, the Belgian legislators have a greater incentive to attract preference votes than their Austrian colleagues. However, the Belgium committee system is considered weak and De Winter, writing about both the committee system and patronage, does not make a connection between the two (De Winter 1996, 1997, 1998: 102–04). Greece does not rank high on either of the two dimensions employed by Mattson and Strøm (1995). Indeed, "parliamentarian efficacy is almost zero," much legislation is delegated to the executive, and government bills are passed in a very short time (Morlino 1998: 68). Overall, the micro logic identified by Cox and McCubbins (2001), does not work in all systems where patronage is important.

Bureaucratic organization

For the sake of simplicity, I distinguish three models of bureaucratic organization: a spoils system, in which officials come and go with the government, the classic Weberian bureaucratic merit model, and the New Public Management (NPM) model. These models are not just behavior regularities but have their institutional underpinning in the constitutions and the laws governing the internal working of the administration (Page and Wright 1999). While the USA is a spoils system in the top layers of the administration, the European countries subscribe to the merit system. Both are increasingly penetrated by NPM principles.

Jobs in the bureaucracy are a patronage resource in themselves. While this is openly recognized under the spoils system, appointments under the other systems can be made in a partisan manner but disguised as merit or technocratic appointments. A qualitative assessment of Western European parliamentary democracies suggests that partisanship has no relevance in making civil service appointments in five countries only

(Denmark, Finland, Ireland, the Netherlands, and Norway) while in Sweden and the UK it affects the appointment of top officials only (Strøm, Müller, and Bergman 2003). The latter, in the terms of Theodor Eschenburg (1961: 12–13), is power patronage (*Herrschaftspatronage*) rather than mass patronage. It serves the purpose of increasing the parties' policy-making capacities and hence the goal to tie a mass following to the party by the means of policy rather than patronage. In the remaining countries political parties have entrenched themselves in the bureaucracy more broadly. In the most clientelistic systems – Austria, Belgium, and Italy – civil service appointments at most levels are routinely made with a strong partisan bias. Belgium and to a lesser extent also Italy were latecomers to the development of modern (Weberian) bureaucracies. In Belgium this type of administration was not introduced (at least on paper) before the 1950s, replacing a pre-modern system of open patronage by ministers and parties (Van Hassel 1975; MacMullen 1979: 217–18). In Italy a modern merit administration was not established until after unification in the second half of the nineteenth century (Hine 1979) and was quickly captured by patronage providing politicians. In contrast, the Austrian administration had a long merit tradition and indeed was the backbone of the Habsburg Empire. Yet, that tradition did not prevent it from becoming politicized and captured by parties in a process that began in the inter-war period and was completed after 1945 (Müller 2006).

Probably more important than jobs in the bureaucracy itself is the fact that bureaucrats control access to other resources that can be used in clientelistic exchange. Under these circumstances parties may find it easy to get civil servants to do them a "favor" and provide resources required for patronage. Using public resources for party or personal purposes should be easiest under the spoils model. After all, politicians and officials share the bonds of co-partisanship and if patronage has the intended effects it will keep both of them in office. Of the countries covered in this chapter the USA comes closest to a spoils system. Yet, merit bureaucracies are not immune against becoming corrupted by their political masters in order to provide patronage. The more the merit system *de facto* has been turned into a party patronage system, the more we can expect civil servants to apply political criteria in their decisions (see e.g., Della Porta and Vannucci 1996: 357–62).

The NPM model contains elements that point in opposite directions with regard to the politicians' capabilities to squeeze patronage resources out of the state. Under the NPM model administrators have fixed goals in terms of outputs or outcomes and goal achievement is the criterion for the evaluation of their performance (Lane 2000; Peters and Pierre 2001). Consequently there should be little room for patronage as it is inefficient and hence undermines the administrators' performance. Yet, the question is whether the goals are always so clearly stated that performance evaluation becomes mechanical. If this is not the case and the performance of the administrators is subject to interpretation by the incumbent politicians, patronage may come back through the backdoor. NPM civil servants with short-term contracts may be more willing to help raise patronage resources than the members of an old-fashioned merit bureaucracy. To the best of my knowledge the still nascent empirical research on the impact of the NPM revolution has not yet addressed this question.

External constraints

The existence of external constraints makes life harder for politicians who are willing to employ all or almost all means as long as they serve their ends. Hence, an independent judiciary, particularly if it also controls the magistrates and displays judicial activism, and an independent audit office, constitute major constraints for party patronage. This is particularly true if the effectiveness of these institutions is increased by investigative journalism and important parliamentary minority rights. Such institutions not only make it more difficult to divert government resources into patronage activities, they also make the other problems of linkage politics identified above more severe. If watchdogs are around it is more difficult to claim credit for action that is illegal or violates official efficiency standards. Likewise, the enforcement of deals by bending the law is less likely under such circumstances. Having said this, I will refrain from repeating the relevance of external constraints in the following sections.

The countries of particular interest in this chapter clearly distinguish themselves with regard to judicial constraints relevant in the patronage context. Italy's magistrates enjoy the greatest independence from politics, as evidenced by the Tangentopoli scandal, and the vigorous attempts to prosecute Prime Minister Berlusconi. Yet, this independence has played out only when a politically motivated cohort of lawyers penetrated the judicial system that was fortunate to receive cooperation from exploited clients (see Della Porta and Vannucci 1996: 362–65; Golden 2002). In Austria judges are independent but magistrates remain under political control; allegedly some corruption cases have not been brought to court because of this construction. In Belgium the judiciary is deeply politicized and several spectacular cases over the last decade have shown that it is not very effective (Van Outrive 1996: 376). Hence, overall, the independence of the judicial system is a serious constraint for clientelism.

Credit claiming

Regardless of whether political actors compete for political support by the means of policy or clientelism, it is crucial for them to get credit for the relevant public decisions. In other words, it is important that the citizens assign responsibility to political actors for what these actors themselves consider desirable (Mayhew 1974: 53). In order to be useful a claim has to be credible. Policy-based credit claiming generally requires that the relevant party is in office or has otherwise a large amount of bargaining power (e.g., as the pivotal party in parliament, or by setting the public agenda). While government office is the best precondition for being able to claim credit for public policies, the case is more complicated in coalition than in single-party governments. Even if specific policies originate from one coalition partner this party may not be able to effectively claim credit for them (see e.g., Marsh and Mitchell 1999). Rather, credit may go to the party with the most visible cabinet offices, or to the party holding the relevant portfolio. While political parties as collective entities may have difficulties claiming credit for public policies this is even more the case for factions and individual politicians. As Mayhew (1974: 59) has noted, for individual Congressmen, "the prime mover role is hard to play on large matters." This is even truer for representatives elsewhere, given that no other legislature is as "transformative" (Polsby 1975) and no other legislatures allow for so much policy entrepreneurship as the US Congress.

When political actors face difficulties in getting credit for policies, they have an incentive to try something else. Hence, they may turn to patronage – provided that the required resources are available – and/or pork-barrel politics. But are these activities inherently better for credit claiming purposes? With regard to pork-barrel politics, the crucial question for credit claiming is: "Who spends?" (Samuels 2002: 848). This question is answered largely by the constitutional division of labor and hence the overall institutional framework.

With regard to patronage the answer to the question whether politicians will be able to claim credit is yes. Typically the relevant behavior of politicians is client-initiated: citizens approach individual politicians or party organizations with very specific problems. They may need a job, housing, or help in a pending administrative procedure. Whatever the outcome, clients will not fail to recognize it. If the clients get what they want, the political actor is likely to be credited with having been the causal force. Politicians, in turn, take care to stress their role in these cases, e.g., by showing their clients letters they have written on their behalf or by letting them know by other means what they are doing in order to help.

Sometimes the relevant politicians hasten to bring the good news of a successful intervention to the clients before official notification or they find ways to remind the clients of their role once the issue has been settled.

Yet, institutions not only impact on the capacities of actors to claim credit, they also define the need to do so. The remainder of this section concentrates on the institutions' impact on the needs of politicians to claim credit for their actions.

Electoral institutions

Electoral systems distinguish themselves by the weight they give to individual candidates relative to the party. The more candidate-centered electoral systems are, the more individual politicians sharing the same party label need to differentiate themselves from one another. Hence they have an incentive to cultivate a personal vote that helps them to survive against intra-party competition and at the same time makes their own fate somewhat independent from that of their party (Cain, Ferejohn, and Fiorina 1987; Geddes 1999: 225; Cox and McCubbins 2001: 48–49). Incumbents can employ two major strategies to win personal votes – clientelism, as defined in this chapter (including ombudsman services) and pork-barrel legislation, bringing public goods to the electoral district (the local production of which may in turn allow for patronage by handing out contracts to specific firms, providing jobs, etc.). If electoral systems determine the need of incumbents to claim credit we should find the more clientelism the more candidate-centered the electoral systems are.

Building on Carey and Shugart (1995) and Mitchell (2000) I distinguish three dimensions of electoral systems that are relevant to their "candidate-centeredness": candidate nomination, district magnitude, and intra-party preference voting. Recall that all specific expectations derived for these three dimensions apply under the *ceteris paribus* clause only.

Candidate nomination. Electoral systems are the more candidate-centered the less parties control candidate nomination. In candidate-centered systems individual politicians acting as political entrepreneurs can enforce their nomination under the party label. Among the set of countries relevant to this chapter, the USA – to the extent that primaries are based on state rather than party rules – is the only case. In all European countries, political parties must formally endorse candidates running under their label. Yet, most European parties apply a decentralized method of candidate selection and in reality local party barons who *de facto* nominate themselves as candidates can come close to the US political entrepreneur. The main difference is that they must be able to control the party organization permanently. While the higher party levels in principle may intervene, they often would need to resort to the most drastic (and often goodwill-destroying) means (such as expelling the candidate from the party) in order to prevent his or her nomination. Leaving aside the USA, the main differences between countries do not rest with the electoral rules but with the specifics of party organization and are beyond the scope of this chapter.

District magnitude. Single-member districts provide greater incentives for incumbents to invest in their personal reputation than multimember districts. Asworeth and Bueno de Mesquita (2006) specifically predict that the team production problem in multi-member districts will lead to the production of less pork for the constituency. The number of countries with single-member districts is slightly greater than those with ballots open to outsiders. In addition to the USA they are used in Britain, France, Germany (for electing half of the MPs), and more recently also in Italy (for electing 75 percent of the MPs). Clientelism predates the introduction of single-member districts in Italy, and otherwise none of the most clientelistic systems uses them.

Preference voting. This dimension refers to the relevance of party-determined ranks of candidates on the party lists and, in the last consequence, the relevance of the party label. If the list structure is fixed (i.e., cannot be changed by the voters), incumbents have no incentive to seek personal credit with the voters. Fixed-list systems exist in all single-member districts (where the party "list" consists of one candidate only), in Germany (also for the other half of the seats), Iceland, Portugal, Spain, and – since 1994 – for a quarter of the seats in Italy. In loosely bound list systems the candidates placed at the top of the party list or close to it (among the "eligible" ranks) enjoy a premium as the list can be changed only by meeting more or less demanding requirements in terms of support for those outside the "eligible" ranks. Much, of course, depends on how demanding these requirements for voter coordination are. The countries that fall in this category are Austria, Belgium, Denmark (if the individual parties decide so), The Netherlands, Norway, and Sweden (which moved from the theoretical possibility of intra-party candidate choice to the most permissive of these systems in 1998). Party-ranking is least critical in open-list systems where the voters alone decide who will take a seat in parliament (i.e., only votes for specific candidates identified by the voters determine the party's parliamentary delegation). Then, party ranking is no more than a suggestion. Under this rule incumbents have a clear incentive to get individual credit with their voters. Open-list systems exist in Denmark (if the individual parties decide so, which increasingly is the case), Finland, and Greece,[7] and were used in Italy before 1994. Finally, some electoral systems allow voters to compose their own lists outside the borders of individual parties. In contrast to Carey and Shugart (1995: 422), I consider these systems as providing greater incentives for candidates to build a personal reputation than systems that allow merely for intra-party preference voting. While it is true that the party label protects candidates when competing with candidates from other parties, real world electoral systems such as the STV and *panachage* systems do not replace intra-party by inter-party candidate competition but *add* the latter to the former and hence allow the voters to "weight-in" other dimensions (e.g., region or gender) as they see fit. Hence, electoral systems that allow for votes across party lists provide greater incentives for seeking a personal reputation than those restricting the choice to candidates of the same party. In the set of countries covered here, Ireland (STV), Luxembourg, and Switzerland (*panachage* systems) belong to this category. Open-list systems in both variants – mere intra-party and intra-party *cum* inter-party – constitute the candidate-centered end of the continuum mapped out here.

Of the four most clientelistic systems two (Italy and Greece) fall in the candidate-centered category. None of these four systems belongs to the closed-list category. The systems with a medium level of party patronage are spread more widely, making up the bulk of countries at *both* ends of the party-centered *vs.* candidate-centered continuum. There is certainly no particularly good fit between the candidate-centeredness of electoral systems and clientelism (see also Gallagher 1985: 371). But what can be said of the actual working of the systems that fall into the "right" (predicted) corners? Is patronage indeed a consequence of the needs and activities of incumbent MPs and their challengers in candidate-centered systems?

Italy provides the best insights and also allows for within-nation comparison. First, preference votes were much more frequent in the South and the islands than in the rest of the country. According to the conventional wisdom this is exactly where mass clientelism was flourishing (Chubb 1982; Putnam 1993).[8] Second, there were significant differences between the parties. The bulk of preference votes always went to the DC, while the share of the PCI after 1949 declined constantly (Wildgen 1985). Intra-party competition for preference votes was indeed more important

---

[7] Preference voting had been abolished for a number of years.
[8] To be sure, the Tangentopoli scandal that eventually brought Italy's so called First Republic to its end began in Milan. However, here the nature of the deal was different and certainly not *mass* clientelism.

in a thoroughly factional party such as the DC (Zuckerman 1979) than in a party subscribing to the principle of "democratic centralism." Moreover, as the permanent party of government at the national level the DC had much better access to patronage resources (Leonardi and Wertman 1989: 223–44). Third, Golden and Chang (2001) have demonstrated by using quantitative data that corruption (as measured by the attempts of the magistrates to bring sitting MPs before the court) and intra-party competition (as measured by the use of preference votes in the respective electoral districts) are highly correlated. Fourth, qualitative evidence suggests that the electoral system impacts on clientelism in the form suggested here (e.g., Allum 1973: ch. 6). This was also the argument of the reformers who introduced the 1992 referendum that abolished preference voting. It remains to be seen what fate party patronage takes in Italy's so-called Second Republic. Unfortunately the removal of preference voting was not a "controlled experiment" given the simultaneous change of other elements of the electoral system and the competitors. In any case, the great variance within Italy suggests that the preference voting system itself is not sufficient to trigger specific candidate strategies and clientelism in particular.

The two remaining countries which are high on patronage, Austria and Belgium, employ weaker preference voting systems. Austria's preference vote system has elected only few candidates to parliament and these clearly were outsiders to the system of mass patronage (Müller 1983). Nevertheless, in the 1980s and 1990s more "typical" candidates (occupying safe seats) have increasingly campaigned for preference votes. The background to this behavior of MPs is that the preference votes have become one of the factors that enter their party's calculation that influence the renomination of a sitting candidate, particularly if there is serious intra-party competition and the incumbent's competitor aims at sending signals to the party by campaigning for preference votes (Müller *et al.* 2001). MPs, just like other party office-holders, used to play an important role in handing out patronage. Yet, the sequence of events suggests that intra-party competition and its institutional foundations are not the driving forces of patronage politics. First, mass party patronage was there before the preference voting system (introduced in 1949). Second, patronage was already in decline before preference votes became more important by first discussing and then introducing electoral reform strengthening the preference vote system in 1992.

The Belgian case is similar to the Austrian. Only a few Belgian MPs have made it to parliament via preference votes, but preference votes do help to ensure renomination by the party organization (De Winter and Dumont 2003). Also, MPs, like other party agents, are involved in patronage politics. Yet, similar to the Austrian case, patronage did not emerge from the needs of MPs to rally a personal following and almost certainly would not disappear if preference voting were abolished while leaving everything else as it is.

Unfortunately, the case of Greece is not well documented in the literature. Yet, in their substantial treatment of clientelism Mavrogordatos (1997) and Pappas (1999) do not even mention the ambitions of individual politicians and intra-party competition as (potential) causal factors. It seems that parties *as organizations* monopolize the patronage linkage with their voters.

Finally, it is worth taking a look at Ireland, which is classified here as displaying a medium level of party patronage but employs one of the most candidate-centered electoral systems, the STV system. Here the personal vote is considerable and MPs act as brokers for their constituency (Marsh 2000: 117–18). Yet, Farrell (2002: 146) compares Ireland with other STV systems and comes to the conclusion that clientelism is not a systematic property of the STV system, arguing that "localism" would not dissipate if the electoral system were changed. Hence, he places a premium on Ireland's political culture, i.e., the demand side. Farrell's comparative perspective does not include Malta, which also employs the STV system. According to one observer (Boissevain 1977) patronage has been in decline for a long time. Yet, the electoral system has remained the same, indicating that STV does not necessarily lead to patronage. However, according to another account, Malta is still very clientelistic and the STV system plays an important role (Hierczy de Miño and Lane 2000: 190).

I will not try to sort out the different interpretations of empirical facts and causal factors here. What this case and the others discussed above in some length suggest is that the direct effects of the electoral systems' rules of candidate selection should not be overestimated. To be sure, candidate-centered systems produce incentives for individual behavior, but it seems it depends on the circumstances how strong these effects are and what kind of behavior they cause. If patronage already is institutionalized, MPs probably will try to get their share. If this is not the case, MPs may concentrate on serving their constituencies by providing collective goods. So, it seems that the specifics of the candidate selection under various electoral systems are neither sufficient nor necessary to explain the prominence of patronage strategies in some countries.

Legislative institutions

Once the representatives are elected, does the internal organization of the legislature impact on their chances for effective credit claiming? More specifically, does it provide incentives for the representatives to concentrate on either policy or patronage, or ombudsman services? Recall that the question of resource allocation, that is whether representatives have the means to exercise real influence on policy or to mobilize patronage resources, has been discussed in the previous section. Here the question is whether the parliamentary stage privileges a policy or patronage strategy by allowing credit claiming.

The main stage of parliament, the plenary debate, is largely reserved for debating policy and invoking the political accountability of the executive. Parties and representatives have ample opportunity to take positions and claim credit for policy (Mayhew 1974), though, as noted above, the great majority of individual representatives are unlikely to benefit. In contrast, parliamentary questions give individual MPs "exclusive" rights on very specific issues. These can be special policy problems, constituency matters, or the concerns of individual clients. Being on record with such questions is a proof that the representative is seriously concerned about the specific matters and puts him or her in a relatively good position to claim credit once the relevant issues are addressed by public policy. However, the instrument of parliamentary question in most cases is considered inappropriate for articulating individual concerns unless they highlight a more general policy problem. Rather, the appropriate means is by a letter to the minister. Given the geographical concentration of those affected by constituency problems, effective credit claiming appears easier in these cases. Thus, if anything, collective goals of local communities (that do not fall in our definition of clientelism) are the most rewarding issue to push for individual representatives in questions. The set-ups for parliamentary questions differ from country to country (Wiberg 1995). However, the differences appear marginal from the point of view of credit claiming, at least until more specific research has demonstrated their relevance.

Bureaucratic organization

Here we can repeat what has been said under this label in the section on resources: unprofessional and/or politicized bureaucracies will not only make it easier for politicians to intervene on behalf of their clients but also to do so openly and claim credit for it. Clearly, the most clientelistic countries share this feature.

Conclusion

In this chapter I have identified three problems of linkage politics that political actors must cope with: controlling the means for policy and/or patronage, credibly claiming credit for their (beneficial) actions, and finally, enforcing the implicit contracts they have with those who benefit from policy and/or patronage so that they get their returns. Institutions impinge on these problems. I have discussed the first two with regard to the question whether policy or patronage is a more rewarding strategy. I have also examined what incentives specific institutions provide to politicians to diverge from the normatively and empirically dominant policy strategy and choose a patronage strategy to build linkages with constituents.

To summarize the results of this chapter: no specific institution is necessary for patronage becoming an important or the dominant linkage strategy. Even less so is a specific institutional configuration sufficient to explain patronage. This is generally in line with the expectations formulated at the outset on the basis of theoretical considerations on the role of institutions and with the conclusions of Kitschelt (2000b: 861) from a less comprehensive review of institutional factors impacting on linkages. Nevertheless it is clear that institutions provide incentives for specific behavior. However, these incentives are not overwhelmingly strong. Hence the relevance of institutions for linkage strategies and linkages is best studied in context with demand and supply side incentives. In critical situations the exact setup of institutions may indeed tip the balance in favor of one or other strategy, yet such occasions will be rare. While the relevance of institutions for explaining the dominant strategies of parties and the general level of patronage remains modest, they are likely to have greater influence on the specific *forms* patronage takes.

12 Clientelism in Japan: the importance and limits of institutional explanations

Ethan Scheiner

Japan is (in)famous for its clientelistic politics, for which the country's electoral institutions are frequently blamed. Indeed, this chapter's analysis of clientelism in Japan is more sympathetic than the other chapters in this volume to institutional explanations for voter–politician linkages. In Japan, electoral rules have helped protect the clientelistic system, as societal pressures to reduce the country's particularistic arrangements run through institutions that privilege those favoring clientelism's maintenance. The most popular institutional arguments surrounding Japanese clientelism tend to focus on the now-defunct but long-used single non-transferable vote in multimember district (SNTV/MMD) electoral systems. SNTV/MMD was useful in helping to organize clientelistic linkages. Nevertheless, just as Müller in this volume argues that no electoral system is likely to determine the nature of voter-politician linkages, I argue that SNTV/MMD was neither necessary nor sufficient for clientelism in Japan.

SNTV/MMD was important in reinforcing clientelistic linkages, but clientelism in Japan was originally due to other factors, especially the internal mobilization of the country's first parties and the organization of landholding. In the postwar period, SNTV/MMD created incentives for new political arrangements that held clientelism at their core, but SNTV/MMD was hardly a sufficient reason for clientelism. The electoral system was utilized throughout the country, but the levels of clientelism varied with differences in social structure, local governmental financial autonomy, and political economy.

This chapter offers support for the principal arguments laid out in the Introduction, and the Müller, and Kitschelt contributions to this volume. Similar to Kitschelt and Wilkinson's argument, the Japanese case highlights the importance of political economy, economic development, and party competition in shaping voter-politician linkages; with the strain clientelistic practices put on the Japanese economy beginning in the late

Portions of this chapter appear in Scheiner (2006: chs. 3 and 8).

1980s, clientelism became increasingly unpalatable to those who did not rely upon clientelistic support for their well being. Seeing clear displeasure with clientelism among urban voters and the more developed sectors of the economy, along with the strong presence of an opposition that competed with the ruling party in cities, Japan's leaders made a greater effort to scale back the clientelistic system.

Voting in Japan

Although some (especially urban) voters focus more on party and programmatic politics, Japanese voters tend to cast ballots according to candidates' personal characteristics and ability to deliver particularistic goods. Curtis notes that Japanese candidates focus on developing their own local organizations and securing the backing of powerful interest groups in the district: "the stress is on constituency service to convince voters that the candidate has the clout in Tokyo to bring the district new roads and bridges, industrial development, and higher living standards" (1992: 228). As Fukui and Fukai write, "Japanese voters are mobilized at election time mainly by the lure of pork-barrel" (1996: 268–69).

Japanese clientelism

Kitschelt's description in this volume of Japan's "predominantly business-mediated clientelism" highlights the core of Japanese linkage patterns, where voters' gains in the exchange are founded foremost on the benefits delivered to their place of business. As Kitschelt explains, clientelistic exchange in Japan tends to run through informal channels and emphasizes financial and regulatory assistance to less competitive businesses rather than social entitlements and public jobs.

Depictions of Japanese politics tell of politicians spending hours attending weddings, funerals, and meetings with members of their district, passing out cash gifts. Voters develop personal relationships with their representatives, and are made aware of the material benefits that will follow from their support (Curtis 1971). Often, this is not so much an exchange as a gesture to make voters feel a welcome link between themselves and their candidates.

However, Japanese clientelism takes on less symbolic forms. Woodall describes Japanese clientelism as "selective allocation of distributive policy benefits by public-sector elites in exchange for the promise of solidarity and mutually beneficial inputs from favored private-sector interests . . . [involving] government subsidies, official price supports and import quotas, targeted tax breaks, regulatory favors in the allocation of trucking routes, and other policy benefits" (1996: 9–10). Sometimes the exchange has little to do with voters, the clearest case being *amakudari*, whereby retired bureaucrats receive high-paying second careers at companies they regulated as bureaucrats.

Richardson (1997) describes Japan as a "party clientelistic state," in which the longtime ruling Liberal Democratic Party (LDP) is a caretaker for its clients (260), especially rice farmers, the small-business sector, geographical regions lacking high-growth industries, and industries in decline. These groups strongly support the LDP, and, are in turn, "amply rewarded from the public coffers" (Pempel 1998: 63).

Distributive goods are at the core of Japanese clientelism. In particular, the government uses public works to fund two of its most important clients: construction industries and farmers who also act as part-time construction workers. In 1997, public works spending in Japan amounted to 8.7 percent of the country's GDP, in contrast to figures of 3.2 percent in France, 2.3 percent in Canada, 2.2 percent in Germany, 2.2 percent in Italy, 1.4 percent in England, and 1.7 percent in the USA (Seaman 2003). In many cases, public works projects appeared to have no other *de facto* goal than funneling money to clienteles, such as construction companies.

The exchange is particularly strong in rural areas. The LDP has long allocated huge subsidies to Japanese farming interests and farmers have been one of the LDP's strongest supporters. Given that even farmers who do not support LDP candidates can benefit from the LDP's agricultural policies and agricultural groups cannot always reliably deliver votes to the LDP, agricultural support, generally speaking, should not be categorized as clientelistic. However, as Kitschelt and Wilkinson's chapter discusses, the fact that much of the support given to specific types of farmers involves a contingent, direct exchange, with voters/farmers predictably supporting the LDP in a "monitorable" fashion suggests that many of these agricultural policies are highly clientelistic.[1]

Mechanisms of clientelistic exchange in Japan

In Japan, clientelism is first and foremost candidate or politician based. Unlike systems such as Austria, where parties deliver patronage directly, in Japan individual politicians are the main link. Candidates' relationships with two types of groups – *kōenkai*, and construction groups, especially land improvement districts – demonstrate this pattern.

---

[1] As further illustration, Kitschelt and Wilkinson discuss how the provision of the yam tariff (a club good) as a benefit to Gunma Prefecture works as an example of clientelistic exchange.

Kōenkai

Most LDP national politicians maintain *kōenkai* (personal support organizations). Designed to support the electoral activities of individual candidates, *kōenkai* are organized hierarchically, with national politicians at the top, leading local politicians and local business notables at the intermediate levels, and voters at the bottom. The largest *kōenkai* contain many tens of thousands of members. The politician at the top provides the *kōenkai* gifts, puts on parties and organizes lavish trips, at essentially no cost to members. More substantially, as Curtis explains, *kōenkai* members "turn to it for various favors and services much as Americans turned to the urban party machine in its heyday" (Curtis 1971: 145). Politicians provide *kōenkai* members with employment, marital introductions, and school placement for their children. Other favors are even weightier, as politicians, for example, donate bottles of expensive *sake* to local organizations and money to help with small-scale construction projects (e.g., roof replacement costs) being pushed by *kōenkai* members (Curtis 1971: 149–50).

In exchange, *kōenkai* members are expected to vote for the candidate, and asked to campaign on the candidate's behalf and provide the names of others whom the *kōenkai* can contact to ask for support.

Public works and land improvement districts

Public works spending, especially on construction, plays a big role in Japan's political economy. Roughly 15 percent of Japan's total GDP is invested in construction (Okuda 2001). Construction companies employ about 10 percent of the workforce (Woodall 1996: 83), and probably a higher percentage in rural areas. Construction is among the LDP's biggest supporters, providing large donations and mobilizing votes for LDP candidates. In return, LDP politicians provide contracts to construction companies.

Although some public works are distributed universally, with little hope of politicians monitoring the exchange, certain types fit the clientelistic category well. Among the clearest cases is land improvement subsidization and the land improvement districts who run the projects. Typically, the national government gives land improvement subsidies to fund specific agriculture-related projects, such as irrigation. Among agricultural interest groups, land improvement groups receive by far the largest subsidy allocation (Mulgan 2000: 81).

For politicians, funding such projects is attractive because of its targetability; politicians can select specific supporters to funnel money to. LDP politicians help their top local political and construction industry clients pursue project subsidies and lobby the central bureaucracies for funding. The local leaders of the municipality being allocated the money ensure that a particular company is given the project. The project itself typically does not cover wide expanses of land and the benefits of the project usually only accrue to a relatively small number of people working for the company. And the land improvement districts regularly kick a percentage back to the Diet (national parliament) members (Mulgan 2000: 407).

The exchange is also appealing to politicians because land improvement groups actively back LDP politicians. The groups have well-developed organizations that specialize in politicians' electoral operations. They have regular contact with farmers and others with influence over the farm vote and, moreover, employ farmers who need part-time construction work to supplement their incomes. Thanks in large part to the government subsidies they receive, the land improvement districts have large sums of money to spend on mobilizing the vote (Mulgan 2000: 405–07). Very importantly, while Japan's leading agricultural cooperatives are often too diffuse to be able to guarantee the delivery of votes, land improvement grants are very targeted and thereby increase the vote collection power of the groups (Mulgan 2000: 515–22).

Monitoring and the impact of local politicians

Kōenkai and land improvement grants allow for targeted allocation of goods, but how can one tell if voters are behaving as they promise? Here, local politicians are particularly useful and, especially in rural areas, national lower house politicians often rely on local politicians to deliver their vote (Curtis 1971; Park 1998). National politicians provide local politicians with funds and lobby the central government on their behalf. In exchange, local politicians mobilize individuals to campaign and voters to cast ballots for the correct candidate. As Curtis notes, "Direct vote-buying is rare in Japan, but paying people who supposedly have the ability to deliver their particular group of supporters is not" (1992: 235).

It is usually impossible to tell for which candidate individual voters cast their ballots. Therefore, as Kitschelt and Wilkinson note in the Introduction, politicians often monitor voters *collectively*. In Japan, much of this collective monitoring is founded on directly monitoring local politicians' efforts on their behalf. For most local level elections in Japan, candidates can win office with as little as two to three hundred votes. In such areas, local candidates are familiar with who their supporters are, and these bases of support tend to be *highly* concentrated geographically (Horiuchi 2005). In national elections, votes are tallied at a larger regional level so it is not possible to tell how many votes each candidate received at the most local levels. Nevertheless, even in national elections in rural areas, ballots are often tallied at the village level with very small populations, at times with total votes cast in the lower hundreds.[2] Given that it is usually well known which local politicians represent and are responsible for mobilizing voters in such villages, observers can see the number of votes won by these local representatives in the areas and compare them to the number won by the Diet candidate.

This monitoring capacity plays a critical part in shaping the success of clientelistic linkages in Japan (Park 1998: 184). Diet members make clear to local politicians that they are aware of the number of votes that are available to be won in their electoral bases and offer to reward them for delivering such votes, through future electoral support and funding from the central government, and threaten to punish them if they fail to do so by isolating them from future support.[3] Local politicians tend to be quite responsive to such carrots and sticks (Park 1998).

When placed within Kitschelt's and Wilkinson's framework, we can see why Japanese politicians have successfully maintained clientelistic linkages. Kitschelt and Wilkinson suggest that conditional exchange relations are most valuable in systems where the exchange is on-going and politicians can monitor individuals. The long-time dominance of the LDP makes the exchange on-going.[4] In addition, monitoring capacity – especially in rural areas – in Japan gives further leverage to politicians in the exchange. Because vote counting areas in Japan are so compact, with only small numbers of voters within them, the process comes to approximate individual- rather than group–level monitoring. Moreover, by often focusing on the behavior of specific local politicians, national politicians actually monitor individual behavior, dramatically increasing their leverage over the exchange.

The factors shaping Japanese clientelism

Although Japan utilized an electoral system, SNTV/MMD, that made clientelistic behavior especially likely, electoral system arguments provide neither necessary nor sufficient explanations for Japan's clientelism.

---

[2] In each district throughout the country, votes are tallied and made public at the sub-district level – at the city, ward, town, or village level – before being summed together.

[3] Collective monitoring also occurs in urban areas (Park 1998), but, given the larger populations in the vote-tallying areas and the fact that voting is more volatile, monitoring is more difficult.

[4] The on-going nature of the relationship under single party dominance therefore is an additional reason that a lack of party competition leads to greater clientelistic behavior.

SNTV/MMD

Under SNTV/MMD, each voter casts one non-transferable ballot for a candidate. In Japan's House of Representatives (HR), each district typically held between three and five seats, and, where M was the number of seats in the district, the top M vote getters each won a seat. The LDP tended to run at least two candidates per district. Despite sharing party affiliation, these two (or more) candidates were rivals, vying for votes in the same district. Under this system, campaigns based on intra-party competition over issues would have proven counter-productive. The system therefore offered a great incentive to emphasize personalistic (Carey and Shugart 1995) and patronage-based campaigns.

Electoral competition plays a critical part in shaping the heavy emphasis on clientelism within this system. However, while Kitschelt and Wilkinson discuss how increased *party* competition leads to greater disbursement of programmatic goods, the heavy competition between the same party *candidates* under SNTV/MMD made clientelistic distribution of goods a logical strategy. The evidence suggests that LDP same-district incumbents differentiated themselves from one another by providing particularistic government resources to different organized interests (McCubbins and Rosenbluth 1995) or geographical regions (Tatebayashi and McKean 2002).[5]

Resource control

Nevertheless, while the SNTV/MMD most certainly reinforced Japanese clientelism, SNTV/MMD does not appear to have brought it about originally.

Ramseyer and Rosenbluth (1995) offer the best-known argument about the impact of SNTV/MMD in prewar Japan, arguing that the prewar, 1925-introduced SNTV/MMD system increased the emphasis on "money" politics in Japanese electoral politics. Such arguments are certainly correct in noting that money politics became more intense and widespread under the 1925 electoral system, but vote buying had grown widespread around 1905. Of course, this does not dispute the impact of SNTV/MMD, as Japan was utilizing an SNTV/MMD system containing between one and thirteen seats per district (Scalapino 1953).

That said, even from the first days of Japanese democratic elections in the late nineteenth and early twentieth centuries, huge sums of money

---

[5] However, some candidates – particularly those with constituents uninterested in pork – are less likely to pursue such a strategy.

were utilized to conduct campaigns, irrespective of the electoral system used (Scalapino 1953). Early Japanese parties, seeking to create links with various rural agricultural and urban commercial interests focused on providing patronage benefits to their electoral districts (Pempel 1978). This was no doubt due to the need to create links to society, but in a way that would not step on the more programmatic concerns of the political elite and bureaucracy.

In some ways, we might interpret Japan's early party organization as occurring much like Shefter's (1994) notion of internal mobilization – elites in the government seeking to gain additional power by creating linkages to society – which, given elites' access to state resources, tended toward patronage-oriented politics.[6] Early leader Itō Hirobumi, for example, took over the leadership of the Liberal Party (*Jiyūtō*) and reorganized it as *Seiyūkai* in 1900 to create party support within the Diet for the government. In the early 1910s, civil service laws were changed to give the *Seiyūkai* greater opportunity to use patronage, and ties between the parties and ruling oligarchy grew fairly close (Berger 1977). Well-known public servants became party members, and the parties' ties to the bureaucracy grew more pronounced. *Seiyūkai* sought to stabilize its electoral base by means of patronage. Japanese parties distributed pork and created links between agricultural interests, who provided votes for conservative parties, and business, which paid for parties' operating expenses. Over time, parties gained greater budgetary control and, in turn, greater ability to provide pork, their means of catering to local economic interests.

To be sure, this discussion offers support for Kitschelt's argument in this volume about the importance of a "developmental state" in shaping the creation of clientelistic linkages under democratization. The emphasis early Japanese parties put on using government resources to aid and mobilize economic interests certainly meshes well with Kitschelt's analysis. Nevertheless, in contrast to Kitschelt's comparative analysis, the Japanese case also suggests the utility of Shefter's framework for understanding the origins of clientelistic linkages. As suggested above, many of the early clientelistic maneuverings of the Japanese government were founded on an effort simply to use the resources available to them to channel support for the new government. The fact that well-known public servants became politicians and used the resources of the state to "purchase" popular support gives this view additional weight.

Given Shefter's observation that, once established, parties' linkage forms tend to remain fairly constant, much of Japanese clientelistic

---

[6] We should not push the analogy with internally mobilized parties too far, since strict civil service laws in the early twentieth century kept the bureaucracy insulated from party control.

politics can be explained by pointing to a path-dependent evolution from before the war. Pempel (1978) notes the continuity between the pre- and postwar eras, especially the fact that the main bases of rural conservatism remained intact and loyal to their prewar politicians. Prewar party behavior was reinforced in the early postwar period as the clientelistic prewar parties were reborn as the Liberals and the Democrats and then the LDP. Made up heavily by former bureaucrats, the LDP had strong ties to the bureaucracy, thereby giving the party exceptional resources that it could use in reinforcing clientelistic linkages.

Socioeconomic organization

While parties' control over state resources played a critical role in shaping early patronage-oriented practices, the great power of landlords in the prewar period cemented clientelistic linkages.

Universal male suffrage came about in 1925. A particular feature of Japan's socio-economy made clientelistic politics especially effective in this context. Throughout much of the country, only rural landlords played any serious role in shaping Japanese electoral politics. Prewar Japan was heavily rural and because of the power rural landlords held over their tenants, most voters had little choice but to follow the voting instructions of their landlords (Curtis 1971: 41–42). This made clientelistic linkages simple to execute: politicians channeled government resources to individual landlords and the landlords made sure their tenants voted for specific politicians.

SNTV/MMD as reinforcement

Given their capacity to deliver votes, targeting specific landlords with direct subsidies would have made sense under any electoral system. However, it was especially attractive to politicians under SNTV/MMD, where building a base of concentrated votes was an efficient path to election. In the postwar period, a change in Japan's socioeconomic organization made SNTV/MMD a more potent influence in reinforcing Japan's clientelistic linkages.

During the early postwar occupation of Japan, the USA instituted land reform to eliminate the concentration of rural land ownership. Conservative politicians no longer had their base of landlords to deliver the vote. In theory, the decline in landlord power could have led politicians to pursue more programmatically oriented behavior in order to generate support. Nevertheless, clientelism remained the norm. In part, continued control over government resources gave conservative politicians incentives to pursue clientelistic linkages.

But SNTV/MMD appears to have been influential as well. Given the incentives created by SNTV/MMD for candidates to differentiate themselves functionally or geographically from fellow partisans, as well as the low vote percentage needed to win office, Japanese politicians had a great incentive to pursue narrowly targeted, reliable bases of support. In this way, SNTV/MMD promoted the change in candidate strategy that took place in the early postwar period, whereby, in place of local landlords, Japanese national politicians turned increasingly to local politicians and *kōenkai* to deliver votes for them (Curtis 1971: 42–43). Clientelistic linkages were at the heart of these relationships.

The impact of social structure, financial centralization, and political economy

Although SNTV/MMD reinforced clientelism, other features were more important in shaping the level of clientelism; even under SNTV/MMD there was much variance (over time and space) in the level of clientelism, suggesting strongly the insufficiency of the electoral system argument.

I discuss the changing levels of support over time for clientelism in greater detail when I deal with political economy (pp. 288–92). In part, this shift was obvious after the 1994 reform of the electoral system, but much of it occurred under the SNTV/MMD system as well. Moreover, clientelistic practices were (and are) more prevalent and looked upon more favorably in rural areas. As discussed throughout this volume, pork-barrel is not equivalent to clientelism. Nevertheless, pork-barrel is a useful "tracer" of clientelism. Using this tracer – as shown in the JES-II public opinion survey – we can see substantial differences in urban and rural areas. In 1993, the survey asked respondents (a), if there was in their district a "candidate who has done something special for the people of this area such as improving roads or acquiring government grants?" and (b), all else equal, if they would be more likely to cast a ballot for a candidate who dedicates himself primarily to national and foreign affairs or one who devotes himself "to activities involving the protection of local interests"? Question (a) provides a useful proxy for the level of clientelistic behavior – there is good reason to believe that where voters more often cite the presence of candidates who provide patronage benefits, clientelistic practices are more common. Given that protection of specifically local interests often involves clientelistic favors, question (b) represents a reasonable approximation of respondents' support for clientelism.

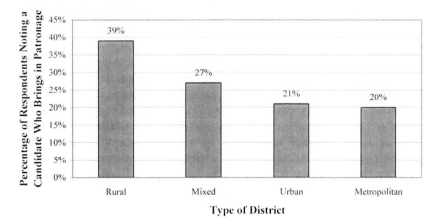

Figure 12.1 Level of urban-ness and presence of candidates who deliver patronage
Source: JES-II public opinion survey

The responses to the questions varied substantially by region. As Figure 12.1 indicates, patronage-oriented behavior appears to have been more widespread in rural areas. As Figure 12.2 shows, respondents in rural areas were markedly more likely to support politicians with a local orientation than were those in more urban areas.[7]

Three principal factors explain these differences: social structure, centralization of government financing, and political economy.

Social structure

Pork-based clientelistic behavior by politicians is more efficient in rural areas; in cities, public works projects usually affect large numbers of people – many of whom do not vote in the area – which makes it more difficult for parties to use the projects to target specific groups of voters. In rural areas, because a larger percentage of beneficiaries of such spending live and vote in the district, it is easier to both target specific, geographically concentrated groups and claim credit for spending. It is not surprising, therefore, that rural candidates' voter bases tend to be more geographically concentrated than those of urban candidates.

Also, as Kitschelt and Wilkinson note in the Introduction, clientelistic exchange is easier to monitor and maintain in places of "rigid, durable social networks." In Japan, rural residents hold closer community ties and

---

[7] Level of urban-ness is determined by population density.

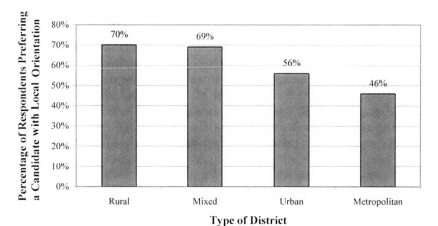

Figure 12.2 Level of urban-ness and preference for candidates with local orientation
Source: JES-II public opinion survey

links to their local political leaders, making it both easier for local leaders to mobilize groups of voters and more effective for national politicians to channel particularistic goods through such leaders to appeal to voters. Rural social networks and the incentives created by SNTV/MMD reinforced one another, as the networks gave rural politicians greater capacity to develop an efficient vote division strategy in the form of geographically targeted bases of support. In contrast, urban residents are less well tied together and therefore politicians in such areas are more inclined to appeal to them through voluntary organizations and direct appeals to the electorate (Curtis 1971: 252).

Social structural factors also played a role in the growing clamor for the elimination of Japan's clientelistic practices. Over the years, demographics of the average Japanese changed to favor far less clientelism. Local communities were more tightly knit in the early postwar period and political and social networks were especially close in rural areas. However, with the increasing flight of voters from the countryside, such links loosened (Mulgan 2000: 382–83), making it more difficult to include many in the clientelistic networks.

Centralization of government financing

Centralization of local government financing also reinforces the already existing clientelistic system and in turn shapes variance in clientelistic practices. Japan's central government is usually the leading financier of local governmental expenditures and the central government avoids funding local governments' wide-sweeping public goods types of projects (Reed 1986). As such policies are relatively unlikely to get funded in much of the country, even when voters approve of more public-goods oriented policy, they have less incentive to cast ballots for local candidates who espouse them. Note, for example, that the major public goods policy push in Japan in the postwar period occurred in the 1960s and 1970s, a time when economic growth increased the autonomy of localities throughout Japan (and decreased their dependence on central government funding).

Similarly, Japanese urban areas usually maintain greater wealth than rural ones, rely less upon the central government for funding and can safely ignore the center's policy "recommendations." As Lyne in this volume argues, programmatic parties are typically attractive only to those with enough assets of their own to not depend on targeted clientelistic benefits. Not surprisingly, therefore, urban areas in Japan typically have a greater programmatic orientation to their policy-making.[8] In these ways, while centralization does not cause clientelistic behavior, centralized funding structure does help maintain it.

Political economy

Variation in support for clientelism over time. The LDP was able to generate electoral success through its support of various groups, especially large firms, professionals, small subcontractors and distributors, and farmers. To the extent that there has been a clear exchange – whereby politicians provide individuals and groups in such industries with targeted favors in return for support, which politicians monitor either through locally based elites or through collective monitoring practices – these relationships clearly approximate clientelism as described in this volume.

In the early postwar decades, even as many larger firms grew internationally competitive, tremendous growth created a positive-sum economy, in which it was possible – and politically advantageous – for the LDP to support all of its major constituents. But the party's ability to maintain the support of disparate groups was dependent upon economic growth and the insulation of the Japanese market. Neither of these factors could be sustained. By the 1990s, Japan's economic bubble had burst and the economy slowed dramatically.

Various pressures prompted changes. Foreign countries and firms exerted weight on Japan to open its markets. In response, Japan liberalized in a number of areas. However, the debate surrounding clientelism

---

[8] For more on clientelism and centralization in Japan, see Scheiner (2006).

appears to have had more domestic roots. Slowed economic growth increased the need for trade-offs between the groups supporting the LDP. Rosenbluth puts some emphasis on the role of Japan's internationally competitive firms fearing a backlash in a more global economy (1996: 148), but domestic distributive struggles (which Rosenbluth also notes) appear to have played the key role in generating a backlash against clientelism in Japan. Urban consumers and efficient businesses grew tired of government pork-barrel and corruption that were placing a strain on Japan's economy and their own pocketbooks. Even with the continued presence of SNTV/MMD in the early 1990s, leading business associations decried LDP clientelistic practices and provided support for anti-LDP alternatives.

Variation in support for clientelism across the country. As Müller indicates in this volume, the characteristics of the potential clients of clientelism influence the nature of linkages, and individual socioeconomic self-interest has played a substantial role in shaping Japanese voters' receptiveness to clientelism. More specifically, Lyne's and Kitschelt's and Wilkinson's chapters suggest that only those with sufficient affluence and relatively low discount rates can afford to support programmatic alternatives. Indeed, Japanese rural residents have socioeconomic characteristics that make them more likely to depend on and benefit from clientelistic exchange, as they cannot wait long for material rewards.

I examine the correlates of support for clientelism in Japan by utilizing as a dependent variable in a probit model the JES-II public opinion survey's variable indicating respondents' support for candidates with a localistic orientation. Given that protection of local interests in Japan typically involves clientelistic favors, this question represents a reasonable approximation of respondents' support for clientelism. *Clientelism support* is coded 0 for those preferring candidates working on national issues and 1 for those preferring local issue oriented candidates.

I expect older citizens and those with less education to support clientelism because they are likely to see clientelistic practices as important in protecting themselves against pressures to become more "efficient": The coefficient on *Age*, a 0–1 dummy variable coded 1 for respondents 55 and older, should be positive, and the coefficient on *Education*, the respondent's level of education, should be negative. Individuals in *Clientelistic Occupation*s, a 0–1 dummy variable coded 1 for respondents working in farming, forestry, fisheries, mining, or transportation should be more likely to support clientelistic practices. I also create *Head Occupation*, a nearly identical variable, but one that identifies the occupation of the head of the respondent's household. In many cases, larger companies are less dependent upon locally based favors, so I expect the coefficient on

Table 12.1 *Correlates of preference for candidates with local orientation*

	Coefficient[a]	(SE)	Coefficient	(SE)
Constant	1.390***	(0.262)	0.628***	(0.180)
Age	−0.011**	(0.003)	0.548*	(0.223)
Age*Education	–		−0.385***	(0.104)
Education	−0.365***	(0.044)	−0.254***	(0.050)
Clientelistic Occupation	0.010	(0.148)	−0.045	(0.150)
Head Occupation	0.475*	(0.216)	0.484*	(0.217)
Work Size	−0.113***	(0.029)	−0.104***	(0.029)
Rural	0.183***	(0.040)	0.193***	(0.040)
N	1125		1125	
LR χ^2 (df=6)	156.18***		165.62***	
Log Likelihood	−690.71		−685.99	
Pseudo R^2	0.1016		0.1077	

$^{*}p < .05, \quad ^{**}p < .01, \quad ^{***}p < .001$

[a]Results of a Probit Model

Work Size, the number of workers employed in the respondent's business, to be negative. Finally, all else being equal, rural voters should be more supportive of localistic and clientelistic practices, so I include *Rural*, a variable indicating the level of rural-ness of the respondent's district,[9] which should have a positive coefficient.

The results are listed in the first column of Table 12.1. The significant negative sign on Age is surprising but is probably due to the fact that older respondents had a lower level of education than younger respondents. I therefore run a second model, in which I also use an interaction term, Age*Education, which leads to a more understandable result. Age is positive and significant, while Age*Education is negative and significant; older Japanese are more likely to have localistic tendencies, but older respondents with high levels of education prefer more "issue"-oriented politics.

The results for the other variables are largely as expected. Except for the non-significant Clientelistic Occupation, the sign on every variable is in the expected direction. Most striking, even controlling for urban-ness, respondents in particular socio-demographic and economic conditions

---

[9] *Rural* is the same variable utilized in Figures 12.1 and 12.2 and is based on a 4-point scale running from metropolitan (1) to rural (4) and helps control for other non-socioeconomic factors (such as tighter or looser social networks) that are specific to more urban or rural areas.

Table 12.2 *Socioeconomic/demographic means by type of district*

	Rural	Mixed	Urban	Metropolitan
Age[a]	0.48	0.39	0.36	0.30
Education[b]	1.79	2.10	2.19	2.50
Clientelistic occupation[c]	0.17	0.10	0.05	0.02
Head occupation[d]	0.14	0.07	0.04	0.03
Work size[e]	2.36	2.50	2.75	2.87

[a]Proportion of the respondents 55 years of age or older.
[b]4 point education level scale where: 1 = Primer or lower secondary, 2 = High School, 3 = Jr. college/trade school, 4 = University and grad school.
[c]Proportion of the respondents working in farming, forestry, fisheries, mining, or transportation.
[d]Proportion of the respondents whose head of household works in farming, forestry, fisheries, mining, or transportation.
[e]5 point scale for the number of people who work in the respondent's place of employment where: 1 = 1–4 people, 2 = 5–29 people, 3 = 30–299 people, 4 = 300–999 people, 5 = 1,000 people or more.
Source: JES-II public opinion survey results.

were more likely to support localistic and presumably clientelistic behavior. Head Occupation and Work Size are both statistically significant and in the expected direction. People from families involved in occupations more dependent upon clientelism's benefits and people working in smaller businesses were more likely to have a clientelistic orientation. The strongest effect was education. According to these results, respondents with only a grade school education had a 76 percent probability of supporting localistic behavior, as compared to 32 percent for individuals with college and graduate school experience.

Average (mean) residents of rural areas hold socioeconomic/ demographic characteristics that make them much more likely to support localistic and clientelistic politics than do average residents of more urban areas. As Table 12.2 indicates, rural Japanese are markedly older, less educated, and more likely to be employed in clientelism-related professions and work in smaller workplaces than urban Japanese. Figure 12.3 plots the likelihood of a resident of each level of urban-ness supporting localistic and clientelistic politics (based on the means in Table 12.2 and the coefficients from Table 12.1).[10] As Figure 12.3 demonstrates, based on their socioeconomic/demographic factors, the average metropolitan

---

[10] The Rural variable is held constant at its mean.

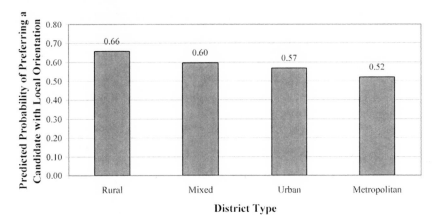

Figure 12.3 Impact of socioeconomic/demographic factors in shaping support for clientelism
Note: Predicted probabilities based on Table 12.1, Column 2 Probit Results (all variables except for "rural")

voter will support localistic politics 50 percent of the time, whereas rural ones will do so nearly 70 percent of the time.

Importance of electoral institutions: protecting clientelism by channeling preferences

I have downplayed the impact of institutions on clientelism, but, as long as institutional rules help protect regions that depend upon clientelistic benefits, institutions can neutralize the impact of political economy; in Japan, the regions most supportive of the clientelistic state have sufficient political clout – especially in the number of seats they hold and the way the seats are allocated – to prevent greater success by anti-clientelistic parties. Therefore, despite a growing backlash against clientelism, the LDP has strong incentives to protect clientelistic arrangements.

Japan's new opposition of the 1990s was founded to a large degree on a backlash against clientelism, and voters displeased with clientelistic practices supported the new parties (Scheiner 2006: ch. 8). Urban voters were antagonistic to Japan's clientelistic system and with the backing of these voters the new parties found success in the cities. However, in rural areas, voters were not only more supportive of Japan's clientelistic system, but often even dependent upon it. Support for clientelism was highly correlated with support for the LDP and its candidates.

In 1994, Japan eliminated SNTV/MMD and replaced it with a mixed-member system that combined single member districts (SMDs) and

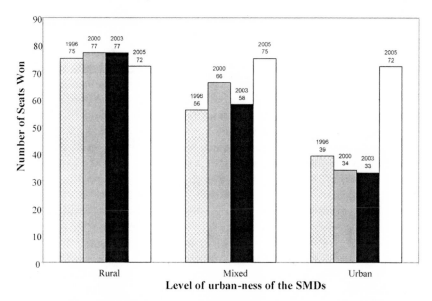

Figure 12.4 Number of SMDs within each district type held by the LDP, 1996–2005
Note: Urban–rural scale based on population density scores determined by the University of Tokyo seminar of Ikuo Kabashima: 1996–2000: 100 seats in each type of district; 2003–05 (extrapolated by author from 1996–2000 categories): 99 rural, 101 mixed, and 100 urban

proportional representation (PR) seats. Largely because of rural support for clientelism, the LDP dominated rural SMD races. Figure 12.4 illustrates LDP success by type of district for SMDs in HR elections in 1996–2005. The figure shows that the LDP won roughly 75 percent of the rural SMDs, but, with the exception of the anomalous 2005 election, did much less well in others. Despite the fact that rural SMDs constitute only about 20 percent of the HR's 480 seats, rural SMD victories provide the LDP with nearly one-third of all the seats it needs to win a majority. The LDP has a great incentive to maintain its support for the clientelistic system in order to maintain this solid base.

Preferences for the clientelistic system are strong in rural areas, but elsewhere they are mixed. In cities, there are more voters who maintain more anti-clientelistic views, but there are also those – individuals who run the countless small and medium-sized businesses, those involved in the construction industry, and members of LDP *kōenkai* – who benefit from the clientelistic system and continue to support the LDP. Therefore, although the anti-clientelistic opposition has found urban success, it has not outweighed the opposition's weak position in the clientelistic countryside.[11]

Part of the rural advantage has been malapportionment. Under SNTV/MMD, rural SMDs received more seats per resident than urban areas, but 1994 electoral reform reduced this, albeit not completely; under a "fairly" apportioned system, urban areas would gain thirteen to fourteen seats that rural areas currently hold, probably leading to a moderate swing in the number of seats held by both the LDP and the opposition. Malapportionment continues to a small degree to help protect the LDP and rural interests.

The candidate-centered small-district electoral system is probably more important. Even in rural districts, the LDP as a party received under 40 percent of the PR vote. The opposition would profit from a more proportional electoral system and, if in power, would push more than the LDP against the clientelistic system. By allowing the LDP to win 75 percent of rural SMDs with only 50 percent of the SMD vote, the small district system gives clientelism- (and LDP-)supporting groups a large bang for their voting buck. Japan's clientelistic, rural areas receive a form of institutional protection that feeds the success of the LDP. Given its support base, the LDP has a great incentive to maintain clientelistic practices.

This suggests an important contrast to Italy and Austria, where the changing political economy led to a public backlash against clientelism that altered the party system (Kitschelt 1995). In Italy, the beginning of the DC's rapid decline occurred under the country's now-defunct PR system. The proportional system made it far easier for other parties to cut into the DC's base of support, even where the DC was at its regional strongest. The same was clearly the case in Austria's PR system.

In Japan, however, the emphasis on SMDs makes it difficult for smaller, less popular options to chip away at the LDP's foundation in rural areas. Electoral institutions did not originally bring about clientelism in Japan, but, by channeling preferences in a particular way, electoral rules helped maintain clientelism when a different electoral system might have led to its downfall.

The decline of clientelism in Japan

Two pieces of institutional continuity from the SNTV/MMD period remain. First, even under the new electoral system, ballots continue to

---

[11] Moreover, as shown by the 2005 HR election – in which the LDP found success in urban areas when Prime Minister Koizumi strongly pushed reform – urban areas are highly competitive and volatile. No party can rely on success there.

be tallied at the same (tiny) municipality levels, thereby continuing to aid monitoring efforts in rural areas. Second, Japanese campaign laws continue to severely limit candidates' and parties' campaign access to television, radio, and print, making it more difficult for candidates and parties to make mass, programmatic appeals. Nevertheless, even with these institutions and the powerful presence of the LDP's rural base, clientelism and its perceived acceptability appear to be in decline in Japan, highlighting Kitschelt's and Wilkinson's point that institutions better explain politician tactics than the larger strategy of linkage building.

In the 1990s and early 2000s, the LDP continued to channel goods to its inefficient, but politically supportive, clienteles. However, especially from the late 1980s, in the face of such "wasteful" spending, economic failure and corruption, public outrage over clientelism grew. As Kitschelt and Wilkinson suggest is the case in general under such conditions, the Japanese media fed this bitterness by framing clientelistic practices as founded on favoritism and corruption. In 2001 this outrage helped lead to the prime ministership of Junichiro Koizumi, who promised the elimination of many such practices.

Because of Japan's urban–rural divide, there is, to use Kitschelt's and Wilkinson's phrasing, great "constituency heterogeneity" in the LDP, and, as a result, with higher levels of Japanese wealth, greater urbanization, and increased party competition in urban areas, pressure on the LDP to reduce its clientelistic practices has been ratcheted up. As Table 12.2 indicates, anti-clientelistic positions and characteristics consistent with such positions increase with each level of urban-ness in Japan. Greater urbanization in Italy and Austria appeared to increase antagonism toward the clientelistic system, which in turn exacted political costs on their ruling regimes (Scheiner 2006). Continued Japanese urbanization will be likely to harm its clientelistic system as well.

Japan's increased wealth is likely to help chip away at the clientelistic system. As Lyne and Kitschelt, and Wilkinson (in this volume) suggest, with increased wealth comes a sense that the short-term benefits to be won from additional public works simply do not matter enough. And, as Kitschelt in this volume argues, when clientelism goes along with a declining economy, the popular acceptability of clientelistic practices declines as well. Especially in times of economic weakness, such as Japan faced from the late 1980s, many simply see no need for – and many see great harm in – spending money on "infrastructure." Such views are particularly strong in areas – especially cities – that do not directly benefit from clientelistic spending.

However, there is reason to think that the interaction between economic development and competition, which Kitschelt and Wilkinson emphasize, is important as well. Based on a rough examination we can see the

correlation between the development/competition interaction and voter–
politician linkages – during the prewar period of lower economic development but relatively high party competition, clientelistic practices were
very much the norm. In the 1960s "miracle growth" period of high development and low competition, clientelistic practices remained very common. The most serious period of shifting against the clientelistic system
emerged under Prime Minister Koizumi, partly in response to the growing threat of the Japanese opposition – in short, during a period of high
economic development *and* more serious party competition. The Democratic Party of Japan (DPJ) emerged in the late 1990s as the leading
opposition party in Japan, campaigned against the clientelistic system,
and in 2003 had the most successful election of any opposition party
in the postwar period. Not surprisingly, under Prime Minister Koizumi,
the LDP responded. Although many in the party opposed harming its
clientelistic base, led by Koizumi the LDP moved to privatize the postal
system, which had long been important to the LDP's rural clientelistic
network, and cut public works spending.

Conclusion

As Müller's chapter notes, institutions offer strong *incentives* for specific
types of behavior, and institutions are likely to play a major part in the
forms patronage takes within a given system. In Japan, the SNTV/MMD
electoral system played a central role in making Japan's clientelistic system heavily candidate-centered, and locality and local politician oriented.
Other institutions, such as the small population vote-counting areas in
rural areas and campaign laws that make it difficult to engage in mass
campaigning in Japan, have clearly played a major part in creating such
emphases.

Japan's electoral institutions have also been important in protecting
the clientelistic system. In any clientelistic system, various voters and
regions will oppose clientelistic practices, especially as the economy grows
increasingly zero-sum. But certain areas remain very supportive of the
clientelistic system. As more regions and voters grow opposed to the
clientelistic system, electoral institutions are important in determining
the extent to which votes from clientelist-supporting areas are sufficient
to protect the regime that maintains clientelism.

That said, there are limits to our ability to use institutions to explain
clientelism in Japan. To explain the origins of clientelism in Japan, we
must look to other factors: the internal mobilization of the country's first
parties, the organization of landholding, and possibly the early developmental state (see Kitschelt's chapter). Particular electoral institutions

such as SNTV/MMD are neither necessary nor sufficient for clientelism. Clientelism has existed in Japan under both SNTV/MMD and mixed-member arrangements, and Japan's current electoral rules help maintain the clientelistic system, but by no means guarantee it.

The perceived acceptability of clientelism in Japan and the government's willingness to engage in clientelistic behavior has varied depending on non-electoral system factors such as a given region's social structure, affluence and financial independence, economic development and the degree of party competition, and the state of the country's political economy. In the short run, political institutions are likely to help maintain the clientelistic system through their protection of rural interests and the LDP. However, it is non-institutional factors that have the greatest power to be the clientelistic system's downfall.

13 The demise of clientelism in affluent capitalist democracies

Herbert Kitschelt

The practice of political clientelism in four stable, affluent, post-industrial countries with democratic practices – Austria, Belgium, Italy, and Japan – goes back to the beginning of the post-World War II period, but has older origins. The persistence of clientelism in these polities is at odds with theories of political development, state formation, and democratic institutions. Such theories would not expect to encounter a prominence of clientelistic linkages in wealthy democracies (all four countries), in countries with early bureaucratic-professional state formation (Austria and Japan) and with democratic institutions inimical to personalist candidate competition (Austria, Belgium).

While the explanatory domain of development theories for clientelism may be impressive in global comparative analysis, it requires a supplement and replacement for these four affluent OECD countries that draws on the analysis of political-economic governance structures and is loosely inspired by the variety of capitalism literature (Hall and Soskice 2001). Given certain conditions, different property rights and governance structures across a range of countries may deliver similar rates of growth and development. Some of these growth-enhancing governance structures involve a political allocation of scarce resources either through outright state ownership and control of productive facilities or the indirect guidance of private market participants through public regulatory and financial inducements.[1] Such arrangements – as well as some institutional designs to deliver social policy benefits – retrospectively turned out to facilitate the growth of clientelistic linkage practices between politicians and electoral constituencies and in some instances may well have been designed to deliver such consequences. State-interventionist modes of

---

[1] Note that this characterization of "market distorting" political-economic institutions is not identical with Hall and Soskice's description of the coordinated market economy (CME), let alone the liberal market economy (LME). CME attributes emphasize the *self-organization of economic market participants*, be they businesses or labor. Direct or indirect state intervention in the economy is in fact not easily accommodated in the CME/LME dichotomy and is quite prominent in a number of hard-to-classify countries.

business governance and/or social policy schemes conducive to clientelistic politics were prevalent in all four of our countries. I argue, however, that particularly the state-interventionist business governance, and
in a less pronounced, more mediated fashion social policy schemes that
further clientelistic politics, have become incompatible with economic
and technological challenges that shaped economic growth during the
last quarter of the twentieth century. In a *marxisant* terminology, clientelism as a political mode of exchange faces demise when its institutional arrangements become fetters stifling the material possibilities of
economic performance. When the forces of production run into a serious contradiction with the prevailing political-institutional relations, then
a period of economic crisis may ensue. Such economic crisis triggers a
political-institutional crisis, revealed in changing configurations of competition among established and new parties, some of which openly attack
clientelism. Intensifying party competition develops its own momentum
beyond purely economic exigencies. Citizens and political elites begin
to alter their modes of linkage building and establish new practices of
democratic political accountability that also enable them to address the
political-economic challenges that originally caused the crisis.

The first part of this chapter outlines diverging profiles of partisan-
based clientelism, either with a direction toward social policy or business
governance in the four countries. For the sake of brevity I summarize only
arguments contained in a longer version of this chapter about the historical genealogy of clientelism and political-economic governance structures
that set these four countries apart from a broader comparison group of
affluent capitalist democracies. The second part then examines symptoms
of crisis of clientelist arrangements in the economic and political realm,
while the third part explores an explanation of this phenomenon together
with rival explanatory accounts. So as not to sample on the dependent
variable, comparisons in all sections draw on a broad set of OECD countries to highlight the specificities of the four clientelistic cases.

Profiles of clientelism

Clientelistic practices of exchange involve at least five different aspects
to a varying degree in the four countries. Two of them concern benefits targeted directly at electoral mass constituencies, namely social policy benefits (public housing, and to a lesser extent differential access
to social insurance benefits for unemployment, old age, and sickness)
and public sector employment in the civil service (patronage). The other
two modes of clientelistic exchange work through business arrangements. On the one hand, the politicized governance of public or publicly

controlled enterprises allows politicians to benefit supporters through public procurement contracts, soft loans, and influence on the hiring policy of such companies. Also in this instance, jobs are at stake. On the other hand, even where governments do not exercise control over enterprises through ownership or contractual relation, politicians may politicize the regulatory process that affects the operation of private businesses (e.g., with regard to subjects such as land zoning, building codes, environmental and health protection, anti-trust and fair-trade regulation). Here mass supporters may indirectly benefit from politicians' benevolence through higher wages, greater job security, and better employment opportunities. Firms may even help "deliver the votes" to their favored politicians and indirectly monitor the clientelistic exchange.

One final aspect of clientelism concerns the extent to which it is formally legally codified or tacitly practiced through informal arrangements. The general presumption in the literature is that clientelism operates in informal ways, but this is not always borne out. Some clientelistic practices may be perfectly legal and therefore harder to discredit politically. An example might be the parties' appointment powers to corporate managing boards of state-owned companies in Austria in the past. Not all clientelistic practices therefore are also instances of corruption in the technical-legal sense.

As a rough simplification, Italy and Austria are instances of *comprehensive clientelism*, where linkages work both through direct material exchanges with voters (jobs, social policy entitlements) and indirectly through political dealings with public and private businesses, albeit in a more formalized fashion in Austria. Japan constitutes a *predominantly business-mediated clientelism*. Voters obtain small gifts through direct exchange, but rather large returns through their affiliation with companies and government agencies participating in the clientelistic exchange circuits. Belgium, finally, represents a more *social clientelism* operated through its pillarized system of social insurance and non-profit services.

Social policy benefits. After World War II, the Italian Christian Democrats captured and managed the social security system to establish clientelistic linkage (Warner 2001: 133). Since the 1920s, in Austria public housing allocations served the same purpose and provided a powerful stimulus to party membership (Kofler 1985: 64). In Belgium, party affiliated non-profit organizations made it possible to supplement and later displace ideological party affiliation with materialistic-clientelistic instrumental exchange (Billiet and Huyse 1984: 144–45; Hellemans 1990: ch. 9). In Japan, the residual size of the welfare state limits, but does not entirely rule out, the clientelistic penetration of social policy. Japan has always maintained a lean welfare state, except during a brief period of intense inter-party competition in the 1970s.

Public sector patronage. Even where relatively few citizens directly benefit from patronage appointments (say, between 1 percent and 5 percent of the labor force), such employment may be important for the diversified employment portfolio strategy of extended families and have a demonstration effect. Civil service patronage is extensive in Austria, Belgium, and Italy and plays a role even in Japan. In Austria, parties carved out fiefdoms in public enterprises according to a principle of proportionality among partisan stripes. Both Belgium and Italy have been called "particracies" because of their civil service penetration by patronage (Deschouwer *et al.* 1996). In Italy, this has meant that many partisan appointees were hired as "temporary" civil servants to circumvent the examination requirements for "permanent" employees. In Belgium, party politicians made the ultimate decisions for social service and administrative organizations (Billiet and Huyse 1984: 143; Hellemans 1990: 243). Such hiring underwent tremendous growth from the 1960s to the 1980s. In Japan, early retirement from the civil service compels civil servants to look for lucrative jobs in private firms whose development and regulation they oversaw as public officials ("amakudari," "descent from heaven"). The professional neutrality of the Japanese civil service may therefore be a fiction (Frank 2000). Moreover, the postal system and particularly its bank have provided partisan jobs for people who often doubled as organizers and operators of the ruling Liberal Democrats.

Public and state subsidized enterprise. Such companies extend patronage and clientelism beyond the range of the civil service both at the level of management and rank and file. By the 1980s, in Italy and Austria, political parties controlled different bits of the substantial state holding and financial companies. State-owned companies in Italy were described as "one-way spoils system" (Amatori 2000: 150). In a similar vein, the two major Austrian parties divided control over different enterprises (cf. Müller 1988). Despite the small Japanese public enterprise sector, *de facto* political influence via regulatory decisions and subsidization of parts of the domestic economy was tied into partisan networks (cf. Uriu 1996). The construction sector, with large indirect impact on employment levels in weak regions, stands out (Okuda 2001; Pempel 1998: 183–85; Scheiner, this volume). Only Belgium has relatively limited business-mediated clientelism. Katzenstein (1985) employs it as an example of "liberal corporatism" with large financially strong corporations. With the crisis of heavy industry from the 1970s on, however, the creation of mixed ownership enterprises provided more openings for a partisan politicization of business practices, particularly when such restructuring efforts were folded into a wider settlement of the ethno-linguistic regional conflict in Belgium (cf. Drumaux 1988).

Regulatory authority. Among the four countries, Japan in particular is known for its weak, politically biased business regulation that awards advantages to rent-seeking, ruling-party affiliated groups. The high informality of the country's regulatory regimes invites much case-by-case administrative discretion and especially lax anti-trust regulation. At least through the mid-1990s, regulatory reform made precious little progress in the Japanese political economy (Carlile and Tilton 1998a: 13). The World Bank's indicator of "regulatory quality," based on a combination of different expert surveys charged with assessing "the incidence of market-unfriendly policies such as price controls or inadequate bank supervision, as well as perception of the burdens imposed by excessive regulation in areas such as foreign trade and business development" (Kaufmann, Kraay, and Zoido-Lobaton 2002: 5), may serve as an indirect tracer of opportunities for partisan affiliated clientelistic linkage building in the regulatory arena. While the extremes for 1997/98 are Iraq (−3.80) at the low end and the United Kingdom (+1.21) at the high end, Japan (+.39) among our four countries is clearly furthest below the OECD average of 21 affluent countries (+0.94; s.d. =0.21). Also Italy (+0.59) and Belgium (+0.79) are below that average, while Austria approximates it (+0.90).

Degree of formality (codification) of clientelistic resource allocation. In some instances, particularistic principles of asset allocation may in fact be legally codified and thus elevated out of the shadowy world of illicit advantages and corrupt practices. Among our countries, this applies foremost to the governance of public corporations in Austria, where the principle of *Proporz* in the recruitment of personnel is often made explicit. But in Belgium also the pillarization of social insurance administration and benefits disbursement has been an entirely above-board, legal arrangement. Legal codification of allocation that in practice amounts to clientelism may limit the potential for public disenchantment and delegitimation of citizen-politician linkages, when compared to the entirely informal comprehensive clientelism prevailing in Italy and the equally informal business-mediated clientelism in Japan.

Table 13.1 summarizes the narrative comparison of the previous paragraphs by assigning high, intermediate, or low scores to each of the five dimensions of clientelism. Italy and Austria are cases of comprehensive clientelism, covering both direct exchange with voters and business-mediated allocation of benefits. These practices are somewhat tempered in Austria because of the administrative codification of *Proporz* practices and the country's judicial-administrative professionalism with a moderately high regulatory quality. Japan is a predominantly business-mediated

Table 13.1 *Determinants of clientelistic exchange: scope and intensity of particularistic linkages*

		Comprehensive clientelism		Business-mediated clientelism	Social clientelism
		Italy	Austria	Japan	Belgium
Direct exchange with voters	social policy benefits	1.0	1.0	0.0	1.0
	civil service patronage	1.0	1.0	0.5	1.0
Business-mediated exchange	public ownership of business and/or public procurement?	1.0	1.0	1.0	0.0
	low quality of business regulation	1.0	0.0	1.0	0.5
Informality of clientelistic exchange?		1.0	0.5	1.0	0.0
Summary score of scope and intensity of clientelism		5.0	3.5	3.5	2.5

clientelism where citizens primarily obtain clientelistic advantages via employment affiliations (e.g., with construction, farming, retail, post office, or ailing/subsidized industrial sectors). The Table may understate Japanese clientelism to the extent that it ignores gift giving to clients in electoral campaigns. Finally, Belgium approximates social clientelism with negligible business-mediated partisan exchange. The legal codification of clientelistic resource allocation in a pillarized democracy may take the sharp edge of arbitrariness and intransparency away from some Belgian clientelistic practices.

In established post-industrial democracies monitoring of clientelistic exchange, let alone enforcement, are not based on heavy-handed violations of the secrecy of the vote. It is rather indirectly based on social pressure, mediated by membership and activism in political parties, unions, businesses, professional associations, and churches. In Italy interest groups (and the Catholic Church) and enterprises received material benefits "in return not just for supporting the DC, but also for ensuring that their members fulfilled their end of the bargain, voting as instructed" (Warner 2001: 139). In Southern Italy, of course, the Mafia might be the most important monitoring and enforcement mechanism creating what Della Porta and Vannucci (1995: 170) call an efficient market for votes through voter intimidation and voter organization. Particularly in Austria, but also in Italy or Belgium, strong party membership and/or small local precinct organization enable party functionaries to monitor small group voting. Party membership is insignificant in Japan, but the candidates' personal local campaign machines keep tabs on small precincts and estimate the votes to be delivered by each unit.

How do our four countries compare to a wider set of established affluent OECD democracies? If we accept judgmental indicators, such as those reported in Blondel and Cotta (1996) and also listed in Müller's contribution to this volume, three large democracies may have a low to moderate incidence of clientelistic practices (France, Germany, and the United States), three further countries exhibit only marginal traits of clientelism (Netherlands, Switzerland, and the United Kingdom) and two Scandinavian countries are virtually clientelism-free (Denmark, Sweden).[2]

Column 1 of Table 13.2 creates judgmental tiers of clientelism based on these three classes of less or non-clientelistic systems, topped off by our three classes of clientelism. For the latter, I employ the summary scores of Table 13.1 as my guide, ranking Italy as the country with the greatest scope and intensity of clientelism, followed by Austria and Japan, and trailed by Belgium. As a matter of concept confirmation, Table 13.2 then reports World Bank scores for the control of corruption, regulatory quality, and the rule of law for 1997/98 and 2000/01. The last rows reveal the correlation between these indicators and the judgmental summary index of clientelism in column 1. I calculate these correlations with Austria included ($N = 12$) and excluded ($N = 11$). Because of Austria's codification of clientelism, against the backdrop of early professional civil service development (see below), Austria's clientelism score is somewhat higher than it should be based on indicators of good governance.

Countries left out from our comparison would not alter the menu of linkage practices. The missing Anglo-Saxon settler democracies (Australia, Canada, New Zealand) all rate as well or better than the United Kingdom on corruption, regulatory quality, or rule of law. The missing Scandinavian countries (Finland, Norway, and tiny Iceland) are in the same neighborhood as the two included cases from that region. Arguably, one could include Portugal and Spain as "near affluent" democracies, though with much less democratic political experience. The values of these two countries on our correlates in Table 13.2 would be in the neighborhood of those of France and Germany, but considerably set apart from our four clientelistic cases.

The correlations calculated in Table 13.2 indicate that corruption almost perfectly traces the intensity of clientelistic practices across the

---

[2] Papakostas (2001: 33) reports there is not even a Swedish term for clientelism, let alone social science research.

Table 13.2 *Correlates of clientelism in advanced capitalist democracies*

	Ranking of clientelism (1)	Control of corruption		Regulatory quality		Rule of law	
		1997/98 (2)	2000/01 (3)	1997/98 (4)	2000/01 (5)	1997/98 (6)	2000/01 (7)
Italy	5	0.80	0.63	0.59	0.59	0.86	0.72
Austria	4	1.46	1.56	0.90	1.19	1.81	1.89
Japan	4	0.72	1.20	0.39	0.64	1.42	1.59
Belgium	3	0.67	1.05	0.79	0.58	0.80	1.34
France	2	1.28	1.15	0.71	0.59	1.08	1.23
Germany	2	1.62	1.38	0.89	1.08	1.48	1.53
United States	2	1.41	1.45	1.14	1.19	1.25	1.58
Netherlands	1	2.03	2.09	1.14	1.50	1.58	1.67
Switzerland	1	2.07	1.91	0.88	1.21	2.00	1.91
United Kingdom	1	1.71	1.86	1.21	1.32	1.69	1.61
Denmark	0	2.13	2.09	1.05	1.09	1.69	1.71
Sweden	0	2.09	2.21	0.85	1.08	1.62	1.70
Average	2.08	1.50	1.55	0.88	1.01	1.49	1.54
Standard deviation	1.62	0.54	0.49	0.24	0.32	0.38	0.32
correlation with ranking of clientelism (without Austria in parentheses)	NA	−0.86 (−0.92)	−0.86 (−0.93)	−0.65 (−0.71)	−0.59 (−0.72)	−0.52 (−0.72)	−0.54 (−0.76)

Source: Kaufman, Kraay, and Zoibo-Lobaton (2002).

sample, provided we bracket the minor exception of Austria. With regulatory quality and the rule of law, the fit is less tight, but still surprisingly strong, again provided we drop Austria and also Japan in the case of rule of law only. The emergence of a professional career civil service before democratic mass enfranchisement in Austria and Japan may account for the two countries' higher regulatory and legal performance. Let us emphasize that the judgmental ranking of clientelistic practices in column 1 of Table 13.2 appears not to be arbitrary. It picks up a variety of political process features we would expect to relate to the nature of democratic citizen-politician linkages. This should inspire some confidence in the measurement of our dependent variable, clientelism.

Clientelism in crisis

Three of the four affluent clientelistic democracies went through an era of fascist rule in the twentieth century after a belated start of industrialization, typically with assistance from an illiberal authoritarian regime. After World War II, all three of them experienced the rise and durable hegemony of a cross-class party under a Christian Democratic or Liberal Democratic label, while developing weak conservative secular market-liberal parties. What distinguishes them from Germany, the country that shares all of these features, yet did not develop pronounced clientelistic politics, is the sometimes indirect and sometimes direct role of the state in industrial investment and development strategies in the post-war decades, whereas Germany had assertive private sector business coordination throughout the post-war period. The fourth clientelistic country, Belgium, displays all the features of the three strongly clientelistic ones to a lesser extent: early industrialization and market self-organization of business; powerful fascist movement, but no fascist regime; strong Christian Democracy, but checked by a medium-strong market-liberal secular party organizing its own societal pillar.

The point here is not to explain the rise of clientelism in a broad comparative context and detail the strategic mechanisms that drive it, but to highlight the importance of features that grow out of the political-economic development of our four countries and that impinge on their crisis years starting in the 1980s: the role of governments in organizing and regulating the economy and the feebleness of political market liberalism. The crisis of clientelism involves the unraveling of both of these features, namely of (1) the politicized public and semi-public economy, and (2) the dominance of Christian (or Liberal Democrat) center-right parties. The crisis of the public economy is typically mirrored in a rise of market-liberal parties. It is not coordinated market capitalism *per se*, but specific arrangements of sectoral and firm–group centered versions of that coordinated capitalism, often intertwined with outright state-run companies or regulatory agencies, that set the stage for direct exchange relations of electoral constituencies with office-seeking politicians delivering particularistic, targeted groups to relevant audiences.

The resulting "particracies" in our four countries began to be confronted with growing public restlessness and outrage over clientelistic arrangements only in the 1980s, even though mass publics had always voiced less satisfaction with democracy in these four countries than just about any other European democracy.[3] In the 1980s, such sentiments translated into the withdrawal of support from established parties and sometimes the rise of new parties. Three mechanisms drove the crisis of clientelism: (1) the declining performance of clientelistically penetrated

---

[3] For figures on satisfaction with democratic institutions in the EU, see Fuchs, Guidorossi, and Svensson (1995).

Table 13.3 *Disaffection with the political system and with established political parties*

	Clientelism score	Confidence in the legislature[a]	Confidence in the civil service[b]	Decline of established parties 1960/69–2000[c]
Italy	5	32	27	−49.6
Austria	4	41	42	−36.3
Japan	4	29	34	−38.7
Belgium	3	43	43	−22.0
France	2	48	49	−25.1
West Germany	2	51	39	−10.1
United States	2	46	59	−4.8[d]
Netherlands	1	52	46	−4.3
Switzerland	1	no data	no data	−21.5[e]
United Kingdom	1	46	44	−13.8
Denmark	0	42	51	−15.6
Sweden	0	47	44	−12.1
correlation with clientelism score		−0.70 (N = 11)	−0.65 (N = 11)	−0.81 (N = 12)

[a]Percent respondents from World Values Survey 1990/91, variable 279, national average.
[b]Percent respondents from World Value Survey 1990/91, variable 280, national average.
[c]Decline of established parties' vote total from the 1960–69 average to the last legislative election before 2000 (United States: presidential election). For calculation see Kitschelt (2002: 192–24).
[d]Presidential elections
[e]The Swiss established party decline is calculated based on the assumption that half of the Swiss People Party's support is anti-established party. Counting the SVP entirely as an established party, the vote loss in Switzerland would be only 9.8 percent, counting it entirely as a new party, that vote loss would be 33.2 percent.

economic sectors, resulting in skyrocketing demands for subsidies; and (2) an intensification of democratic political competition over linkage mechanisms in which the defenders of clientelism increasingly fought rearguard battles. (3) Once there was a receptive audience to challenge established modes of citizen-politician accountability, the mass media served as catalysts to broadcast and amplify political discontent with democracy.

Table 13.3 provides a snapshot of public confidence in legislatures and the civil service, the key arenas involved in the struggle over clientelistic politics, detailing how unpopular democratic institutions were in the heavily clientelistic countries compared to other OECD members. Moreover the last column of Table 13.3 shows that indeed it is in the most clientelistic countries that decline in support for the established large parties of the 1960s is the greatest by 2000. First, young educated urban service sector voters, particularly women, defected to left-libertarian parties (Kitschelt 1994). Later, new radical right or right-wing populist parties benefited from the defection of other groups from established parties, such as younger lower and medium-skilled males (Kitschelt 1995). The resulting reorganization of partisan alignments was dramatic in two of the four party systems and moderately strong in the other two polities. In each instance, it intensified competition between two blocs of parties trying to displace each other in the control of the executive.

In Austria, the rise of the right-wing populist Freedom Party from 1987 to its peak in 1999 at 27 percent of the vote forced both clientelistic parties, the Austrian People's Party (ÖVP) and the Austrian Social Democrats (SPÖ) to abandon their preferred clientelistic linkage techniques (cf. Müller 2002). In the course of this transformation, the ÖVP took a decidedly neoliberal turn that made the party give up much of its cross-class appeal customary for Christian Democratic parties after World War II. In a somewhat different vein, the cross-class and long-time hegemonic Christian Democrats in Italy disappeared entirely and gave rise to a bipolar reconfiguration of the Italian party system around a center-right and a center-left sector of party alliances (cf. D'Alimonte and Bartolini 1997). What emerged on the right was an entirely new "business party" around a wealthy media tycoon who constructed a new electoral vehicle as a marketing device without an organizational infrastructure with deep roots (Newell and Bull 1997: 92–3).

In Japan, the postwar hegemonic Liberal Democrats lost the support of a very large share of their former constituencies. But it has been more difficult to build a new contender credible to large audiences to confront a weakened Liberal Democratic Party (see Scheiner 2006, and in this volume). The Japan Socialist Party (JSP) itself was sufficiently compromised by clientelistic involvements to go down in the maelstrom of opposition to the "old" Japanese politics. After ten years of trial-and-error, the Japanese Democratic Party appears to hold out the promise of becoming a counterweight to the LDP, but in a centralist system it is difficult to establish a credible competitor whose lead politicians cannot gain credibility in subnational governments.

In Belgium, finally, the established parties lost voters in several waves, first to ethnolinguistic parties in the 1970s, then to left-libertarian parties in the 1980s, and finally in the 1990s to a radical right-authoritarian party in Flanders that clearly also invoked the theme of particracy to rally support. Nevertheless, the established parties' loss of support has not been as dramatic as in the cases of business-mediated or comprehensive clientelism.

In addition to defection from established parties, lower voter turnout became another mode of expressing disaffection with clientelism. Protest against clientelism may well have been a powerful force driving down voter turnout, net of the well-known institutional, strategic, and organizational variables that affect variance of turnout in space and time (Powell 1986; Jackman 1987; Gray and Caul 2000). As Table 13.4 illustrates, decline in established party vote share and turnout in national legislative elections (respectively presidential elections in the US) go hand-in-hand. Of course, because Belgium and Italy had compulsory voting, their vote loss has been less pronounced than one might otherwise have expected. For each country, I calculate a regression of actual turnout levels on the passage of years (i = 1, 2, ...) since 1970. The turnout figures (T) in Table 13.4 indicate the difference between electoral turnout closest to 1970 and the expected turnout in the last election before 2000. Cross-nationally, the correlation between decline in established party share and decline in turnout is moderate, if we include all twelve countries (r = +0.56), but receives a boost from setting aside Belgium and Italy with their compulsory vote systems (r = +0.75; N = 10).

In the 1960s parties with high levels of clientelism also tended to have higher than average turnout levels. This makes sense because voters had to demonstrate their support for the parties that targeted benefits to them. By 2000, there was a negative correlation between clientelism score and turnout levels. If we employ a country's clientelism score as predictor of its changed rate of voter turnout from the average in the 1960s to the last election before 2000, the correlation is moderately negative when we include the compulsory voting polities (r = −0.50), strongly negative when we confine ourselves to the voluntary vote polities only (r = −0.75). Clientelism coincides with a sharp drop in voter turnout over the last third of the twentieth century.[4]

The data presented here pretty clearly establish that clientelistic citizen-politician linkages in advanced capitalist democracies have been in trouble since the 1980s. But none of the indicators I have employed establishes a causal mechanism to account for this process so far. We have observed only the facts, namely that large proportions of the voting and non-voting

---

[4] This relationship remains robust, even if we add five further advanced post-industrial democracies, although two of them are outliers for idiosyncratic reasons (Finland and New Zealand, as compared to Australia, Canada, and Norway). The association is still a respectable +0.67 (N = 17), although structural economic crises unrelated to clientelism in both Finland and New Zealand triggered more increases in voter abstention (Finland) or declines in established party support (New Zealand) than the countries' low clientelism scores would have led us to expect. My analysis drops very small countries (Iceland, Luxembourg) and economic and/or political late developers (Greece, Ireland, Portugal, Spain).

Table 13.4 *Decline of established parties and voter turnout*

		Decline of voter turnout (T) from the first election in the 1970s to the last election in the 1990s[a]			
		0–5	5–10	10–15	15–20
Decline in established party support (EP)[b] 1960/69–2000	0–15	United Kingdom (T: −3.4/EP: −13.8)	Netherlands (T: −8.2/EP: −4.3) United States (T: −8.0/EP: −4.8) Germany (T: −7.0/EP: −10.1) Sweden (T: −7.4/EP: −12.1)	Switzerland (T: −14.3/EP: −21.5) France (T: −14.8/EP: −25.1) Austria (T: −14.6/EP: −36.3) Italy (T: −11.2/EP: −49.6)	Japan (T: −20.0/EP: −38.9)
	15–30	Denmark (T: −0.6/EP: −15.6)			
	>30	Belgium (T: −1.2/EP: −22.0)			

[a] Percent decline, predicted regression score
[b] Percent decline in legislative elections
Source: International IDEA Voter Turnout website at http://www.idea.int/vt/index.cfm

electorate have become disaffected with clientelistic practices and abandoned the parties identified with such practices. It is now time to probe into possible causes for this development.

Causes of clientelism's demise

The crisis of clientelism is essentially a political-economic phenomenon, primarily but not exclusively focused on business-mediated clientelism serving narrow rent-seeking industrial-sectoral groups with privileged access to public resources through support for/penetration by the established political parties. The decline of clientelistic parties is hence most pronounced in the comprehensively clientelistic polities of Italy and Austria, but also very steep in the exclusively business-mediated clientelism of Japan. Parties supporting Belgium's social clientelism have suffered relatively less, and some of this decline is due to exogenous, unrelated issues related to Belgium's ethnolinguistic conflict.

The industries involved in clientelistic politics have been on the relative and absolute decline since the 1970s. As they become progressively feebler, the maintenance of political exchange requires an escalating amount of public resources. The intensifying scramble for scarce resources places clientelism in the public limelight of the media and precipitates the erosion, if not collapse, of clientelistic business-mediated exchanges. Social clientelism is more indirectly affected by a general fiscal environment of retrenchment of benefits since the 1980s. New political forces of both the right and left have challenged contribution and benefits schemes and political practices.

The "clientelistic moment" in the 1940s and 1950s when centrist parties with cross-class alliances in Austria, Belgium, and Italy built or at least expanded business-mediated clientelistic empires occurred at a time when heavy industries, engineering, construction, finance, and infrastructure (telecommunications, transportation) were considered the lead industries pushing economic growth. It is these industries in which direct and indirect state intervention with associated clientelistic practices went much further than in light consumer products industries or consumer and business related services, let alone the much later developing high technology industries and services revolving around the revolution of information technology, data processing, or bioengineering. Clientelistic political practices entrenched themselves in what from the perspective of the 1980s and 1990s became ailing sunset industries with declining profitability and an employment overhang. Prompted by the weakening micro-economics of the government owned or regulated economic sectors, the clientelistic forces intensified their pressures to extract subsidies from the public purse. In Austria and Italy these problems show up in the crisis of public sector industries, in Japan in the crisis of formally private sectors benefiting from public procurement, subsidies, or regulatory favoritism that distorted market prices and prevented the correct appraisal of financial risks.

In each of these cases, the clientelistic political penetration of strong industrial sectors reached its high watermark from the 1950s to the 1970s by engineering a containment, if not closure, of opportunities for party competition. Conversely, the decline of clientelism involves an intensification of party competition in the sense that small changes in the electoral performance of individual parties may translate into large shifts in the governing party (coalition). What Katz and Mair (1995) characterize as "cartel parties," namely parties that can effectively insulate themselves from competition, even if they do not respond to voter preferences, is not a progressively more common phenomenon in European politics, but is closely wedded to the significance of clientelistic politics in some post-World War II advanced capitalist democracies.[5] The decline of clientelism, in fact, has been intimately linked with the erosion of a single or two-party coalition hegemony/duopoly in government in each of these four countries. This applies to Social Democracy and People's Party in Austria, Christian Democrats in Belgium and Italy, and Liberal Democrats in Japan. Whereas these parties ruled without interruption for most of the post-World War II period until the early 1990s, they then experienced significant stretches of confinement to the legislative opposition benches, or outright electoral collapse in the Italian case.

To put these developments into perspective, consider the relative share of public enterprise in the business sector of advanced capitalist democracies, as measured by the scope of public ownership across industrial sectors (column 1, Table 13.5) and the fixed capital formation by the public business sector as a percentage of total capital formation (columns 2–5, Table 13.5). Only the two comprehensive clientelistic countries out of our set of four – Austria and Italy – show a large state-owned sector. State ownership is neither a necessary nor a sufficient condition for clientelistic practices, as is indicated by the relatively high scores of public ownership in France and the United Kingdom with evidently less or non-clientelistic politics. This may be so because both countries provide a partially or wholly market-liberal capitalist environment with an atmosphere, corporate organization, and interest groups in which collusion and cooperation, as preconditions of clientelistic politics, do not thrive. Interestingly, the French and UK figures also show the greatest decline

---

[5] For a critique of Katz and Mair (1995), see Koole (1996) and Kitschelt (2000a).

Table 13.5 *State involvement in the public sector, 1970–1990*

	State ownership in up to eight industries in the 1980s[a]		Fixed capital formation by the public business sector in OECD countries (percent of total capital formation)[b]			
	%		1970	1980	1990	Change 1970–90
Italy	75	(4.5/6)	14	15	13	−1
Austria	100	(7/7)	n.d.	19	21	[+2]
Japan	4	(0.25/7)	10	9.5	6	−4
Belgium	29	(2/7)	12	13	10	−2
France	72	(5/7)	16	14	12	−4
Germany	44	(3.5/8)	12	11	n.d.	[−1]
United States	3	(.25/8)	4	4.5	3.5	−0.5
Netherlands	50	(3/6)	15	12.5	n.d.	[−2.5]
Switzerland	n.d.		n.d.	n.d.	n.d.	n.d.
United Kingdom	77	(6.25/8)	12	11	6	−6
Denmark	n.d.		9	8	13	+4
Sweden	58	(3.5/6)	n.d.	15	10	[−5]

[a] Based on Vickers and Wright (1988: 10). A total of eight industries is scored: Electricity, gas, oil, coal, steel, ships, motor, and airlines. Based on scoring published in the *Economist*, industries receive 0.25, 0.50, 0.75 or 1.00 point scores for public ownership. The total score in the table reflects the summed index of public ownership in all the up to eight industries that exist in a country.
Source: Boix (1998: 55) based on OECD data.

in public sector involvement in these more liberal capitalist polities over the 1970–90 period (see last column of Table 13.5). By contrast, in those CMEs where clientelism penetrates a substantial publicly owned or regulated enterprise sector, it proves more "sticky" than elsewhere because rent-seeking partisan interests are configured around the state apparatus and block political reform, even when economic considerations suggest the rationalization, downsizing, and privatization of declining industries.

The weakening of the Austrian state-owned industries and the politicians' slow embracing of privatization and depoliticization of industrial enterprises constitutes an often-recounted story (Müller and Meth-Cohn 1994; Stiefel 2000). The critical causal relation runs from declining micro-economic performance of the large state holding companies to a politicization of the clientelistic managerial structures and employment practices/privileges of Austrian state capitalism and from there eventually on to electorally mediated political pressures to dismantle public property and the clientelistic governance techniques. It required, however, the intensification of partisan competition through the strategic reorientation and increasing support gathered by a right-wing populist anti-statist

Table 13.6 *Japan's government fixed capital formation (as a percent of GDP) in comparative perspective*

	Japan	France	Germany	Italy	United States	United Kingdom
1970	4.5	3.6	4.4	3.0	2.6	4.7
1975	5.3	3.7	3.6	3.4	2.1	4.7
1980	6.3	3.1	3.4	3.2	1.7	2.4
1985	4.7	3.1	2.3	3.7	1.7	1.9
1990	5.0	3.3	2.2	3.3	1.7	2.3
1995	6.4	3.5	2.3	2.3	1.8	2.1
					(1994)	(1994)

Source: Okuda (2001: 3), based on UN data.

party, the Austrian Freedom Party, to force the clientelistic ÖVP (People's Party) and SPÖ (Social Democratic Party) coalition into privatizations and a decoupling of state-owned business and financial institutions from political partisan penetration.

A similar trajectory of financial hemorrhage in state-owned, patronage penetrated state holding companies, followed by a politicization of clientelistic governance, unfolded in Italy from the 1980s on (see Amatori 2000; Cassese 1994). Here the lead clientelistic parties saw privatization as a threat to their clientelistic capacity to procure jobs for followers (Cassese 1994: 137). Their ultimate collapse in 1994 under a cloud of corruption scandals that exposed the clientelistic networks opened the way to more political-economic reform.

In Table 13.5, Japan's business-oriented clientelism does not surface because governments shape business fortunes and clientelistic exchange less through ownership relations than public procurement contracts, particularly in the construction sector, and through regulatory protection and favoritism. The internationally outstanding level of high government fixed capital formation in Japan is almost entirely due to the exorbitant size of the country's public procurement dependent construction sector (Table 13.6). The gap between falling public works budgetary outlays in most OECD democracies and seesawing or rising expenditures in Japan is clearly visible. It contributed to a level of gross public sector debt in Japan that by the turn of the century had reached levels unparalleled by any other capitalist economy under peace-time conditions.

The single greatest problem of Japan's economy, however, may have been its anti-competitive regulatory policies (cf. Porter, Takeuchi, and Skakibara 2000: 140). These regulatory practices have enabled banks, life insurance companies and industrial enterprises to allocate vast resources in high-risk, low marginal return investments, often with direct financial participation of the government run postal savings bank and with various instruments of fiscal and tax policy. The patronage networks radiating from the ruling Liberal Democrats have facilitated and lubricated this process. Hence, economic problems in the affected sectors creating an imperative for economic and political reform shook up the ruling party. As Pempel (1998: 14) states, "[i]ncreased politicization of the regulatory process, massive mismanagement of the domestic economy, corruption scandals, and political opportunism all combined in the mid-1990s to break apart the LDP, overhaul the electoral system for the Lower House, and completely reorder the party system."

At the same time, the difficulty of creating an effective opposition party in Japan that voters could look upon as a credible government alternative to the ruling Liberal Democrats, gave the incumbent hegemon a lease on life. Given the limited increase of partisan competitiveness in Japanese elections from 1994 to the turn of the century, the reforms pushed by the Liberal Democratic Koizumi government after 2001 were piecemeal and cautious. An intensification of party competition with the rise of the Democratic Party in 2004 prompted a moderate acceleration of reforms against the clientelistic networks of reciprocity that was ratified in Koizumi's victory over the old guard in the LDP in the 2005 Lower House election. For the reforms to continue and accelerate, however, sustained competitive pressure on the LDP may be needed to hold the remaining defenders of the clientelistic economy inside the LDP establishment at bay.

Belgium's social clientelism has encountered political-economic problems primarily through a run-away fiscal deficit and debt ratio of the public sector to sustain its partisan associated social insurance pillars. Business-mediated clientelism that generated bad economic outcomes in Austria, Italy, and Japan was not as virulent in Belgium, even though Belgium had its share of problems to deal with the political partisan ramifications of its steel and coal crisis. But the accumulation of big public debts was mostly due to efforts to compensate labor market participants for higher unemployment after the oil crises and in the context of a party system in which complex multiparty coalitions, in association with patronage networks in the social service administrations, hampered efforts to achieve fiscal stabilization.

The economic crisis of the 1980s contributed to the declining role of the Christian Democrats and the feasibility of government coalitions without participation of this hitherto hegemonic party. Competitiveness in Belgian politics increased particularly under the impact of intermittently increasing support for the market-liberal parties in key elections during the last decades of the twentieth century.

Alternative explanations

To recap the argument, the differential importance of business-mediated clientelism drives my explanation of the timing as well as of the intensity of growing opposition to established clientelistic practices in the four countries. That challenge is intense in Austria, Italy, and Japan. They have in common business-mediated clientelism, but not social clientelism, a feature pronounced only in Austria and Italy. In the contrasting case of weak business-mediated clientelism, Belgium, anti-clientelistic mobilization is more restrained. Let me now turn to alternative explanations of the demise of clientelism in our four advanced capitalist democracies with intense clientelism, none of which fits the cross-national and temporal patterns of challenge experienced across these four cases.

The first alternative explanation has to do with the *ratcheting up of the cost of clientelism-driven electoral campaigns*. This argument is consistent with a "developmentalist" hypothesis that citizens' opportunity costs for embracing clientelistic exchange become greater with affluence and education. The empirical evidence, however, fits only Italy and Japan. Scholars have widely commented on the "astronomical costs" of Japanese election campaigns in the 1990s (cf. Pempel 1998: 141, 184). In a similar vein, Italy incurred the massive costs of the clientelistic machines that by the later 1980s may well have exceeded 1.5 percent of total GDP every year (Rhodes 1997: 71).[6] There is little evidence, however, that campaign expenditures spun out of control in other clientelistic countries with less personalistic electoral systems, such as Austria and Belgium.

A second explanation homes in on the *post-industrial, middle-class professional, urban character of the anti-clientelistic revolt in Japan and Northern Italy or in the urban areas of Austria*, particularly in Vienna. While it is true that these social strata have furnished an over-proportional share of the anti-clientelistic constituency, this observation is fully consistent with a political-economic theory of opposition to rent-seeking groups. Clientelistic benefits bypassed the sectors in which middle-class professionals are typically situated. But the anti-clientelistic revolt also extended to segments of the working class who did not benefit from job protection and the benefits of political network status, particularly among the young low-skilled, low-political affiliation manual workers. The exclusive privileges enjoyed by participants in sectors relying on business-mediated clientelism generated resentment among labor market participants at all

---

[6] The percent GDP estimate is based on Rhodes's source according to which Italian parties were estimated to have obtained illegally about 3,400 billion lire per year in the late 1980s.

skill levels, provided they were situated in firms outside the clientelistic networks.

Third, *macro-economic developments* in our four countries and beyond affect, but do not directly supply, a satisfactory explanation of anti-clientelistic mobilization. The interaction between general economic climate and the micro-economics of business-mediated clientelism is always critical to generate an empirically adequate theoretical account of the challenge to and the demise of clientelism. This can be shown by comparing four macro-economic indicators to the patterns of anti-clientelistic mobilization in our four countries.

(1) High *public sector deficits* may be a possible result of rent-seeking clientelistic practices, but they are neither a necessary nor a sufficient consequence of clientelism or a cause of its decline. The take-off periods for anti-clientelistic politics are not necessarily contingent upon the advent of fiscal imbalance in the public sector. In Italy and Belgium, large fiscal deficits began to accumulate in the 1970s and antedated the public assault on clientelism by more than a decade. Conversely, Austria and Japan did not experience very high public sector deficits until the early 1990s when the anti-clientelistic challenge was well under way. It is the micro- and meso-economic conditions of clientelistic firms and sectors more so than the performance of the whole economy that is decisive for anti-clientelistic mobilization.

(2) In a similar vein, the incidence of *declining economic growth and rising unemployment* does not match the onset of anti-clientelistic mobilization. Japan's economic growth looked great throughout the 1980s (3.4 percent/a on a per capita basis) and even into the early 1990s, when the real estate bubble burst and anti-clientelistic electoral politics went into full swing.[7] Italy had one of the best per capita growth figures behind Japan in the Western hemisphere throughout the 1980s (2.3 percent/a compared to 2.1 percent/a in the United States and Germany) and experienced a major fall only after clientelism had already become intensely contentious. Also, Austria's economic growth rate of 2.0 percent per capita in the 1980s was average for OECD countries. Among the four countries, Belgium had the comparatively worst economic performance in the 1980s, yet displayed the least increase in resistance to clientelistic politics.

(3) A similar lack of consistency can be found in the relationship between the challenge and demise of clientelism and the *movement of annual trade and balance of accounts figures*. Throughout the 1980s,

---

[7] Per capita economic growth figures are calculated from the information provided by the World Bank's World Development Indicators website.

Austria's and Italy's exports thrived and their balances of accounts were only mildly in deficit. Belgium performed similarly well. In Japan, an appreciating yen and a movement of manufacturing to low-wage Asian neighbor countries led to a decline and stagnation of Japan's share in the world's export markets, but combined with a very strongly positive national balance of accounts. Some have argued that foreign pressures to open up Japanese markets to trade worked through electoral system reform which then would terminate clientelistic practices of rent-seeking and improve economic efficiency (Rosenbluth 1996). But the new electoral system did not close the door to clientelistic direct exchange relations. Furthermore, there is little evidence suggesting that trade exposure of the most clientelistic sectors and/or concerns about external competitiveness in the most export-oriented industries ever was a mobilizing factor in the anti-clientelistic campaign.

(4) Those who identify globalization of economies as a prime cause of domestic political-economic crisis and change often home in on the *removal of capital market regulation* that permits domestic capital to roam abroad in search of better rates of return or to extract profit-enhancing concessions from their domestic work force by threatening to pursue this strategy. Yet again, changes in the capital market openness in the 1990s show little relationship to the intensity of anti-clientelistic mobilization.[8] In the country with the weakest challenge to clientelism, Belgium, capital market openness leaped forward the most from 1985 to 1990 (from 10.0 to the maximum value 14.0), whereas in Japan there was no change at all (score 10.5) and in Austria only a marginal opening (from 11.5 to 12.5). Only Italy fits a proposition that holds capital market opening responsible for the collapse of business-mediated clientelism because it experienced a rather sharp opening (from 10.5 to 13.5 on the openness index from 1985 to 1990).

Maybe domestic realignments of citizen-politician linkage mechanisms respond to major political-economic regime shifts in international regional or global arenas that reveal the full impact of international forces on domestic political arrangements. One candidate for this argument is the increasing integration of the European Union. For Italy, a plausible case can be made that the growing fiscal and regulatory authority of the European Union, particularly in matters such as anti-trust, government procurement, and subsidies to state-regulated or state-owned industries, restrained the range of operation of clientelistic politics in the 1990s. This

[8] I am drawing here on Dennis Quinn's well-known index of capital exchange controls that ranges from 0 to 14, as reported by Scharpf and Schmidt (2000: 368–69) for the years 1970 to 1993.

shift of control led to a "hollowing out" of politicized public control over the economy, but simultaneously also a "hardening" of the state against interest group capture (cf. Della Sala 1997). Setting aside Belgium with little business-mediated clientelism, a similar argument as for Italy would not work in the case of then non-EU members Austria and Japan. The anti-clientelistic wave in Austria started long before the prospects of EU entry were imminent. Japan, of course, did not even participate in the construction of a regional economic zone that could have forced domestic regulatory policies to change.

Beyond macro-economics, a fourth and final argument invokes the *fall of communism in 1989* as a primary cause for the demise of clientelism in advanced capitalist democracies. This argument rests on the assumption that hegemonic center parties, organizing a cross-class compromise, had to hold socialist and communist challengers at bay with a wide range of techniques, including a business-mediated clientelism in which private enterprise would fund anti-communist parties as an insurance policy against the socialization of the means of production. The disappearance of the communist threat internally and externally made clientelistic containment strategies superfluous and made business reticent to contribute to clientelistic parties (Rhodes 1997: 67–68). This proposition rings true for the Italian and Japanese cases, but cannot accommodate Austria. In both Italy and Japan, communist or socialist parties engaged in a sufficiently radical rhetoric and their bourgeois competitors made them out to be sufficiently "anti-system" throughout much of the time period from the 1950s to the 1970s to enable clientelistic ruling parties to mobilize corporate backers in the pursuit of a common anti-communist purpose. But Austria lacked a salient anti-system party and nevertheless experienced a challenge to clientelism in exactly the same time period as Italy and Japan. Given the commonality of micro-economic difficulties in the most rent-seeking sectors of business-mediated clientelistic politics in all three countries, the disappearance of anti-communist political sentiments can only be a minor supplementary force that hastened the demise of clientelism in Italy and Japan.

Conclusion: a future for clientelism in affluent democracies?

The comparative analysis of citizen-politician linkage practices in democratic countries would benefit from better descriptive measures of linkages, from larger comparison samples, and from more detailed, refined theories that could flesh out the strategic constellations of political and economic actors shaping the choice of linkage modes. Within the confines of available data and broad theoretical perspectives, this chapter has tried to account for the rise and demise of clientelistic linkage practices in four advanced capitalist democracies against the backdrop of different, more programmatic politics in other rich established OECD democracies.

This chapter delivers four messages. First, it is theoretically useful to dissociate a variety of patterns of clientelism contingent upon the precise nature of the exchanges between politicians and constituencies that prevail (business-mediated, social, and comprehensive clientelism). Second, in a most similar systems comparison of advanced capitalist democracies, it is not economic development that accounts for the emergence and decline of varying linkage practices and not even the nature of formal democratic institutions. Instead, it is political-economic governance structures and competitive configurations among partisan forces that shape modes of democratic linkage. Third, and more specifically, clientelistic politics occurs in variants of "coordinated market capitalism," but the latter may have been only a necessary, yet not a sufficient condition for clientelistic politics to have become prominent after World War II. Coordinated capitalism created a business atmosphere ("corporate culture") and a mobilization of collective actors in the economy, both on the business and the labor side, who potentially seek out clientelistic arrangements. The decline of clientelism has been one facet of the erosion of coordinated capitalism more generally in many of its empirical contours. In fact, where clientelism prevails, coordinated capitalism may be under particularly intense siege. This does not imply, of course, that liberal market capitalism is the answer. Both types of capitalism and hybrids in between the ideal types have their drawbacks and may promote an era of experimentation and recombination of elements of corporate governance and macro-political economic politics the ultimate outcome of which cannot yet be anticipated.

This brings me to my fourth and final point. Both the rise and the demise of clientelism in advanced capitalist democracies is deeply enmeshed in the reorganization of political-economic governance more generally and of the parties involved in this process more specifically. What has started to happen since the 1980s in the advanced post-industrial capitalisms with clientelistic features is an increasing defection of citizens from accepting the benefits of clientelistic ties. Direct and indirect costs of political clientelism appear too high to many citizens to tolerate rent-seeking social forces that extract targeted material rewards from political parties in exchange for their voter allegiance. Both in the era of the rise as well as the demise of clientelistic democracy a realignment in the configuration of partisan competitors on the political stage takes place. This process challenges the established incumbent parties and their political and economic networks of popular support. In the current conjuncture, however, it may be too early to judge what is likely to emerge from this process of rearranging and recasting citizen-politician linkages of accountability.

14 A research agenda for the study of citizen-politician linkages and democratic accountability

Herbert Kitschelt and Steven I. Wilkinson

The systematic study of citizen-politician linkage mechanisms of accountability and responsiveness is challenging because we lack good comparative and historical data on both the exchanges involved, as well as on the non-clientelistic factors that might potentially also explain the political or economic outcomes in which we're interested. There are obvious reasons for voters and politicians to hide information on clientelistic exchanges: to deter competitors, to avoid social opprobrium, as well as to avoid prosecution. So in the absence of good data social scientists have been forced to rely on often-excellent qualitative studies on specific practices in individual countries, or on indirect quantitative tracers of such practices enabled by the idiosyncratic data opportunities in a single country.

The studies assembled in this book, as well as the Introduction, primarily speak to the theoretical questions of (1) how to conceptualize alternative citizen-politician linkage mechanisms in democratic polities and (2) how to explain the empirical variation in linkage practices across polities and parties as our dependent variable. Empirically, the studies rely on qualitative cross-national assessments (e.g., contributions by Kitschelt, Levitsky, Müller, and van de Walle), on unique subnational quantitative measures not available in a cross-national framework (such as in Magaloni, Diaz-Cayeros, and Estévez, Wilkinson, Lyne, or in Scheiner), or on observation-based narratives (such as Krishna, Chandra, or Levitsky). Given this state of affairs, we need to start thinking about how to make advances in empirical research on democratic linkage mechanisms beyond the status quo.

In this conclusion, therefore, instead of summarizing the previous chapters, we will address what we regard as the steps necessary to advance the study of clientelism beyond what is possible here. The first part of the conclusion deals with conceptual and empirical issues of data collection, particularly a proposal to collect systematic data about the nature of political linkage mechanisms across democracies which would be sufficient to enable us to test rival theories. The second part of the conclusion discusses the theoretical purposes for which such a dataset might be deployed. The study of principal-agent relations and political account-ability in democracies is intrinsically valuable for both positive and normative reasons. Assembling cross-national data on linkage relations would be even more rewarding, however, if they could be employed to explain political-economic processes and *outcomes*, such as fiscal policies, economic growth, and social equity. In the second part of this conclusion, we speculate on the relationships we might uncover with such data.

Systematic data on citizen-politician linkages

The content analysis of party manifestoes (Budge *et al.* 2001) as well as expert judgments of parties' policy positions (Huber and Inglehart 1995; Laver and Benoit, forthcoming; Laver and Hunt 1992) have generated systematic data on the programmatic appeals of parties in a considerable number of countries. Corresponding data on clientelistic politics are missing. Many democracies in developing countries have not been mapped either in programmatic or clientelistic terms.

We can employ several indicators to assess whether programmatic linkages are present. First, if parties' mean positions on salient issue (bundles) systematically diverge. Second, if on such policy issue (bundles) politicians inside the same party show less variance than politicians belonging to different parties. Third, if politicians are able to map their party positions on the formal left-right scale. Fourth, if politicians' mean party positions correspond to those of their partisan electorates.[1] Fifth, if actual policy outputs and outcomes vary with the partisan stripes of governments (e.g., Castles 1982; Garrett 1998; Klingemann, Hofferbert, and Budge, 1994).

The absence of measures of clientelistic linkages would be no problem if we could safely postulate a one-to-one trade-off with programmatic politics. But this is unlikely to be the case. Some democratic polities may involve both programmatic and clientelistic politics, others neither. If there is a trade-off between clientelism and programmatic competition, it is likely to be far from perfect. All this necessitates that we develop independent measures of clientelistic linkage.

The difficulties in obtaining valid and reliable data about citizen-politician linkages are particularly severe for those scholars who – unlike social anthropologists – wish not to supply thick descriptions of political exchange in a small number of places, but rather a broad comparative map

---

[1] Of course, inter-party differences in the preference schedules of their electoral followings may be entirely due to the systematic partisan bias of critical, rational voter minorities who explicitly link their partisan choice to the bundles of policy promises offered by the parties. Majorities of citizens may still cast their vote in an unreflective fashion.

of linkage practices in order to explain variation in modes of democratic accountability. Let us distinguish among three general classes of problems in the empirical analysis of clientelism: first, the *conceptual identification* of clientelistic principal-agent accountability (contingent exchange or not?); second, the *subjective interpretation* of contingent exchange by the patrons (instrumental or not?); third, the *strategic misrepresentation* of such exchange relations primarily by the political agents. Problems of conceptual identification haunt all modes of data collection on clientelism. Problems of subjective interpretation are particularly virulent in mass surveys. Issues of strategic misrepresentation come up primarily in data collection from politicians themselves.

Conceptual identification

As we discussed in the Introduction, clientelistic politics that involves the contingent exchange of political support for targeted benefits is easier to identify if benefits accrue to individual voters or businesses (jobs, contracts, etc.), but much harder to separate from policy linkage where politicians deliver *local club goods*, such as infrastructure projects. To the extent that *specific* localities get *preferential* access to such facilities *contingent* upon the electoral choices of small groups of voters and contributors to parties and candidates, the production of local public goods constitutes the currency of clientelistic politics. How should we draw the line between a general collective club good and such clientelistic targeted club goods? Asking voters directly (e.g., in surveys) is difficult, as they may have reasons to interpret political accountability in non-instrumental terms (see below). Moreover, they may be sufficiently myopic in their range of experiences to be unable to tell whether benefits accrued to them as a matter of general policy or targeted favoritism. Asking politicians is futile, as they have an obvious strategic interest in misrepresenting the reasons for their decisions to supply targeted benefits to local constituencies (see below).

If political actors themselves are rarely suitable sources of unbiased and cross-nationally comparable information to determine levels of clientelistic or programmatic citizen-politician linkages, we might resort to "objective" data about resource allocation through political exchange as a way out of our predicament. Contributions to our book are highly inventive in their pursuit of this avenue. Magaloni *et al.*, for example, examine local patterns of allocating targeted and decomposable resources that can be distributed in discretionary fashion to particular individuals and small groups. Lyne draws on patterns of legislative roll call voters in the Brazilian Congress, and Hale compares the electoral success of different types of candidates in Russia's Duma elections. While each of these methods and measures may be suitable as a valid indicator of linkage practices within a particular country, they are so wedded to the intricacies of a local institutional setting that none of them can be easily transferred and applied to a larger set of countries in a cross-national study of democratic linkage mechanisms.

A further alternative with greater cross-national reach and comparability may be offered by expert surveys in which professionals observing local political allocation are asked to assess prevailing practices of political exchange. It is plausible that they are in as good or better a position to gauge whether in their country local club goods accrue to communities as a matter of general public policy, or more as a reward for political services to particular parties or individual politicians.

Subjective interpretation

Research on clientelistic politics runs into the problem that actors often interpret what observers would term clientelism in very different terms. Even social anthropologists who have spent years conducting fieldwork in Latin American municipalities and elsewhere have emphasized the difficulty of "proving" the existence of clientelism (cf. Auyero 2000; Gay 1994). Even though there are targeted and instrumental exchanges between individual voters or small groups of voters and politicians or parties competing for electoral support, often no direct on-the-spot transfer of goods and monitoring of individual compliance takes place. In many cases the search for "smoking gun" evidence therefore remains futile. As the Introduction to this volume argues and Müller's contribution exemplifies, social networks and associations often exercise indirect monitoring and enforcement, mediated by local neighborhood organizers or party precinct captains expected to "deliver" contingents of voters. Group membership intertwines instrumental benefits with affective group identifications and thus reduces the problem of monitoring.[2] Local brokers may ultimately cut defectors off from benefits based on social clues and circumstantial evidence more than on direct observation of non-compliance with a clientelistic bargain followed by immediate punishment.

In social-network-based clientelism, citizens usually do not reflect on linkages to politicians in terms of instrumental exchange (cf. Auyero

---

[2] For other examples of patron-client networks that mix affective and instrumental motivations, see Scott (1972) and Milne (1973: 901). However, while Scott and Milne saw these affective ties as stemming from traditional norms and cultures, we agree with Auyero that they can also stem from much more recent social and political mobilizations in both developing *and* developed states.

2000: ch. 5). "Soft" monitoring and incentives, together with the presence of brokers and politicians in the same community, make clients interpret political accountability in terms of solidary relations that grow out of the broker's positive contributions to her constituencies. As Auyero (2001: 177) concludes, "[t]he truth of clientelism is collectively repressed by both brokers and clients." Close affective relations between citizens and patrons go hand in hand with materially significant exchange relations, such as appointments to public sector jobs or favoritism in the provision of local infrastructure (clean water, sewers, paved roads, school facilities), and enable citizens to interpret such relations in communitarian terms: "Reciprocity and calculation exist, but demands for recognition within the inner circle are more significant" (Auyero 2001: 180).

Because of these problems of interpretation, as well as the fact that payments may be given by patrons to clients before, during, or after an election, it may be difficult to generate useful information about clientelistic exchange through either econometric methods or population surveys. Within individual countries, concrete questions concerning valuation or receipt of targeted material advantages from politicians may sometimes work.[3] But for the purposes of cross-national research, the nature of targeted goods and the likely survey response bias in each country may vary too much across polities to generate meaningful comparisons.

Strategic misrepresentation

Politicians, even more than voters, may want to conceal the presence of clientelistic exchange. Even those politicians who manifestly organize clientelistic exchanges may sense a certain contempt for the crude practice of paying voters off with selective incentives and may therefore misrepresent such practices, when asked directly to specify the nature of their dealings with electoral constituencies. Politicians may treat direct questions about clientelism – like corruption – as valence questions on which they suspect most citizens and observers to be on one side of the issue (against). Hence they present their own practices as devoid of clientelism, but may attribute such practices to their competitors and opponents.[4]

---

[3] This was demonstrated by Wantchekon (2003) through a field experiment in Benin. Stokes (2005) employs an Argentinean questionnaire in which interviewees were asked whether local political figures would help them with problems, such as finding a job, and whether they had received campaign gifts from a party candidate.

[4] For the pitfalls of using political players as the main source of information about corruption or pork, see Barry Ames's (2001: 34) experiences in Brazil. In a similar vein, a survey among Russian legislators fielded by Kitschelt and Smyth (2002) included a question about clientelistic exchange. The response pattern was that of valence competition: respondents attributed clientelistic practices to other parties, but not to their own.

Furthermore, where legal prohibitions exist against clientelistic exchanges, even if widely ignored in practice, politicians may abstain from being too open, lest their admissions be used against them by their (equally clientelistic) political rivals.

Expert surveys as an alternative?

Surveys among small panels of "experts" who have monitored the political practices of their own polity over considerable periods of time and partaken in the "collective experience" of social scientific research, as documented in academic and journalistic books about politics in their countries, may in part get us beyond the obstacles of identifying, interpreting, and correctly representing citizen-politician relations in a polity. One might envision a cross-national study with expert panels numbering between ten and twenty respondents in each of the currently seventy to ninety polities with more than one million inhabitants on earth with a sufficient cumulative record of democratic competition to warrant a survey of citizen-politician linkages.

Each country expert panel would rate the parties and aggregate averages for all parties in their polity on several modules of questions. The first module would deal with direct and indirect personal and small-group-targeted political exchanges involving private and local club goods and services. A second module would deal with direct and indirect personal and small group monitoring techniques that enable politicians and voters to determine whether exchanges have been consummated or not. Ideally, each of these modules would not simply provide aggregate measures for polities at large, but specify clientelistic practices by party and subnational variation. Also an intertemporal comparison (clientelism now and ten years ago?) might be useful.

A third module would address the organizational structures of parties in order to assess their capabilities to provide direct or indirect monitoring of clients and/or to coordinate programmatic policy stances. A fourth and final module would ask experts to indicate the presence, salience, and nature of parties' policy stances in order to provide a baseline indicating whether and how clientelistic and programmatic linkage practices coincide or operate as trade-offs in democratic party competition. This module may also include an assessment of the extent to which parties choose to appeal to the personal qualities of their leaders, net of programmatic or clientelistic politics, as a technique to attract voters.

After the first round of data collection, in order to increase the reliability and comparability of the expert assessments, average expert ratings of all parties on all variables could be fed back to the juries for reconsideration ("Delphi method"). Each country's expert group should also obtain mean ratings generated by juries covering other countries. Based on this information, respondents should have a chance to revise their initial personal scores and comment on the profiles of mean scores for their own country.[5]

All such cross-national research is beset by the anchor point problem (cf. King *et al.* 2003). Based on their personal parochial experience and particularities of semantic connotations of specific concepts employed in the translation of questionnaires, respondents may interpret the endpoints of quantitative judgment scales differently. Hence the comparison of cross-national means and differences is meaningless. What may strike citizens in country A as a sign of strong clientelistic practices may not even make it onto the radar screen of most respondents in country B. The Danes may interpret a practice as scandalously clientelistic that would hardly register in traditionally clientelistic polities such as Italy.

Expert surveys do not permit us to avoid the anchor point problem entirely, but they may help in several ways. First of all, political science and public policy experts tend to be less parochial in their knowledge of political practices and thus base their anchor point on a broader range of experiences. Second, given the specific opportunities of an expert survey, the research instrument can flesh out the meaning of the end points of rating scales in greater detail than in a population survey. A convergence in the perception of the rating scales for different linkage practices can be achieved only if questions are relatively concrete and accompanied by descriptions of what sorts of political behavior must be present to score practices near one or the other extreme points on a variety of scales developed to capture clientelistic practices. This descriptive elaboration of the meaning of scales through empirical examples may approximate for an expert survey, what King *et al.* (2003) call "vignettes," the elaboration of exemplary behavior or opinions to which respondents assign scale values. Third, given their own exposure to multiple political entities, experts may have a greater capacity to identify clientelistic practices as well as to interpret political exchange as clientelistic than average citizens. And finally, given that experts are not directly political players with ambitions to acquire power in their own countries' party competition, they may be less tempted to misrepresent prevailing practices of vote-getting strategically.

Compared to localized ethnographic research of citizen-politician linkages, of course, there is at least one weakness that broad cross-national research can never overcome. In pursuit of the objective to expand the

---

[5] See Linstone and Turoff (1975) for the origin of the method and a description of its applications.

scope of comparison, empirical research inevitably must sacrifice a great deal of the subtlety and specificity of the social anthropologists' localized observations. Broadly comparative studies inevitably generate large measurement error. Moreover, they are beset by aggregation problems, for example when a single empirical characterization of a linkage practice is meant to represent the average behavior of myriads of citizens and politicians across entire political parties or all politicians and parties in a polity. Nevertheless, these trade-offs between scope and depth are unavoidable given financially restrictive research budgets and time for observation. Given the paucity of encompassing datasets, we opt for the pursuit of such a set of observations even in the full knowledge of measurement error and distortion through aggregation of observations.

Consequences of alternative democratic linkage practices

One reason for the high level of current interest in clientelism, as we point out in the Introduction, is the assumption, which we explore below, that it is damaging for governance, economic growth, and income inequality. It is also believed to be bad for democracy, because it decreases the legitimacy of elected leaders and makes citizens unwilling to defend it from authoritarian threats. But is clientelism really this harmful? Without in any way wishing to make a normative argument in its favor, we argue here that such broad statements about the negative consequences of clientelism are based on little empirical evidence. There *are* in fact contexts in which clientelism seems to deliver rather satisfactory outcomes in terms of economic growth and distributional equity. Furthermore, clientelistic democracies often persist for long time periods, even if distrust of political institutions and popular cynicism about the way authoritative decisions are made in the polity is widespread.

Political-economic consequences of democratic linkage mechanisms: growth and distributive justice

Clientelism is believed to be incompatible with a liberal market-based framework for allocating scarce resources. Clientelistic politics locks in rent-seeking interests who gain market-distorting advantages through the authoritative allocation of scarce resources that rewards them for their services and contributions to particular political patrons and parties (Kurer 1996). Clientelism is also blamed for allocating scarce resources to the "wrong" goods. Instead of supplying *public goods* that benefit society as a whole, regardless of how this or that individual and small interest group is voting, clientelistic politicians produce and distribute *private* and *club goods* whose benefits they are able to target on supporters of their personal political career or at least on the fortunes of their own party. The disbursement of private and club goods may be inefficient and unproductive, even though politically opportunistic. Moreover, its distributive effects are such that they reward organized, wealthy special interests. These beneficiaries, in turn, supply politicians with the funds necessary to co-opt and to pay off a vast mass of poor voters with meager, direct benefits that are economically detrimental in the long run because they displace the supply of public goods. Over time, clientelism thus tends to reproduce and reinforce income inequality, asset concentration, and socioeconomic disempowerment of the overwhelming share of a country's citizens.

The presence of clientelistic linkages of accountability and responsiveness supplies a micrologic to account for macro-economic and political phenomena observed in a number of prominent studies. A case in point may be the econometrically rather robust finding of a strong statistical association between high income inequality and low economic growth (see Aghion and Wilkinson 1998; Alesina and Perotti 1996; Alesina and Rodrik 1994; Landa and Kapstein 1999, for a review). Political clientelism may induce both income inequality and inefficient patterns of public resource allocation that result in low economic growth. In a similar vein, a large literature observes a close association between "bad governance" – conceived as the absence of the rule of law, the insecurity and unpredictability of property rights, and the lack of civil liberties – and low economic performance (cf. Acemoglu, Johnson, and Robinson 2001; Easterly 2001; Easterly and Levine 2002; Knack 2003; Laporta *et al.* 1999; Rodrik *et al.* 2002). The targeted allocation of resources to partisan supporters practiced by clientelistic exchange relations often involves a violation of the rule of law, based on universalistic norms enabling market participants to predict the conduct of state agents, and commonly leads to outright corruption.

Furthermore, the Introduction and the chapters by Chandra and Wilkinson in this book note that ethnocultural networks offer opportunities for politicians to construct clientelistic exchange relations. Such clientelistic practices, in turn, may explain why political units characterized by the mobilization of competing ethnocultural networks may be inefficient in supplying collective goods (Alesina, Baqir, and Easterly 1999). This inefficiency negatively affects economic growth.

Because we lack a set of reliable and valid cross-national data on citizen-politician linkage strategies in democratic polities, none of the hypotheses about the association between modes of democratic citizen-politician linkage and economic performance can currently be tested. Nevertheless, let us now indicate some general problems with the easy assumptions that are often made about the links between clientelism and levels of growth and inequality.

First, does clientelism provide greater benefits to rent-seeking groups than programmatic competition? In answering this question, we should remember that one of the key findings of an earlier literature on the politics of clientelism (cf. Scott 1969, 1972) was that the very fact of democratic competition and an open electoral marketplace in which politicians vied for the support of voter constituencies helped place limits on the exploitation of clients by patrons and ensured that some minimum level of resources was provided to non-clients as well as clients. This observation is consistent with more recent work by Quinn and Woolley (2001), who find that democracies do not deliver systematically better or worse economic performance than authoritarian regimes, but that they have *less variation in performance*. Competitive mechanisms make politicians responsive to special interests, but also restrain their pursuit of predatory practices, such as clientelism, concentrating most of the benefits on a small economically and politically dominant group of unimaginably wealthy asset holders, while paying off everyone else with very small benefits to avert an imminent insurrection. Democracies thus deliver neither stellar nor awful economic results. Basic imperatives of competition and transparency limit the range of outcomes that can be associated with *both* clientelistic and programmatic modes of citizen-politician linkage.

Next, we should bear in mind that politicians may channel resources to particular groups in societies even under programmatic party competition. Consider a highly fragmented programmatic party system where politicians cannot predict or monitor and enforce the conduct of voters in response to targeted material incentives. Politicians heading the many small parties in such a system may try to diversify their policy appeals in order to carve out rather reliable core partisan electorates by catering to the material interests of well-defined rent-seeking categories of market participants. Party system fragmentation may thus also promote the provision of club goods (rather than public goods) in a way that hurts economic performance.

Such rent-seeking constituencies may include large companies and economic sectors whose economic success in a market environment requires subsidies and protections (agriculture, heavy industry, etc.), the civil service whose products are not priced in competitive markets, or particular geographical regions that may exhibit a unique agglomeration of weak economic sectors, but whose political representatives are powerful operators in making and breaking governments. Electoral laws and institutional rules of political representation may enhance the leverage of such regional and sectoral special interests.[6] The intricacies of government coalition building and coalition cabinet maintenance in a programmatic multiparty system may magnify the bargaining leverage of special interest parties and thus generate very high levels of benefits allocated to rent-seeking constituencies.[7] In other words, clientelism may be a *sufficient* condition to service strong rent-seeking demands, but it is far from being a *necessary* condition for a democratic polity to award large prizes to rent-seeking interests.

A second broad question is whether clientelism in democracies increases or decreases social inequality. In fact, among post-industrial capitalist democracies, those with higher levels of clientelism *do not* seem to exhibit higher levels of inequality and/or smaller redistributive social programs than countries with more programmatic party competition. Japan is often heralded as one of the more egalitarian capitalist societies, almost on a par with social democratic Scandinavia, even though it has experienced clientelistic politics paired with development of only a small welfare state. By contrast, Austria and Belgium have combined their clientelistic partisan exchanges with broad redistributive social policies. In these instances, clientelism goes with large welfare states, but also with extensive redistribution toward the worst-off households. Among clientelistic wealthy democratic polities, only Italy's income inequality tends to be worse than that of the average OECD member in the 1980s. Even then, however, Italian inequality is similar to that of largely non-clientelistic democracies such as Canada, France, Switzerland, and the United States.[8] In fact, World Bank figures for the mid-1990s show that Austria, Belgium, Japan, and even Italy are among the world's most egalitarian countries, far ahead of Britain, France, Germany, or the United States. South Korea also has rather high levels of equality on a par with the average of most advanced capitalist democracies, although it has a comparatively modest per capita GDP. Among less developed countries, there also appears to be only a modest, if any correlation between clientelism and income inequality. For example, Chile, as a polity with a reputation for comparatively less clientelism and more programmatic divisions in democratic party politics both before and after the Pinochet dictatorship

---

[6] See Rogowski (1987) on electoral laws and protectionist economic interests.

[7] Maybe for this reason Alesina and Tabellini (1990) find that very complex government coalitions generate greater fiscal deficits. They do not, however, control for the effect of citizen-politician linkage strategies.

[8] For data on income inequality, see Huber and Stephens (2001: 109) and Moller *et al.* (2003: 15).

than just about every other Latin American democracy,[9] currently displays extreme income inequality that is almost as high as that of Brazil and Colombia, higher than that of Mexico, and much higher than inequality in Bolivia, the Dominican Republic, Ecuador, Peru, or Venezuela, all countries with a reputation for intense clientelism in domestic party politics.[10] Moreover, inequality in Chile is unlikely to be a consequence of the decades of dictatorship, because it preceded the breakdown of democracy in 1973.

Of course, these impressionistic bivariate observations and comparisons do not replace a sophisticated multivariate econometric exploration of the impact of linkage mechanisms in democratic politics on patterns of income inequality. As we have argued already, such an undertaking presupposes data on linkage patterns that are currently unavailable. Nevertheless, at first sight, the hypothesis that democratic clientelism fuels inequality seems implausible.

As Medina and Stokes (in this volume) argue, clientelism may sometimes reveal and reinforce the presence of asymmetric relations of electoral competition between a hegemonic incumbent and an underdog challenger in the opposition that may cement high levels of inequality. Yet the political-economic impact of open, competitive clientelism in which more than one party has a reputation for delivering selective benefits to its constituents is far less certain. Under such circumstances clientelistic politics may be a mechanism to compensate vote-rich, but asset-poor and market-vulnerable constituencies for accepting socioeconomic dislocation and hardship due to economic development and trade openness. It should not be forgotten that clientelistic handouts may often be the most important significant benefit that poor people in peripheral regions may desire and be able to obtain from politicians, something that may be responsible for the fact that the poor in India and several Latin American countries vote at higher levels than the rich.[11]

Let us turn finally to the association between democratic linkages of accountability, authoritative resource allocation, and economic performance in terms of allocation efficiency and growth. We concede that, on

---

[9] This does not imply that Chile is free of clientelism. Several studies of Chile have highlighted the coexistence of clientelist and programmatic strategies, for instance after the incorporation of the working class through socialist politics in 1932 (Scully 1995: 113–14).

[10] For a comparison of all countries based on Gini coefficients from the early to mid-1990s, see World Bank (2000a: 282–83).

[11] A point made by politician-economist Cesar Gaviria, a former president of Colombia and general secretary of the Organization of American States, on a panel discussing the conduct of political parties in the democracies of less developed countries.

average, the prevalence of clientelism may foster more satisfaction of rent-seeking interests, worse governance, and weaker economic performance than polities with mostly programmatic competition. But we think that the relationship may be conditioned on several other factors. We have suggested as much in our treatment of political-economic determinants of citizen-politician relations in the Introduction. Furthermore, based on Kitschelt's chapter about clientelism in advanced capitalist democracies, clientelistic polities such as Austria, Belgium, Italy, and Japan in economic terms performed as well as or better than countries with predominantly programmatic patterns of party competition for much of the post-World War II period, even if we control for the boost laggards receive from catching up to the world innovation frontier from a relatively low level of per capita GDP in the 1950s. The same observation could be made about current clientelistic practices and economic fortunes in some less developed democratic countries. Why may this be so?

The relative burden clientelism imposes on economic development may vary with the nature of the challenges of development and growth different countries are facing given the status quo of their political economies. In affluent democracies, the costs of maintaining clientelistic exchange as central mode of democratic citizen-politician linkage may depend on the nature of the global economic innovation frontier and global relations of economic competition at a particular point in time. Consider several factors that may create variance in the performance of clientelistic democracies some of which may matter more in less developed countries lagging behind the world's technical-economic innovation frontier, others more in countries near the world innovation frontier. In each instance, let us keep in mind the baseline that democratic competition for political office as such places a restraint on the extent of clientelism, as it does on bad governance or corruption.

At low levels of development, even small investments in universalistically disbursed public goods – e.g., basic education, hygiene and health related environmental protection, and efficacy and competence of judiciary and state bureaucracy – may give economic growth a big boost. Furthermore, and without going out on a limb with an unqualified endorsement of "strategic trade theories," some selective benefits that may be tied into clientelistic politics, such as tariff protection, export subsidies, and access to capital at below-market rates, may in fact constitute a growth enhancing strategy that helps certain domestic companies and entire industrial sectors to gain comparative advantage in global markets where they had none before, particularly when paired with a currency regime that encourages exports. Evidently, not every measure of trade protection and every industrial subsidy pays off in terms of economic growth, as the experience of import substituting industrialization shows. Nevertheless, the initial success of ISI strategies from the 1930s to the 1960s, and of associated practices of clientelistic political accountability, whenever ISI countries adopted modes of democratic competition at least intermittently, suggests that sometimes servicing rent-seeking interests may not be diminishing growth by much or even be growth enhancing.[12] In this vein, some of the economies growing fastest from low levels of economic development, such as the Southeast Asian tigers from the 1960s to the 1980s and also the next generation of tiger cubs experiencing their economic take-off in the 1980s and 1990s (such as Thailand or Malaysia), have exhibited moderately high to very high levels of clientelistic rather than programmatic political competition, whenever they have practiced political democracy. This clientelism articulates itself in financial favors extended to business interests and in a selective protection of domestic producers from foreign competitors, but apparently did not dramatically dampen economic growth as long as it was combined with strong incentives for producers to export and compete in world markets.[13]

Clientelism that services rent-seeking interests may turn into a more severe bottleneck for political economic development as countries become affluent and reach the global innovation frontier. Now more intensive investments in collective goods and freely available regional club goods become vital in order to promote economic excellence. Rent-seeking interests, entrenched through clientelistic exchange relations, may stifle efficient resource allocation. Again, however, there may be contingencies that shape the relative effect of clientelism on the economic fortunes of particular polities in rather diverse ways. Let us propose a weak and a strong version of the argument.

According to the *weak version*, a certain level of clientelism does not endanger economic growth very much, as long as there are highly dynamic sectors in a polity that are protected from clientelism and that deliver sufficient resources to cross-subsidize clientelistic sectors, if only indirectly through taxes and higher costs of inputs they buy from clientelistic sectors (e.g., in terms of food consumed by their employees, construction,

---

[12] Of course, from a perspective of global welfare enhancement that does not take the distribution of welfare gains into account, most trade restrictions and export subsidies will appear to be economically inefficient. Individual countries with clientelistic political economies externalize these costs to other countries or less valued domestic constituencies.

[13] As Haggard (1990) points out, the difference between protectionist ISI and export-led industrialization is not that the latter abides by liberal free trade principles, but that its protections of domestic producers work through undervalued rather than overvalued currencies, targeted capital market supports for promising firms, and a selective use of tariffs.

transportation, and communications inputs). For this reason, the Austrian, Italian, or Japanese economies with sectors displaying a considerable amount of state regulation and state ownership penetrated by clientelistic partisan politics did well, as long as (1) other efficient sectors performed well, and (2) the costs and losses incurred by inefficiencies in the clientelistic sectors did not spin out of control. As Kitschelt argues in his analysis, it was the economic performance crisis of the 1980s and 1990s, particularly in the clientelistic sectors, but also beyond, that finally made clientelism in advanced capitalist countries politically controversial, *not* any general characteristics of a country's political economic structure. In Japan, for example, clientelistic economic sectors – such as agriculture, construction, and retail – were always inefficient. But this inefficiency began to impose greater burdens on the economy as the cost of clientelism went up and as efficient non-clientelistic sectors began to generate fewer resources that could be absorbed by the clientelistic sectors. If a country encounters this kind of declining performance in its economic lead sectors, or growing demand for subsidies in the clientelistic sectors, then economic crisis may trigger a political crisis of clientelistic politics.[14]

But there is also a stronger version of the political economic argument we touched upon in the Introduction when we discussed political-economic causes of clientelism and would like to restate here. We start from the following inductive, empirical question: is it just by accident that political clientelism in affluent capitalist democracies occurs primarily in what Soskice (1999) and Hall and Soskice (2001) characterize as cooperative market economies (CME), set against alternative institutional arrangements in liberal market economies (LME)?

We should emphasize upfront that neither CME nor LME capitalism entails far-reaching government intervention. CME, just like LME, is pretty much a self-regulatory web of institutions governed by owners of different assets (capital, labor). What differ between the two types are the contractual facilities employed to combine asset owners in and around the marketplace. The weak version of the political economy argument about the consequences of clientelism claims that *politicization of market relations through direct state intervention (regulatory, management, ownership)* opens the door to clientelism and economic efficiency. According to that weak version, this is economically relatively harmless as long as a polity also has strong, economically successful, self-regulated sectors of

---

[14] We implicitly ignore the counterfactual that Japan might have had even higher rates of economic growth in the 1970s, 1980s, and especially the 1990s, had it done away with clientelistic exchange relations early on.

the economy, *no matter* whether they are based on CME or LME institutional arrangements. By contrast, the strong political economy argument about the economic consequences of clientelism argues (1) that one mode of capitalism – CME capitalism – is more hospitable to clientelism and (2) that the costs of clientelism in CME economies depend on the nature of the lead growth sectors in economies in a particular era. If the most dynamic industrial sectors lend themselves to CME institutions, then clientelism is relatively harmless. If, however, CME institutions thrive in sectors and niches of the world economy that are not very dynamic in terms of growth, clientelism becomes politically controversial. As people begin to attack CME institutions as "fetters" of economic development, they also target clientelistic practices in such sectors.

Cooperative market capitalism tends to find its organizational expression in the dominance of large oligopolistic companies or company networks over entire sectors, intertwined with banks as providers of capital. The companies rely on stable factor markets and cooperative industrial relations granting wage earners long-term labor contracts. Under CME conditions, firms focus on incremental innovation placing a premium on cumulative learning under conditions of stable input (labor, capital) parameters. Personnel turnover is low, managerial decisions are made in a collegial fashion on corporate boards and in consultation with active owners, and the operational and managerial labor force often acquires occupational skills more in the industry or company than in external formal educational and professional institutes (cf. Soskice 1999; Hall and Soskice 2001). CME capitalism is said to work particularly well in industries such as the production of consumer durables (such as automobiles), plant equipment and machinery, instruments, chemicals and pharmaceuticals, and a host of crafts products, particularly high-quality items. By contrast, LME capitalism involves arm's length, short-term spot-market exchange relations and more fluid organizational structures. Labor contracts are flexible and industrial relations are more conflictual. LME capitalism relies on equity capital markets, external professional skills acquired in educational institutions, and managerial hierarchies subject to more rapid turnover and external recruitment. LME-governed firms show more inclination to pursue radical innovation. Furthermore, there is more innovation through company turnover and the growth of entirely new companies. LME capitalism works best in industries that rely on low-skill labor or on high-skill, general professional employees, on technological challenges that prompt trial-and-error radical innovation, and on product markets with rapidly shifting demand structures. LME institutions are said to do well in sectors such as information and communication technologies and biotechnologies, in areas where consumption is highly charged symbolically (fashion, furnishings, vacation travel, entertainment, other personal services) and in financial services (investment financing).

If CME capitalism is more hospitable to clientelism than LME capitalism, such clientelistic structures should have been relatively harmless during what Freeman and Louca (2001: 257–300) characterize as the post-World War II long cycle of economic growth through mass consumer goods and transportation equipment, together with the underlying sectors of machinery, steel, and oil. As the economic prowess of such lead industries began to sag in the 1980s and 1990s and new lead industries began to arise that were less hospitable to clientelism, such practices of political exchange became politically controversial, as voices in CME capitalist countries grew louder to adopt LME institutions and strategies of economic growth.

There are at least two possible arguments to advance the case that CME capitalism may tolerate more politicization of personnel decisions and capital allocation with relatively lower losses than LME capitalism, at least as long as CME compatible industries are leading sectors of economic growth. First, under conditions of organizational stability and coordinated governance in CME capitalism, it would be easier for partisan networks to entrench supporters in organizational hierarchies than in the comparatively more volatile arrangements typical of LME capitalism. Second, because a considerable share of the skills and capabilities that make CME industries productive rely on local managerial knowledge and local vocational learning, CME industries can upgrade the skills and capabilities of clientelistically recruited wage earners and managers incrementally and thus make even politicized patronage arrangements work comparatively efficiently.

All of this, however, is of no avail when CME prone industries decline relative to LME prone industries. National public policies may then try to change institutional frameworks of economic self-governance so as to discourage CME in favor of LME practices. In that process, new policies also begin to target clientelistic arrangements as impediments to economic performance. According to the "strong" political economy argument, then, relative economic decline in CME dominated capitalism is caused by clientelism only *in interaction with the movement of the world economic innovation frontier* from industries the efficiency of which benefits from CME institutions (automobiles, consumer durables, etc.) to sectors and industries where LME institutions clearly perform better ("high technology," personal and financial services, etc.). As long as this shift does not take place, clientelism is relatively harmless.

The main message of our hypothesis-generating exercise is that the relationship between citizen-politician exchanges that establish democratic responsiveness and accountability and economic performance is complicated. We can conceive of a number of causal chains through which political principal-agent relations exercise a contingent effect on economic performance in developing countries situated behind the world innovation frontier as well as in advanced capitalist polities located near that frontier.

Consequences for democratic regime stability

Do linkage mechanisms influence satisfaction with democracy and ultimately the willingness of citizens to defend or to abandon democracy, were they to face a challenge by a determined band of authoritarian insurrectionists? Population surveys in affluent capitalist democracies bear out the fact that levels of satisfaction with the functioning of democracy in a country are closely linked to the nature of its predominant linkage patterns between democratic principals and agents. As Kitschelt's contribution suggests, perceptions of democratic institutions tend to be most cynical and disenchanted in the more clientelistic countries among the tier of wealthy capitalist democracies. In a similar vein, a twelve-country comparative study of Latin American patterns of party competition shows that the levels of confidence citizens express in the practice of democracy in their own country are lowest where programmatic party competition is weak. This provides at least some indirect plausibility for the proposition that cynicism is directly related to the presence of clientelistic citizen-politician linkages.[15] We can think of several reasons why this might be so. Clientelism with its targeted, direct exchanges between politicians and electoral constituencies that are frequently associated with outright corruption violates basic commonsense standards of fair democratic procedure and equality before the law. Furthermore, the practices of monitoring and enforcing clientelistic exchanges sometimes infringe on citizens' civil and political rights, such as the secrecy of the ballot.

But does this assertion also imply that clientelistic democracies are inherently less stable than democracies in which programmatic citizen linkages prevail? We answer this question in a fashion that mirrors our development of hypotheses concerning the economic

---

[15] This relationship is explored in detail in the penultimate chapter to Kitschelt *et al.* (2001) with Latin American survey data from 1998. It should be emphasized, however, that that study largely infers the existence of clientelism by determining whether programmatic party competition is weak.

consequences attributable to different citizen-politician linkage mechanisms in democracies: whether the combination of clientelism and public cynicism about democratic institutions promotes a democratic breakdown depends on a number of contingencies. There are conditions under which democratic clientelism may yield durable democratic systems even in the face of widespread cynicism about democratic practices. Considerations of expediency and self-interest make it possible to sustain an institutionalized pattern of exchange that manifestly violates widespread normative sensibilities about equality and fairness in democratic procedure. Those who might challenge the clientelistic arrangements may have too few resources to overcome collective action problems in order to disrupt the dominant practices and/or the clientelistic benefits appear just too enticing. The combined work of stick and carrot may keep clientelism in place. Under such circumstances, all participants have well-considered instrumental reasons to stick to the existing practices, when compared to the benefits of potential alternatives, such as programmatic linkages within democratic party competition or the abolition of democracy in favor of some authoritarian regime.

Let us expand on a stimulating recent article by Alicia Adsera and Carles Boix (2002) on the relationship between economic openness (trade), political regime form (democracy or not), and the welfare state. Democratic linkage mechanisms do not figure in their analysis. We will add them to show the contingency under which clientelism may make a difference for democratic stability and under which a combination of trade, political regime, and social redistribution may prevail that is not anticipated by Adsera and Boix.

The article is based on a straightforward logic. To get citizens to accept the economic vulnerabilities incurred by trade openness, rulers must either repress or bribe them. Whereas authoritarian rule suggests repression, democracy necessitates social protection. Under authoritarian conditions, trade openness can be combined with a residual welfare state providing little economic protection to those exposed to new market vulnerabilities. If people rebel, the coercive power of the state moves against them. By contrast, democracies cannot afford the repressive strategy. As already Cameron (1978) and Katzenstein (1985) argued, citizens accept trade openness in democracies as long as they are compensated through a comprehensive, risk-hedging welfare state. Where this welfare state is not forthcoming, for whatever reason, trade issues gain high salience on the political agenda and generally promote a protectionist political economy.

Our Table 14.1 gives the three empirically feasible combinations discussed in Adsera and Boix's (2002) paper. Our simple combinatorics of dummy variables leaves out five combinations, some of which are

Table 14.1 *Adapting Adsera's and Boix's (2002) hypothesized typology of possible combinations of democracy, trade openness, and welfare protections to take the linkage structure into account*

	Democracy?	Free trade?	Encompassing welfare state?
Viable combinations	Yes	Yes	Yes
	Yes	No	No
	No	Yes	No
Unviable combination ("Impossibility theorem")	Yes	Yes	No
Viability through clientelism?	Yes	Yes	No, but clientelism

theoretically and/or empirically irrelevant.[16] But at least one of the combinations is highly interesting and explicitly ruled out by Adsera's and Boix's logic. To overstate their case a bit, this logic climaxes in the "impossibility theorem" that politicians cannot construct a trade-open democracy *without* an encompassing, risk-hedging welfare state. Adsera and Boix (2002: 240–41) make this case empirically plausible with data that begin in 1950 and end in 1990. Since the mid-1980s, however, the world has experienced not only a wave of democratization, but also an associated surge of market liberalization much of which entailed trade liberalization. Politicians did not, however, combine this trade opening with a parallel construction of risk-hedging and compensating social policy in most of the new democracies. How is this possible, given the logic proposed by Adsera and Boix?

One possibility is that all those new democracies enjoy such strong comparative advantages in critical economic sectors that majorities embrace trade openness even at the price of higher volatility and increased competition. A second response is that political turmoil in a number of trade liberalizing new democracies – from Argentina and Bolivia via India and Indonesia to Venezuela – proves Adsera's and Boix's point. While we might not (yet) see the outright collapse of trade-open democracies lacking a system of social safeguards, it is only a matter of time before this becomes common. Irregular executive succession, exemplified by countries such as Argentina and Bolivia, is only the prelude to the downfall

---

[16] Among them, we have the combinations of (1) low trade openness, authoritarianism, and little hedging through the welfare state; (2) closed authoritarian regimes with risk hedging welfare states (the former socialist bloc polities?); (3) trade-open welfare states without democracy; and (4) closed democratic welfare states.

of democracy. Furthermore, the growing number of half-way houses between democracy and dictatorship may provide evidence for the difficulty of combining democracy and trade openness without a risk-hedging welfare state. Beyond these demand-side arguments, there is a third supply-side possibility suggested by Boix's (2003) recent book on *Democracy and Inequality*. There may be no political-economic elites available to stage an anti-democratic coup or a revolution. Under conditions of trade and capital market openness wealthy owners of movable assets do not have to fear that domestic democracy may lead to their domestic expropriation. Anticipating the exit option of asset holders, democratic politicians can change asset distributions only at the margin and therefore lack the political leverage and access to resources needed to construct an encompassing welfare state on the West European model. This deprives the rank-and-file of a well-connected stratum of political entrepreneurs that could help them overcome collective action problems and organize the struggle against the democratic regime.

There is, however, a fourth possibility that follows from our analysis and is indirectly consistent with Adsera and Boix (2002). Indeed, for democracy to prevail, citizens who accept trade openness will expect some compensation for the new market risks they are incurring. But this hedging does not necessarily take the shape of universalistic social policy protecting much of a country's population from the negative potential side-effects of trade openness. Instead, the new compensation may manifest itself in clientelistic side-payments provided by liberalization's winners to particularly aggrieved target constituencies. Clientelism constitutes a process of cooptation that appeals at least to citizens with fairly high discount rates about the future benefits to be derived from a successful regime change or a victorious campaign to introduce a compensatory welfare state. The ubiquity of clientelism may therefore stabilize the political regime in the face of economic vulnerability, if not decline. As Levitsky's chapter shows, politicians such as Menem in Argentina, Fujimori in Peru, or Salinas de Gotari in Mexico in the 1980s and 1990s compensated particularly endangered electoral constituencies with a warm shower of clientelistic inducements.

Przeworski *et al.* (2000: 124, 133) find only weak indications that economic growth rates influence transitions from democracy to dictatorship and they tend to be confined to presidentialist democracies. If we consider the nature of citizen-politician linkages, maybe a more subtle analysis might become feasible. It may be the case that in the presence of encompassing clientelism democratic regime stability is even more impervious to economic growth rates. If economic crises hit democracies without clientelistic side-payments to critical electoral constituencies, then citizens may embrace radical movements to change the political status quo. Clientelism averts programmatic polarization. It is uncertain, however, whether the direct effect of clientelism on stabilizing democracy is trumped by the possible indirect effect of clientelism reducing economic growth in many polities, and presidentialist democracies with strong clientelism may reduce economic growth so much that they are more prone to collapse and transition to dictatorship.

Our conclusion has aimed at raising questions, not answering them. In order to work through this and many other fascinating consequences of citizen-politician linkages of accountability and responsiveness in democracies, it will first be necessary to construct a viable dataset about such linkages. Let us hope that renewed interest in questions of democratic linkage will generate a critical mass of scholars who invest their research time in that enterprise.

References

Abós, Alvaro. 1986. *El posperonismo*. Buenos Aires: Editorial Legasa.

Acemoglu, Daron, Johnson, Simon and Robinson, James A. 2001. "The colonial origins of comparative development: An empirical investigation," *American Economic Review* 91: 1369–401.

Adserà, Alicia, and Boix, Carles. 2002. "Trade, democracy, and the size of the public sector: The political underpinnings of openness," *International Organization* 56: 229–62.

Afanas'ev, M. N. 1997. *Klientelizm i Rossiiskaia Gosudarstvennost'*. Moscow: Moscow Social Science Foundation.

Aghion, Philippe and Wilkinson, Jeffrey G. 1998. *Growth, inequality, and globalization*. Cambridge: Cambridge University Press.

Alarcón-Olguín, Victor. 1994. "The PRI under Salinas de Gortari's presidency," Paper prepared for the XVIII International Congress of the Latin American Studies Association, Atlanta, GA, 10–12 March.

Aldrich, John H. 1993. "Rational choice and turnout," *American Journal of Political Science* 37: 246–78.

  1995. *Why parties? The origin and transformation of party politics in America*. Chicago: Chicago University Press.

Alesina, Alberto, and Perotti, R. 1996. "Income distribution, political instability, and investment," *European Economic Review* 40: 1203–28.

Alesina, Alberto and Rodrik, Dani. 1994. "Distributive politics and economic growth," *Quarterly Journal of Economics* 109: 465–91.

Alesina, Alberto and Tabellini, Guido. 1990. "A positive theory of fiscal deficits and government debt," *Review of Economic Studies* 57: 403–14.

Alesina, Alberto, Baquir, R. and Easterly, William 1999. "Public goods and ethnic divisions," *Quarterly Journal of Economics* 114: 143–84.

Allum, A. 1973. *Politics and society in post-war Naples*. Cambridge: Cambridge University Press.

Almond, Gabriel and Verba, Sidney. 1965. *The civic culture: Political attitudes and democracy in five nations*. Boston: Little, Brown.

Alvarez, Norma. 1999. "Nuevos estilos – viejas costumbres: Las prácticas electorales de la UCR y el PJ en Misiones 1955–1995," Unpublished manuscript, Department of History, Universidad Nacional de Misiones, Posadas, Argentina.

Amatori, Franco. 2000. "Beyond state and market: Italy's futile search for a third way," in *The rise and fall of state-owned enterprise in the western world* (ed.) Pier Angelo Tonninelli. Cambridge: Cambridge University Press, 128–56.

Ames, Barry. 1970. "Bases of support for Mexico's dominant party," *American Political Science Review* 64:153–67.

1987. *Political survival: Politicians and public policy in Latin America*. Berkeley: University of California Press.

2001. *The deadlock of democracy in Brazil*. Ann Arbor: University of Michigan Press.

Amorim Neto, Octavio, and Santos, Fabiano. 2001, Fabiano G. M. "The executive connection: Presidentially defined factions and party discipline in Brazil," *Party Politics* 7: 213–34.

Apter, David. 1966. *The politics of modernization*. Chicago: University of Chicago Press.

Ashworth, Scott and Bueno de Mesquita, Ethan. Forthcoming. "Delivering the goods: Legislative particularism in different electoral and institutional settings," *Journal of Politics* 68.

Auyero, Javier. 1998. "Re-membering Peronism: An ethnographic account of the relational character of political memory," Paper delivered at the XXI International Congress of the Latin American Studies Association, Chicago, 24–26 December.

2000. *Poor people's politics. Peronist survival networks and the legacy of Evita*. Durham, NC: Duke University Press.

Bailey, Frederick G. 1957. *Caste and the economic frontier*. Manchester: Manchester University Press.

1960. *Tribe, caste and nation: A study of political activity and political change in highland Orissa*. Manchester: Manchester University Press.

Bajpai, Nirupam and Jeffrey D. Sachs. 1999. "The state of state government finances in India." Harvard Institute for International Development. Development Discussion Paper No. 719, September. www.cid.harvard.edu/hiid/719.pdf.

Bako-Arifari, Nassirou. 2001. "La corruption au port de Cotonou: Douaniers et intermédiares," *Politique Africaine* 83: 38–58.

Banégas, Richard. 1998. "Marchandisation du vote, citoyenneté et consolidation démocratique au Bénin," *Politique Africaine* 69: 75–88.

Banfield, Edward C. 1958. *The moral basis of a backward society*. New York: Free Press.

Banfield, Edward C. and Wilson, James Q. 1963. *City politics*. Cambridge, MA: Harvard University Press. 1965.

Barrett, Patrick S. 2001. "Labour policy, labour-business relations and the transition to democracy in Chile," *Journal of Latin American Studies* 33: 561–97.

Barro, Robert J. 1997. *Determinants of economic growth*. Cambridge, MA: MIT Press.

Barth, Frederik. 1969. "Introduction," in *Ethnic groups and boundaries: The social organization of cultural difference*, ed. Frederik Barth. Boston: Little, Brown and Company: 9–38.

Bates, Robert H. 1981. *Markets and states in tropical Africa: The political basis of agricultural policies*. Berkeley: University of California Press.

1983. "Modernization, ethnic competition and the rationality of politics in contemporary Africa," in *State versus ethnic claims: African policy dilemmas*, ed. Donald Rothchild and Victor Olorunsola. Boulder: Westview. 152–71.

Bayart, Jean-François. 1979. *L'État au Cameroun*. Paris: Presses de la Fondation Nationale des Sciences Politiques.

1989. *L'Etat en Afrique: la politique du ventre*. Paris: Fayard.

Bayly, C. A. 1988. *Indian society and the making of the British empire*. Cambridge: Cambridge University Press.

Belloni, Frank, Caciagli, Mario, and Mattina, Liborio. 1979. "The mass clientelism party: The Christian Democratic Party in Catania and in Southern Italy," *European Journal of Political Research* 7: 235–75.

Benton, Allyson Lucinda. 2001. "The stability of provincial party systems in Argentina: Regional economies, revenue sharing, and provincial politics during economic reform," in *"Patronage games: Economic reform, political institutions, and the decline of party stability in Latin America,"* Ph.D. Thesis, Department of Political Science, University of California, Los Angeles.

Berger, Gordon Mark. 1977. *Parties out of power in Japan, 1931–1941*. Princeton: Princeton University Press.

Bezerra, Marcos Otávio. 1999. *Em nome das "Bases", política, favor e dependência Pessoal*. Rio de Janeiro: Relume Dumará.

Bienen, Henry. 1967. *Tanzania: Party transformation and economic development*. Princeton: Princeton University Press.

1974. *Kenya: The politics of participation and control*. Princeton: Princeton University Press.

1979. *Armies and parties in Africa*. New York: Africana Publishing.

Billiet, Jaak and Huyse, Luc. 1984. "Verzorgingsstaat en Verzuiling: Een Dubbelzinnige Relatie," *Tijdschrift voor Sociologie* 5: 129–51.

Blondel, Jean. 1996. "Britain. A textbook case of government – supporting party relationship," in *Party and government: An inquiry into the relationship between governments and supporting parties in liberal democracies*, ed. Jean Blondel and Maurizio Cotta. Houndmills: Macmillan.

Blondel, Jean and Cotta, Maurizio (eds.) 1996. *Party and government: An inquiry into the relationship between governments and supporting parties in liberal democracies*. Houndmills: Macmillan.

Bodie, Zvi, Kane, Alex, and Marcus, Alan. 2001. *Investments*, 5th edn. Boston: McGraw-Hill.

Boissevain, Jeremy. 1977. "When the saints go marching out: Reflections on the decline of patronage in Malta," in *Patrons and clients in Mediterranean societies*, ed. Ernest Gellner and John Waterbury. London: Duckworth.

Boix, Carles. 2003. *Democracy and redistribution*. Cambridge: Cambridge University Press.

Boix, Carles and Stokes, Susan C. 2003. "Endogenous democratization," *World Politics* 55: 517–49.

Brass, Paul 1994. *The politics of India since independence*. Cambridge: Cambridge University Press.

Bratton, Michael and Lambright, Gina. 2001. "Uganda's referendum 2000: The silent boycott," *African Affairs* 100: 429–52.

Bratton, Michael and van de Walle, Nicolas. 1997. *Democratic experiments in Africa*. Cambridge: Cambridge University Press.

Bräutigam, Deborah. 1997. "Institutions, economic reform, and democratic consolidation in Mauritius," *Comparative Politics* 30: 45–62.

Brown, Judith. 2003. *Nehru: A political life*. Oxford: Oxford University Press.

Brown, Marguerite. 1988. *Local politics: The law of the fishes: Development through political change in Medak District, Andhra Pradesh (South India)*. Oxford: Oxford University Press.

Bruhn, Kathleen. 1996. "Social spending and political support: The 'lessons' of the National Solidarity Program in Mexico," *Comparative Politics* 26: 151–77.

1997. *Taking on Goliath: The emergence of a new left party and the struggle for democracy in Mexico*. University Park, PA: Pennsylvania State University Press.

Buchanan, James M. and Tullock, Gordon. 1962. *The calculus of consent*. Ann Arbor: University of Michigan Press.

Budge, Ian, Klingemann, Hans-Dieter, Volkens, Andrea, Bara, Judith, and Tanenbaum, Eric. 2001. *Mapping policy preferences. Estimates for parties, electors, and governments 1945–1998*. Oxford: Oxford University Press.

Buijtenhuijs, Robert. 1994. "Les partis politiques Africains, ont-ils des projets de société? L'Exemple du Tchad," *Politique Africaine* 56.

Bunsha, Dionne. 2002. "The rise of print," *Frontline*, July 6–19.

Burgess, Katrina. 1998. "Alliances under stress: Economic reform and party–union relations in Mexico, Spain, and Venezuela," Ph.D. dissertation. Department of Political Science, Princeton University.

2004. *Choosing sides: Party–union relations under stress in a globalizing world*. Pittsburgh: University of Pittsburgh Press.

Burgwal, Gerrit. 1993. *Caciquismo, paralelismo and clientelismo: The history of a Quito squatter settlement*. Amsterdam: Institute of Cultural Anthropology/Sociology of Development, Vrije Universiteit Urban Research Working Papers no. 3.

1995. "Struggle of the poor. Neighborhood organization and clientelist practice in a Quito Ecuador squatter settlement," Ph.D. thesis, University of Amsterdam.

Burnell, Peter. 2001. "The party system and party politics in Zambia: Continuities past, present and future," *African Affairs* 100: 239–63.

Burstein, Paul. 1976. "Political patronage and party choice among Israeli voters," *Journal of Politics* 38: 1023–32.

Cain, Bruce, Ferejohn, John, and Fiorina, Morris. 1987. *The personal vote: Constituency service and electoral independence*. Cambridge, MA: Harvard University Press.

Calderón Alzati and Cazés, Daniel. 1996. *Las elecciones presidenciales de 1994*. Mexico City: La Jornada Ediciones.

Callaghy, Thomas. 1984. *The state–society struggle: Zaire in comparative perspective*. New York: Columbia University Press.

Callahan, William A. and McCargo, Duncan. 1996. "Vote-buying in Thailand's northeast: The July 1995 general election," *Asian Survey* 36: 376–92.

Callow, Alexander. 1976. *The city boss in America: An interpretive reader*. Oxford: Oxford University Press.

Calvo, Ernesto and Murillo, Maria Victoria. 2004. "Who delivers? Partisan clients in the Argentine electoral market?" *American Journal of Political Science* 48: 742–57.

Cameron, David. 1978. "The expansion of the political economy: A comparative analysis," *American Political Science Review* 72: 1243–61.

Cantón, Dario. 1986. *El pueblo legislador: Las elecciones de 1983*. Buenos Aires: Centro Editor de América Latina.

Carey, John M. 2000. "Parchment, equilibria, and institutions," *Comparative Political Studies* 33: 735–61.

2005. "Political institutions, competing principals, and party unity in legislative voting," Berkeley, CA: Institute of Governmental Studies, University of California, Berkeley, working paper #2.

Carey, John M. and Shugart, Matthew Soberg. 1995. "Incentives to cultivate a personal vote: A rank ordering of electoral formulas," *Electoral Studies* 14: 414–39.

Carlile, Lonny E. and Tilton, Mark C. 1998a. "Regulatory reform and the developmental state," in *Is Japan really changing its ways?*, ed. Lonny E. Carlile and Mark C. Tilton. Washington, DC: Brookings. 1–15.

1998b. "Is Japan really changing?" In *Is Japan really changing its ways?*, ed. Lonny E. Carlile and Mark C. Tilton. Washington, DC: Brookings. 197–218.

Cassese, Sabino. 1994. "Italy: Privatization announced, semi-privatizations and pseudoprivatizations," in *Privatization in Western Europe*, ed. Vincent Wright. London: Pinter. 122–37.

Castells, Manuel and Portes, Alejandro. 1989. "World underneath: The origins, dynamics, and effects of the informal economy," in *The informal economy: Studies in advanced and less developed countries*, ed. Alejandro Portes, Manuel Castells, and Lauren A. Benton. Baltimore: The Johns Hopkins University Press.

Castles, Francis G. (ed.) 1982. *The impact of parties: Politics and policies in democratic capitalist states*. Beverly Hills: Sage.

Catterberg, Edgardo. 1991. *Argentina confronts politics: Political culture and public opinion in the Argentine transition to democracy*. Boulder: Lynne Rienner.

Catterberg, Edgardo and Braun, Maria. 1989. "Las elecciones presidenciales Argentinas del 14 de Mayo de 1989: La ruta a la normalidad," *Desarrollo Económico* 115: 361–74.

Chabal, Patrick and Daloz, Jean Pierre. 1999. *Africa works*. London: James Currey.

Chandra, Kanchan. 2004. *Why ethnic parties succeed: Patronage and ethnic headcounts in India*. Cambridge: Cambridge University Press.

Chubb, Judith. 1981. "The social bases of an urban political machine: The case of Palermo," *Political Science Quarterly* 96: 107–25.

1982. *Patronage, power, and poverty in Southern Italy*. Cambridge: Cambridge University Press.

Clapham, Christopher. 1982. "Clientelism and the state," in *Private patronage and public power*, ed. Clapham. New York: Palgrave Macmillan. 1–36.

Collier, Ruth Berins. 1982. *Regimes in tropical Africa*. Berkeley: University of California Press.

1992. *The contradictory alliance: State–labor relations and regime change in Mexico*. Berkeley: International and Area Studies.

Consejo Nacional de Población. 1993. *Indicadores socioeconómicos e indice de marginación municipal, 1990.* Mexico: CONAPO-CNA.

Cooper, Joseph, Brady, David W., and Hurley, Patricia A. 1977. "The electoral basis of party voting: Patterns and trends in the U.S. House of Representatives," in *The impact of the electoral process,* ed. Louis Maisel and Joseph Cooper. Beverly Hills: Sage.

Coppedge, Michael. 1988. "La politica interna de Acción Democrática durante la crisis economica," *Cuadernos del CENDES* 7: 159–79.

1994. *Strong parties and lame ducks: Presidential partyarchy and factionalism in Venezuela.* Stanford: Stanford University Press.

Cornelius, Wayne. 1975. *Poverty and politics of the migrant poor in Mexico City.* Stanford: Stanford University Press.

1977. "Leaders, followers, and official patrons in urban Mexico," in *Friends, followers and factions: Readings in political clientelism,* ed. Steffen Schmidt, James C. Scott, and Carl Lande. Berkeley: University of California Press.

1996. *Mexican politics in transition: The breakdown of a one-party dominant regime.* San Diego: Center for US-Mexican Studies.

Cornelius, Wayne A., Craig, Ann L., and Fox, Jonathan (eds.) 1994. *Transforming state–society relations in Mexico: The national solidarity strategy.* Center for US-Mexican Studies, University of California, San Diego.

Coulon, Christophe. 1988. "Senegal: Development and fragility of a semi democracy," in *Democracy in developing countries: Volume Two, Africa,* eds. Larry Diamond, Juan J. Linz, and Seymour Martin Lipset. Boulder, CO: Lynne Rienner Press. 411–48.

Cox, Gary W. 1997. *Making votes count: Strategic coordination in the world's electoral systems.* Cambridge: Cambridge University Press.

Cox, Gary W. and McCubbins, Matthew D. 1993. *Legislative leviathan: Party government in the House.* Berkeley: University of California Press.

2001. "The institutional determinants of economic policy outcomes," in *Presidents, parliaments, and policy,* ed. Stephan Haggard and Mathew D. McCubbins. Cambridge: Cambridge University Press.

Cox, Gary W. and Rosenbluth, Francis M. 1995. "The structural determinants of electoral cohesiveness: England, Japan, and the United States," in *Structure and policy in Japan and the United States,* ed. Peter F. Cowhey and Mathew D. McCubbins. Cambridge: Cambridge University Press.

Crain, W. Mark, Messenheimer, Harold, and Tollison, Robert D. 1993. "The probability of being president," *Review of Economics and Statistics* 75: 683–89.

Crook, Richard. 1989. "Patrimonialism, administrative effectiveness and economic development in Côte d'Ivoire," *African Affairs* 88: 205–28.

1997. "Winning coalitions and ethno-regional politics: The failure of the 1990 and 1995 elections in Côte d'Ivoire," *African Affairs* 96: 215–42.

Cruise O'Brien, Donal. 1975. *Saints and politicians: essays in the organisation of a Senegalese peasant society.* Cambridge: Cambridge University Press.

Curtis, Gerald. 1971. *Election campaigning Japanese style.* New York: Columbia University Press.

1992. "Japan," in *Electioneering: A comparative study of continuity and change,* ed. David Butler and Austin Ranney. Oxford: Clarendon Press.

D'Alimente, Roberto and Bartolini, Stefano. 1997. "Electoral transition and party system change in Italy," *West European Politics* 20: 110–34.

Dahl, Robert A. 1961. *Who governs? Democracy and power in an American city.* New Haven: Yale University Press.

1971. *Polyarchy.* New Haven: Yale University Press.

Dahlberg, Matz and Johansson, Eva. 2002. "On the vote-purchasing behavior of incumbent governments," *American Political Science Review* 96: 27–40.

Dalton, Russell J., Flanagan, Scott C., and Beck, Paul Allen. 1984. "Electoral change in advanced industrial democracies," in *Electoral change in advanced industrial democracies: Realignment or dealignment?*, ed. Russell J. Dalton, Scott C. Flanagan, and Paul Allen Beck. Princeton: Princeton University Press.

Danevad, Andreas. 1995. "Responsiveness in Botswana politics: Do elections matter?" *Journal of Modern African Studies* 33: 381–402.

De Winter, Lieven. 1997. "Intra- and extra-parliamentary role attitudes and behavior of Belgian MPs," in *Members of Parliament in Western Europe*, ed. Wolfgang C. Müller and Thomas Saalfeld. London: Frank Cass.

1998. "Parliament and government in Belgium: Prisoners of partitocracy," in *Parliaments and governments in Western Europe*, ed. Philip Norton. London: Frank Cass.

De Winter, Lieven and Dumont, Patrick. 2003. "Belgium: Delegation and accountability under partitocratic rule," in *Delegation and accountability in parliamentary democracies*, ed. Kaare Strøm, Wolfgang C. Müller, and Torbjörn Bergman. Oxford: Oxford University Press.

De Winter, Lieven, Della Porta, Donatella, and Deschouwer, Kris. 1996. "Comparing similar countries: Belgium and Italy," *Res Publica* 38: 215–36.

Della Porta, Donatella, and Vannucci, Alberto. 1995. "Politics, the mafia, and the market for corrupt exchanges," in *Italian politics: Funding the First Republic*, ed. Carol Mershon and Gianfranco Pasquino. Boulder: Westview Press. 165–85.

1996. "Controlling political corruption in Italy. What did not work, what can be done?" *Res Publica* 38: 353–69.

Della Sala, Vincent. 1997 "Hollowing out and hardening the state: European integration and the Italian economy," *West European Politics* 20: 14–33.

Deschouwer, Kris. 1999. "In der Falle gefangen: Belgiens Parteien und ihre Reaktionen auf abnehmende Wählerloyalitäten," in *Parteien auf komplexen Wählermärkten*, ed. Peter Mair, Wolfang C. Müller, and Fritz Plasser. Vienna: Signum.

Deschouwer, Kris, Dewinter, Lieven, and Della Porta, Donatella. 1996. "Partitocracies between crises and reforms: The cases of Belgium and Italy," Special issue of *Res Publica* 38.

Diamond, Larry. 1996. "Is the third wave over?" *Journal of Democracy* 7: 20–37.

Diaz-Cayeros, Alberto, Magaloni, Beatriz and Estévez, Federico. 2003. "Electoral risk and redistributive politics in Mexico and the United States," Paper presented at the Midwest Political Science Association Meeting, Chicago, April 3–6.

Diaz-Cayeros, Alberto, Magaloni, Beatriz, and Weingast, Barry. 2002. "Democratization and the economy in Mexico: Equilibrium (PRI) hegemony and its demise," Stanford: Stanford University. Typescript.

Dirks, Nicholas B. 2001. *Castes of mind: Colonialism and the making of modern India*. Princeton: Princeton University Press.

Dixit, Avinash, and Londregan, John. 1996. "The determinants of success of special interests in redistributive politics," *Journal of Politics* 58: 1132–55.

Downs, Anthony. 1957. *An economic theory of democracy*. New York: Harper and Row.

Dresser, Denise. 1991. *Neopopulist solutions to neoliberal problems: Mexico's National Solidarity Program*. Current Issue Brief No. 3. La Jolla: Center for US–Mexican Studies.

   1994. "Bringing the poor back in: National Solidarity as a strategy of regime legitimation," in *Transforming state–society relations in Mexico: The National Solidarity Strategy*, ed. Wayne A. Cornelius, Ann. L. Craig, and Jonathan Fox. La Jolla: Center for US–Mexican Relations.

Dreze, Jean and Sen, Amartya. 1995. *India: Economic development and social opportunity*. Oxford: Oxford University Press.

   1997. *Indian development: Selected regional perspectives*. Oxford: Oxford University Press.

Drumaux, Anne. 1988. "Privatisation in Belgium: The national and international context," *West European Politics* 11: 74–86.

Easterly, William. 2001. *The elusive quest for growth*. Cambridge, MA: MIT Press.

Easterly, William and Levine, Ross. 2002. "Tropics, germs, and crops: How endowments influence economic development," *NBER Working Paper No. 9106*.

Eboko, Fred. 1999. "Les élites politiques au Cameroun: Le renouvellement sans renouveau?," in *Le non-renouvellement des élites en Afrique Subsaharienne*, ed. Jean-Pascal Daloz. Bordeaux: Centre D'Etude d'Afrique Noire.

Echeverri-Gent, John. 1993. *The state and the poor: Public policy and political development in India and the United States*. Berkeley: University of California Press.

Ellner, Steve. 1989. "Organized labor's political influence and party ties in Venezuela: Acción Democrática and its labor leadership," *Journal of Inter-American Studies and World Affairs* 31: 91–129.

   1993. *Organized labor in Venezuela, 1958–1991: Behavior and concerns in a democratic setting*. Wilmington, DE: Scholarly Resources, Inc.

   1996. "Political party factionalism and democracy in Venezuela," *Latin American Perspectives* 23: 87–109.

Erie, Steven E. 1988. *Rainbow's end: Irish-Americans and the dilemmas of urban machine politics, 1840–1985*. Berkeley: University of California Press.

Eschenburg, Theodor. 1961. *Ämterpatronage*. Stuttgart: Curt E. Schwab.

Esping-Andersen, Gøsta. 1990. *The three worlds of welfare capitalism*. Princeton: Princeton University Press.

   1999. "Politics without class: Postindustrial cleavages in Europe and America," in *Continuity and change in contemporary capitalism*, ed. Herbert Kitschelt, Peter Lange, Gary Marks, and John D. Stephens. Cambridge: Cambridge University Press.

Fama, Eugene and French, Kenneth. 1996. "Multifactor explanations of asset pricing anomalies," *Journal of Finance* 51: 55–86.

Farrell, David M. 2002. *Electoral systems*. Houndmills: Palgrave.

Fauré, Y. and Médard, J. C. (ed.) 1982. *Etat et bourgeoisie en Côte d'Ivoire*. Paris: Karthala.

Ferejohn, John. 1986. "Incumbent performance and electoral control," *Public Choice* 50: 5.

1999. "Accountability and authority: Towards a theory of political accountability," in *Democracy, accountability, and representation*, ed. Adam Przeworski, Susan Stokes, and Bernard Manin. Cambridge: Cambridge University Press. 131–53.

Figueiredo, Argelina Cheibub and Limongi, Fernando. 2000. "Presidential power, legislative organization, and party behavior in Brazil," *Comparative Politics* 32: 151–70.

Finegold, Kenneth. 1995. *Experts and politicians reform: Challenges to machine politics in New York, Cleveland, and Chicago*. Princeton: Princeton University Press.

Fiorina, Morris. 1976. "The voting decision: Instrumental and expressive aspects," *Journal of Politics* 38: 390–413.

Fox, Jonathan. 1994. "The difficult transition from clientelism to citizenship," *World Politics* 46: 151–84.

Fox, Richard G. 1969. *From zamindar to ballot box: Community change in a north Indian market town*. Ithaca, NY: Cornell University Press.

Frank, Stephen. 2000. "Bureaucrats for rent: How old-boy networks have undermined the strength of the Japanese state." Ph.D. thesis, Duke University, Department of Political Science.

Frankel, F. and Rao, M. S. A. 1989. *Dominance and state power in modern India: decline of a social order, Volume 1*. Oxford: Oxford University Press.

Franklin, Mark. 2004. *Voter turnout and the dynamics of electoral competition in established democracies*. Cambridge: Cambridge University Press.

Freeman, Chris and Louca, Francisco. 2001. *As time goes by: From the industrial revolutions to the information revolution*. Oxford: Oxford University Press.

Fuchs, Dieter, Guidorossi, Giovanna, and Svensson, Palle. 1995. "Support for the democratic system," in *Citizens and the state*, ed. Hans-Dieter Klingemann and Dieter Fuchs. Oxford: Oxford University Press. 323–54.

Fukui, Haruhiro and Fukai, Shigeko N. 1996. "Pork barrel politics, networks, and local economic development in contemporary Japan," *Asian Survey* 36: 268–86.

Fukuyama, Francis. 1995. "Social capital and the global economy," *Foreign Affairs* 74: 89–103.

Fussel, Paul. 1984. *Class: A guide through the American status system*. New York: Ballantine.

Gallagher, Michael. 1985. "The voters decide?: Preferential voting in European list systems," *European Journal of Political Research* 13: 365–78.

Garrett, Geoffrey. 1998. *Partisan politics in the global economy*. New York: Cambridge University Press.

Garrido, Luis Javier. 1982. *El partido de la Revolución Institucionalizada 1928–1945*. Mexico City: Siglo XXI.

Gay, Robert. 1994. *Popular organization and democracy in Rio de Janeiro: A tale of two favelas*. Philadelphia: Temple University Press.

Geddes, Barbara. 1991. "A game theoretical model of reform in Latin American democracies," *American Political Science Review* 85: 371–92.

1994. *Politicians' dilemma: Building state capacity in Latin America.* Berkeley: University of California Press.

1999. "Comparisons in the context of a game theoretic argument," in *Critical comparisons in politics and culture,* ed. John R. Bowen and Roger Petersen. Cambridge: Cambridge University Press.

Geddes, Barbara and Neto, Artur Ribeiro. 1992. "Institutional sources of corruption in Brazil," *Third World Quarterly* 13: 641–61.

Gellner, Ernest. 1983. *Nations and nationalism.* Ithaca, NY: Cornell University Press.

Gibson, Edward. 1997. "The populist road to market reform: Policy and electoral coalitions in Mexico and Argentina," *World Politics* 49: 339–70.

Gibson, Edward and Calvo, Ernesto. 2000. "Federalism and low-maintenance constituencies: Territorial dimensions of economic reform in Argentina," *Studies in Comparative International Development* 35: 32–55.

Giuliani, Marco. 1997. "Measures of consensual law-making: Italian 'Consociativismo'," *South European Society & Politics* 2: 66–96.

Glaeser, Edward L., La Porta, Rafael, Lopez-De-Silanes, Florencio, and Shleifer, Andrei. 2004. "Do institutions cause growth?" *Journal of Economic Growth* 9: 271–303.

Golden, Miriam A. 2002. "Does globalization reduce corruption? Some political consequences of economic integration," Paper presented to the Annual Meeting of the American Political Science Association, August 29–September 1, 2002, Boston, MA.

Golden, Miriam A. and Chang, Eric C. C. 2001. "Competitive corruption: Factional conflict and political malfeasance in postwar Italian Christian Democracy," *World Politics* 53: 588–622.

Golosov, Grigorii V. 1997. "Russian political parties and the 'bosses': Evidence from the 1994 provincial elections in Western Siberia," *Party Politics* 3: 5–21.

Good, Kenneth. 1994. "Corruption and mismanagement in Botswana: A best-case example?," *Journal of Modern African Studies* 32: 499–521.

Gordin, Jorge. 2002. "The political and partisan determinants of patronage in Latin America 1969–1994: A comparative analysis," *European Journal of Political Research* 41: 513–49.

Gosnell, Harold F. 1968 [1937]. *Machine politics Chicago model.* Chicago: University of Chicago Press.

Government of India, Planning Commission. 2001. *Annual Plan 2000–2001.* New Delhi, Government of India.

2002. *Economic survey 2001–2002.* New Delhi: Economic Division, Ministry of Finance, Government of India.

Gray, Mark and Caul, Miki. 2000. "Declining voter turnout in advanced industrial democracies, 1950–1997: The effect of declining group mobilization," *Comparative Political Studies* 33: 1091–122.

Gray, Obika. 2004. *Demeaned but empowered: The social power of the urban poor in Jamaica.* Kingston: University of the West Indies Press.

Greif, Avner. 2006. *Historical institutional analysis.* Cambridge: Cambridge University Press.

Guillermoprieto, Alma. 2002. "Letter from Colombia: Waiting for war," *The New Yorker*, May 13, 48–55.

Haggard, Stephan. 1990. *Pathways from the periphery.* Ithaca, NY: Cornell University Press.

Haggard, Stephan and Kaufman, Robert (ed.) 1992. *The politics of adjustment.* Princeton: Princeton University Press.

Hale, Henry E. 2003. "Explaining machine politics in Russia's regions: Economy, ethnicity, and legacy," *Post-Soviet Affairs* 19: 228–63.

    2005. "The makeup and breakup of ethnofederal States: Why Russia survives where the USSR fell," *Perspectives on Politics* 3: 55–70.

Hall, Peter A. and Soskice, David. 2001. "An introduction to varieties of capitalism," in *Varieties of capitalism: The institutional foundations of comparative advantage*, ed. Peter A. Hall and David Soskice. Oxford: Oxford University Press. 1–68.

Hardin, Russell. 1995. *One for all: The logic of group conflict.* Princeton: Princeton University Press.

Harmel, Robert and Janda, Kenneth. 1982. *Parties and their environment.* New York: Longman.

Hechter, Michael. 1987. *Principles of group solidarity.* Berkeley: University of California Press.

Hellemans, Staf. 1990. *Strijd om de moderniteit.* Leuven: Universitaire Pers Leuven.

Hernández, Alfonso. 2001. "The political economy of the governorship," unpublished paper, ITESO, Guadalajara, Mexico.

Hernández Rodríguez, Rogelio. 1991. "La reforma interna y los conflictos en el PRI," *Foro Internacional* 31: 222–49.

Herring, Ronald J. 1983. *Land to the tiller: The political economy of agrarian reform in South Asia.* New Haven: Yale University Press.

Hibou, Béatrice (ed.) 1999. *La Privatisation des états.* Paris: Karthala.

Hierczy de Miño, Wolfgang and Lane, John C. 2000. "Malta: STV in a two-party system," in *Elections in Australia, Ireland, and Malta under the single transferable vote*, ed. Shaun Bowler and Bernard Grofman. Ann Arbor: University of Michigan Press.

Hine, David. 1979. "Italy," in *Government and administration in Western Europe*, ed. R. F. Ridley. Oxford: Martin Robertson.

    1993. *Governing Italy: The politics of bargained pluralism.* Oxford: Clarendon Press.

Hirschleifer, Jack and Riley, John. 1992. *The analytics of uncertainty and information.* Cambridge: Cambridge University Press.

Hiskey, Jonathan. 1999. "Does democracy matter? Electoral competition and local development in Mexico," Ph.D. dissertation, University of Pittsburgh.

Hodgkin, Thomas. 1961. *African political parties.* London: Penguin.

Hopkin, Jonathan and Mastropaolo, Alfio. 2001. "From patronage to clientelism: Comparing the Italian and Spanish experiences," in *Clientelism, interests, and democratic representation*, ed. Simona Piattoni. Cambridge: Cambridge University Press.

Horiuchi, Yusaku. 2001. "Turnout twist: Higher voter turnout in lower-level elections". Unpublished Ph.D. dissertation, MIT.

Horowitz, Donald. 1985. *Ethnic groups in conflict.* Berkeley: University of California Press.

Howell, Chris and Daley, Anthony. 1992. "The transformation of political exchange," *International Journal of Political Economy* 22: 3–16.

Huber, Evelyne, and Stephens, John D. 2001. *Development and crisis of the welfare state: Parties and policies in global markets.* Chicago: University of Chicago Press.

Huber, John and Inglehart, Ronald. 1995. "Expert interpretations of party space and party locations in 42 societies," *Party Politics* 1: 73–111.

Huber, John D. and Shipan, Charles R. 2002. *Deliberate discretion? Institutional foundations of bureaucratic autonomy in modern democracies.* Cambridge: Cambridge University Press.

Huntington, Samuel. 1968. *Political order in changing societies.* New Haven: Yale University Press.

1993. *The third wave: Democratization in the late twentieth century.* Norman: University of Oklahoma Press.

Inglehart, Ronald. 1977. *The silent revolution.* Princeton: Princeton University Press.

Inkles, Alex and Smith, David H. 1974. *Becoming modern: Individual change.* Cambridge, MA: Harvard University Press.

International Monetary Fund. 2001. "India, recent economic development and selected issues," June 5: 87–88.

Jackman, Robert. 1987. "Political institutions and voter turnout in the industrial democracies," *American Political Science Review* 81: 405–23.

James, Daniel. 1988. *Resistance and integration: Peronism and the Argentine working class, 1946–1976.* Cambridge: Cambridge University Press.

Jerusalem Post. 2001. "Hillary and the Hassidim," March 16.

Johnston, Michael. 1979. "Patrons and clients, jobs and machines: A case study of the uses of patronage," *American Political Science Review* 73: 385–98.

Jomo, K. S. and Gomez, E. T. 1999. *Malaysia's political economy: Politics, patronage and profits.* Cambridge: Cambridge University Press.

Joseph, Richard. 1987. *Democracy and prebendal politics in Nigeria.* Cambridge: Cambridge University Press.

Kang, David C. 2002. *Crony capitalism: Corruption and development in South Korea and the Philippines.* Cambridge: Cambridge University Press.

Karanth, G. K. 1997. "Caste in contemporary rural India," in *Caste: Its twentieth century avatar,* ed. M. N. Srinivas. New Delhi: Penguin Books. 87–109.

Kasfir, Nelson. 1971. *The shrinking political arena: Participation and ethnicity in African politics.* Berkeley: University of California Press.

Kaspin, Deborah. 1995. "The politics of ethnicity in Malawi's democratic transition," *Journal of Modern African Studies* 33: 595–620.

Katz, Richard S. 1980. *A theory of parties and electoral systems.* Baltimore: Johns Hopkins University Press.

1990. "Party as linkage: A vestigial function?" *European Journal of Political Research* 18: 141–61.

Katz, Richard S. and Mair, Peter. 1995 "Changing models of party organization and party democracy: The emergence of the cartel party," *Party Politics* 1: 5–28.

Katzenstein, Peter. 1985. *Small states in world markets*. Ithaca, NY: Cornell University Press.

Kaufmann, Daniel, Kraay, Aart, and Zoido-Lobaton, Pablo. 2002. *Governance matters II. Updated indicators for 2000/01*. The World Bank. Development Research Group. Policy Research Working Paper 2772.

Kearney, Robert. 1973. *The politics of Ceylon (Sri Lanka)*. Ithaca: Cornell University Press.

Keefer, Phil. 2003. "Clientelism, development and democracy," Washington, DC: World Bank. Typescript.

Kiewiet, D. Roderick, and McCubbins, Mathew D. 1991. *The logic of delegation: Congressional parties and the appropriations process*. Chicago: University of Chicago Press.

King, Gary. 1998. *Unifying political methodology*. Ann Arbor: University of Michigan Press.

King, Gary, Keohane, Robert O., and Verba, Sidney. 1994. *Designing social inquiry: Scientific inference in qualitative research*. Princeton: Princeton University Press.

King, Gary, Murray, Christopher J. L., Salomon, Joshua A., and Tandon, Ajay. 2003. "Enhancing the validity and cross-cultural comparability of measurement in survey research," *American Political Science Review* 98: 191–207.

Kirchheimer, Otto. 1966. "The transformation of western European party systems," in *Political parties and political development*, ed. Joseph LaPalombara and Myron Weiner. Princeton: Princeton University Press.

Kitschelt, Herbert. 1994. *The transformation of European social democracy*. Cambridge: Cambridge University Press.

  1995. *The radical right in Western Europe*. Ann Arbor: University of Michigan Press.

  2000a. "Linkages between citizens and politicians in democratic polities," *Comparative Political Studies* 33: 845–79.

  2000b. "Citizens, politicians, and party cartellization: Political representation and state failure in post-industrial democracies," *European Journal of Political Research* 37: 149–79.

  Forthcoming. "Party systems," in *Oxford Handbook of Comparative Politics*, ed. Carles Boix and Susan Stokes. Oxford: Oxford University Press.

Kitschelt, Herbert, and Smyth, Regina. 2002. "Programmatic party cohesion in emerging post-communist democracies: Russia in comparative context," *Comparative Political Studies* 35: 1228–56.

Kitschelt, Herbert, Hawkins Kirk, Rosas Guillermo, and Zechmeister, Liz. 2006. "Party competition in Latin America," unpublished manuscript.

Kitschelt, Herbert, Mansfeldova, Zdenka, Markowski, Radoslaw, and Toka, Gabor. 1999. *Post-communist party systems: Competition, representation, and inter-party cooperation*. Cambridge: Cambridge University Press.

Klesner, Joseph L. 1994. "Realignment or dealignment? Consequences of economic crisis and restructuring for the Mexican party system," in *Politics of* economic restructuring: State–society relations and regime change in Mexico, eds. Maria Lorena Cook, Kevin Middlebrook, and Juan Molinar. La Jolla: Center for US–Mexican Studies, University of California at San Diego.

1996. "¿Realineación o desalineación? Consecuencias de la crisis y la reestructuración economica para el sistema partidiario Mexicano," in Las dimensiones politicas de reestructuración Mexicana, ed. Maria Lorena Cook, Kevin Middlebrook and Juan Molinar. México: Cal y Arena. 251–91.

Klingemann, Hans-Dieter, Hofferbert, Richard, and Budge, Ian. 1994. Parties, policies, and democracy. Boulder: Westview Press.

Knack, Stephen. 2003. (ed.) Democracy, governance and growth. Ann Arbor: University of Michigan Press.

Kochanek, Stanley A. 1987. "Briefcase politics in India: The Congress Party and the business elite," Asian Survey 27:1278–301.

Koelble, Thomas. 1991. The left unraveled: Social democracy and the new left challenge. Durham: Duke University Press.

1992. "Recasting social democracy in Europe: A nested games explanation of strategic adjustment in political parties," Politics and Society 20: 51–70.

Kofler, Anton. 1985. Parteiengesellschaft im Umbruch: Partizipationsprobleme von Grossparteien. Vienna: Böhlau.

Kohli, Atul. 1987. The state and poverty in India: The politics of reform. Cambridge: Cambridge University Press.

1990. Democracy and discontent: India's growing crisis of governability. Cambridge: Cambridge University Press.

Koole, Ruud. 1996. "Cadre, catch-all or cartel? A comment on the notion of the cartel party," Party Politics 2: 507–23.

Kothari, Rajni. 1988. State against democracy: In search of humane governance. Delhi: Ajanta Publishers.

1998. "Rise of the Dalits and the renewed debate on caste," in State and politics in India, ed. Partha Chatterjee. Oxford: Oxford University Press. 439–58.

Krishna, Anirudh. 2002a. Active social capital: Tracing the roots of democracy and development. New York: Columbia University Press.

2002b. "Enhancing political participation in democracies: What is the role of social capital?" Comparative Political Studies 35: 437–60.

Kristinsson, Gunnar Helgi. 2001. "Clientelism in a cold climate: The case of Iceland," in Clientelism, interests, and democratic representation, ed. Simona Piattoni. Cambridge: Cambridge University Press.

Kuhn, Berthold. 1998. Participatory development in rural India. New Delhi: Radiant Publishers.

Kumar Singh, Ajit. 2000. "UP budget 2000–2001: Fiscal crisis deepens," Economic and Political Weekly (Mumbai) April 29, 1512–13.

Kurer, Oskar. 1996. "The political foundations of economic development policies," Journal of Development Studies 32: 645–68.

Kurtzman, David Harold. 1935. "Methods of controlling votes in Philadelphia," Ph.D. dissertation, University of Pennsylvania.

Laakso, Markku and Taagepera, Rein. 1979. "Effective number of parties: A measure with application to west Europe," Comparative Political Studies 12: 3–27.

Landa, Dimitri and Kapstein, Ethan. 2001. "Inequality, growth, and democracy," *World Politics* 53: 264–96.

Lane, Jan-Erik. 2000. *New public management*. London: Routledge.

Lane, Jan-Erik and Ersson, Svante. 1999. *The new institutional politics: Performance and outcomes*. London: Routledge.

La Porta, R., Lopez-de-Silanes, F., Shleifer, A., and Vishny, R. W. 1999. "The quality of government," *Journal of Law, Economics and Organization* 15: 222–79.

Laver, Michael and Hunt, Ben. 1992. *Party and policy competition*. London: Routledge.

Lawson, Kay (ed.) 1980. *Political parties and linkage*. New Haven: Yale University Press.

Leal, Victor Nunes. 1977. *Coronelismo: The municipality and representative government in Brazil*. Cambridge: Cambridge University Press.

Lemarchand, René. 1972. "Political clientilism and ethnicity in tropical Africa: Competing solidarities in nation building," *American Political Science Review* 66: 68–90.

1988. "The state, the parallel economy and the changing structure of patronage systems," in *The precarious balance: State and society in Africa*, ed. Donald Rothchild and Naomi Chazan. Boulder: Westview Press. 149–70.

Lemarchand, René, and Legg, Keith. 1972. "Political clientelism and development: A preliminary analysis," *Comparative Politics* 4: 149–78.

Leonardi, Roberto and Wertman, David A. 1989. *Italian Christian Democracy*. Houndmills: Macmillan.

Lerner, Daniel. 1958. "The grocer and the chief: A parable," in *The passing of traditional society*. Glencoe, IL: Free Press.

Levi, Margaret. 1988. *Of rule and revenue*. Cambridge: Cambridge University Press.

Levitsky, Steven. 1999. "From laborism to liberalism: Institutionalization and labor-based party adaptation in Argentina 1983–1997," Ph.D. dissertation, Department of Political Science, University of California, Berkeley.

2001. "A 'disorganized organization': Informal organization and the persistence of local party structures in Argentine Peronism," *Journal of Latin American Studies* 33: 29–65.

2003. *Transforming labor-based parties in Latin America: Argentine Peronism in comparative perspective*. Cambridge: Cambridge University Press.

Lewis, Peter. 1996. "From prebendalism to predation: The political economy of decline in Nigeria," *Journal of Modern African Studies* 34: 79–103.

Lewis, W. Arthur. 1978. *The evolution of the international economic order*. Princeton: Princeton University Press.

Lienert, Ian and Modi, Jitendra. 1997. "A decade of civil service reform in sub-Saharan Africa," IMF Working Paper WP/97/179. International Monetary Fund, Fiscal Affairs Department.

Lijphart, Arend. 1977. *Democracy in plural societies: A comparative explanation*. New Haven: Yale University Press.

1994. *Electoral systems and party systems: A study of twenty-seven democracies, 1945–1990*. Oxford: Oxford University Press.

1999. *Patterns of democracy*. New Haven: Yale University Press.

Limongi, Fernando, and Cheibub Figueredo, Argelina. 1995. "Partidos politicos na Câmara dos Deputados: 1989–1994," *Dados* 38: 497–525.

Lindbeck, Assar, and Weibull, Jörgen. 1987. "Balanced-budget redistribution as the outcome of political competition," *Public Choice* 52: 273–97.

Lindberg, C. Staffan. 2001. "Our time to chop: Elections 2000 in Ghana," Presentation to the Annual Meetings of the African Studies Association, Houston, Texas, 15–18 November.

Linstone, Harold A. and Turoff, Murray. 1975. *The delphi method: Techniques and applications.* Reading: Addison-Wesley.

Linz, Juan. 1994. "Presidential or parliamentary democracy: Does it make a difference?," 3–87, in *The failure of presidential democracy,* ed. Arturo Valenzuela and Juan Linz. Baltimore: The Johns Hopkins University Press.

Lipset, Seymour M. 1960. *Political man: The social bases of politics.* Garden City, NY: Doubleday.

1994. "The social requisites of democracy revisited," *American Sociological Review* 59:1–22.

Lipset, Seymour M., and Rokkan, Stein. 1967. "Cleavages, structures, and voters alignments: An introduction," in *Party systems and voter alignments,* ed. Seymour Martin Lipset and Stein Rokkan. New York: Free Press.

Lohmann, Susanne. 1998. "Federalism and central bank independence: The politics of German monetary policy, 1957–1992," *World Politics* 50: 401–46.

Lowi, Theodore J. 1964. *At the pleasure of the mayor: Patronage and power in New York City 1898–1959.* New York: The Free Press of Glencoe.

Lyne, Mona M. 2004. "Endogenous institutions: Electoral law and internal party dynamics in Brazil," Paper presented at the 2004 American Political Science Association Annual Convention, Chicago.

2006. "The voter's dilemma and democratic accountability in Brazil and Venezuela: A transaction cost theory of electoral sanctioning." Manuscript.

MacMullen, A. L. 1979. "Belgium," in *Government and administration in Western Europe,* ed. R. F. Ridley. Oxford: Martin Robertson.

Magaloni, Beatriz. 2005. "The demise of Mexico's one-party dominant regime: Elite choices and the masses in the establishment of democracy," in *The third wave of democratization in Latin America: Advances and setbacks,* ed. Frances Hagopian and Scott Mainwaring. Cambridge: Cambridge University Press.

Forthcoming. *Voting for autocracy.* Cambridge: Cambridge University Press.

Mainwaring, Scott. 1992. "Brazilian party underdevelopment in comparative perspective," *Political Science Quarterly* 107: 677–708.

1995. "Brazil: Weak parties, feckless democracy," in *Building democratic institutions: Party systems in Latin America,* ed. Scott Mainwaring and Timothy Scully. Stanford: Stanford University Press.

1999. *Rethinking party systems in the third wave of democratization: The case of Brazil.* Stanford: Stanford University Press.

Mainwaring, Scott and Perez-Liñán, Anibal. 1997. "Party discipline in multiparty systems: A methodological note and an analysis of the Brazilian Constitutional Congress," *Legislative Studies Quarterly* 22: 471–93.

Manor, James. 1997. "Karnataka: Caste, class, dominance and politics in a cohesive society," in *State and politics in India*, ed. P. Chafferjee. Oxford: Oxford University Press. 262–73.

2000. "Small-time political fixers in India's states," *Asian Survey* 40: 816–35.

Manow, Philip. 2002. "Was erklärt politische Patronage in den Ländern Westeuropas? Defizite des politischen Wettbewerbs oder historisch-formative Phasen der Massendemokratisierung," *Politische Vierteljahresschrift* 43: 20–45.

Marsh, Michael. 2000. "Candidate centered but party wrapped: Campaigning in Ireland under STV," in *Elections in Australia, Ireland, and Malta under the single transferable vote*, ed. Shaun Bowler and Bernhard Grofman. Ann Arbor: University of Michigan Press.

Marsh, Michael and Mitchell, Paul. 1999. "Office, votes, and then policy: Choices for political parties in the Republic of Ireland, 1981–1992," in *Policy, office, or votes?*, ed. Wolfgang C. Müller and Kaare Strøm. Cambridge: Cambridge University Press.

Martz, John D. 1966. *Acción Democrática: Evolution of a modern political party in Venezuela*. Princeton: Princeton University Press.

Mattson, Ingvar and Strøm, Kaare. 1995. "Parliamentary committees," in *Parliaments and majority rule in Western Europe*, ed. Herbert Döring. New York: St. Martin's Press.

Mavrogordatos, George T. 1997. "From traditional clientelism to machine politics: The impact of PASOK populism in Greece," *South European Society & Politics* 2: 1–26.

Mayer, Adrian. 1997. "Caste in an Indian village: Change and continuity 1954–1992," in *Caste today*, ed. C. J. Fuller. Oxford: Oxford University Press. 32–64.

Mayhew, David R. 1974. *Congress: The electoral connection*. New Haven: Yale University Press.

McCarthy, Mary Alice. 1997. "Center-left parties in Chile: Party–labor relations under a minimalist state," Paper presented at the annual meeting of the Midwest Political Science Association, Chicago, IL, April 10–12.

McCubbins, Mathew D., and Rosenbluth, Frances. 1995. "Party provision for personal politics: Dividing the vote in Japan," in *Structure and policy in Japan and the United States*, ed. Peter F. Cowhey and Mathew D. McCubbins. Cambridge: Cambridge University Press.

McGuire, James W. 1997. *Peronism without Peron: Unions, parties, and democracy in Argentina*. Stanford: Stanford University Press.

Medina, Luis Fernando, and Stokes, Susan C. 2002. "Clientelism as political monopoly," Unpublished manuscript, Political Science Department, University of Chicago.

Middlebrook, Kevin. 1995. *The paradox of revolution*. Baltimore: The Johns Hopkins University Press.

Migdal, Joel S. 1988. *Strong societies and weak states*. Princeton: Princeton University Press.

Mijeski, Kenneth. 1977. "Costa Rica: The shrinking of the presidency?," in *Presidential power in Latin American politics*, ed. Thomas V. Di Bacco. New York: Praeger.

Milne, R. S. 1973. "Patrons, clients and ethnicity: The case of Sarawak and Sabah in Malaysia," *Asian Survey* 13: 891–907.

Mitchell, Paul. 2000. "Voters and their representatives: Electoral institutions and delegation in Parliamentary Democracies," *European Journal of Political Research* 37: 335–51.

Mitra, Subrata K. 1991. "Room to maneuver in the middle: Local elites, political action, and the state in India," *World Politics* 43: 390–413.

    1992. *Power, protest and participation: Local elites and the politics of development in India.* London: Routledge.

Molinar Horcasitas, Juan. 1991. *El tiempo de la legitimidad: Elecciones, autoritarismo y democracia en Mexico.* Mexico City: Cal y Arena.

Molinar Horcasitas, Juan and Weldon, Jeffrey A. 1994. "Electoral determinants and consequences of National Solidarity," in *Transforming state–society relations in Mexico: The National solidarity strategy,* ed. Wayne A. Cornelius, Ann. L. Craig, and Jonathan Fox. La Jolla: Center for US–Mexican Relations.

Moller, Stefanie, Bradley, David, Huber, Evelyne, Nielson, François, and Stephens, John D. 2003. "Determinants of relative poverty in advanced capitalist democracies," *American Sociological Review* 68: 22–51.

Mora y Araujo, Manuel and Llorente, Ignacio (eds). 1980. *El voto Peronista: Ensayos de sociologia electoral argentina.* Buenos Aires: Editorial Sudamericana.

Morgenstern, Scott. 2004. *Patterns of legislative politics.* Cambridge: Cambridge University Press.

Morgenthau, Ruth Schachter. 1964. *Political parties in West Africa.* Oxford: Clarendon Press.

Morlino, Leonardo. 1998. *Democracy between consolidation and crisis: Parties, groups, and citizens in southern Europe.* Oxford: Oxford University Press.

Morris, Stephen D. 1995. *Political reformism in Mexico: An overview of contemporary Mexican politics.* Boulder: Lynne Rienner.

Morris-Jones, W. H. 1967. *The government and politics of India.* New York: Anchor Books.

Mulgan, Aurelia George. 2000. *The politics of agriculture in Japan.* New York: Routledge.

Müller, Wolfgang C. 1983. "Direktwahl und Parteiensystem," *Österreichisches Jahrbuch für Politik*: 83–112.

    1988. "Privatising in a corporatist economy: The politics of privatisation in Austria," *West European Politics* 11: 101–16.

    1989. "Party patronage in Austria," in *The Austrian party system,* ed. Anton Pelinka and Fritz Plasser. Boulder: Westview.

    2000. "Patronage by national governments," in *The nature of party government,* ed. Jean Blondel and Maurizio Cotta. Houndmills: Palgrave-Macmillan.

    2006. "The changing role of the Austrian civil service: The impact of politicisation, public sector reform, and Europeanisation," in *From the service state to the enabling state,* ed. Edward C. Page. Houndmills: Palgrave-Macmillan.

Müller, Wolfgang C. and Meth-Cohn, Delia. 1994. "Looking reality in the eye: The politics of privatization in Austria," in *Privatization in Austria,* ed. Vincent Wright. New York: Pinter Publishers. 160–79.

Müller, Wolfgang C., Jenny, Marcelo, Steininger, Barbara, Dolezal, Martin, Philipp, Wilfried, and Preisl-Westphal, Sabine. 2001. *Die österreichischen Abgeordneten*. Vienna: WUV-Fakultas.

Murillo, María Victoria. 2001. *Partisan coalitions and labor competition in Latin America: Trade unions and market reforms*. Cambridge: Cambridge University Press.

Narain, Iqbal (ed.) 1976. *State politics in India*. Meerut: Meenakshi Prakashan.

Nayak, Radhika, Saxena, N. C. and Farrington, John. 2002. *Reaching the poor: The influence of policy and administrative processes on the implementation of government poverty schemes in India*. ODI Working Paper 175, September.

Newell, James L., and Bull, Martin. 1997. "Party organization and alliances in Italy in the 1990s: A revolution of sorts," *West European Politics* 20: 3–53.

Nian, Senati. 2002. "Rural revolution," *The Hindu*, June 23.

North, Douglass C. 1990. *Institutions, institutional change and economic performance*. Cambridge: Cambridge University Press.

Nugent, Paul. 2001. "Winners, losers and also-rans: Money, moral authority, and voting patterns in the Ghana 2000 elections," *African Affairs* 100: 405–28.

O'Donnell, Guillermo. 1979. "Tensions in the bureaucratic authoritarian state and the question of democracy," in *The new authoritarianism in Latin America*, ed. David Collier. Princeton: Princeton University Press.

O'Gorman, Frank. 1984. "Electoral deference in 'unreformed' England: 1760–1832," *Journal of Modern History* 56: 391–429.

Okuda, Takako. 2001. "Mechanism and dynamics of Japanese clientelism: Examination of politics of pork barrel politics in the 1990s," Unpublished Master's thesis, Duke University.

Olson, Mancur, Jr. 1965. *The logic of collective action*. Cambridge, MA: Harvard University Press.

Orttung, Robert W. 2002. "Business and politics in Russia's regions," paper prepared for the 2002 Annual Meeting of the American Association for the Advancement of Slavic Studies, Pittsburgh, PA.

Overseas Development Institute. 2002. "Panchayati Raj and natural resources management: How to decentralize management over natural resources. Karnataka: Situation analysis and literature review," Working Document: 22–23.

Pacheco Mendez, Guadalupe. 1991. "Los sectores del PRI en las elecciones de 1988," Mexican Studies/*Estudios Mexicanos* 7: 253–82.

Page, Edward C. and Wright, Vincent (eds.) 1999. *Bureaucratic elites in western European states*. Oxford: Oxford University Press.

Palomino, Hector. 1987. *Cambios ocupacionales y sociales en Argentina, 1947–1985*. Buenos Aires: CISEA.

Panebianco, Angelo. 1988. *Political parties: Organization and power*. Cambridge: Cambridge University Press.

Panini, M. N. 1997. "The political economy of caste," in *Caste: Its twentieth century avatar*, ed. M. N. Srinivas. New Delhi: Penguin Books. 28–68.

Papakostas, Apostolis. 2001. "Why is there no clientelism in Scandinavia? A comparison of the Swedish and Greek sequences of development," in *Clientelism, interests, and democratic representation*, ed. Simona Piattoni. Cambridge: Cambridge University Press. 31–53.

Pappas, Takis S. 1999. *Making party democracy in Greece*. Houndmills: Macmillan.

Park, Chan Wook. 1998. "Legislators and their constituents in South Korea: The pattern of district representation," *Asian Survey* 28: 1049–65.

Park, Cheol Hee. 1998. "Electoral strategies in urban Japan: How institutional change affects strategic choices," unpublished Ph.D. dissertation, Columbia University.

Pempel, T. J. 1978. "Political parties and social change: The Japanese experience," in *Political parties: Development and decay*, ed. Louis Maisel and Joseph Cooper. London: Sage Publications.

Persson, Torsten, Tabellini, Guido, and Trebbi, Francesco. 2001. "Electoral rules and corruption," *NBER Working Paper* 8154.

Peters, B. Guy and Pierre, Jon (eds.) 2001. *Politicians, bureaucrats, and administrative reform*. London: Routledge.

Piattoni, Simona (ed.) 2001. *Clientelism, interests, and democratic representation*. Cambridge: Cambridge University Press.

Plumb, David. 1998. "El partido por la democracia: The birth of Chile's post-materialist catch-all Left," *Party Politics* 4: 93–106.

Polsby, Nelson W. 1975. "Legislatures," in *Handbook of political science. Volume 5. Governmental institutions and processes*, ed. Fred I. Greenstein and Nelson W. Polsby. Reading, MA: Addison-Wesley.

Porter, Michael E., Takeuchi, Hirotaka, and Sakakibara, Mariko. 2000. *Can Japan compete?* Cambridge, MA: Perseus.

Posner, Daniel. N. 1998. "The institutional origins of ethnic politics in Zambia," Ph.D. Dissertation, Department of Government, Harvard University.

Post, Kenneth. 1963. *The Nigerian federal election of 1959*. Oxford: Oxford University Press.

Powell, G. Bingham. 1986. "American voter turnout in comparative perspective," *American Political Science Review* 80: 17–43.

   2000. *Elections as instruments of democracy: Majoritarian and proportional visions*. New Haven: Yale University Press.

   2004. "Political representation in comparative politics," *Annual Review of Political Science* 7: 273–96.

Powell, John Duncan. 1970. "Peasant society and clientelist politics," *American Political Science Review* 64: 411–25.

Przeworski, Adam. 1991. *Democracy and the market: Political and economic reforms in Eastern Europe and Latin America*. Cambridge: Cambridge University Press.

Przeworski, Adam, and Sprague, John. 1986. *Paper stones: A history of electoral socialism*. Chicago: University of Chicago Press.

Przeworski, Adam, Alvarez, Michael E., Cheibub, Jose Antonio, and Limongi, Fernando. 2000. *Democracy and development: Political institutions and well-being in the world, 1950–1990*. Cambridge: Cambridge University Press.

Putnam, Robert D. 1993. *Making democracy work: Civic traditions in modern Italy*. Princeton: Princeton University Press.

Quinn, Dennis and Woolley, John T. 2001. "Democracy and national economic performance: The preference for stability," *American Journal of Political Science* 45: 634–51.

Raftopoulos, Brian. 2001. "Le mouvement syndical et émergence de l'opposition politique au Zimbabwe," *Politique Africaine* 81.

Ramseyer, J. Mark, and Rosenbluth, Frances M. 1995. *The politics of oligarchy: Institutional choice in imperial Japan*. Cambridge: Cambridge University Press.

1993. *Japan's political marketplace*. Cambridge, MA: Harvard University Press.

Reddaway, P. and Orttung, R. W. 2004. *Dynamics of Russian politics: Putin's reform of federal-regional relations*. Lanham: Rowman & Littlefield.

Reddy, G. Ram and Haragopal, G. 1985. "The Pyraveerkar: The 'fixer' in rural India," *Asian Survey* 25: 1147–62.

Reed, Steven R. 1986. *Japanese prefectures and policymaking*. Pittsburgh: University of Pittsburgh Press.

Rehfeld, Andrew. 2000. "Silence of the land: An historical and normative analysis of territorial representation in the United States," Ph.D. dissertation, Department of Political Science, University of Chicago.

Reno, William. 1995. *Corruption and state politics in Sierra Leone*. Cambridge: Cambridge University Press.

Rhodes, Martin. 1997. "Financing party politics in Italy: A case of systemic corruption," *West European Politics* 20: 54–80.

Richardson, Bradley. 1997. *Japanese democracy: Power, coordination, and performance*. New Haven: Yale University Press.

Riker, William H. 1980. "Implications from the disequilibrium of majority rule for the study of institutions," *American Political Science Review* 74: 432–46.

Riordon, William. 1994. *Plunkitt of Tammany Hall*. Boston: Bedford Books.

Roberts, Kenneth M. 1994. "Renovation in the revolution? Dictatorship, democracy, and political change in the Chilean left," Kellogg Institute Working Paper 203. Notre Dame: The Helen Kellogg Institute for International Studies.

1995. "Neoliberalism and the transformation of populism in Latin America: The Peruvian case," *World Politics* 48: 82–116.

1998a. *Deepening democracy? The modern left and social movements in Chile and Peru*. Stanford: Stanford University Press.

1998b. "The Chilean party system and social cleavages in the neoliberal era," Paper prepared for delivery at the XXI International Congress of the Latin American Studies Association, Chicago, 24–26 September, 1998.

2002. "Social inequalities without class inequalities in Latin America's neoliberal era," *Studies in Comparative International Development* 36: 3–33.

Roberts, Kenneth M. and Arce, Moises. 1998. "Neoliberalism and lower-class voting behavior in Peru," *Comparative Political Studies* 31: 217–46.

Roberts, Kenneth M., and Wibbels, Erik. 1999. "Party systems and electoral volatility in Latin America: A test of economic, institutional, and structural explanations," *American Political Science Review* 93: 575–90.

Robinson, James A. and Verdier, Thierry. 2001. "The political economy of clientelism," Manuscript, University of California, Berkeley, CA.

Robinson, Marguerite S. 1988. *Local politics: The law of fishes*. Oxford: Oxford University Press.

Rodden, Jonathan and Wibbels, Erik. 2002. "Beyond the fiction of federalism," *World Politics* 54: 491–531.

Rodrik, Dani, Subramanian, Arvind and Trebbi, Francesco. 2002. "Institutions rule: The primacy of institutions over geography and integration in economic development," Revised paper, John F. Kennedy School of Government, Harvard University.

Rogowski, Ronald. 1987. "Trade and the variety of democratic institutions," *International Organization* 41: 203–23.

Roniger, Luis. 1981. "Clientelism and patron-client relations: A bibliography," in *Political clientelism, patronage and development*, ed. Shmuel N. Eisenstadt and Rene Lemarchand. Beverly Hills: Sage. 297–329.

Rosenbluth, Frances M. 1996. "Internationalization and electoral politics in Japan," in *Internationalization and domestic politics*, ed. Robert O. Keohane and Helen V. Milner. Cambridge: Cambridge University Press. 137–56.

Rothchild, Donald. 1985. "State ethnic relations in middle Africa," in *African independence: the first 25 years*, ed. Gwendolyn Carter and Patrick O'Meara. Bloomington: Indiana University Press.

Rothchild, Donald and Olorunsola, V. A. (eds.) 1982. *State versus ethnic claims: African policy dilemmas*. Boulder: Westview Press.

Roy, A. D. 1952. "Safety first and the holding of assets," *Econometrica* 20: 431–49.

Roy, Aruna and Dey, Nikhil. 2001. "Chasing a right," *Frontline* 18, 7 (March 31–April 13).

Rudolph, L. I. and Rudolph, S. H. 1967. *The modernity of tradition: Political development in India*. Chicago: University of Chicago Press.

Samuels, David J. 2002. "Pork barreling is not credit claiming or advertising: Campaign finance and the sources of the personal vote in Brazil," *Journal of Politics* 64: 845–63.

Samuels, David and Snyder, Richard. 2001. "The value of a vote: Malapportionment in comparative perspective," *British Journal of Political Science* 31: 651–71.

Sandbrook, Richard. 1972. "Patrons, clients and factions: New dimensions of conflict analysis in Africa," *Canadian Journal of Political Science* 5: 104–19.

Saxena. S. B. and Charan, A. S. 1973. "Dingri (Udaipur District, Rajasthan): A village in the vicinity of a new rail link." *Indian Village Studies No. 18*, Agro-Economic Research Center. Vallabh Vidyanagar Gujarat: Sadar Patel University.

Scalapino, Robert A. 1953. *Democracy and the party movement in prewar Japan*. Berkeley: University of California Press.

Schady, Norbert. 2000. "The political economy of expenditures by the Peruvian Social Fund FONCODES, 1991–95," *American Political Science Review* 94: 289–303.

Schaffer, Frederic. 1998. *Democracy in translation*. Ithaca: Cornell University Press.

Scharpf, Fritz W. 1997. *Games real actors play*. Boulder: Westview.

Scharpf, Fritz W. and Schmidt, Vivien A. 2000. *Welfare and work in the open economy: From vulnerability to competitiveness*. Oxford: Oxford University Press.

Schatzberg, Michael. 2001. *Political legitimacy in Middle Africa: Father, family, food.* Bloomington: Indiana University Press.

Scheiner, Ethan. 2001. "The limits of anti-clientelist appeals: Opposition failure in Japan," Paper prepared for delivery at the 2001 Annual Meeting of the American Political Science Association, San Francisco, August 30–September 2.

——— 2006. *Democracy without competition in Japan: Opposition failure in a one-party dominant state.* Cambridge: Cambridge University Press.

Scott, James C. 1969. "Corruption, machine politics, and political change," *American Political Science Review* 62: 1142–58.

——— 1972. "Patron–client politics and political change in Southeast Asia," *American Political Science Review* 66: 91–113.

Scully, Timothy R. 1995. "Reconstituting party politics in Chile," in *Building democratic institutions. Party systems in Latin America,* ed. Scott Mainwaring and Timothy R. Scully. Stanford: Stanford University Press. 100–37.

Seaman, Scott R. 2003. "Crumbling foundations: Japan's public works policies and democracy in the 1990s," unpublished Ph.D dissertation, Duke University.

Sen, Amartya. 1999. *Development as freedom.* New York: Random House.

Sharpe, W. 1964. "Capital asset prices: A theory of market equilibrium under conditions of risk," *Journal of Finance* 19: 425–42.

Sheffer, Gabriel. 1978. "Elite cartel, vertical domination, and grassroots discontent in Israel," in *Territorial politics in industrial nations,* ed. Sidney Tarrow, Peter J. Katzenstein, Luigi Graziano. New York: Praeger Publishers.

Shefter, Martin 1977. "Party and patronage: Germany, England, and Italy," *Politics and Society* 7: 403–51.

——— 1994. *Political parties and the state: The American historical experience.* Princeton: Princeton University Press.

Shepsle, Kenneth A. 1986. "Institutional equilibrium and equilibrium institutions," in *Political science. The science of politics,* ed. Herbert F. Weisberg. New York: Agathon Press.

——— 1989. "Studying institutions: Some lessons from the rational choice approach," *Journal of Theoretical Politics* 1: 131–47.

Shepsle, K. A. and Bonchek, M. S. 1997. *Analyzing politics: Rationality, behavior, and institutions.* New York: W.W. Norton.

Shepsle, Kenneth A. and Weingast, Barry R. 1987. "The institutional foundation of committee power," *American Political Science Review* 81: 85–104.

Sheth, D. L. 1999. "Secularisation of caste and making of new middle class," *Economic and Political Weekly,* August 21–28, 2502–10.

Shugart, Matthew Soberg. 1998. "The inverse relationship between party strength and executive strength: A theory of politicians' constitutional choices," *British Journal of Political Science* 28: 1–29.

Shugart, Matthew Soberg and Carey, John M. 1992. *Presidents and assemblies: Constitutional design and electoral dynamics.* Cambridge: Cambridge University Press.

Singh, Rajendra. 1988. *Land, power and people: Rural elite in transition 1801–1970.* London: Sage Publications.

Singh, Vikas, Gehlot, Bhupendra, Start, Daniel and Johnson, Craig. 2003. "Out of reach: Local politics and the disbursement of development funds in Madhya Pradesh," Overseas Development Institute Working Paper May 2003 (www.odi.org.uk/publications/working_papers/WP200.pdf).

Sisson, Richard. 1972. *The Congress Party in Rajasthan: Political integration and institution-building in an Indian state*. Berkeley: University of California Press.

Smith, William. 1989. *Authoritarianism and the crisis of the Argentine political economy*. Stanford: Stanford University Press.

Somjee, A. H. 1959. *Voting behaviour in an Indian village*. Political Science Series no. 2. Baroda: M.S. University of Baroda, 1959.

Soskice, David. 1999. "Divergent production regimes: Coordinated and uncoordinated market economies in the 1980s and 1990s," in *Continuity and change in contemporary capitalism*, ed. Herbert Kitschelt, Peter Lange, Gary Marks, and John Stephens. Cambridge: Cambridge University Press. 101–34.

Stiefel, Dieter. 2000. "Fifty years of state-owned industry in Austria, 1946–1996," in *The rise and fall of state-owned enterprise in the western world*, ed. Pier Angelo Toninelli. Cambridge: Cambridge University Press. 237–52.

Stigler, George J. 1972. "Economic competition and political competition," *Public Choice* 13: 91–106.

Stokes, Susan C. 1995. *Cultures in conflict: Social movements and the state in Peru*. Berkeley: University of California Press.

2003. "Perverse accountability: Monitoring voters and buying votes," Paper prepared for Presentation at the Annual Meeting of the American Political Science Association, Philadelphia, August 28–31.

2005. "Perverse accountability: A formal model of machine politics with evidence from Argentina," *American Political Science Review* 99: 315–26.

Stone, Carl. 1986. *Class, state, and democracy in Jamaica*. New York: Praeger.

Stoner-Weiss, Kathryn. 1999. "Central weakness and provincial autonomy," *Post-Soviet Affairs* 15: 87–104.

Strøm, Kaare. 1990. "A behavioral theory of competitive political parties," *American Journal of Political Science* 34: 565–98.

Strøm, Kaare, Müller, Wolfgang C., and Bergman, Torbjörn (eds.) 2003. *Delegation and accountability in parliamentary democracies*. Oxford: Oxford University Press.

Subha, K. 1997. *Karnataka Panchayat elections 1995: Process, issues and membership profile*. New Delhi: Concept Publishing/Institute of Social Sciences.

Swenden, Wilfried. 2002. "Asymmetric federalism and coalition-making in Belgium," *Publius* 32: 67–87.

Szwarcberg, Mariela L. 2001. "Feeding loyalties: An analysis of clientelism, the case of the Manzaneras," unpublished manuscript, Universidad Torcuato di Tella.

Taagepera, Rein, and Shugart, Matthew Soberg. 1989. *Seats and votes: The effects and determinants of electoral systems*. New Haven: Yale University Press.

Tarrow, Sidney. 1977. *Between center and periphery: Grassroots politicians in Italy and France*. New Haven: Yale University Press.

Tatebayashi, Masahiko, and McKean, Margaret. 2001. "Vote division and policy differentiation strategies of LDP members under SNTV/MMD in Japan,"

Prepared for the Conference on Citizen-Elite Linkages, March 30–April 1 2001, Duke University.

Throup, David W., and Charles Hornsby. 1998. *Multi-party politics in Kenya: The Kenyatta & Moi states & the triumph of the system in the 1992 Election*. Oxford: J. Currey.

Tilly, Charles. 1975. *The formation of nation states in western Europe*. Princeton: Princeton University Press.

Torre, Juan Carlos. 1983. *Los sindicalistas en el gobierno, 1973–1976*. Buenos Aires: Centro Editor de America Latina.

Treisman, Daniel. 2000. "The causes of corruption: A cross-national study," *Journal of Public Economics* 76: 399–457.

Treisman, Daniel S. 1999. *After the deluge*. Ann Arbor: University of Michigan Press.

Tsebelis, George. 1990. *Nested games: Rational choice in comparative politics*. Berkeley: University of California Press.

2002. *Veto players: An introduction to institutional analysis*. Princeton: Princeton University Press.

Uphoff, Norman and Ilchman, Warren. 1972. *The political economy of development: Theoretical and empirical contributions*. Berkeley: University of California Press.

Uriu, Robert M. 1996. *Troubled industries: Confronting economic change in Japan*. Ithaca: Cornell University Press.

Urquizo, Yolanda. 1999. Unpublished manuscript, Universidad Nacional de Misiones.

van de Walle, Nicolas. 1993. "The politics of non-reform in Cameroon," in *Hemmed in: Responses to Africa's economic decline*, ed. Thomas Callaghy and John Ravenhill. New York: Columbia University Press. 357–97.

2001. *African economies and the politics of permanent crisis, 1979–1999*. Cambridge: Cambridge University Press.

Van Hassel, Hugo. 1975. "Belgian civil servants and political decision making," in *The mandarins of western Europe*, ed. Mattei Dogan. New York: Sage.

Van Outrive, Lode. 1996. "The political role of the judiciary," *Res Publica* 38: 371–84.

Villalón, Leonardo. 1994. "Democratizing a quasi democracy: The Senegalese elections of 1993," *African Affairs* 93: 163–93.

Villarreal, Juan. 1987. "Changes in Argentine society: The heritage of the dictatorship," in *From military rule to liberal democracy in Argentina*, ed. Monica Peralta-Ramos and Carlos Waisman. Boulder: Westview Press.

Waisbord, Silvio. 1995. *El gran desfile: Campañas electorales y medios de comunicación en Argentina*. Buenos Aires: Sudamericana.

Wantchekon, Leonard. 2003. "Clientelism and voting behavior: Evidence from a field experiment in Benin," *World Politics* 55: 399–422.

Warner, Carolyn M. 1997. "Political parties and the opportunity costs of patronage," *Party Politics* 3: 533–48.

2001. "Mass parties and clientelism in France and Italy," in *Clientelism, interests and democratic representation*, ed. Simona Piattoni. Cambridge: Cambridge University Press. 122–51.

Washbrook, David. 1973. "Country politics: Madras 1880 to 1930," *Modern Asian Studies* 7: 475–531.

Weber, Eugen. 1976. *Peasants into Frenchmen*. Stanford: Stanford University Press.

Weiner, Myron. 1967. *Party building in a new nation: The Indian National Congress*. Chicago: Chicago University Press.

1986. "The political economy of industrial growth in India," *World Politics* 38: 596–610.

Weingast, Barry R. 1995. "The economic role of political institutions: Market-preserving federalism and economic development," *Journal of Law, Economics, and Organization* 11: 1–31.

1996. "Political institutions: Rational choice perspectives," in *A new handbook of political science*, ed. Robert E. Goodin and Hans-Dieter Klingemann. Oxford: Oxford University Press.

2000. "A comparative theory of federal economic performance," *APSA-CP Newsletter*, Winter, 6–11.

Weingast, Barry R. and Marshall, William J. 1988. "The industrial organization of Congress: Or why legislatures, like firms, are not organized as markets," *Journal of Political Economy* 96:132–63.

Weingrod, Alex. 1968. "Patrons, patronage and political parties," in *Comparative Studies in Society and History* 10: 377–400. Also published in *Friends, followers and factions; A reader in political clientelism*, ed. Steffen W. Schmidt, Laura Guasti, Carl H. Landé and James C. Scott. Berkeley: University of California Press.

Weldon, Jeffrey. 1997. "Political sources of presidencialismo in Mexico," in *Presidentialism and democracy in Latin America*, ed. Scott Mainwaring and Matthew Soberg Shugart. Cambridge: Cambridge University Press.

Whyte, J. H. 1965. "Landlord influence at elections in Ireland, 1760–1885," *English Historical Review* 80: 740–60.

Wiberg, Matti. 1995. "Parliamentary questions," in *Parliaments and majority rule in western Europe*, ed. Herbert Döring. New York: St. Martin's Press.

Widner, Jennifer. 1992. *The rise of the party-state in Kenya*. Berkeley: University of California Press.

Wildgen, John K. 1985. "Preference voting and intraparty competition in Italy: Some new evidence on the Communist–Christian Democratic stalemate," *Journal of Politics* 47: 947–57.

Wilkinson, Steven I. 2004. *Votes and violence: Electoral competition and ethnic riots in India*. Cambridge: Cambridge University Press.

Wolfinger, Raymond E. 1972. "Why political machines have not withered away and other revisionist thoughts," *Journal of Politics* 34: 365–98.

Woodall, Brian. 1996. *Japan under construction: Corruption, politics, and public works*. Berkeley: University of California Press.

World Bank. 1999. *World development report 1999/2000*. Washington, DC: World Bank.

2000a. *Entering the 21st century*. Washington, DC: World Bank.

2000b. *Overview of rural decentralization in India, Volume II*," Washington, DC: World Bank.

2003. *India: Sustaining reform, reducing poverty.* Report No. 25797-IN. Washington, DC: World Bank.

Yadav, Yogendra. 1996. "Reconfiguration in Indian politics: State assembly elections, 1993–95," *Economic and Political Weekly* 95–104.

Zamítiz, Héctor. 1991. "La reforma del PRI en el contexto de la reforma del estado: Actores y dinámica política de la XIV Asamblea Nacional," *Estudios Políticos* 6: 109–39.

Zucker, Lynne G. 1977. "The role of institutionalization in cultural persistence," *American Sociological Review* 42: 726–43.

Zuckerman, Alan. 1979. *The politics of faction.* New Haven: Yale University Press.

Index

LaVergne, TN USA
05 December 2009
165916LV00007B/15/P